Consensus in International Law

Consensus in International Law

Critical History, Queer Reimaginings

CLAERWEN O'HARA
Lecturer, Melbourne Law School, University of Melbourne, Australia

OXFORD
UNIVERSITY PRESS

OXFORD
UNIVERSITY PRESS

Great Clarendon Street, Oxford, OX2 6DP,
United Kingdom

Oxford University Press is a department of the University of Oxford.
It furthers the University's objective of excellence in research, scholarship,
and education by publishing worldwide. Oxford is a registered trade mark of
Oxford University Press in the UK and in certain other countries.

Published in the United States of America by Oxford University Press
546 Fifth Avenue, New York, NY 10036, United States of America.

British Library Cataloguing in Publication Data
Data available

Library of Congress Control Number: 2026939774

ISBN 9780198948612

DOI: 10.1093/9780198948643.001.0001

Printed and bound by
CPI Group (UK) Ltd., Croydon, CR0 4YY

The manufacturer's authorized representative in the EU for product safety is
Oxford University Press España S.A. of Parque Empresarial San Fernando de Henares,
Avenida de Castilla, 2 – 28830 Madrid (www.oup.es/en or product.safety@oup.com).
OUP España S.A. also acts as importer into Spain of products made by the manufacturer.

MIX
Paper | Supporting
responsible forestry
FSC® C013604
FSC
www.fsc.org

Acknowledgements

This book was written on the stolen lands of the Wurundjeri Woi-wurrung people of the Kulin Nation in Naarm (Melbourne, Australia). I acknowledge that their sovereignty was never ceded and pay my respects to their elders past and present.

This project began as a doctoral thesis, which I undertook at Melbourne Law School between 2018 and 2022. I am endlessly grateful to my PhD supervisors, Sundhya Pahuja and Hilary Charlesworth. Through your care, insight, and humour, you helped me to find my academic voice. Any clarity or rigour in this book has been achieved in no small part due to your supervision. I also wish to thank Dianne Otto and Ann Genovese for their mentorship and guidance, both during the PhD and beyond. I have learned so much from your generosity and can only hope that one day I might live up to your example of how to do feminist work in academia.

During my PhD, I benefited from the companionship and support of an exceptional group of graduate researchers and early career scholars, including, in no particular order, André Dao, Tim Lindgren, Johanna Commins, Robi Rado, Caitlin Murphy, Alex Dela Cruz, Nina Araneta-Alana, Haris Jamil, Sanam Amin, Luís Bogliolo, Tobias Barkley, Darshan Datar, Anna Saunders, Tess Whitton, Liam Elphick, Balawyn Jones, Lisa Archbold, Ntina Tzouvala, James Parker, Shane Chalmers, Cait Storr, and Adil Hasan Khan. I was particularly lucky to be completing my PhD alongside Danish Sheikh and Odette Mazel, who were also exploring the law through the lens of queer theory in their own doctoral research. And a very special thanks to my PhD sibling, Valeria Vázquez Guevara, who generously read over every piece of work with which I was struggling, who was there with me in both the good times and the bad, and who has become a very dear friend.

Thank you to my PhD examiners, Donatella Alessandrini and Andrew Lang, whose insightful and detailed engagement with my thesis provided a guiding light in the process of turning it into a book. Thanks also to Anne Orford and Jenny Morgan for their helpful comments as my academic advisors at different points during my candidature, as well as to Shaun McVeigh, Peter Rush, and Sean Cooney for acting as chairs of my PhD Advisory Committee.

Much of the thinking about how to transform my doctoral thesis into a book occurred while I was employed as a lecturer at La Trobe Law School between 2022 and 2025. I am grateful for the friendship, support, and ideas of my La Trobe colleagues during that time, including Kathleen Birrell, Madelaine Chiam, Julia Dehm, Martin Clark, Luis Eslava, Anita Mackay, Marc Trabsky, Fiona Kelly, and

Lorne Neudorf. Thank you in particular to Maria Elander for reading over my book proposal and encouraging me to take the next step.

Since returning to Melbourne Law School in 2025, I have benefited from the kindness and thinking of new colleagues, including Richard Joyce, Oishik Sircar, and Debolina Dutta. I am also very grateful for the mentorship and support I have received from scholars at other institutions, including that of Tamsin Phillipa Paige, Anna Hood, and Gina Heathcote. In addition, I would like to thank those scholars who took a particular interest in my work along the way, inspiring me to keep moving forward with this project, including Matthew Nicholson, Rob Howse, and Jens Theilen. I am also thankful for all the help and support I received from my editorial team at Oxford University Press and, in particular, that of Robert Cavooris and Mirza Rizwaan Ahmad.

Finally, I wish to thank Dan and Ori—words cannot do justice to my gratitude for your unwavering support on both this journey and many others. It is you who give me hope in the future.

Earlier versions of some portions of this book have appeared in print before. An earlier version of Chapter 2 and some parts of Chapters 3 and 6 appear in Claerwen O'Hara, 'Consensus Decision-Making and Democratic Discourse in the World Trade Organisation and General Agreement on Tariffs and Trade 1947' (2021) 9(1) *London Review of International Law* 37–68. Some parts of Chapter 3 appear in Claerwen O'Hara, 'Consensus and Diversity in the World Trade Organization: A Queer Perspective' (2022) 116 *American Journal of International Law Unbound* 32–37. An earlier version of Chapter 5 appears in Claerwen O'Hara, 'Consensus, Difference and Sexuality: Que(e)rying the European Court of Human Rights' Concept of "European Consensus"' (2021) 32 *Law and Critique* 91–114.

Contents

1

Consensus in International Law

Orientation, Theory, Method

1.1 Between Ambiguity and Celebration: The Idea of Consensus in International Law

The idea of 'consensus' is everywhere in international law. International organizations ranging from the United Nations to the World Trade Organization use a method of decision-making called 'consensus'.[1] Customary international law is sometimes described as based on an 'international consensus'.[2] The word 'consensus' appears throughout the names of international development policies and agreements, both informally, as in the case of the 'Washington Consensus',[3] as well as formally, as in the titles of the 'Monterrey Consensus'[4] and the 'European Consensus on Development'.[5] In the area of international human rights law, some scholars have turned from 'natural law' to 'consensus' as a primary justification for human rights,[6] and regional human rights courts, such as the European Court of Human Rights and the Inter-American Court of Human Rights, use a method of

[1] The WTO's consensus principle is enshrined in Article IX:1 of the Marrakesh Agreement Establishing the World Trade Organization, opened for signature 15 April 1994, 1867 UNTS 154 (entered into force 1 January 1995) (WTO Agreement). Although the United Nations General Assembly's use of consensus decision-making is not formalized, the majority of its resolutions now tend to be adopted without a vote; see, eg, Henry G Schermers and Niels M Blokker, *International Institutional Law* (5th edn, Martinus Nijhoff 2011) 536.

[2] See, eg, Brigitte Stern, 'Custom at the Heart of International Law' (2001) 11 Duke Journal of Comparative and International Law 89, 106–07; J Patrick Kelly, 'The Twilight of Customary International Law' (2000) 40 Virginia Journal of International Law 449, 508–16.

[3] The term 'Washington Consensus' was coined by economist John Williamson in 1989 to describe a set of economic policies promoted by the World Bank, International Monetary Fund, and US Treasury at the time. For an overview, see John Williamson, 'A Short History of the Washington Consensus' (2009) 15 Law and Business Review of the Americas 7.

[4] United Nations, The Monterrey Consensus: Report of the International Conference on Financing for Development, UN Doc A/CONF.198/11 (18–22 March 2002).

[5] There have been two: the first European Consensus on Development (2005) and the second European Consensus on Development (2017). These set out the framework for action for development cooperation between the European Union and its Member States. For the most recent, see The New European Consensus on Development—'Our World, Our Dignity, Our Future': Joint Statement by the Council and Representatives of the Governments of the Member States Meeting within the Council, the European Parliament and the European Commission (8 June 2017), available: <https://ec.europa.eu/europeaid/new-european-consensus-development-our-world-our-dignity-our-future_en>.

[6] Marie-Bénédicte Dembour, 'What Are Human Rights? Four Schools of Thought' (2010) 32 Human Rights Quarterly 1, 19.

Consensus in International Law. Claerwen O'Hara, Oxford University Press. © Claerwen O'Hara 2026.
DOI: 10.1093/9780198948643.003.0001

treaty interpretation known as 'consensus'.[7] Even in the 2020s, when global contestation is on the rise and fears about the future of international law abound,[8] international legal scholars continue to emphasize the significance of consensus in international law. In 2023, for example, Bruce Cronin advanced a consensus-based theory of international law, in which he argued that 'in limited and well-defined areas of international law, states have begun to recognize the authority of collective international consensus over individual state consent as the source of some legal rules'.[9]

Across these different contexts, consensus is often depicted in a positive light. Over the World Trade Organization's lifetime, for example, commentators have argued that the organization's use of consensus decision-making not only lends 'democratic legitimacy' to its decisions,[10] but is the reason the World Trade Organization itself is 'often viewed as one of the most democratic and Member-driven organizations of our time'.[11] Likewise, scholars have claimed that the European Court of Human Rights' use of 'European consensus' as a method of treaty interpretation offers 'democratic legitimation' to the choices that it makes by allowing the Court to engage with the preferences of the Council of Europe Member States.[12] For those worrying about the current state of international law, consensus is sometimes presented as the glue of the international order, which is now becoming unstuck.[13]

And yet, 'consensus' is an elusive idea. Indeed, one does not have to go too far back to find a time when it was doubted whether consensus could even be defined in international law. In 1973, for example, the Chairman of the United Nations Committee on the Peaceful Uses of the Sea-Bed and the Ocean Floor, Hamilton

[7] For an overview of the European Court of Human Rights' concept of 'European consensus', see Kanstantsin Dzehtsiarou, *European Consensus and the Legitimacy of the European Court of Human Rights* (Cambridge University Press 2015). For an overview of the Inter-American Court of Human Rights' use of consensus, see Lucas Lixinski, 'The Consensus Method of Interpretation by the Inter-American Court of Human Rights' (2017) 3 Canadian Journal of Comparative & Contemporary Law 65.

[8] See, eg, Linda Kinstler, 'Are We Witnessing the Death of International Law?' *The Guardian* (London, 26 June 2025) <https://www.theguardian.com/law/2025/jun/26/are-we-witnessing-the-death-of-international-law>.

[9] Bruce Cronin, *Purging the Odious Scourge of Atrocities: The Limits of Consent in International Law* (Oxford University Press 2023) 3.

[10] John Jackson, *Sovereignty, the WTO and Changing Fundamentals of International Law* (Cambridge University Press 2006) 114.

[11] Rajesh Babu, 'Decision Making in the WTO: From Negotiated Law-Making to Judicial Law-Making' in Julien Chaisse and Tsai-Yu Lin (eds), *International Economic Law and Governance* (Oxford University Press 2016) 487.

[12] See, eg, Dzehtsiarou (n 7) 211.

[13] See, eg, the following statement by an anonymous German professor of international law in 2025: 'this order has (or had?) at its core a mutual trust in a minimal consensus, a trust largely shaped by the shared memory of the two World Wars of the 20th century. Today, that trust is being squandered by key players; the minimal consensus is visibly crumbling', quoted in Maxim Bönnemann and Eva Maria Bredler, '"Wavering Between Hope and Despair": Reflections from within German International Law Scholarship' (*Verfassungsblog*, 20 June 2025) <https://verfassungsblog.de/between-hope-and-despair/>.

Amerasinghe, cast doubt on the possibility of writing 'into the rules of procedure a rule to the effect that there should be a consensus, because a consensus is beyond definition; it is impossible of definition'.[14] Even today, articles and books on consensus in international law frequently open with remarks about the slipperiness of the concept. The first chapter of a 2019 edited collection on European consensus, for example, begins as follows: '"Consensus" is a "riddle, wrapped in a mystery, inside an enigma"... [T]he precise nature and extent of the agreement that underpins consensus is elusive.'[15]

When international lawyers and legal scholars have sought to pin down the nature and extent of consensus as a state of agreement, they have usually placed it somewhere in between a simple majority and unanimity. In 1970, Richard Falk wrote that consensus means 'an overwhelming majority, a convergence of international opinion, a predominance of view; it means considerably more than a simple majority, but something less than unanimity'.[16] In other words, for Falk, it denoted an agreement that is widespread, but not quite complete.

Others have asserted that consensus in international law is better viewed as a process of decision-making. In their entry on 'consensus' in the Max Planck Encyclopaedia of Public International Law, for example, Rüdiger Wolfrum and Jakob Pichon write: 'Consensus is sometimes being understood as a decision-making procedure established under this term or as a decision taken on the basis of this procedure. The appropriate use of the term should be the reference to the procedure.'[17] Wolfrum and Pichon go on to focus on the most common consensus procedure in international law, consensus decision-making between states, which they define as 'a procedure for adopting a decision or a statement without proceeding to a formal vote ... [T]he only requirement is that no formal objection is voiced.'[18]

While this procedural account of consensus may seem more straightforward than the definition of consensus provided by Falk above, the level of agreement involved is still unclear. As Wolfrum and Pichon emphasize, a decision adopted 'by consensus is not necessarily accepted by all members. Rather, it is simply not rejected by any members.'[19] Wolfrum and Pichon's account of consensus also does not capture other modes of decision-making in international law that carry the

[14] Hamilton Shirley Amerasinghe, Sri Lanka, quoted in Louis B Sohn, 'Voting Procedures in United Nations Conferences for the Codification of International Law' (1975) 69 The American Journal of International Law 310, 333.

[15] Panos Kapotas and Vassilis P Tzevelekos, 'How (Difficult Is It) to Build Consensus on (European) Consensus?' in Panos Kapotas and Vassilis P Tzevelekos (eds), *Building Consensus on European Consensus: Judicial Interpretation of Human Rights in Europe and Beyond* (Cambridge University Press 2019) 1.

[16] Richard A Falk, *Status of Law in International Society* (Princeton University Press 1970) 134.

[17] Rüdiger Wolfrum and Jakob Pichon, 'Consensus', *Max Planck Encyclopaedia of Public International Law* (Oxford University Press 2010).

[18] ibid.

[19] ibid.

name 'consensus' but do revolve around a lack of objection, such as the use of comparative analysis by the European Court of Human Rights and Inter-American Court of Human Rights to identify a regional or international 'consensus'.

The central puzzle in this book is how did something considered 'elusive', a 'mystery', and, at times, 'beyond definition' come to be not only everywhere in international law, but also celebrated? And what is the effect of that combination of celebration and uncertainty? Whose voices are elevated through the association between ideas of consensus and 'democratic legitimacy' and whose are papered over through its conceptual imprecision? What structures, practices, and discourses might the idea of consensus uphold or reinforce, and what might it mask? In sum, what work does the idea of consensus do in international law?

The answer I provide is that the idea of consensus operates as a technique of authorization in international law. More specifically, I argue that the idea of consensus lends authority to international practices and decisions by gesturing towards a widespread, yet unfixed, level of agreement. In my account, the gesture towards a widespread agreement works to imbue international decision-making with an air of equality and project visions of unity onto a final decision. This accounts for the positive aura surrounding both the idea of consensus in international law and the institutions that invoke it. At the same time, the unfixed nature of the agreement means that the idea of consensus can be applied flexibly, including in situations in which no such equality or unity exists. This flexibility has enabled the idea of consensus to appear throughout international law, across a range of legal and institutional contexts, some of which look very different from one another. It has also meant that, as an authorizing device, consensus is at once potent and precarious, for the discourses of 'legitimacy', 'democracy', and 'unity' that it generates do not always match the reality on the ground.

1.2 A Tale of Two Institutions: Consensus in the Multilateral Trade Regime and the European Court of Human Rights

This book explores the idea of consensus in international law through two different uses of consensus. These are: (1) consensus decision-making in the General Agreement on Tariffs and Trade (1947)[20] (GATT) and the World Trade Organization (WTO); and (2) the concept of 'European consensus' in the European Court of Human Rights (ECtHR). These case studies were selected because they represent two of the main legal mobilizations of the idea of consensus in international law, which are, at least on the face of it, quite distinct from one another: consensus as a method of decision-making between states and consensus as

[20] Opened for signature 30 October 1947, 55 UNTS 194.

a method of treaty interpretation. In the GATT/WTO, consensus primarily refers to a method of decision-making between states, based around a lack of voting. The Marrakesh Agreement Establishing the World Trade Organization provides that a decision is deemed to have been reached by consensus in the WTO 'if no Member, present at the meeting when the decision is taken, formally objects to the proposed decision'.[21] 'European consensus', by contrast, is a term used to describe an interpretive method created by the ECtHR. Broadly, it refers to the ECtHR's practice of undertaking a comparative analysis of the laws and practices of the Member States of the Council of Europe in order to determine whether they would support a particular reading of the European Convention on Human Rights[22] (ECHR). For the ECtHR, a 'European consensus' exists when a majority of Member States take a similar approach to a particular human rights issue.[23]

In addition to their different uses of consensus, the GATT/WTO and ECtHR are two very different institutions. The WTO is an international trade organization that grew out of the GATT, which is now composed of 166 Members from across the world. It facilitates the negotiation of trade treaties, the settlement of trade-related disputes, and the monitoring of trade policy. The ECtHR is a regional human rights court, which has jurisdiction over alleged violations of the ECHR in the forty-six Member States of the Council of Europe. Yet, despite the differences between these institutions and their uses of consensus, both consensus decision-making in the GATT/WTO and the ECtHR's concept of European consensus have been depicted in a similar light. As we saw above, both have been described as 'legitimacy' and 'democracy'-enhancing.[24] Using these two case studies thus allows the book to drill down into the work that consensus, as an idea, does in international law, across different legal and institutional contexts.

In adopting a case studies approach, the book does not purport to provide a comprehensive account of consensus in international law. However, focusing on two examples of consensus in two different institutions has other benefits. It allows for a nuanced and textured account of how the idea of consensus has been mobilized in a given institutional setting, and the effects of that mobilization, in a way that would not be possible in a book attempting to cover the great many uses of consensus in international law or one oriented towards the formulation of an abstract model.[25] What is more, through the detailed accounts of consensus

[21] WTO Agreement (n 1) fn 1.

[22] European Convention on Human Rights and Fundamental Freedoms, as amended by Protocols Nos 11 and 14, opened for signature 4 November 1950, ETS 5 (entered into force 3 September 1953).

[23] See, eg, Luzius Wildhaber, Arnaldur Hjartarson, and Stephen Donnelly, 'No Consensus on Consensus? The Practice of the European Court of Human Rights' (2013) 33 Human Rights Law Journal 248.

[24] Jackson (n 10) 114; Dzehtsiarou (n 7) 211.

[25] On the benefits of a 'narrow focus on a few episodes involving a handful of organizations', see Guy Fiti Sinclair, *To Reform the World: International Organizations and the Making of Modern States* (Oxford University Press 2017) 12.

offered with respect to each institution, an uncannily similar story emerges, which provides insight into the work that the idea of consensus does in international law more broadly.

Taking a historical approach, the book locates the emergence of consensus as a technique of authorization in both the GATT and ECtHR in the 1970s. This was a time when the authority of these two institutions had come under challenge and alternative accounts of international law were being put forward, which claimed to be more democratic than the existing system. In the field of trade, states in the global South were using their newfound majoritarian power in international institutions to push for a more egalitarian global economy in the form of the 'New International Economic Order' (NIEO). In the field of human rights, new social movements, such as those associated with the sexual revolution and gay and women's liberation, were signalling a desire for an international law that better reflected their views and values. I contend that leaning on the idea of consensus through a rebranding of the 'sense of the meeting' procedure, in the case of the GATT, and the development of a comparative method of treaty interpretation, in the case of the ECtHR, helped to shore up the authority of both institutions by enabling them to claim that they spoke in the name of 'the many'. However, by blurring who exactly 'the many' were or would be at the point of decision-making, this shift did little to change the existing power structures within those institutions.

Over time, the authorizing work of consensus in these two institutions expanded. In addition to securing the authority of the ECtHR and the GATT/WTO themselves, it began to author and authorize legal discourses that worked to hold certain regimes of social and economic normativity in place. This is because, by routinely grounding claims about the world in the idea of consensus, these institutions were able to conceal different and dissenting viewpoints, making it appear as if those claims were the only ones that could have been made. In the context of the multilateral trade regime, I illustrate this by focusing on how the claim that the final outcome of the Uruguay Round of trade negotiations (1986–93) represented an 'international consensus' bolstered the sense that there was no alternative to the neoliberal orientation underpinning the new WTO system. In the context of the European human rights system, I do so by focusing on how the ECtHR's claims about the existence or non-existence of a region-wide 'sexual consensus' have reinforced normative assumptions about what sexuality, family-making, and Europeanness should look like.

Through these two modes of authorization, I claim that consensus became an important tool of 'worldmaking',[26] particularly in the post-Cold War era. But while it has had significant effects, grounding the authority of international institutions and their legal regimes in claims of consensus has also proved to be fragile. And,

[26] 'Worldmaking' refers to the discursive, visual and other practices that we use to give shape to the world(s) we inhabit, see Nelson Goodman, *Ways of Worldmaking* (Hackett Publishing 1978).

as this book shows, through its projection of visions of representation and homogeneity that have not always matched the way in which the practices and decisions it described were experienced on the ground, consensus has been a contributing factor in some of the backlash and instability facing the WTO and ECtHR today.

1.3 Existing Accounts of Consensus in International Law

Perhaps owing to both its prevalence and its mystique, there is extensive literature on the idea of consensus in international law. This literature can be divided into two categories, which reflect the agreement-based and procedural accounts of consensus that we saw earlier. First, there are those who understand consensus as a state of international agreement. Francisco Pascual-Vives calls this the 'substantive' account of consensus in international law.[27] In this account, consensus is seen as 'a general (but not unanimous) agreement among the subjects of public international law'.[28]

This 'substantive' account of consensus in international law underpins claims that consensus is the basis of customary international law. Kelly, for example, argues that whereas customary international law was originally grounded in a 'classical consent' theory, which held that custom was derived from the tacit consent of each state, it is now based on a 'consensus theory', premised on the 'common consent . . . [of] the overwhelming majority of states'.[29] This is also the account of consensus that Cronin has in mind in his theory of consensus-based international law, which holds that 'the regulation of certain acts of state violence committed within its own borders can be legally binding on governments in the absence of either explicit consent or a common customary practice',[30] if the principles in question are supported by a 'widespread agreement among the members of the international community'.[31]

A substantive account of consensus is also found amongst scholars who use the idea of consensus to assert the universality of a particular area of international law. Chowdhury, for example, asserts that '[t]he human rights instruments and covenants, as conceptualized in UDHR [Universal Declaration of Human Rights] and other major UN conventions, exhibit common narrative standards based on the widest attainable consensus among nations with diverse cultural traditions, religious doctrines, and ideological systems'.[32] For many international human rights

[27] Francisco Pascual-Vives, *Consensus-Based Interpretation of Regional Human Rights Treaties* (Brill 2019) 13–14: Chapter 1 'The Notion of Consensus in Public International Law'.
[28] ibid 14.
[29] Kelly (n 2) 509–11.
[30] Cronin (n 9) 4.
[31] ibid 37.
[32] Nayeefa Chowdhury, 'The Quest for Universal Human Rights: A Brief Comparative Study of Universal Declarations of Human Rights by the UN and the Islamic Council of Europe' (2008) 12 International Journal of Human Rights 347, 349.

lawyers, this putative cross-cultural international consensus supports the universality of human rights.[33] Some scholars go even further, arguing that 'the entire architecture of the international global order is premised on consensus'.[34]

Sometimes, these agreement-based accounts of consensus in international law are linked back to a specific procedural history, such as an international court's use of comparative analysis or an international organization's use of consensus decision-making. In arguing that human rights are now 'officially "universalized"',[35] for example, Alves emphasizes the fact that the Vienna Declaration and Programme of Action[36] was adopted at the United Nations (UN) World Conference on Human Rights in 1993 by more than 170 states 'by consensus without a vote or reservations'.[37] For others, consensus in international law is something that can be inferred without a formal decision-making process. Donnelly, for instance, sees the 'overlapping international consensus'[38] on the rights in the Universal Declaration of Human Rights[39] (UDHR) as simply the result of 'most leading elements in almost all contemporary societies endors[ing] the idea that every human being has certain equal and inalienable rights'.[40]

Though scholars in this category generally consider the idea of a widespread international agreement to be desirable,[41] there are some critics. In the context of the ECtHR's use of European consensus, for example, scholars such as Brauch, Benvenisti, and Shahid criticize the Court's reliance on the views of the majority of people in the majority of Member States, arguing that it threatens the rights of minority groups.[42] These scholars do not necessarily contest the idea that the ECtHR's consensus-based decisions reflect a Europe-wide 'general agreement'.[43]

[33] For an overview of this position, see Joe Hoover, 'Rereading the Universal Declaration of Human Rights: Plurality and Contestation, Not Consensus' (2013) 12 Journal of Human Rights 217.

[34] Marina Aksenova, 'Quantum Leaps of International Law' in Barrie Sander and Jason Rundall (eds), *Symposium: COVID-19 and International Law* (Opinio Juris 2020).

[35] Jose A Lindgren Alves, 'The Declaration of Human Rights in Postmodernity' (2000) 22 Human Rights Quarterly 478, 498.

[36] Vienna Declaration and Programme of Action, UN Doc A/CONF.157/23 (12 July 2993).

[37] Alves (n 35) 482.

[38] Jack Donnelly, *Universal Human Rights in Theory and Practice* (3rd edn, Cornell University Press 2013) 65.

[39] Universal Declaration of Human Rights, GA Res A/RES/3/217 A (10 December 1948).

[40] Donnelly (n 38) 70.

[41] For a summary of this view, see Kathryn McNeilly, *Human Rights and Radical Social Transformation: Futurity, Alterity, Power* (Routledge 2018) 79.

[42] Jeffrey A Brauch, 'The Dangerous Search for an Elusive Consensus: What the Supreme Court Should Learn from the European Court of Human Rights' (2009) 52 Howard Law Journal 277, 288–90; Eyal Benvenisti, 'Margin of Appreciation, Consensus, and Universal Standards' (1999) 31 New York University Journal of International Law and Politics 843, 851–52; Masuma Shahid, 'The Right to Same-Sex Marriage: Assessing the European Court of Human Rights' Consensus-Based Analysis in Recent Judgments Concerning Equal Marriage Rights' (2017) 10 Erasmus Law Review 184.

[43] Echoing Francisco Pascual-Vives' distinction between the 'substantive' and 'formal' accounts of consensus in public international law, see Pascual-Vives (n 27), Dzehtsiarou calls this the 'substantive criticism' of European consensus because it 'attacks normative value of European consensus and its appropriateness in human rights adjudication'. Dzehtsiarou contrasts this line of critique with what he calls the 'procedural criticism', which is concerned with the Court's 'method, namely how consensus is identified and applied', see Dzehtsiarou (n 7) 115.

Rather, their concern is that, not being a complete agreement, such an approach may not always reflect minority views. Consequently, in their view, the Court 'stops short of fulfilling the crucial task of becoming the external guardian against the tyranny by majorities'.[44]

Second, there are scholars who understand consensus as a process of international decision-making. Pascual-Vives calls this the 'formal account' of consensus in international law.[45] For scholars in this camp, the meaning of consensus is determined by the procedural rules that are applied before a claim of international consensus is made. As Kaptos and Tzevelekos write:

> [Consensus] spans from anything between a broad, shared understanding (in the sense of concurrence, like-mindedness or general opinion) to (explicit or implied) unanimity that entails a veto power for anyone who participates in the consensus-making process. Different shades of consensus exist between the two extremes of this continuum, *depending on the 'looseness' or 'rigidity' of the rules of its formation*.[46]

This understanding of consensus is shared by many scholars who focus on consensus decision-making in international organizations. In her article on the role of consensus in GATT/WTO decision-making,[47] for example, Mary Footer explains that although 'the use of the word "consensus" in the domestic context and in international relations frequently gives rise to ambiguity', she is using it to mean 'decisions of international organizations, or other international institutions, that have been adopted by acclamation [i.e. without a vote]'.[48] Likewise, writing on the practice of taking 'decisions by consensus' in international organizations like the UN, World Health Organization, International Maritime Organization, and WTO, Alan Boyle and Christine Chinkin write, '[w]hat do we mean by consensus in such cases? Unlike a unanimous decision, consensus is arrived at without a vote. It does not follow that all participants are necessarily in favour of such a decision.'[49]

Many international lawyers and legal scholars view consensus decision-making in a positive light. This is because it is understood to afford all participating parties the opportunity to reject a given decision, while simultaneously encouraging the resolution of differences through negotiation. Boyle and Chinkin, for example, argue that the 'consensus process tends to democratise decision-making' by ensuring that no participating state is ignored, and every state compromises.[50]

44 Benvenisti (n 42) 852.

45 Pascual-Vives (n 27) 13.

46 Kapotas and Tzevelekos (n 15) 1 [emphasis added].

47 Mary E Footer, 'The Role of Consensus in GATT/WTO Decision-Making' (1997) 17 Northwestern Journal of International Law & Business 653.

48 ibid 658.

49 Alan Boyle and Christine Chinkin, *The Making of International Law* (Oxford University Press 2007) 157.

50 ibid 159–60.

Similarly, John Jackson asserts that consensus decision-making in the GATT/WTO:

> . . . forces the membership to achieve as wide an acceptance of new measures as possible, thus lending democratic legitimacy to measures that are finally adopted. It therefore forces the richer and more powerful members of the organization to take into consideration the needs and opinions of all parts of the organization, including the poorer and less powerful governments.[51]

Some scholars are more critical. Steinberg, for example, argues that despite all the talk of 'sovereign equality' in connection with the use of consensus decision-making in the GATT/WTO, in practice, most rounds of trade negotiations 'have been concluded through power-based bargaining that has yielded asymmetrical contracts favoring the interests of powerful states'.[52] A growing number of scholars also raise concerns about the functionality of consensus decision-making, arguing that it is leading to cumbersome and ineffective decision-making in organizations such as the WTO.[53]

Commentators on the ECtHR's use of European consensus as a method of treaty interpretation also tend to focus on the process of decision-making that precedes the Court's claim of consensus—namely, its use of comparative research and analysis. Former ECtHR vice-president Christos Rozakis defines 'European consensus' in the following terms: 'The concept of "European consensus" is used to denote the result of comparative research regarding the presence or absence of common ground, especially in the law and practice of parties to the Convention on which the Court can found its conclusions.'[54] Similarly, for Kanstantsin Dzehtsiarou, '[t]he concept of European consensus in the case law of the ECtHR may be defined as a general agreement among the majority of Member States of the Council of Europe about certain rules and principles identified through comparative research of national and international law and practice.'[55] As we can see

[51] Jackson (n 10) 114.

[52] Richard H Steinberg, 'In the Shadow of Law or Power? Consensus-Based Bargaining and Outcomes in the GATT/WTO' (2002) 56 International Organization 339, 341.

[53] See, eg, Gabrielle Marceau, 'Never Waste a Good Crisis: The End of the WTO Dream, or the Beginning of Something Greater?' (2020) 17 International Organizations Law Review 345, 347; Euan MacMillan, 'Explaining Rising Regionalism and Failing Multilateralism: Consensus Decision-Making and Expanding WTO Membership' (2014) 11 International Economics and Economic Policy 599; Debra Steger, 'The Future of the WTO: The Case for Institutional Reform' (2009) 12 Journal of International Economic Law 803; Claus-Dieter Ehlermann and Lothar Ehring, 'Are WTO Decision-Making Procedures Adequate for Making, Revising, and Implementing Worldwide and "Plurilateral" Rules?' in Ernst-Ulrich Petersmann and James Harrison (eds), *Reforming the World Trading System: Legitimacy, Efficiency, and Democratic Governance* (Oxford University Press 2005).

[54] Christos Rozakis, 'Foreword' in Panos Kapotas and Vassilis P Tzevelekos (eds), *Building Consensus on European Consensus: Judicial Interpretation of Human Rights in Europe and Beyond* (Cambridge University Press 2019) xi.

[55] Kanstantsin Dzehtsiarou, 'European Consensus and the Evolutive Interpretation of the European Convention on Human Rights' (2011) 12 German Law Journal 1730, 1733.

through Rozakis and Dzehtsiarou's references to a 'common ground' and 'general agreement', such definitions of European consensus also tend to blur with the agreement-based accounts of consensus that we saw earlier.[56]

As with the use of consensus decision-making in international organizations, the ECtHR's concept of 'European consensus' is often greeted by commentators with 'effusive enthusiasm'.[57] Helfer, for example, praises European consensus as a method that allows the ECtHR 'to interpret the Convention as a modern document which is responsive to progressive European conditions and attitudes'.[58] Dzehtsiarou contends that European consensus enhances the legitimacy of the ECtHR by creating 'a means of dialogue' between the Court and the Contracting Parties, thereby enabling the Court to secure their implicit consent for a particular reading of the ECHR.[59] Some commentators have, however, expressed concern about the vague and inconsistent manner in which the ECtHR identifies and applies European consensus.[60] In their view, the ECtHR's approach would be greatly improved by 'a clear, consistent and, to a reasonable extent, predictable definition of consensus'.[61]

Yet, throughout the literature on consensus in international law, it seems that few have stepped back to consider the work that the inconsistency and uncertainty surrounding the idea of consensus does. That is, rather than lingering in the 'site of enunciation'[62] and asking what kinds of authority take shape through the contradictions, gaps, and dissonances embedded in the idea of consensus, the main approach has been to try to pin consensus down, as either a state of agreement or a process of decision-making, and then to make assessments about whether the use of consensus in a particular legal context is positive or negative—usually landing on the side of positive.

There are some notable exceptions. In an article on consensus claims in international legal scholarship, Lianne Boer argues that '[c]onsensus evades capture; and this might be precisely where its strength lies'.[63] By searching through the

[56] Some scholars also explicitly adopt an agreement-based account of European consensus. See, eg, Pascual-Vives (n 27).

[57] Paolo G Carozza, 'Uses and Misuses of Comparative Law in International Human Rights: Some Reflections on the Jurisprudence of the European Court of Human Rights' (1998) 73 Notre Dame Law Review 1217, 1218.

[58] Laurence R Helfer, 'Finding a Consensus on Equality: The Homosexual Age of Consent and the European Convention on Human Rights' (1990) 65 New York University Law Review 1044, 1056.

[59] Dzehtsiarou (n 7) 6.

[60] See, eg, Howard Charles Yourow, 'Margin of Appreciation Doctrine in the Dynamics of European Human Rights Jurisprudence' (1987) 3 Connecticut Journal of International Law 111, 158; Laurence R Helfer, 'Consensus, Coherence and the European Convention on Human Rights' (1993) 26 Cornell International Law Journal 133, 135.

[61] Dzehtsiarou (n 7) 11.

[62] Peter Rush, 'An Altered Jurisdiction: Corporeal Traces of Law' (1997) 6 Griffith Law Review 144, 150.

[63] Lianne JM Boer, '"The greater part of jurisconsults": On Consensus Claims and Their Footnotes in Legal Scholarship' (2016) 29 Leiden Journal of International Law 1021, 1031.

footnotes of over two dozen claims about the 'majority view' of scholars or the 'generally accepted' interpretation in academic writings on cyber-attacks and Article 2(4) of the UN Charter, Boer finds that most are grounded in references to the same small pool of scholars. However, she notes that the fact that 'consensus seems to evaporate the moment we attempt to substantiate it'[64] does not seem to take away from the sense that 'consensus claims carry the weight of collective scholarly authority'.[65] As a result, they can still operate as a form of 'closure', with serious consequences for 'who is given a voice in the debate, and whose voice remains in the dark'.[66]

Similar insights can be found in Kathryn McNeilly's monograph *Human Rights and Radical Social Transformation: Futurity, Alterity, Power*, which argues that the consensus narratives built around the UDHR and Vienna Declaration and Programme of Action 'have been central to the power of human rights in the contemporary period'.[67] According to McNeilly, this is because such narratives function to close off debate by obscuring the disagreements that underlie human rights and presenting the field as 'settled'.[68] In her view, conflicts over human rights will never be finished, so we must turn away from an emphasis on consensus in international human rights law and instead embrace the more unstable and futural notion of human rights 'to come'.[69]

Also writing in the context of human rights, Jens Theilen's monograph *European Consensus Between Strategy and Principle: The Uses of Vertically Comparative Legal Reasoning in Regional Human Rights Adjudication* contends that, contrary to the dominant narrative in which European consensus is presented as providing an objective benchmark within the ECtHR reasoning, this technique of interpretation forms part of the structures of argument that render human rights law indeterminate.[70] By emphasizing its indeterminacy, Theilen aims to expose the way the ECtHR's particular use of European consensus has served to entrench the status quo and shut off critical engagement with European power structures by focusing on the way things are in the present and portraying the Court's conclusions as apolitical.[71] Theilen suggests that a better approach would be for the ECtHR to use 'comparative law as a way of unearthing contradictions within European public culture',[72] as this would lead to a more transformative and open-ended account of human rights.

[64] ibid.
[65] ibid 1039.
[66] ibid 1042.
[67] McNeilly (n 41) 78.
[68] ibid 78–79.
[69] ibid 79–80.
[70] Jens T Theilen, *European Consensus Between Strategy and Principle: The Uses of Vertically Comparative Legal Reasoning in Regional Human Rights Adjudication* (Nomos 2021).
[71] ibid 425–28.
[72] ibid 439.

This book joins Boer, McNeilly, and Theilen in contesting the idea that consensus is ever truly reachable or determinable. It builds on the important groundwork they have laid in relation to international legal scholarship and human rights by extending their perspective to a broader study of the idea of consensus in international law, which not only cuts across two different legal and institutional contexts, but also pays attention to both the consensus narratives that exist in international law and the practices that work to ground those narratives. In addition, this book brings these scholars' various insights about the relationship between the illusory nature of consensus and power into sharper focus by concentrating on one specific form of power: authority.

1.4 A Different Approach: Reading for Authority and Alterity

To explore the work that the combination of ambiguity and celebration surrounding the idea of consensus does in international law, this book adopts a unique theoretical approach informed by jurisdictional thinking and queer theory. This approach enables me to draw out the practices and discourses that the idea of consensus works to naturalize and reinforce, as well as those that it helps to mask, by reading for both authority and alterity. In the following subsections, I provide an overview of the theories and methods that inform my approach.

1.4.1 Attending to Practices of Authority and Authorization through Jurisdictional Thinking

Taking heed of the various references to 'legitimacy' in association with consensus, this project began with an intuition that there is a relationship between consensus and practices of authority and authorization in international law. Authority is understood here as a relation of power or hierarchy that seems 'right' or 'legitimate'.[73] Political thinker Hannah Arendt defines authority as a relation 'between the one who commands and the one who obeys' in which what the two 'have in common is the hierarchy itself, whose rightness and legitimacy both recognize'.[74] Arendt contrasts authority with both coercion and reason.[75] Whereas coercion involves subordination through domination and reason involves persuasion between equals, authority gives people reasons to submit.[76] Authorization is the process

[73] Shaunnagh Dorsett and Shaun McVeigh, *Jurisdiction* (Routledge-Cavendish 2012) 10: 'while authority can be understood in many ways according to different political and jurisprudential traditions, it has broadly been concerned with the explanation of the legitimate means of affiliation and subordination.'

[74] Hannah Arendt, *Between Past and Future* (Penguin Books 1997) 93.

[75] ibid.

[76] Dorsett and McVeigh (n 73) 10, summarizing Arendt.

through which a relation of power acquires its sense of rightness or legitimacy, giving people reasons to submit. This process relies on practices of representation, which give visual and textual form to authority.[77] Consider, for example, the use of a coronation chair to stage and perform the transfer of authority from one monarch to another[78] or the conquistadores' practice of reading out a Spanish royal proclamation in the Americas in the fifteenth and sixteenth centuries 'to legally authorise Hispanics either to rule over Native Americans . . . or to wage a just war against them and claim possession of their labour and land as the victor's right'.[79]

In paying attention to authority and authorization, this book draws on 'jurisdictional thinking', which Shaunnagh Dorsett and Shaun McVeigh describe as a way of approaching law that 'gives us a distinct way of representing authority' by attending to the discursive and material forms that law takes.[80] Or, as Sundhya Pahuja, quoting Peter Rush,[81] puts it, jurisdictional thinking allows us to 'linger in the "site or space of enunciation" in which authority takes shape and is set into motion'.[82] Lingering in this site involves focusing on aspects of law that are often relegated to historical accounts of a particular field of law or to the area of procedural law, such as those symbolic vocabularies and ritualized behaviours that work to distinguish 'the legal' from other socio-political registers.[83] Given that consensus is both a language that pervades international law and one that is often attached to various procedures, jurisdictional thinking provides a lens through which the work that consensus does in international law can become visible, particularly in terms of its relationship to authority and authorization.

Some international legal scholars who attend to practices of authorization have focused on the authority of international organizations. In her book *International Authority and the Responsibility to Protect*, for example, Anne Orford argues that the doctrine of 'responsibility to protect', which links ideas of sovereignty to ideas of protection, has led to an expansion of international executive authority exercised by the UN.[84] Others have used jurisdictional thinking to explore how the dominant system of law that we currently call 'international law' came to assert itself as the *only* international law and the consequences of that process of authorization.

[77] ibid 12–14. However, note that, in this context, '[r]epresentation is an activity rather than simply an image', ibid 14. It is about 'staging and performance', ibid 13.

[78] Dorsett and McVeigh (n 73) 13.

[79] Maïa Pal, *Jurisdictional Accumulation: An Early Modern History of Law, Empires, and Capital* (Cambridge University Press 2020) 240.

[80] Dorsett and McVeigh (n 73) 5. See also Cait Storr, *International Status in the Shadow of Empire: Nauru and the Histories of International Law* (Cambridge University Press 2020) 15.

[81] Rush (n 62) 150: 'Jurisdiction is not so much a discourse, not so much a statement of the law, but a site or space of enunciation. It refers first and foremost to the power and authority to speak in the name of law and only subsequently to the fact that the law is stated—and stated to be something or someone.'

[82] Sundhya Pahuja, 'Laws of Encounter: A Jurisdictional Account of International Law' (2013) 1 London Review of International Law 63, 69.

[83] Storr (n 80) 16.

[84] Anne Orford, *International Authority and the Responsibility to Protect* (Cambridge University Press 2011). On the expansion of institutional authority in international law, see also Sinclair (n 25).

In her article 'Laws of Encounter: A Jurisdictional Account of International Law', for example, Pahuja redescribes sovereignty as 'an historically particular way of claiming, actualising and exercising lawful authority'.[85] Pahuja argues that, combined with the universalization of the nation state and a temporal organization of difference through the idea of 'development', this mode of claiming authority helped to conceal other laws of encounter and spread a European international law across the globe.

In this book, I analyse the relationship between consensus and authority in international law using both of these lenses. On the one hand, I explore how consensus has interacted with, shaped, and reinforced the authority of the two international bodies under analysis: the GATT/WTO and the ECtHR. To do so, I trace the emergence and development of each institution's use of consensus and the work it has done over time, particularly with respect to the narratives surrounding the two institutions. On the other hand, I consider the relationship between consensus and the dominance of certain international legal ideas and discourses. In the context of the GATT/WTO, I concentrate on the way in which the final consensus reached in the Uruguay Round of multilateral trade negotiations (1986–1993) helped to naturalize a particular vision of international economic law. In relation to the ECtHR, I focus on how the Court's concept of European consensus has reinforced certain legal constructions of sexuality.

1.4.2 Reading for Difference: International Law through the Lens of Queer Theory

In exploring the work that consensus does in international law, this book is concerned not only with what consensus authorizes, but also with what it deauthorizes, disciplines, and conceals. This concern is common amongst jurisdictional thinkers, particularly in the field of international law.[86] Scholars who take up Third World Approaches to International Law (TWAIL), and Indigenous legal scholars working with this sensibility[87] have drawn attention to the way in which colonial and neo-colonial jurisprudence has facilitated the misrecognition of international legal conflicts or non-Western law as 'social', 'cultural', or 'political' in nature.[88] These scholars resist this process of deauthorization by attending to

[85] Pahuja (n 82) 74.

[86] For an overview, see Shaun McVeigh, 'Critical Approaches to Jurisdiction and International Law' in Stephen Allen and others (eds), *The Oxford Handbook of Jurisdiction in International Law* (Oxford University Press 2019) 202–04: 'Plural Authorities and Encounters'.

[87] On the way 'jurisdictional thinking is better understood less as a theory of law than as a sensibility that attends to the practices of authorization', see Storr (n 80) 15.

[88] See, eg, Christine Black, Shaun McVeigh and Richard Johnstone, 'Of the South' (2007) 16 Griffith Law Review 299; Pahuja (n 82); Sundhya Pahuja and Anna Saunders, 'Rival Worlds and the Place of the Corporation in International Law' in Jochen von Bernstorff and Philipp Dann (eds), *The Battle for*

different jurisdictional arrangements and emphasizing a plurality of juridical authorities. In this book, I too take seriously the idea of a multiplicity of international laws. In particular, I pay attention to how the uses of consensus by the GATT/WTO and ECtHR have helped to disguise or diffuse other deployments of international law, from the international law advanced by states in the global South in connection with their vision for a NIEO to the use of 'people's tribunals' by protest groups in Europe in the 1960s and 1970s.[89]

However, in this book, I also consider the impact of consensus in international law on forms of difference that go beyond law, including economic, social, and sexual difference. This allows the book to explore the broader worldmaking dimension of consensus in international law.[90] To undertake this exploration, I draw on insights from queer theory, which is a theoretical lens that seeks to 'make strange'[91] ideas and practices that are considered to be 'the normal, the legitimate, the dominant'[92] and render visible the alterity that lies beneath. Queer theory grew out of the work of feminist theorists such as Judith Butler and Eve Kosofsky Sedgwick in the early 1990s[93] and builds on the post-structuralist thought of Michel Foucault.[94] Although queer theory refers to a diverse body of work, a number of key features can be distilled, including a rejection of essentialist and binary thinking, a mission to resist and destabilize regimes of normativity, and, most significantly for this book, a radical embrace of difference.[95]

These features of queer theory are most commonly applied in relation to gender and sexuality. In this context, queer theorists have challenged the binaries of man/woman and heterosexual/homosexual and emphasized the 'open mesh

International Law: South-North Perspectives on the Decolonization Era (Oxford University Press 2019); Sundhya Pahuja, 'Letters from Bandung: Encounters with Another International Law' in Luis Eslava, Michael Fakhri and Vasuki Nesiah (eds), *Bandung, Global History, and International Law: Critical Pasts and Pending Futures* (Cambridge University Press 2017); Mark McMillan, 'Koowarta and the Rival Indigenous International: Our Place as Indigenous Peoples in the International' (2014) 23 Griffith Law Review 110.

[89] In taking seriously the jurisdiction claimed by people's tribunals, I am taking up the central insight in Tim Lindgren's doctoral thesis, 'An International Law of Peoples: The International Rights of Nature Tribunal and International Law' (University of Melbourne 2024).

[90] For a discussion of law's worldmaking power in connection with jurisdictional thinking, see, eg, Pahuja and Saunders (n 88); Shaun McVeigh and Sundhya Pahuja, 'Thinking with Jurisdiction: Shaun McVeigh and Sundhya Pahuja in Conversation' (2022) 82 Zeitschrift für ausländisches öffentliches Recht und Völkerrecht/Heidelberg Journal of International Law 299, 302.

[91] Nikki Sullivan, *A Critical Introduction to Queer Theory* (New York University Press 2003) vi.

[92] David M Halperin, *Saint Foucault: Towards a Gay Hagiography* (Oxford University Press 1995) 62.

[93] Judith Butler, *Gender Trouble: Feminism and the Subversion of Identity* (Routledge 1990); Eve Kosofsky Sedgwick, *Tendencies* (Duke University Press 1993); Eve Kosofsky Sedgwick, *Epistemology of the Closet* (1st edn, University of California Press 2008).

[94] See, in particular, Michel Foucault, *The History of Sexuality Vol 1: An Introduction* (Robert Hurley tr, Pantheon 1980).

[95] Claerwen O'Hara, 'Queer Legal Theory' in Harry Hobbs and Jeremy Patrick (eds), *Beyond Doctrine: Alternative and Critical Approaches to Law* (Federation Press 2025) 221.

of possibilities' that exists 'when the constituent elements of anyone's gender, of anyone's sexuality aren't made (or can't be made) to signify monolithically'.[96] These insights have been picked up by scholars of international law, and, in particular, those working in the fields of international and regional human rights law, who point out how legal categories such as 'sexual orientation' and 'gender identity' can constrain difference by relying on binary and essentialist thinking and patrolling the boundaries of what constitutes a valid or meaningful experience of gender and sexuality.[97] The aim of such critiques, as one of the leading scholars in the field, Dianne Otto, writes, is to open up space 'to celebrate human sexuality and gender expression in all its diversity and fluidity'.[98]

But queer theory has also been extended beyond the realm of gender and sexuality.[99] For example, in their work on 'queering the economy', J.K. Gibson-Graham reads the economic landscape 'for difference, rather than dominance'[100] in order to recover the 'rich and prolific disarray'[101] of non-capitalist practices that have been obscured by the hegemony of globalized neoliberal capitalism. Using a slightly different approach, Kapoor seeks to align queer and Third World political projects by pointing out that 'both result from the same orientalist hetero-normative discourse'[102] and 'operate from the margins, questioning normalising power mechanisms and social order, while upholding a deviant, non-conformist and non-assimilationist politics'.[103] Kapoor then goes on to sketch a 'queer Third World' politics, which calls for the global South to revisit 'its political roots in non-alignment'[104] and embrace a position of difference so as to denaturalize the prevailing global economic system.

[96] Sedgwick, *Tendencies* (n 93) 9.

[97] See, eg, Matthew Waites, 'Critique of "Sexual Orientation" and "Gender Identity" in Human Rights Discourse: Global Queer Politics Beyond the Yogyakarta Principles' (2009) 51 Contemporary Politics 137; Wayne Morgan, 'Queering International Human Rights Law' in Carl Stychin and Didi Herman (eds), *Law and Sexuality* (University of Minnesota Press 2000); Dianne Otto, 'Queering Gender [Identity] in International Law' (2015) 33 Nordic Journal of International Law 299; Michele Grigolo, 'Sexualities and the ECHR: Introducing the Universal Sexual Legal Subject' (2003) 14 European Journal of International Law 1023; Damian A Gonzalez-Salzberg, *Sexuality and Transsexuality under the European Convention on Human Rights: A Queer Reading of Human Rights Law* (Hart Publishing 2019); Giovanna Gilleri, *Sex, Gender and International Human Rights Law: Contesting Binaries* (Routledge 2023); Tamsin Phillipa Paige and Claerwen O'Hara (eds), *Queer Encounters with International Law: Lives, Communities, Subjectivities* (Routledge 2024).

[98] Dianne Otto, 'Introduction: Embracing Queer Curiosity' in Dianne Otto (ed), *Queering International Law: Possibilities, Alliances, Complicities, Risks* (Routledge 2018) 1, 1.

[99] On this trend, see Claerwen O'Hara and Tamsin Phillipa Paige, 'Reaching Out Towards the Horizon: Queer Engagements with International Law Beyond Queer Theory's Site of Origin', *Queer Engagements with International Law: Times, Spaces, Imaginings* (Routledge 2024); Claerwen O'Hara, 'Queer Approaches to International Economic Law' in *Elgar Encyclopedia of International Economic Law* (Edward Elgar 2024).

[100] JK Gibson-Graham, *A Postcapitalist Politics* (University of Minnesota Press 2006) xxxi–xxxii.

[101] JK Gibson-Graham, *The End of Capitalism (As We Knew It): A Feminist Critique of Political Economy* (2nd edn, University of Minnesota Press 2006) xxxix.

[102] Ilan Kapoor, 'The Queer Third World' (2015) 36 Third World Quarterly 1611, 1619.

[103] ibid 1612.

[104] ibid 1621.

International legal scholars have also taken up queer theory to critique and challenge dominant concepts or logics in international law not directly related to gender and sexuality, from international law's narrow conception of peace[105] and colonial conception of temporality[106] to its emphasis on the value-laden concept of the nation state[107] and denial of subjectivity to oceans and the environment.[108] Across these different contexts, queer theory is used not only to dislodge and denaturalize ideas that are taken for granted by exposing the narrow thinking upon which they are built, but also to demonstrate how the world could be (and often already is) otherwise by looking for different approaches and ways of being in the 'gaps, overlaps, dissonances and resonances, lapses and excesses of meaning'[109] that exist in any given context.

In this book, I use queer theory in relation to both sexuality-related and non-sexuality-related topics. In my reading of the ECtHR's case law relating to sexuality, I engage in a more 'traditional' application of queer theory to show how the Court's claims of European consensus have lent authority to narrow constructions of sexuality, helping to close off spaces for sexual difference and uphold the dominant sexual order. In my exploration of narratives that emerged from the fact that the Uruguay Round of GATT trade negotiations were concluded through consensus, I draw on insights from queer theory to think through how this apparent 'lining up' of voices worked to deauthorize and conceal economic practices and imaginaries that did not conform to the dominant neoliberal model. In this context, it is economic heterodoxy and its advocates that I read as queer. Though my use of queer theory is sometimes more subtle when applied to international economic law, it has been no less significant in informing my thinking. Finally, queer theory's radical embrace of difference is at the heart of my proposal, in the last chapter, to move beyond some of the issues described in

[105] Dianne Otto, 'Rethinking "Peace" in International Law and Politics From a Queer Feminist Perspective' (2020) 126 Feminist Review 19; Dianne Otto, 'Queerly Troubling International Law's Vision of "Peace"' (2022) 116 AJIL Unbound 22; Philipp Kastner and Elisabeth Roy Trudel, 'Unsettling International Law and Peace-Making: An Encounter with Queer Theory' (2020) 33 Leiden Journal of International Law 911.

[106] Vanja Hamzić, 'International Law, Coloniality, and the Temporal Otherwise' in Claerwen O'Hara and Tamsin Phillipa Paige (eds), *Queer Engagements with International Law: Times, Spaces and Imaginings* (Routledge 2024); Rahul Rao, *Out of Time: The Queer Politics of Postcoloniality* (Oxford University Press 2020); Caitlin Biddolph, 'Queering Temporalities of International Criminal Justice: Srebrenica Remembrance and the International Criminal Tribunal for the Former Yugoslavia (ICTY)' (2020) 29 Griffith Law Review 401.

[107] Dianne Otto, 'Resisting the Heteronormative Imaginary of the Nation-State: Rethinking Kinship and Border Protection' in Dianne Otto (ed), *Queering International Law: Possibilities, Alliances, Complicities, Risks* (Routledge 2018).

[108] See, eg, Gina Heathcote, 'Oceans versus Ghost Fleets' in Claerwen O'Hara and Tamsin Phillipa Paige (eds), *Queer Engagements with International Law: Times, Spaces and Imaginings* (Routledge 2024); Emily Jones, 'Challenging International Environmental Law's Heteronormativity and Anthropocentrism: Towards Queer Kinship' in Claerwen O'Hara and Tamsin Phillipa Paige (eds), *Queer Engagements with International Law: Times, Spaces and Imaginings* (Routledge 2024).

[109] Sedgwick, *Tendencies* (n 93) 9.

this book by (re)imagining the international as a meeting place for a plurality of worlds.

By using queer theory to uncover the different and dissenting viewpoints that lie beneath claims of consensus in international law, this book aims not only to shed light on what is at stake in those claims, but also to unsettle the practices of authorization with which they are associated. As Buss writes, putting queer theory into conversation with authority in the context of international law raises 'a series of questions that attempt to challenge—possibly queer—the normative foundations upon which debates about international legal authority and its future are premised',[110] opening up alternative possibilities.

1.4.3 Locating and Exploring the Discourses of International Law

In relation to both of my case studies, I follow many queer theorists in using critical discourse analysis, which is a methodology that maps patterns in speech and text to draw out the co-constitutive relationship between those patterns and configurations of power.[111] Critical discourse analysis goes about this task by placing texts and utterances in their broader context and reading them through that context. More specifically, I use a form of critical discourse analysis called the 'discourse-historical' approach, which relies on documents on public record, rather than interviews or other forms of ethnography.[112] When applied to international law, this approach involves considering how the words in a treaty, judgment, or meeting record emanate from, and, in turn, reinforce, a particular institutional and normative world, located in a given moment in time.[113] In this case of the book, I use critical discourse analysis to attend to the ways in which claims of consensus made by the GATT/WTO and ECtHR have intermingled with institutional representations and social perceptions of those institutions. I also use critical discourse analysis to explore how those claims of consensus have been shaped by, and have given shape to, discourses relating to the global economy, sexuality, and international and regional identities.

In employing this approach, I engage with a broader archive than one would typically find in a more doctrinal legal analysis. Like other international legal

[110] Doris E Buss, 'Queering International Legal Authority' (2007) 101 Proceedings of the Annual American Society of International Law Meeting 122, 125.

[111] Claudio Ramírez, 'Ethos and Critical Discourse Analysis: From Power to Solidarity' (2013) 13 Contextes. On how this approach is commonly used by queer theorists see Kath Browne and Catherine J Nash, 'Queer Methods and Methodologies: An Introduction' in Kath Browne and Catherine J Nash (eds), *Queer Methods and Methodologies: Intersecting Queer Theories and Social Science Research* (Routledge 2016) 6.

[112] Tamsin Phillipa Paige, *Petulant and Contrary: Approaches by the Permanent Five Members of the UN Security Council to the Concept of 'Threat to the Peace' Under Article 39 of the UN Charter* (Brill Nijhoff 2019) 36–37.

[113] For an example of the application of critical discourse analysis to international law, see ibid.

scholars working with critical and socio-legal approaches, I accept that 'the logic and language of international law appears in multiple sites and guises, extending far beyond the traditionally recognized sources of treaty, custom, and judicial decisions'.[114] As such, the documents I rely upon as part of my critical discourse analysis span formal legal sources, such as the ECtHR's judgments, as well as sources not always considered part of the 'official' legal archive but in which the broader discourses of international law still reside, such as speeches made at WTO Ministerial Meetings and in the Parliamentary Assembly of the Council of Europe, other scholars' oral histories of GATT/WTO negotiations and ECtHR applications, and newspaper articles depicting how various institutional practices or decisions were publicly received at a particular moment in time.

1.5 Consensus as a Technique of Authorization

Adopting a queer jurisdictional approach allows this book to provide a different account of consensus in international law to that prevailing in the existing literature. Rather than depicting consensus in international law as a particular process of decision-making or a state of agreement, I present it as a historically specific technique of authorization, which works by gesturing towards a widespread, yet unfixed and often unquantifiable, level of agreement. This does not mean that I overlook the procedures that international institutions have developed to ground their claims of consensus. I accept, and indeed the book goes into great detail about, the way in which claims of consensus in international law are often linked back to certain decision-making processes, such as the taking of a decision without a vote, in the case of the GATT/WTO, or a comparative analysis of the laws and practices of the Member States of the Council of Europe, in the case of the ECtHR. However, in my view, these processes or procedures are best viewed as practices or rituals,[115] which help to stabilize a larger authorizing process, the crux of which is the gesture towards the elusive idea of a 'general agreement'.

By redescribing consensus as a technique of authorization, this book offers a new way of thinking about consensus in international law that not only allows us to step back and see the world that consensus has helped to author and authorize, but also to ask whether we accept what we see. One aim of jurisdictional thinking is to invite lawyers to take responsibility for the practices of authorization in which we participate. As Pahuja writes, '[i]t means we must choose our law, rather than assuming any one law is simply already there before we arrive ... For international

[114] See Sinclair (n 25) 8.

[115] On rituals and ritualism in international law, see, eg, Hilary Charlesworth and Emma Larking (eds), *Human Rights and the Universal Periodic Review: Rituals and Ritualism* (Cambridge University Press 2015).

lawyers, this means taking responsibility for the practices our own conduct as jurists authorises.'[116] In revealing the legal, institutional, and social arrangements consensus has helped to hold in place, this book gives international lawyers and international legal scholars an opportunity to decide whether we wish to continue portraying consensus as an attainable state of agreement or praising the rituals that work to stabilize a claim of consensus, knowing how doing so is likely to shape and reshape the world.

This book also comes at a time when the post-Cold War international legal order seems to be unravelling and international institutions such as the WTO and ECtHR are facing backlash and instability. In December 2019, the WTO was 'dejudicialized' as a result of the United States (US)—once one of the organization's strongest supporters—blocking consensus on appointments to the WTO Appellate Body until it no longer had the quorum to rule on appeal.[117] In recent years, the US has also 'gained a renewed appreciation for tariffs and export restrictions as methods of industrial sabotage . . . even if this embrace means ignoring or directly undermining the authority of the WTO'.[118] Since the early 2010s, the ECtHR has been the subject of sustained criticism from a number of Council of Europe Member States,[119] leading to two Declarations and a Protocol aimed at reeling in the Court's power.[120] By demonstrating how the authority of these institutions and their legal discourses has been built, at least in part, on claims of democracy and sameness that have sat uneasily with the reality on the ground, this book sheds light on some of the causes of the crises they are facing today. In drawing a connection between consensus and some of the problems that beset international law in our present moment, the book also cautions against a sense of nostalgia for an era of international law based around consensus claims as we attempt to chart a pathway towards a better future.

[116] Pahuja (n 82) 92–93.

[117] For the term 'dejudicialized' in relation to the Appellate Body impasse, see Richard H Steinberg, 'The Impending Dejudicialization of the WTO Dispute Settlement System?' (2018) 112 American Society for International Law Proceedings 316. The Appellate Body (AB) requires a quorum of three, see Understanding on Rules and Procedures Governing the Settlement of Disputes 1994, 1869 UNTS 299, Article 17:1. On 11 December 2019, the AB's membership fell to one. However, two AB members stayed on until June 2020 to complete a report.

[118] Ntina Tzouvala, 'On Tariffs and the Ends of International Economic Law' (*LPE Project*, 29 April 2025) <https://lpeproject.org/blog/on-tariffs-and-the-ends-of-international-economic-law/>.

[119] For an overview of some of the criticism being directed at the European Court of Human Rights, see, eg, Patricia Popelier, Sarah Lambrecht, and Koen Lemmens (eds), *Criticism of the European Court of Human Rights: Shifting the Convention System: Counter-Dynamics at the National and EU Level* (Intersentia 2016).

[120] See the Brighton Declaration (20 April 2012), available at <https://www.echr.coe.int/Documents/2012_Brighton_FinalDeclaration_ENG.pdf>; the Copenhagen Declaration (13 April 2018), available at <https://rm.coe.int/copenhagen-declaration/16807b915c>; and Protocol No. 15 Amending the Convention for the Protection of Human Rights and Fundamental Freedoms, opened for signature 24 June 2013, CETS 213, 2013 (entered into force 1 August 2021).

1.6 Overview of the Monograph

This book is in three parts. The first part, which comprises Chapters 2 and 3, explores the idea of consensus in the GATT/WTO. **Chapter 2** is focused on the relationship between the multilateral trade regime's claim to operate according to something called 'consensus decision-making' and the institutional authority of the GATT/WTO. Taking the form of a historical narrative, it begins with an account of how the GATT Contracting Parties began taking decisions by the 'sense of the meeting' in lieu of a formal vote in the 1950s. The chapter then traces how, over the 1960s and 1970s, the GATT's 'sense of the meeting' procedure was gradually transformed into something known and celebrated as 'consensus'. The chapter contextualizes this shift within the period of decolonization that had recently taken place, which had not only resulted in there being significantly more states from the global South in many international organizations than there were from the global North, but also saw the authority of the GATT come under challenge through demands by the decolonized states for a more egalitarian international economic order. The chapter argues that the GATT's claim to take its decisions 'by consensus' helped to shore up that institution's authority amid these changes by imbuing it with an egalitarian aura.

The chapter then examines the relationship between consensus and the authority of the WTO. It describes how, in the shift from the GATT to the WTO, the nature of 'consensus decision-making' changed, leading to decision-making difficulties. The chapter then tracks how the WTO responded to these difficulties by wrapping its use of consensus decision-making in a discourse of 'democracy'. The final part of Chapter 2 focuses on two other forms of consensus decision-making in the WTO—negative consensus and judicial consensus—and how they facilitated the rise of the WTO Appellate Body. The chapter shows how, over the history of the multilateral trade regime, the idea of consensus has routinely functioned to stabilize the authority of the GATT/WTO and the organs contained therein, while simultaneously working to siphon power away from the majority of its Members and their constituencies.

Chapter 3 then moves away from the various procedures that carry the name 'consensus' in the GATT/WTO to consider the authorizing work that consensus, as a claimed outcome, has performed in the multilateral trade regime. To do this, the chapter focuses on the Uruguay Round of multilateral trade negotiations, which lasted from 1986 until 1994 and culminated in the agreement to establish the WTO. The chapter examines the narratives that emerged from the claim that those negotiations were concluded by consensus. It draws out the way in which the WTO's consensual origins became an important part of that institution's mythology, helping to portray the new trade regime as a product of international unity and agreement. Through an engagement with queer theory, it also considers how the final Uruguay Round consensus worked to ground and authorize post-Cold

War discourses proclaiming the 'triumph' of free market capitalism by making it appear as if there were no longer any opposition or economic alternatives left.

In the second part of the book, which comprises Chapters 4 and 5, I turn to the relationship between consensus and authority in the European human rights system. As with the multilateral trade regime, I begin by focusing on institutional authority before moving to an account of how the idea of consensus has worked to authorize certain legal ideas and discourses. **Chapter 4** considers the relationship between the authority of the ECtHR and its claim to base its decisions on a 'European consensus'. Like Chapter 2, this chapter takes a historical approach. It provides an account of the ECtHR's turn to a comparative method of treaty interpretation in the 1970s as a means of interpreting the ECHR as a 'living instrument'. The chapter contextualizes this development within the social and political upheaval that had occurred in Europe in the 1960s and 1970s, which saw not only the emergence of a different set of values to those underpinning the ECHR, but also a desire for a more democratized international law. Although the ECtHR's new interpretive method was vague and discretionary, I argue that it became associated with ideas of 'progress' and 'public voice', helping to establish a positive reputation for the Court. The chapter then traces how the ECtHR's comparative method developed over time, eventually becoming known as 'European consensus' and associated with ideas of democracy. I contend that these discursive shifts helped to bolster the authority of the European human rights system, ultimately contributing to the Member States' decision to expand and reinforce the ECtHR's jurisdiction at the end of the twentieth century.

Chapter 5 considers the effects that flow from the ECtHR's claims about the existence or non-existence of a European consensus on a particular matter through a case study on sexuality rights. This chapter argues that by routinely making claims about a region-wide sexual consensus, the ECtHR has helped to lend authority to a set of narrow ideas about the way sexuality, family-making, and Europeanness may be expressed. As a result, the ECtHR's claims of European consensus have functioned to uphold and sustain heteronormative power relations, notwithstanding the role this interpretive technique has played in the recognition of new rights for lesbian, gay, bisexual, transgender, and intersex people under the ECHR. Drawing on insights from queer theory, this discussion is carried out through a critical analysis of a selection of decisions relating to sexuality made by the ECtHR and the European Commission on Human Rights.

In the third part, which comprises Chapters 6 and 7, I bring the book to a close by considering recent problems associated with the practices and discourses of consensus in the WTO and ECtHR, as well how we might move beyond a consensus-oriented approach to international law. **Chapter 6** explores the role of consensus in recent crises in the WTO and ECtHR. In relation to the WTO, it focuses on the US' unilateral decision to paralyze the Appellate Body through the WTO's consensus procedure in 2019. In relation to the ECtHR, it examines backlash towards the Court from several Council of Europe Member States, with a particular focus on the United Kingdom and Russia. This chapter argues that the gap between the discourses of democracy and homogeneity that came to surround each institution's use of consensus and the experience of those practices and decisions on the ground is at the heart of some of the problems facing both the WTO and ECtHR today.

In **Chapter 7**, I consider how we might approach international law in a way that could better accommodate all the diversity that exists in the world. I contend that overcoming the issues described in the book is not as simple as abandoning the use of decision-making methods called 'consensus', although there could be benefits to doing so. Rather, in my view, what is needed is a shift in imagination in which the goal of the world or a particular region routinely reaching a widespread agreement is decentred. To achieve this shift, I argue in favour of a vision of the international as a 'meeting place' for a plurality of peoples and their laws. The chapter then illustrates what this meeting place could look like by providing a series of vignettes of predominantly historical examples in which states or groups of people have approached the international in ways that come close to resembling such a meeting place.

The vignettes I provide include state-based attempts to create international organizations that are more open to multipolarity and legal pluralism, from the UN Conference on Trade and Development's function as a meeting place for the Cold War's different worlds in the 1960s and 1970s, to the more recent attempt by a coalition of Latin American states known as the Bolivarian Alliance of the Peoples of Our America, or 'ALBA', to open up existing international organizations, including the WTO, to the voices and visions of law of people on the outside. They also include experiments with alternative international practices and arrangements through non-state-based initiatives, from the International Tribunal on Crimes against Women, a feminist people's tribunal held in Brussels in 1976, to the use of 'encounters' by the Zapatistas, a Mexico-based insurgent group, as a way to bring a transnational network of activists and rebels together. While all the examples I provide are flawed in some way, together they provide a repository of framings and procedures that are more open to difference and plurality than the current international legal framework. In this way, they offer a basis for reimagining international law in queerer directions into the future.

2
Consensus Decision-Making and the Authority of the General Agreement on Tariffs and Trade and World Trade Organization

2.1 Introduction

In 2019, I attended the World Trade Organization's (WTO) fifth 'open day'.[1] This was a day when the WTO opened its doors to the public, giving them 'a chance to discover the WTO in all its facets—historical, cultural and international'.[2] Arriving in Geneva on a sunny June morning after an overnight bus ride from Barcelona, I was interested to see how the WTO would present itself to the public. Not long into then-Director-General Roberto Azevêdo's opening speech, he emphasized that the WTO operated by 'consensus', which, he informed us, meant that it was a 'member driven' organization. The prominence the Director-General gave the WTO's principal method of decision-making, as well as the language he used to describe it, echoed what I had read on the organization's website. A page entitled 'Whose WTO is it anyway?' opens with the following statement: 'The WTO is "member-driven", with decisions taken by consensus among all member governments'.[3] According to the website, this makes the WTO 'different' from (and, implicitly, better than) 'some other international organizations such as the World Bank and International Monetary Fund' because 'power is not delegated to a board of directors or the organization's head'; '[a]ll major decisions are made by the membership as a whole'.[4]

An older information pack dispelling misconceptions about the WTO makes the point even more forcefully, explaining that the WTO is not 'a dictatorial tool

[1] World Trade Organisation, 'Open Day 2019' (2019) <https://www.wto.org/english/forums_e/open_day_e/open_day19_e.htm>.

[2] This is how WTO Director-General Pascal Lamy had described the event at the WTO's first open day ten years earlier, see World Trade Organisation, 'WTO Opens Its Doors to the Public' (31 August 2009) <https://www.wto.org/english/news_e/pres09_e/pr570_e.htm>.

[3] World Trade Organisation, 'Whose WTO Is It Anyway?' <https://www.wto.org/english/thewto_e/whatis_e/tif_e/org1_e.htm>.

[4] ibid.

Consensus in International Law. Claerwen O'Hara, Oxford University Press. © Claerwen O'Hara 2026.
DOI: 10.1093/9780198948643.003.0002

of the rich and powerful'.[5] Rather, 'decisions taken in the WTO are negotiated, accountable and *democratic*'[6] because they are 'generally made by consensus among all members'.[7] Across these statements, a certain importance was being placed on the WTO's use of consensus decision-making. For representatives of the organization, it seemed, this decision-making practice was part of the reason why the WTO had the 'right' and 'legitimacy' to govern in the field of international trade. In other words, consensus was an important part of the WTO's authority.

This chapter explores the relationship between WTO's claim to take decisions 'by consensus' and the institutional authority of the multilateral trade regime. As will be recalled from the previous chapter, I am using the term 'authority' to mean a relation of power or hierarchy that seems 'right' or 'legitimate'.[8] Taking a historical approach, the chapter traces how a practice of decision-making known as 'consensus' came about in the WTO and its predecessor, the General Agreement on Tariffs and Trade (1947)[9] (GATT), and the way that practice became associated with ideas of 'legitimacy', 'equality', and even 'democracy', reinforcing the multilateral trade regime's authority.

The chapter argues that consensus became linked to the authority of the GATT over the course of the 1960s and 1970s, when a rise in the number of newly independent states and a decline in European power saw a series of struggles take place between rival accounts of international law.[10] During this period, states in the global South began using their newfound majoritarian power in international institutions to push for a more egalitarian international economic order. In response, states in the global North presented the idea of striving for a widespread international agreement called a 'consensus' as a 'realistic' way of achieving inter-state equality. In this context, the GATT's weighted and informal 'sense of the meeting' procedure, which had been in use since the 1950s, was gradually reframed as something known as 'consensus decision-making'. This reframing helped to shore up the authority of the GATT by imbuing it with an egalitarian aura.

Over the following decades, and often in response to moments of contestation, representatives of the GATT/WTO continued to return to, and to build on, the narrative of equality that had been constructed around consensus decision-making—for example, by adding the language 'democracy'—until consensus became an integral part of the multilateral trade regime's authority. And yet, throughout this

5 World Trade Organisation, '10 Common Misunderstandings About the WTO' (*Institute for Agriculture and Trade Policy*, 30 November 1999) <https://www.iatp.org/documents/10-common-misunderstandings-about-the-wto>.

6 ibid [emphasis added].

7 ibid.

8 Shaunnagh Dorsett and Shaun McVeigh, *Jurisdiction* (Routledge-Cavendish 2012) 10.

9 Opened for signature 30 October 1947, 55 UNTS 194.

10 Sundhya Pahuja and Anna Saunders, 'Rival Worlds and the Place of the Corporation in International Law' in Jochen von Bernstorff and Philipp Dann (eds), *The Battle for International Law: South–North Perspectives on the Decolonization Era* (Oxford University Press 2019) 141.

history, the decision-making practices that came to carry the name 'consensus' in the GATT/WTO often resulted in outcomes that many considered *unequal* or *undemocratic*, creating a gap between the discourses upon which the multilateral trade regime's authority increasingly relied and the way its decision-making practices were experienced on the ground.

This chapter is in three sections. The first section focuses on the relationship between consensus and the authority of the GATT. It traces how, over the 1960s and 1970s, GATT's 'sense of the meeting' was transformed into the GATT's 'consensus' procedure, paying close attention to the way in which this shift was shaped by debates over inter-state equality during that period. The second part examines the relationship between consensus decision-making and the authority of the WTO, which replaced the GATT in 1995. It describes how, in the move from the GATT to the WTO, the nature of consensus decision-making changed, leading to decision-making difficulties. The WTO responded to these difficulties by deploying a discourse of democracy around its use of consensus decision-making in the early 2000s. The final part of the chapter explores two other forms of consensus decision-making that came about with the transition to the WTO: negative consensus and judicial consensus. It demonstrates how these decision-making practices attracted similar discourses of 'legitimacy', 'equality', and 'democracy', all the while facilitating a fundamental shift in the functioning of the WTO, in which judicial decision-making effectively came to replace political decision-making over the course of the 2000s and 2010s.

2.2 Consensus Decision-Making in the General Agreement on Tariffs and Trade and Discourses of Inter-State Equality

2.2.1 The GATT's 'Sense of the Meeting' Procedure

The General Agreement on Tariffs and Trade of 1947 was a treaty governing international trade relations, which was applied on a provisional basis from 1948 until the establishment of the WTO in 1995.[11] Its drafters originally intended it to be a temporary instrument, which would later be incorporated into the Havana Charter for an International Trade Organization[12] (Havana Charter)—an agreement establishing a new international organization on trade.[13] Drafted in 1947

[11] Protocol of Provisional Application to the General Agreement on Tariffs and Trade, 30 October 1947, 55 UNTS 308 (entered into force 1 January 1948).

[12] Final Act and Related Documents, United Nations Conference on Trade and Employment, Havana Cuba, 21 November 1947–24 March 1948, UN Doc E/CONF.2/78 ('Havana Charter').

[13] Oliver Long, *Law and Its Limitations in the GATT Multilateral Trade System* (Kluwer Academic Publishers 1987) 11.

by the United States (US) and 'a small nuclear group'[14] of states that it assembled, the GATT's aim was to protect already negotiated tariff concessions while details of the new international organization were being finalized.[15] These states envisaged the International Trade Organization (ITO), as it was to be known, as a 'third pillar' of the US-dominated, post-war international economic order, sitting alongside the International Monetary Fund (IMF) and International Bank for Reconstruction and Development (IBRD).[16] At the Havana Conference on Trade and Employment in 1948, fifty-six states agreed to the ITO by signing the Havana Charter. However, as the Havana Charter never attained the approval of the US Congress, it failed to come into existence.[17] In the vacuum left behind, the GATT Contracting Parties transformed that sketchy and provisional treaty into 'what it was never intended to be'[18]—the main multilateral framework for regulating and negotiating tariffs and other trade matters.[19]

The GATT formally provided for majority voting on a 'one state, one vote' basis. Article XXV:4 required most decisions to be taken by a simple majority vote; Articles XXV:5 and XXX:1 required a two-thirds majority for decisions on waivers and most amendments,[20] respectively. This decision-making structure contrasted with that of the IMF and IBRD, which used weighted voting. Zamora asserts that this distinction arose because the drafters of the GATT paid 'scant attention' to its decision-making provisions, believing the instrument to be an interim measure.[21] This assertion is supported by the negotiating history, which reveals that the US and UK quickly accepted majority voting in the GATT in February 1947,[22] despite both having proposals for weighted voting in the ITO on the table at that time.[23] Nevertheless, the final text of the Havana Charter ended up providing for majority voting in the ITO itself.[24] Kaya argues that the Havana Charter's equal voting provisions added to its unpopularity within the US, contributing to its failure to pass Congress.[25]

[14] Douglas A Irwin, Petros C Mavroidis, and Alan O Sykes, *The Genesis of the GATT* (Cambridge University Press 2011) 62. Those states were the United Kingdom, Canada, Australia, New Zealand, South Africa, France, the Netherlands, Belgium, China, Brazil, and India.

[15] ibid 80.

[16] Long (n 13) 1.

[17] Karin Kock, *International Trade Policy and the Gatt 1947–1967* (Almqvist & Wiksell 1969) 57–60.

[18] John Jackson, 'Review: Oliver Long, Law and Its Limitations in the GATT Multilateral Trade System' (1988) 82 American Journal of International Law 653, 653.

[19] Long (n 13) 1–5; Jackson (n 18) 163.

[20] Amendments to Part 1, Article XXIX, and Article XXX required unanimity.

[21] Stephen Zamora, 'Voting in International Economic Organizations' (1980) 74 American Journal of International Law 566, 579.

[22] Drafting Committee of the Preparatory Committee of the UN Conference on Trade and Employment, Suggested Amendments to the Draft General Agreement Submitted by the Delegate for the United States and the Draft Declaration Submitted by the Delegate for the United Kingdom, E/PC/T/C.6/65 (10 February 1947) 2.

[23] Drafting Committee of the Preparatory Committee of the UN Conference on Trade and Employment, *First Report of the Administrative Sub-Committee (Report on Executive Board Membership and Voting)*, E/PC/T/C.6/62 (10 February 1947), Appendices 1–3.

[24] Havana Charter (n 12), Article 75.

[25] Ayse Kaya, 'Designing the Multilateral Trading System: Voting Equality at the International Trade Organization' (2016) 15 World Trade Review 25, 28.

Once the GATT was up and running, the Contracting Parties began to dispense with the GATT's formal voting rules. From the early 1950s, they started taking decisions by 'the sense of the meeting' in lieu of a formal vote[26]—a decision-making method that would later become known as 'consensus'. One of the earliest records of the GATT's move to this procedure is a 1953 report of the Working Party on the 'Arrangements for Japanese Participation', which provides: 'the CONTRACTING PARTIES do not usually proceed to a formal vote in reaching decisions; generally, the Chairman takes the "sense of meeting".'[27] This phrase appears again in a resolution on the participation of Switzerland in 1958[28] and the resolution on the participation of Israel in 1959.[29] Under the 'sense of the meeting' procedure, the chairperson would seek a 'compromise between the different propositions, and propos[e] it for adoption without putting the matter to a vote'.[30] If no Contracting Party formally disagreed with the proposal, a decision was considered reached.[31]

Scholars have advanced numerous reasons for the GATT's move to the 'sense of the meeting' procedure. One is that it enabled the Contracting Parties to avoid voting on controversial matters.[32] Another is that it provided flexibility in decision-making, especially in relation to non-Contracting Parties' participation.[33] A third explanation, which garners significant scholarly support, is that the 'sense of the meeting' emerged within the GATT as a substitute for weighted voting.[34] The 'sense of the meeting' procedure can have a weighted effect on decision-making because, in the absence of formal voting rules, powerful states have more opportunity to use their market size and/or geopolitical power to influence the decision-making process.[35] As the only way to prevent a decision from being adopted under

[26] Mary E Footer, 'The Role of Consensus in GATT/WTO Decision-Making' (1997) 17 Northwestern Journal of International Law & Business 653, 665.

[27] GATT Doc G/55/Rev.1 (1953), cited in ibid.

[28] Participation of Switzerland in the Thirteenth Session of the Contracting Parties: Recommendation by the Intersessional Committee, GATT Doc W.13/3 (16 October 1958) [1].

[29] Summary of the Tenth Meeting, Contracting Parties Fourteenth Session, GATT Doc SR.14/10 (10 June 1959), 120. However, note that a vote took place on this occasion with one abstention (Pakistan) and one vote against (Indonesia).

[30] Henry G Schermers and Niels M Blokker, *International Institutional Law* (5th edn, Martinus Nijhoff 2011) 539, describing how the 'sense of the meeting' procedure operates.

[31] ibid.

[32] See, eg, Long (n 13) 55.

[33] See, eg, John Jackson, *World Trade and the Law of GATT: A Legal Analysis of the General Agreement on Tariffs and Trade* (Bobbs-Merrill 1969) 123.

[34] See, eg, Peter Drahos, 'Weaving Webs of Influence: The United States, Free Trade Agreements and Dispute Resolution' (2007) 41 Journal of World Trade 191, 194; Claus-Dieter Ehlermann and Lothar Ehring, 'Are WTO Decision-Making Procedures Adequate for Making, Revising, and Implementing Worldwide and "Plurilateral" Rules?' in Ernst-Ulrich Petersmann and James Harrison (eds), *Reforming the World Trading System: Legitimacy, Efficiency, and Democratic Governance* (Oxford University Press 2005) 513; Footer (n 26) 668; John Jackson, 'Designing and Implementing Effective Dispute Settlement Procedures: WTO Dispute Settlement, Appraisal and Prospects' in Anne O Krueger (ed), *The WTO as an International Organization* (University of Chicago Press 1998) 177.

[35] Asif H Qureshi, *The World Trade Organization: Implementing International Trade Norms* (Manchester University Press 1996) 6–7.

this procedure is to block it—a move that can come with political and economic costs—powerful states are also in a better position to maintain an objection to a proposed decision.[36]

As time went on, the GATT's emphasis on the 'sense of the meeting' procedure increased. By the 1960s, the Contracting Parties had dispensed with voting entirely for all decisions other than those relating to waivers or accession.[37] By the 1970s, the GATT Secretariat had begun to promote the Contracting Parties' use of what was now being called 'consensus decision-making'. For example, in contrast to the commentaries on earlier rounds of trade negotiations, which make little mention of the Contracting Parties' decision-making method, the term 'consensus' appears throughout the press release on the results of the Tokyo Round (1973–79), with approving statements such as 'the outcome has been very satisfactory. A series of consensus agreements has been reached.'[38]

To understand the almost complete substitution of voting with consensus decision-making within the GATT in the 1960s, as well as the Secretariat's increasing promotion of it in the 1970s, we must look to the surrounding historical context. The wave of decolonization that had taken place between the late 1940s and the mid-1970s meant there were now more states from the global South in many multilateral institutions than there were states from the North.[39] By 1970, for example, the GATT had seventy-seven Contracting Parties, fifty-two of which were considered 'developing' countries.[40] In this context, international lawyers in the global North began promoting the idea of taking decisions without a vote as a way to preserve the power of wealthy states in international institutions, while also appearing to adhere to the principle of sovereign equality. In 1978, for example, Jonathan Charney, an American legal academic and member of the US delegation at the Third UN Conference on the Law of the Sea (UNCLOS III), wrote:

> The consensus system assures that decision-making . . . will not be dominated by the numerical superiority of any group of nations. Rather, procedural significance will be given to the variations in the power of nations. Since it is difficult to obtain acceptance of voting systems that overtly recognize the differences in nations' importance, the consensus approach permits the maintenance of an

[36] Drahos explains this effect within the GATT as follows: 'A powerful player such as the United States could better absorb the costs of negating consensus, more credibly threaten the negation of consensus and find more ways to exert pressure in order to obtain consensus', see Drahos (n 34) 194. See also Ehlermann and Ehring (n 34) 513.

[37] Richard H Steinberg, 'In the Shadow of Law or Power? Consensus-Based Bargaining and Outcomes in the GATT/WTO' (2002) 56 International Organization 339, 344.

[38] GATT Annual Session Acts on Tokyo Round Results and Sets Future Work Programme, GATT Doc GATT/1253 (30 November 1979) 2.

[39] Schermers and Blokker (n 30) 546.

[40] Roshani M Gunewardene, 'GATT and the Developing World: Is a New Principle of Trade Liberalization Needed?' (1991) 15 Maryland Journal of International Law 45, 47, fn 10.

egalitarian procedure which in practice may assure that multilateral negotiations reflect the real geopolitical power of the participating nations.[41]

Views such as these led non-voting to become increasingly popular in international organizations and conferences in the 1960s and 1970s,[42] and effectively replace voting altogether within the GATT.

But the emphasis on an international decision-making procedure that increasingly carried the name 'consensus' did more than offer states in the global North a pragmatic solution to the South's numerical superiority. In my argument, consensus became a technique through which states in the North could flatten, reshape, and subvert an alternative international legal imaginary that was being articulated by states in the global South at the time and reassert the authority of existing international legal and economic arrangements. In order to understand how consensus became a tool of authorization and deauthorization during this period, it is necessary to put the GATT to one side for a moment and revisit the so-called battle for international law of the decolonization era,[43] which was primarily waged in other international fora.

2.2.2 The New International Economic Order, Consensus, and Competing Ideas of Inter-State Equality

In the 1960s and 1970s, states in the global South used their newfound majority power in bodies such as the UN General Assembly (UNGA) to call for a 'New International Economic Order' (NIEO).[44] This was expressed in a series of resolutions in the UNGA, including the Declaration on Permanent Sovereignty Over Natural Resources (1962),[45] the Declaration on the Establishment of a New International Economic Order and Programme of Action (1974),[46] the

[41] Jonathan Charney, 'United States Interests in a Convention on the Law of the Sea: The Case for Continued Efforts' (1978) 11 Vanderbilt University Journal of Transnational Law 39, 43.

[42] David Kennedy, 'The Move to Institutions' in Jan Klabbers (ed), *International Organizations* (2nd edn, Routledge 2016) 126–32.

[43] Jochen von Bernstorff and Philipp Dann (eds), *The Battle for International Law: South–North Perspectives on the Decolonization Era* (Oxford University Press 2019).

[44] The term 'new international economic order' was coined by Raúl Prebisch in 1963, see Adom Getachew, *Worldmaking after Empire: The Rise and Fall of Self-Determination* (Princeton University Press 2019) 161. However, Anghie writes that its political origins 'can be traced back at least to the Bandung Conference in 1955 and its attempts to foster solidarity among newly independent', see Antony Anghie, 'Legal Aspects of the New International Economic Order' (2015) 6 Humanity 145, 146. On the way states in the South used their numbers in bodies such as the UNGA to put forward this vision, see ibid.

[45] GA Res 1803 (XVII), UN Doc. A/RES/1803/(XVII) (14 December 1962). Adopted by eighty-seven votes in favour; two against; twelve abstentions.

[46] GA Res 3201 (S-VI), UN Doc A/RES/3201/(S-VI) and GA Res 3202 (S-VI), UN Doc A/RES/3202/(S-VI) (1 May 1974) ('NIEO Declaration'). Adopted by 'consensus' but with five reservations, see 'Reservations Entered by the United States, German Federal Republic, France, Japan, and the United Kingdom', 13 ILM 744 (1974).

Charter of Economic Rights and Duties of States (1974),[47] and the Resolution on Development and International Economic Co-Operation (1975).[48] States in the South also pursued the NIEO through the United Nations Conference on Trade and Development (UNCTAD), which began as a one-off conference in Geneva in 1964 but subsequently became a permanent organ of the UN. For many states in the South, UNCTAD offered an important institutional alternative to the GATT, which they considered to be a product of a Eurocentric international order.[49]

The core of the NIEO was a pursuit of greater inter-state equality. As Gilman writes:

> The economic proposals of the NIEO and the legal ideas for their implementation were, in the end, merely instruments in the service of the political goal of creating true global democracy of equal (and equally) sovereign states, thereby completing the process of decolonization.[50]

There were two components to the NIEO's vision for inter-state equality. First, states in the South claimed a right to 'full and effective'[51] participatory equality in international economic decision-making. In relation to this right, states in the South appeared to favour majority voting. In the Joint Declaration of the Group of Seventy-Seven (1964), for example, a coalition of states predominantly from Africa, Asia, and Latin America—known as the 'Group of 77' (G77)—expressed support for simple and special majority voting in UNCTAD on the grounds that they 'attach[ed] cardinal importance to democratic procedures which afford no position of privilege in the economic and financial, no less than in the political, sphere'.[52] Second, proponents of the NIEO demanded greater substantive equality within the global economy through measures such as development assistance and preferential treatment in trade agreements.[53] This stemmed from the view that formal equality alone was not enough to render them full participants within the international economic order.[54]

[47] GA Res 3281(XXIX), UN Doc A/RES/3281(XXIX) (12 December 1974). Adopted with 120 votes in favour; 6 against; 10 abstentions.

[48] GA Res 3362 (S-VII), UN Doc A/RES/3362/(S-VII) (16 September 1975). Adopted by 'consensus' but 'some wording was not acceptable to the U.S. or other industrial nations, and these objections were to be read into the record of the Special Session', see Karen A Hudes, 'Towards a New International Economic Order' (1975) 2 Yale Journal of International Law 88, 153.

[49] Getachew (n 44) 164.

[50] Nils Gilman, 'The New International Economic Order: A Reintroduction' (2015) 6 Humanity 1, 6.

[51] See, eg, Article 4(c), NIEO Declaration (n 46).

[52] Joint Declaration of the Seventy-Seven Developing Countries, 15 June 1964, available at <https://www.g77.org/doc/Joint%20Declaration.html>.

[53] See, eg, Article 4(n) and (o) NIEO Declaration (n 46).

[54] Getachew (n 44) 163–64.

The fact that the legal and political project associated with the NIEO could be viewed as 'a scaling up of the democracy principle to the international level'[55] was a problem for states in the North, which wished to maintain existing economic arrangements without appearing to undermine such democratic aims.[56] This unease can be seen in France's reservation to the Declaration on the Establishment of a NIEO in 1974, in which it claimed that the 'programme naturally ha[d] the approval of a country such as France, which is not unaware of how history is made up of revolutions',[57] before going on to outline its concerns with the resolution in question. If states in the North were to reassert the authority of existing international economic arrangements, they would need to present an alternative international democratic imaginary. And, for this purpose, they appear to have settled on consensus.

The rhetorical push for consensus began at the first UNCTAD in 1964. During the Conference, there was a dispute over the decision-making rules to be applied.[58] Western states, led by the US, put forward a proposal that the Conference's recommendations should be adopted by a two-thirds majority of members, *including a majority of the twelve principal trading states*, because, despite being in the minority, their economies represented around 80 per cent of world trade.[59] States in the global South, supported by the Socialist Bloc, rejected this proposal and instead argued for majority voting based on the principle of 'one state, one vote'.[60] Eventually, a compromise was reached. Decisions would be taken by a two-thirds majority vote but there would be the option of a 'conciliation' procedure before a vote, whereby, at the request of a member, a Conciliation Committee would assist the members to reach a compromise.[61] Though a vote could still take place afterwards, voting was banned within the Conciliation Committee.[62] The conciliation procedure also aimed to limit the need for voting by finding a proposal that was acceptable to all sides.[63]

States in the global North framed the object of avoiding majority voting at the first UNCTAD in terms of the need to reach something called 'consensus'. In his closing statement at the Conference, the head of the Swiss delegation, Hans Schaffner, said that while the formation of opinions within coalitions like the G77 could be a 'useful

[55] Quinn Slobodian, *Globalists: The End of Empire and the Birth of Neoliberalism* (Harvard University Press 2018) 220. See also Gilman (n 50) 6.

[56] On the way the NIEO and UNCTAD presented a 'serious challenge' to the hegemony of the GATT framework, see Michael Strange, 'Discursivity of Global Governance: Vestiges of "'Democracy'" in the World Trade Organization' (2011) 36 Alternatives: Global, Local, Political 240, 250.

[57] See, eg, the French Reservation to the NIEO Declaration in Reservations (n 46) 754.

[58] Ugo Villani, 'Conciliation and Consensus in UNCTAD' (1976) 2 Italian Yearbook of International Law 61, 61.

[59] ibid 62.

[60] ibid 63.

[61] Schermers and Blokker (n 30) 537–38.

[62] Villani (n 58) 71.

[63] ibid 77.

preliminary step',[64] 'success . . . will depend on something that no one can define but that everyone understands: the broadest consensus possible'.[65] Likewise, in his closing statement, Edward Heath, the UK's Secretary of State for Industry, Trade, and Regional Development, praised the idea of consensus in the following terms:

> . . . majorities, though easier to obtain, are not as effective as a real consensus of opinion. This is what is required if solid progress is to be made . . . [A]n agreed consensus of view may be less dramatic than a majority of a hundred votes, but it is more likely to feed the hungry, which is our common task. For we must keep always in the forefront of our minds what is our real purpose.[66]

Here, we see the idea of striving for a widespread, but apparently undefinable, agreement called 'consensus' being put forward as a more 'effective' way of addressing the global South's economic concerns than a majority vote.

The following year, in 1965, British international lawyer and legal scholar Clarence Wilfred Jenks[67] wrote an essay on decision-making in international organizations, in which he grouped UNCTAD's conciliation procedure together with other non-voting procedures, including the 'sense of the meeting' procedure, under the heading 'consensus'.[68] Jenks observed that '[i]n the search for a new compromise between ease and responsibility of action the concept of consensus as the most appropriate basis for important decisions has attracted an increasing measure of attention'.[69] Like the European representatives at UNCTAD, he saw this shift as necessary for effective decision-making in the postcolonial era: 'A wider acceptance of the principle of consensus represents the only realistic approach to many of our difficulties'.[70] Though Jenks did not define 'consensus', he did not appear to see it as referring to any specific procedure. Rather, for him, it seemed to describe a goal or ethos that guided certain modes of international decision-making. In his account, this principle had a long history in international law:

> Historically, international law owes much to the concept of a general consensus; customary international law has grown out of, and developed by means of, such

[64] Schaffner quoted in Proceedings of the United Nations Conference on Trade and Development: Final Act and Report (Vol 2), UN Doc. E/CONF.46/141 (1964), 530.

[65] ibid [emphasis added].

[66] Heath quoted in ibid, 539.

[67] Jenks went on to become Director-General of the International Labour Organization in 1970.

[68] Wilfred C Jenks, 'Unanimity, the Veto, Weighted Voting, Special and Simple Majorities and Consensus as Modes of Decision in International Organisations', *Cambridge Essays in International Law—Essays in Honour of Lord McNair* (Cambridge University Press 1965) 55–62. Note that the 'sense of meeting' procedure that Jenks described as 'consensus' was that of the Executive Board of the IMF, rather than the GATT, see ibid 56. In 1946, the IMF inserted Rule C-10 into the Rules and Regulations of the Executive Board of the IMF, which states that 'the chairman shall ordinarily ascertain the sense of the meeting in lieu of a formal vote'. See Footer (n 26) 665.

[69] Jenks (n 68) 55.

[70] ibid 63.

> as consensus; the old diplomacy, which we tend to think of as operating on the principle of unanimity, was at its best a collegial conduct of affairs by consensus.[71]

By redescribing consensus as a longstanding international legal principle, Jenks helped to weave it into the existing fabric of international law, imbuing it with the authority of time.[72]

In the 1970s, as the South's push for international legal and economic change gathered momentum, states in the global North became more adamant about the need to put an end to majority voting. In particular, the US was greatly concerned by the adoption of the NIEO-related Charter of Economic Rights and Duties in September 1974 in the UNGA, with 120 states voting in favour, 10 abstentions, and 6 states—Belgium, Denmark, West Germany, Luxembourg, the UK, and the US—voting against.[73] In March 1975, Daniel Moynihan, the US Ambassador to India at the time, wrote an article in which he argued that 'the discovery that a vast majority of the nations of the world feel there are claims which can be made on the wealth of individual nations' was 'both considerable and threatening', especially to the US, 'which regularly finds itself in a minority'.[74] He went on to claim that the US, having learnt to 'deal with Communism' in world affairs, now needed to find ways to address 'the tyranny of the ... "new majority"' and the international 'socialism' that it was breeding.[75] On the basis of this article, US President Gerald Ford appointed Moynihan as US Ambassador to the UN.[76]

From that point onwards, the US' support for a system of international economic law underpinned by the idea of consensus seemed to move from scattered statements of encouragement to a policy.[77] In September 1975, Moynihan, now US Ambassador to the UN, presented a speech on behalf of US Secretary of State

71 ibid 56.

72 On the relationship between authority and time, see Dorsett and McVeigh (n 8) 33, discussing how the doctrine of precedent in the common law tradition creates 'a relation between past, present and future'.

73 Charter of Economic Rights and Duties (n 47).

74 Daniel Moynihan, 'The United States in Opposition' (1975) 59 Commentary, available at <https://www.commentary.org/articles/daniel-moynihan/the-united-states-in-opposition/>.

75 ibid. The US' growing concern about the South's use of majority blocs was also reflected by its response to the Charter of Economic Rights and Duties (n 47), in which the US 'suggested that it might reconsider its vote ... if additional negotiations could reach an agreed consensus on those issues vital to "countries whose numbers may be small but whose significance in economic relations and development can hardly be ignored"'. See Charles N Brower and John B Tepe, 'The Charter of Economic Rights and Duties of States: A Reflection or Rejection of International Law?' (1976) 9 International Lawyer 295, 300.

76 The declassified record of President Ford's first meeting with Moynihan reveals that US Secretary of State Henry Kissinger said to the President: '[t]hat Commentary article is one of the most important articles in a long time. That is why it is essential to have him [Moynihan] at the UN', see *Memorandum of Conversation*, Washington, April 12, 1975, 10:45 am, available at <https://history.state.gov/historicaldocuments/frus1969-76ve14p1/d22>.

77 On the way Kissinger's 1975 speech represented a turning point in US policy towards the NIEO, see Daniel J Sargent, 'North/South: The United States Responds to the New International Economic Order' (2015) 6 Humanity 201, 210.

Henry Kissinger entitled 'Global Consensus and Economic Development'.[78] In this speech, Kissinger warned that 'the division of the planet between North and South, between rich and poor, could become as grim as the darkest days of the cold war',[79] eventually leading to 'the erosion of international institutions . . . and failed development.'[80] To avoid this outcome, Kissinger argued, there was a need for a global 'consensus on the realities and principles of the development effort',[81] built upon 'the equality and cooperation of states'.[82] He then outlined a number of principles for international economic decision-making, one of which was that the methods of participation 'must be realistic'.[83] In this regard, Kissinger stated that '[t]he genuine diversity of interests that exists among states must not be submerged by bloc discipline or in artificial, unrepresentative majorities. For only genuine consensus can generate effective action.'[84]

In this speech, Kissinger not only continued the narrative, established in the mid-1960s, that reaching an international consensus was the only 'effective' means through which to address the South's economic concerns. He also posited consensus as a more 'realistic' model for participatory equality in international decision-making, presenting it as more 'representative' and less 'divisive' than majority voting, while still just as capable of ensuring 'the equality . . . of states'. Moreover, although Kissinger did not endorse any particular procedure, his support for a non-majoritarian mode of decision-making that could generate a 'consensus' seemed to point towards the non-voting procedures that were being called 'consensus' at the time. In the years that followed, a body of international legal scholarship sprang up, explicitly championing consensus decision-making as the most effective way of securing international cooperation,[85] as well as the most realistic way of achieving 'the practice of global democracy of some sort'.[86] And it was against this backdrop that the GATT Secretariat began treating its weighted 'sense of the meeting' procedure—now framed as 'consensus'—as a virtue, mentioning it with approval in its press releases.

[78] Henry Kissinger, 'Global Consensus and Economic Development' (delivered by Moynihan at the Seventh Special Session of the UNGA), *Department of State Bulletin* (1975). Note that this was the same session at which the Resolution on Development and International Economic Co-Operation (1975) (n 48) was passed.

[79] Kissinger (n 78) 425.

[80] ibid.

[81] ibid 426.

[82] ibid 425.

[83] ibid 440.

[84] ibid.

[85] See, eg, Eric Suy, 'The Meaning of Consensus in Multilateral Diplomacy' in Robert J Akkerman, Peter J Krieken, and Charles O Pannenbourg (eds), *Declarations on Principles: A Quest for Universal Peace* (A W Sijthoff 1977) 260; Sidney Weintraub, 'North–South Dialogue at the United Nations: How the UN Votes on Economic Issues' (1977) 53 International Affairs 188, 188.

[86] Barry Buzan, 'Negotiating by Consensus: Developments in Technique at the United Nations Conference on the Law of the Sea' (1981) 75 The American Journal of International Law 324, 328.

States in the South did not all agree with the idea that consensus decision-making could fulfil their demand for participatory equality. In 1973, for example, several Southern delegations opposed a proposal, put forward by the Soviet Union and supported by the US, to minimize voting in order to reach consensus at UNCLOS III due to the consensus procedure's potential to operate as a veto power, thus undermining decision-making equality.[87] The representative for Kenya, Frank Njenga, for example, stated that the principle of '[e]quality of States is completely inconsistent with the power of any State to veto proposals commanding the support of an overwhelming number of States . . . as would be the case with a consensus procedure'.[88] The representative for China, Ling Qing, was more scathing:

> [A] super-Power, under the smokescreen of practising 'consensus', asserted that the rules of a new law of the sea would have international observance only if they were supported by all countries . . . The intent of these remarks is all too obvious: that is, as long as this super-Power alone does not agree, the Conference cannot be held and the new law of the sea cannot be established. Is this not typical hegemonism? . . . In our opinion, consultations are desirable; but there certainly should be some method of voting in formulating a new law of the sea. The Chinese delegation firmly opposes the attempt . . . to impose on the Conference the so-called principle of 'consensus' which is tantamount to a veto.[89]

Writing on international decision-making in the context of the NIEO in 1979, Algerian diplomat and jurist, Mohammed Bedjaoui characterized consensus decision-making as an 'enormous concession' of the part of the 'majority states', which had come about as a way for the 'industrialized countries' to 'get around majority rule'.[90] Like Njenga and Qing, he considered that the turn to consensus decision-making had introduced 'a new form of "veto"'[91] into international organizations.

However, states in the South did seem open to the idea that striving for a widespread international agreement might offer them the most 'realistic' pathway for achieving economic equality. After all, they were conscious that if they wanted to see significant economic change, they would need to secure the cooperation of the wealthy states. As UNCTAD Secretary-General Raúl Prebisch put it: 'There is obviously no immediate practical purpose in adopting recommendations by a simple majority of the developing countries but without the favourable votes of the

[87] See Louis B Sohn, 'Voting Procedures in United Nations Conferences for the Codification of International Law' (1975) 69 The American Journal of International Law 310, 335–36.

[88] First Committee, Third United Nations Conference on the Law of the Sea, 1929th Meeting, UN Doc A/C.1/PV.1929 (18 October 1973) [50].

[89] First Committee, Third United Nations Conference on the Law of the Sea, 1932nd Meeting, UN Doc A/C.1/PV.1932 (22 October 1973) [61].

[90] Mohammed Bedjaoui, *Towards a New International Economic Order* (Holmes & Meier 1979) 171.

[91] ibid 168.

developed countries, when the execution of those recommendations depends on their acceptance by the latter.'[92] Consequently, states in the South began seeking consensus on some of their own NIEO-related resolutions. In May 1974, for example, the South succeeded in having the Declaration on the Establishment of a NIEO adopted by the UNGA without a vote.[93] However, the Declaration was accompanied by five reservations from states in the North,[94] including one from the US objecting to the use of the term 'consensus'.[95] In the US' account, the passage of the Declaration without a vote could not be called a 'consensus' because, while the US 'did not choose to voice objection to the resolution presented', '[t]o label some of these highly controversial conclusions as agreed [was] not only idle; it [was] self-deceiving'.[96] In this reservation, we see that what 'consensus' meant to the US, at least at this time, was not simply a decision taken without a vote. Rather, for the US, it was a general agreement that could only exist when it too was in accordance.

2.2.3 The GATT's Consensus Procedure and the Global South

It is here that we return to the GATT. In the 1960s, states in the global South had largely avoided using the GATT as part of their attempts to establish the NIEO, instead preferring the UNGA and UNCTAD, where they benefited from the voting rules[97] and the idea of reimagining international trade seemed more possible.[98] In the 1970s, however, states in the South began to engage more actively with the GATT as part of their pursuit of a more equitable global economy. In 1971, for example, they successfully negotiated a ten-year waiver to the GATT, which allowed the 'developed contracting parties . . . to accord preferential tariff treatment to products originating in developing countries and territories'.[99] Once the Tokyo Round of GATT trade negotiations (1973–79) was under way, states such as India and Egypt used the negotiations as a platform to advance the NIEO. In 1975, for example, Ambassador K. B. Lall of India proposed a 'study on possible techniques for re-ordering our mutual relations to expand production in and enlarge exchange of goods with and amongst the developing countries'.[100] In 1976, Egyptian representative M. A. B Hamza called for several measures to 'ameliorate

[92] Quoted in UNCTAD Proceedings (1964) (n 64), 553.
[93] See the NIEO Declaration (n 46).
[94] The other states that entered reservations were the UK, France, Japan, and West Germany.
[95] See Reservations (n 46).
[96] ibid 745.
[97] Anghie (n 44) 146.
[98] On the view amongst many in the South in the 1960s that the GATT needed a complete overhaul, Luis Eslava, 'The Developmental State: Independence, Dependency, and the History of the South' in Jochen von Bernstorff and Philipp Dann (eds), *The Battle for International Law: South–North Perspectives on the Decolonization Era* (Oxford University Press 2019) 89.
[99] Generalized System of Trade Preferences, GATT Doc L/3545 (25 June 1971).
[100] Statement of the Representative of India, GATT Doc CG.18/WA (25 November 1975), 5.

the critical situation of the developing countries'.[101] In both of these statements, the representatives for India and Egypt referred to the UNGA Resolution on Development and International Economic Co-Operation (1975),[102] thereby building a bridge between the GATT and NIEO-related developments in other international fora.

While the South's turn to the GATT in the 1970s may have been influenced by the praise that had started to surround its use of consensus decision-making, it also appears to have been predicated on a belief that these states could use their numerical power to offset the weighted nature of that procedure. After all, they had succeeded in having the Declaration on the Establishment of a NIEO adopted without a vote in the UNGA in 1974, even if the US had objected to the use of the term 'consensus'. States in the South seem to have taken the view that, with enough planning, the GATT's consensus procedure could work in their favour.[103] To secure their success, the Informal Group of Developing Countries—the South's coalition within the GATT—met regularly in the final months of the Tokyo Round to coordinate their strategy.[104] They also called on UNCTAD to give them 'technical assistance . . . to facilitate their effective participation in the negotiations'.[105]

States in the South enjoyed some successes during the Tokyo Round. Most notably, in 1979, they won the right to 'differential and more favourable treatment' on a permanent basis[106]—just as they had originally demanded as part of the NIEO. These gains were not, however, purely the result of numerical superiority and UNCTAD assistance. While states in the North resented what they saw as the '"UNCTADization" of the GATT'[107] during the 1970s, they ultimately chose against using coercive tactics to dominate the agenda-setting process.[108] This was due to the Cold War context of the Tokyo Round, in which the US was concerned about the geopolitical alignment of the global South, especially after Soviet support for their efforts to strengthen UNCTAD in the 1960s.[109] As a result, the US wanted as many Southern states in the GATT system as possible. Allowing them some leverage in its consensus procedure formed part of this strategy.[110]

The provisional nature of the global South's influence within the GATT in the 1970s became clear during the Uruguay Round (1986–94) when, with a rapidly

[101] Statement by the Representative of Egypt, GATT Doc CG.IS/W/6 (24 February 1976), 2.
[102] ibid 1; Statement of the Representative of India (n 100) 5–6.
[103] Steinberg (n 37) 357.
[104] ibid.
[105] Recent Trends in International Trade and Development, UNCTAD Res 91(IV), UN Doc TD/218 (30 May 1976) [16].
[106] Decision on Differential and More Favourable Treatment, Reciprocity and Fuller Participation of Developing Countries, GATT Doc L/4903 (28 November 1979).
[107] Steinberg (n 37) 359.
[108] ibid.
[109] ibid 345.
[110] ibid 356–59.

shifting geopolitical landscape, states in the South felt the full weighted nature of its consensus procedure come down upon them. First, in the lead-up to the Uruguay Round, the US, European Communities (EC), Canada, and Japan formed a group known as the 'Quad'.[111] By bringing the largest economies together, this group was able to wield significant influence over the GATT's consensus procedure before and during the official negotiations.[112] In contrast, states in the South entered the Uruguay Round in a weaker and less unified position due to the debt crisis of the 1980s and the structural adjustment programmes (SAPs) that followed.[113] The SAPs, which were conditions imposed by financial institutions such as the IMF and World Bank in return for bailout loans, restructured Southern economies in ways that made them more export-dependent.[114] This not only made it harder for some states in the South to resist the North's trade liberalization proposals in the way they had in previous Rounds,[115] but also fractured groups such as the G77[116] and the GATT Informal Group of Developing Countries,[117] rendering the South more vulnerable to the North's 'divide and coerce'[118] tactics once the Uruguay Round was under way.

During the Uruguay Round, the Quad's influence was also facilitated through the use of 'Green Room' meetings, which were small, informal gatherings that had been used within the GATT since the Tokyo Round as a way to facilitate 'consensus building'.[119] Green Room meetings usually consisted of twenty to thirty-five states and would include states in the 'inner circle of power',[120] as well as a 'roughly

[111] For an overview of the Quad, see Theodore Cohn, *Governing Global Trade: International Institutions in Conflict and Convergence* (Routledge 2002) 123–67.

[112] An official WTO publication notes that '[u]ntil the mid-1990s, the "Quad"—the US, EU, Japan and Canada, then the largest traders—were seen as the most powerful consensus brokers', see World Trade Organization, *10 Things The WTO Can Do* (2012) 38, available at <https://www.wto.org/english/res_e/publications_e/wtocan_e.pdf>.

[113] Donatella Alessandrini, *Developing Countries and the Multilateral Trade Regime: The Failure and Promise of the WTO's Development Mission* (Hart Publishing 2010) 105. See also John Toye, 'Assessing the G77: 50 Years After UNCTAD and 40 Years After the NIEO' (2014) 35 Third World Quarterly 1759, 1767.

[114] Alessandrini (n 113) 105.

[115] ibid. See also Toye (n 113) 1767.

[116] In the context of the G77, Toye explains that '[d]ebt problems . . . pulled the Latin Americans and Africans apart because their crises followed very different trajectories', the former's debts mainly being to private sector banks, the latter's to public sector institutions, see Toye (n 113) 1767. While states from the South had never negotiated as the G77 within the GATT, they had been guided by its policy objectives and bolstered in their negotiating position by its political weight, see Amrita Narlikar, *International Trade and Developing Countries: Bargaining Coalitions in the GATT & WTO* (Taylor & Francis 2005) 62.

[117] This can be seen, for example, in the split between the G10 (Argentina, Brazil, Egypt, India, Yugoslavia, Cuba, Nigeria, Nicaragua, Peru, and Tanzania) and the remainder of the Informal Group of Developing Countries in the lead-up to the Uruguay Round over the former's hardline position on services, for an overview see Narlikar (n 116) 74–76.

[118] BS Chimni, 'Political Economy of the Uruguay Round of Negotiations: A Perspective' (1992) 29 International Studies 135, 142.

[119] Kristen Hopewell, *Breaking the WTO: How Emerging Powers Disrupted the Neoliberal Project* (Stanford University Press 2016) 47.

[120] ibid.

representative subset'[121] of the remainder of the GATT's Contracting Parties. From within these informal meetings, the Quad was able to expand outwards an agreement that it had reached on an issue.[122] As Cold War tensions thawed, states in the North also became less hesitant about resorting to coercive tactics to achieve their trade policy objectives. In 1988, for example, the US passed legislation enhancing Section 301 of the US Trade Act of 1974.[123] This new provision, known colloquially as 'Super 301',[124] allowed the US to take unilateral retaliatory action against states not only for violating international trade agreements, but also for conduct that 'unjustifiably' or 'unreasonably' burdened US commerce.[125]

Throughout the Uruguay Round negotiations, the US used the threat of these unilateral trade sanctions to pressure states into accepting its proposals.[126] For example, in order to break the unity of India and Brazil in their opposition to the proposed Trade-Related Intellectual Property Rights (TRIPS) Agreement,[127] the US began a Section 301 investigation against Brazil over patent protection for pharmaceutical products in 1987 and increased tariffs on Brazilian goods the following year.[128] This led Brazil to drop its opposition to the TRIPS Agreement in 1990, isolating India and paving the way for a consensus on the TRIPS Agreement to be reached.[129]

In addition, the US and EC pushed for all the proposed Uruguay Round agreements, as well as a framework agreement establishing the WTO, to be accepted as a 'single undertaking'.[130] This meant that rather than being able to pick and choose between agreements, states had to sign on to the whole package on 'all-or-nothing basis'.[131] The 'single undertaking' principle had come about with the launch of the Uruguay Round as a procedural device, which required all agreements relating to goods, intellectual property, and investment 'to be negotiated, adopted and implemented by all negotiating parties at the same time'.[132] However, as the end of the

[121] Steinberg (n 37) 355.
[122] Hopewell (n 119) 62.
[123] ibid 57.
[124] A Lynne Puckett and William L Reynolds, 'Rules, Sanctions and Enforcement under Section 301: At Odds with the WTO?' (1996) 90 American Journal of International Law 675, 680.
[125] Hopewell (n 119) 57.
[126] Chimni (n 118) 143.
[127] Agreement on Trade-Related Aspects of Intellectual Property Rights, Marrakesh Agreement Establishing the World Trade Organisation, Annex 1C, opened for signature 15 April 1994, 1869 UNTS 299 (entered into force 1 January 1995).
[128] Peter Drahos and John Braithwaite, *Information Feudalism: Who Owns the Knowledge Economy?* (Earthscan 2002) 136.
[129] ibid.
[130] Steinberg (n 37) 360.
[131] Tadgh Ó Laoghaire, 'Making Offers They Can't Refuse: Consensus and Domination in the WTO' (2018) 5 Moral Philosophy and Politics 227, 245. The US presented this plan to the EC in October 1990, which then agreed to back it, see Steinberg (n 37) 360.
[132] Miguel Rodríguez Mendoza and Marie Wilke, 'Revisiting the Single Undertaking: Towards a More Balanced Approach to WTO Negotiations' in Carolyn Deere Birkbeck (ed), *Making Global Trade Governance Work for Development: Perspectives and Priorities from Developing Countries* (Cambridge University Press 2011) 490 [emphasis removed].

Uruguay Round neared, the US and EC gave this principle teeth by declaring that they would both withdraw from the GATT 1947 upon joining the WTO.[133] This meant that if other states wished to preserve their existing trade relationship with the world's largest economies, they had no choice but to sign onto the proposed trade organization and accept the 'single undertaking'.[134]

The Uruguay Round concluded in 1994 with an agreement to establish the WTO, along with several other far-reaching trade agreements. These agreements favoured the global North—requiring liberalization in areas in which the US and Europe had an advantage, such as services, while requiring very little liberalization in areas in which they did not, such as agriculture.[135] The Uruguay Agreements also watered down the principle of 'special and differential treatment' that had underpinned the GATT since the 1970s, emphasizing uniform trade rules instead.[136] Upon realizing what they had agreed to, many states in the South expressed dissatisfaction with the results of the Uruguay Round.[137] They felt that they had made considerable concessions without having gained much in return. As one observer from the South later put it in an interview with Kristen Hopewell: 'We felt we came out of the Round with empty pockets. We had our list of what we wanted and they had theirs. They got almost everything on theirs and we got almost none of ours.'[138]

Corporate lobbying of Northern governments during the Uruguay Round,[139] combined with the economic philosophy of US and European trade policymakers at the time, also meant that the resulting trade regime took on a neoliberal character. While the meaning of 'neoliberalism' remains contested,[140] I am using it to refer to a political and economic agenda that emphasizes trade liberalization, deregulation, and privatization, while also embracing the use of law and institutions as a way to 'encase' the market from political interference.[141] The new WTO system reflected this orientation in a number of ways. First, the WTO's creation brought with it a new judicialized dispute settlement procedure, which would be both compulsory and binding.[142] Second, the Uruguay Round Agreements expanded the

133 Ó Laoghaire (n 131) 245.

134 ibid. See also Steinberg (n 37) 360.

135 Alessandrini (n 113) 132–57.

136 Chantal Thomas, 'The Death of Doha? Forensics of Democratic Governance, Distributive Justice, and Development in the WTO' in Chi Carmody, Frank J Garcia, and John Linarelli (eds), *Global Justice and International Economic Law: Opportunities and Prospects* (Cambridge University Press 2012) 188.

137 Hopewell (n 119) 71.

138 Quoted in ibid 69. This interview was conducted in 2010.

139 On the 'unprecedented' involvement of the corporate sector in the Uruguay Round negotiations, see Alessandrini (n 113) 106. This issue is discussed further in Chapter 3.

140 Slobodian (n 55) 2.

141 On the idea of neoliberalism as 'encasement', see ibid 5–7. On the relationship between neoliberalism and legalism in the context of trade, see also Ntina Tzouvala, 'Neoliberalism as Legalism: International Economic Law and the Rise of the Judiciary' in Ben Golder and Daniel McLoughlin (eds), *The Politics of Legality in a Neoliberal Age* (Routledge 2017); Andrew Lang, *World Trade Law After Neoliberalism: Re-Imagining the Global Economic Order* (Oxford University Press 2011).

142 Dani Rodrik, *The Globalization Paradox: Democracy and the Future of the World Economy* (WW Norton 2011) 78–79.

multilateral trade regime into new areas, including services, agriculture, intellectual property, and investment.[143] Third, they deepened its reach by requiring the removal or harmonization of a range of new 'beyond-the-border' trade barriers.[144] This meant WTO law would now regulate multiple policy areas previously belonging to the domestic sphere—marking a shift towards what Rodrik describes as 'deep integration'.[145]

Not only was this trade regime a far cry from the 'socialist globalization'[146] the global South had once envisaged as part of the NIEO, but the extensive 'beyond-the-border' measures contained in the Uruguay Agreements required states in the South to undertake significant legal and institutional changes to harmonize their regulatory systems with those in the North.[147] These changes proved extremely costly in terms of both human and material resources.[148] Consequently, almost as soon as the Uruguay Round was over, the states in the South began calling on the WTO to address what became known as the 'implementation issues'.[149]

The outcome of the Uruguay Round revealed just how much the GATT's consensus procedure was skewed in favour of economic power. And yet, by this time, some states in the South appear to have accepted the idea that it *could* offer them 'realistic' participatory equality. Indeed, when the US proposed that the WTO formally adopt consensus as its primary decision-making method at the end of the Uruguay Round, it was actively backed by some states in the South, such as India.[150] The US, for its part, put forward this proposal after initially considering a more explicitly weighted procedure,[151] partly because it saw that 'consensus-based decision-making, rooted in the principle of sovereign equality, had powerful normative appeal'.[152] In other words, the US seemed to understand that, in the battle of ideas over inter-state equality, its illusory, consensus-based version had won, and

143 Kh Menjor Singh, *World Trade Organization and the Third World* (Mittal Publications 2005) 15.
144 ibid.
145 Rodrik (n 142) 83.
146 Johanna Bockman, 'Socialist Globalization against Capitalist Neocolonialism: The Economic Ideas behind the New International Economic Order' (2015) 6 Humanity 109. Note, however, that the radicality of the state-based 'welfare world' of the NIEO should not be overstated, see Getachew (n 44) 142–75. See also Dianne Otto, 'Subalternity and International Law: The Problems of Global Community and the Incommensurability of Difference' (1996) 5 Social & Legal Studies 337.
147 Sylvia Ostry, 'The Uruguay Round North-South Grand Bargain: Implications for Future Negotiations', *The Political Economy of International Trade Law: Essays in Honor of Robert E. Hudec* (Cambridge University Press 2002) 288.
148 Hopewell (n 119) 68.
149 For an overview, see World Trade Organisation, 'Implementation Issues' (*Hong Kong Ministerial: Briefing Notes*, 2005) <https://www.wto.org/english/thewto_e/minist_e/min05_e/brief_e/brief18_e.htm>.
150 Craig VanGrasstek, *The History and Future of the World Trade Organization* (World Trade Organization 2013) 65.
151 Chakravarthi Raghavan, *Recolonization: GATT, the Uruguay Round & the Third World* (Zed Books 1990) 208; Steinberg (n 37) 364.
152 Hopewell (n 119) 59.

the idea of consensus was now integral to the authority of the multilateral trade regime.

Consensus decision-making was thus enshrined in the Marrakesh Agreement Establishing the World Trade Organization (WTO Agreement).[153] The way in which consensus has functioned in the WTO is explored in the next section. However, it is worth noting here that, as time went on, the WTO began to mobilize a discourse around its consensus procedure that no longer simply responded to the NIEO's call for inter-state equality, but instead sought to erase the memory of the NIEO altogether. For example, in an address to the UN Conference on Least Developed Countries in 2001, WTO Director-General Mike Moore stated:

> History is a grim master. Colonial oppression gave way as freedom marched forward. Then, so many were cursed with that seductive phantom of hope, Marxist economics. That hoax and tragedy was followed by another great tragedy, the cold war. The cold war gave leaders grim leverage—that leverage is gone... But... poor and developing countries have a new form of leverage in a new arena, the WTO. Ours is an Organization where Members have equal powers because we operate on a basis of consensus.[154]

In Moore's account of history, the South's pursuit of a NIEO in the 1960s and 1970s is wholly absent, reduced to nothing more than a fleeting moment of Marxist folly and 'grim' Cold War leverage. Instead, he presents the WTO, with its use of consensus decision-making, as the first time 'poor and developing countries' had truly glimpsed equality. With institutional discourses such as these, the memory of the NIEO began to fade within the walls of the WTO, its demands for participatory and substantive equality gradually buried beneath a pile of consensus rhetoric.

2.3 Consensus Decision-Making in the World Trade Organization and Discourses of Democracy

2.3.1 The WTO's Codification of the Consensus Procedure

As noted above, during the Uruguay Round, the GATT Contracting Parties decided to enshrine consensus decision-making in the WTO Agreement. Article IX:1 of that agreement provides that 'the WTO shall continue the practice of decision-making by consensus followed under GATT 1947'. The WTO Agreement also goes

[153] Marrakesh Agreement Establishing the World Trade Organisation, opened for signature 15 April 1994, 1867 UNTS 154 (entered into force 1 January 1995) ('WTO Agreement'), Article IX:1.

[154] Mike Moore, 'The WTO and LDCs: Delivering a Better Future Through Trade' (17 May 2001) <https://www.wto.org/english/news_e/spmm_e/spmm63_e.htm>.

further in its provision for consensus decision-making than that practised under the GATT 1947. For example, under the GATT, waiver decisions were routinely taken by vote.[155] In contrast, Article IX:3 of the WTO Agreement provides that a vote shall only take place on waiver decisions if the Members cannot reach consensus in a period of ninety days. In addition, a footnote to Article IX:3 states that any decision to grant a waiver in relation to transition periods or staged implementation 'shall be taken only by consensus'.[156] Consensus decision-making is also expressly required for amendments to the Uruguay Agreements[157] and decisions by the Dispute Settlement Body under the Dispute Settlement Understanding.[158] However, the WTO Agreement still provides for voting in certain circumstances. In the event that consensus cannot be reached, Article IX:1 provides that the matter shall be decided by a simple majority vote. Article IX:2 also requires that authoritative interpretations of the Uruguay Agreements be made by a three-fourths majority vote.

In addition to codifying and extending the GATT's practice of consensus decision-making, the WTO Agreement also defined consensus. Footnote 1 provides that 'The body concerned shall be deemed to have decided by consensus on a matter submitted for its consideration, if no Member, present at the meeting when the decision is taken, formally objects to the proposed decision'.[159] This marked a shift away from the practice of consensus under the GATT, where there had been some uncertainty about whether a consensus could be declared when a small number of states formally objected to the proposed decision. In 1988, for example, Australia suggested that because 'consensus was not unanimity',[160] the GATT chairperson could conclude that a consensus existed even if one or two states formally disagreed.[161] This ambiguity is also reflected in scholarship. In 1986, Patterson wrote: 'In the GATT framework . . . an agreement is reached when those who do not agree either keep quiet . . . *or are so few or so small in terms of their interest in the issue that their agreement is not regarded . . . as essential*'.[162]

[155] Isabel Feichtner, 'The Waiver Power of the WTO: Opening the WTO for Political Debate on the Reconciliation of Competing Interests' (2009) 20 European Journal of International Law 615, 619.

[156] WTO Agreement (n 153) fn 4.

[157] ibid, Article X:1.

[158] Article 2:4 of the Understanding on Rules and Procedures Governing the Settlement of Disputes, Annex 2 of the WTO Agreement (n 153).

[159] WTO Agreement (n 153) fn 1.

[160] Quoted in 'Institutions and Procedure', *GATT Analytical Index* (6th edn, World Trade Organization 1995) 1108.

[161] ibid 1109. Other GATT Contracting Parties, however, objected to this assertion. For example, India, supported by Brazil, Mexico, Jamaica and Peru, stated that, in its view, '[i]f a contracting party chose to contest a consensus . . . it was then not possible for the Chairman of any GATT body to conclude that a consensus did exist', ibid.

[162] Gardner Patterson, 'The GATT and Negotiating International Trade Rules' in Alan K Henrikson (ed), *Negotiating World Order: The Artisanship and Architecture of Global Diplomacy* (Scholarly Resources, 1986) 181, 184 [emphasis added].

There are a number of reasons why consensus decision-making was codified, extended, and defined in the WTO Agreement. One reason, which I touched on earlier, was that consensus decision-making now carried an egalitarian appeal, helping to shore up the authority of the new trade institution. But another was that the newly defined consensus procedure would make it difficult to alter the Uruguay Agreements. In 1991, during the Uruguay Round, the EC and Canada had put forward a draft of what would eventually become the WTO Agreement.[163] The draft effectively replicated the decision-making provisions in the GATT 1947 by providing for majority voting.[164] Ehlermann and Ehring report that this worried the US.[165] It feared that if consensus remained an informal practice, the US' sovereignty would be undermined if the Uruguay Agreements could be modified through 'quickly formed majorities'.[166] The US was also concerned that 'developing countries would try to use the . . . voting rules to get out of their obligations later on'.[167] As such, one of the US' main objectives was to change the text to make it 'as difficult as possible to take decisions'.[168]

After considering other decision-making options, the US appears to have pushed for consensus to become the WTO's principal decision-making procedure in order to 'lock in' the new multilateral trade regime. By defining consensus as when '*no* Member, present at the meeting . . . formally objects to the proposed decision', the WTO Agreement now clarified that the only barriers to blocking a consensus would be a lack of formality or presence. While these criteria could still disadvantage the WTO's poorest Members,[169] they would generally slow down the decision-making process and protect outnumbered states.[170] That the codification of the consensus procedure was intended to have a conservative effect is shown in GATT Director-General Peter Sutherland's repeated assurances, in the months between the signing of the Uruguay Agreements and their approval by the US Congress, that the 'procedures of the WTO offer[ed] much more protection against unwanted change'.[171] A number of scholars also contend that consensus

[163] VanGrasstek (n 150) 65.

[164] ibid.

[165] Ehlermann and Ehring (n 34) 508.

[166] ibid 509; Alexandru Grigorescu, *Democratic Intergovernmental Organizations: Normative Pressures and Decision-Making Rules* (Cambridge University Press 2015) 116.

[167] Ehlermann and Ehring (n 34) 509.

[168] ibid.

[169] On the way formality and presence can disadvantage poorer WTO Members, see Amrita Narlikar, 'The Politics of Participation: Decision-Making Processes and Developing Countries in the World Trade Organisation' (2002) 91 The Round Table 171, 175.

[170] Schermers and Blokker argue that it is more difficult for international meetings 'to neglect the formal objections by one participant if there [is] an adopted *rule* that decisions [can] only be adopted by consensus', rather than a *practice* of taking decisions by consensus, see Schermers and Blokker (n 30) 542 [emphasis in the original].

[171] 'Sutherland Dismisses Fears that the World Trade Organization Will Infringe Sovereignty as Unfounded', GATT Press Release, GATT/1634 (30 May 1994) 6; Peter Sutherland, A New Framework for International Economic Relations, GATT/1640 (16 June 1994) 8.

decision-making was extended to waivers and became the only decision-making method for waivers relating to implementation as a way to allay the US' concerns about states in the South later 'getting out' of their commitments.[172]

2.3.2 The WTO's Consensus Procedure and the Emergence of a Discourse of Democracy

The US' attempts to ensure that decision-making would be difficult did not, however, mean that it was opposed to any change within the WTO system. Almost as soon as the Uruguay Round had ended, the US trade policy elite began advocating for a new round of negotiations 'to push forward where the neo-liberal agenda had been pushed back during the Uruguay Round'.[173] In this regard, the US seems to have envisaged the WTO's consensus procedure as a one-way valve; designed to prevent any roll-back of the Uruguay Agreements, but not to stand in the way of further trade liberalization. Indeed, emboldened by their success in the Uruguay Round, the wealthy states seemed to be of the view that the consensus procedure was still sufficiently weighted in their favour to enable the launch of a new round.[174] And so, at the 1999 Ministerial Conference in Seattle, they sought to launch the 'Millennium Round' of trade negotiations.

The Seattle Ministerial was a failure. Negotiators from the US and Europe overestimated the level of influence they could exert through the WTO's consensus procedure, especially in the face of continued discontent from states in the global South regarding the outcome of the Uruguay Round. Even when the wealthy states resorted to their tactic of convening a secret Green Room meeting to steer the negotiations towards their desired outcome, excluded delegates from the South located the room and tried to force their way in.[175] If anything, such tactics on the part of the Northern powers only exacerbated the unwillingness of the majority of the Membership to agree to a new round.[176] This can be seen in the statement of the African Group, issued on the last morning of the Seattle Ministerial: 'There is no transparency in the proceedings and African countries are being marginalized and generally excluded . . . We will not be able to join the consensus required to meet the objectives of this Ministerial Conference'.[177] Similarly, the Dominican

[172] Ehlermann and Ehring (n 34) 509; Isabel Feichtner, *The Law and Politics of WTO Waivers: Stability and Flexibility in Public International Law* (Cambridge University Press 2011) 216.

[173] Robert Howse, 'The World Trade Organization 20 Years On: Global Governance by Judiciary' (2016) 27 European Journal of International Law 9, 21.

[174] ibid.

[175] John S Odell, 'Breaking Deadlocks in International Institutional Negotiations: The WTO, Seattle, and Doha' (2009) 53 International Studies Quarterly 273, 286.

[176] BS Chimni, 'World Trade Organization, Democracy and Development: A View from the South' (2006) 40 Journal of World Trade 5, 15.

[177] Cited in Odell (n 175) 286–87.

Republic's ambassador said of the Seattle Ministerial: 'They still think the WTO is a club. They still think 20 countries can decide for the rest of us.'[178] Amidst all this outrage, states in the North were unable to obtain the consensus needed to launch a new round of negotiations.[179] This failure rattled both the US and the WTO Secretariat.[180] They feared that if they could not commence a new round, 'the WTO would be seen as ineffectual and become irrelevant'.[181]

To maintain the authority of the WTO, Director-General Mike Moore mobilized a discourse of democracy around its use of consensus decision-making. This discourse drew on the idea of inter-state equality that had been deployed in relation to consensus decision-making in the 1970s, but it was now much more explicit in its invocation of the concept of 'democracy'. In 2000, for example, Moore declared that 'the consensus principle[,] which is at the heart of the WTO system ... is a fundamental democratic guarantee'.[182] Likewise, in 2002, Moore said: 'What the consensus rule embodies is the right to sovereignty, free choice, self-government—in other words "democracy" in its most basic sense.'[183] Soon, the WTO Secretariat joined in, putting together information packs with statements such as: 'Decisions in the WTO are generally by consensus. In principle, that's even more democratic than majority rule because no decision is taken until everyone agrees.'[184] These claims could also be found in the WTO's Annual Reports: 'The WTO functions on the basis of consensus ... [This] gives negotiating agendas a solid basis in democratic legitimacy and accountability.'[185]

This discourse of democracy had a dual purpose. First, it was used to rationalize the Seattle failure, as well as the general difficulties the Members were encountering with respect to consensus decision-making. In this usage, the cumbersome nature of the WTO's consensus procedure was portrayed as simply the price the institution had to pay for being 'hyper-democratic'.[186] In 2001, Moore said: 'Of course, [the WTO's consensus procedure] ... means deals sometimes take a long time to broker. With so many stakeholders ... the processes are difficult and laborious ... But it is democratic and it does ensure all our members participate fully.'[187] In 2005, once Moore was no longer Director-General, he went even further:

[178] ibid 286.
[179] Hopewell (n 119) 73.
[180] ibid.
[181] ibid.
[182] Mike Moore, 'The WTO Is Back On Track for Trade and Development' (16 February 2000) <https://www.wto.org/english/news_e/spmm_e/spmm24_e.htm>.
[183] Mike Moore, 'Democracy, Development and the WTO' (26 March 2002) <https://www.wto.org/english/news_e/spmm_e/spmm82_e.htm>.
[184] WTO Secretariat, '10 Common Misunderstandings about the WTO' (2003), cited in Strange (n 56) 246–47.
[185] World Trade Organisation, Annual Report (2001) 5.
[186] 'Who Elected the WTO?' *The Economist* (29 September 2001) <https://www.economist.com/special-report/2001/09/29/who-elected-the-wto>.
[187] Mike Moore, 'Trade, Development and Democracy: The Need for Reform of the WTO' (10 April 2001) <https://www.wto.org/english/news_e/spmm_e/spmm57_e.htm>.

> Despite what some of the media people say, the WTO is extremely democratic, even *too democratic*. Everything must be done by consensus, everybody must agree . . . and once you reach an agreement all those agreements must be ratified by everyone's parliament.[188]

Northern media outlets toed a similar line. In 2001, for example, an article appeared in the *Economist* with the opening line: 'The WTO is no would-be tyrant. It is democratic to a fault.'[189]

Second, Moore used this democracy discourse to boost the WTO's legitimacy in the eyes of civil society groups and state representatives from the South. This was mainly carried out through comparisons with other international organizations. For example, Moore emphasized the way in which the WTO's decision-making differed from that in the UN, with statements such as 'all WTO agreements are reached by a consensus . . . We have no security council. Every country has a veto.'[190] He also stressed that, unlike IMF and World Bank, the WTO made 'no provisions for . . . "weighted" voting.'[191] These comparisons enabled Moore to claim that, even with its Green Room meetings, the WTO was 'the most democratic international body in existence today.'[192]

Despite all this enthusiasm about consensus—or perhaps because of it—the WTO continued to experience decision-making difficulties. While states in the South eventually agreed to a new round at the Doha Ministerial in 2001, they may have done so more as a result of the shock of 9/11, which had happened two months earlier, than any newfound spirit of consensus.[193] In the years that followed, the Doha Round negotiations were characterized by deadlock and breakdown as states in the South refused to be 'bulldozed'[194] by the North as they felt they had been during the Uruguay Round.[195] With India and Brazil at the helm, and later China too, states in the South led a sustained revolt against the US and European Union (EU), refusing to agree to their proposals and forcing their own onto the agenda.[196] While the multilateral trade regime's use of consensus decision-making

[188] 'Former WTO Head Michael Moore Talks About Who Benefits From Trade Reforms', *Radio Free Europe/Radio Liberty* (online, 11 October 2005) <https://www.rferl.org/a/1062035.html> [emphasis added].

[189] 'Who Elected the WTO?' (n 186).

[190] Moore (n 187).

[191] Mike Moore, 'The Democratic Roots of the World Trade Organization' in Patrick FJ Macrory, Arthur E Appleton, and Michael G Plummer (eds), *The World Trade Organization: Legal, Economic and Political Analysis*, vol 1 (Springer 2005) 41.

[192] ibid 47.

[193] Hopewell (n 119) 74.

[194] ibid 92.

[195] For an overview of the North–South Doha deadlock see Sungjoon Cho, 'The Demise of Development in the Doha Round Negotiations' (2010) 45 Texas International Law Journal 573.

[196] See generally, Hopewell (n 119) 77–104. Most of the Doha Round's stalemate centred on the issue of agriculture.

had previously given the US and EU a de facto veto power,[197] states in the South found that it could now give them one too, especially if they operated in organized and united coalitions.[198] Eventually, the impasse between the North and South saw the Doha Round negotiations collapse in 2008.

In Hopewell's view, the South's ability to resist the North's proposals constituted a significant power shift within the multilateral trade regime.[199] And yet, the result has been that neither side really achieved what they wanted—including, in the case of some states in the South, a loosening of their Uruguay commitments.[200] Instead, decision-making by 'veto vs veto', combined with a gradual reinterpretation of the 'single undertaking' principle during the Doha Round to mean '*nothing can be agreed until everything is agreed*',[201] has entrapped both the North and South within 'the straitjacket of the WTO single package',[202] unable to move forwards or backwards. A handful of agreements have come into being over the WTO's life-time. In 2005, for example, the Members agreed to amend the TRIPS Agreement to enable poorer WTO Members to access generic medicines produced in other countries.[203] At the 2013 Bali Ministerial Conference, the Members also reached consensus on the Trade Facilitation Agreement.[204] Even as the Doha Round was officially being put to death at the 2015 Nairobi Ministerial, the WTO Members agreed to the 'Nairobi Package' on the abolition of agricultural export subsidies.[205] But, for the most part, the WTO Members have been in perpetual stalemate since its inception. This has caused the WTO to become stuck in time. As the EU put it in 2018: 'since 1995, the world has changed; the WTO has not.'[206]

[197] Patterson (n 162) 185.

[198] Some important coalitions that emerged during the Doha Round were the G-21 and the G-33. The G-21 is a a coalition of states in the global South led by Brazil and India that formed at the Cancun Ministerial Meeting in 2003. At Cancun, the G-21 united to block the US and EU's joint proposal on agriculture and put forward their own counterproposal targeting US and EU agriculture subsidies. This contributed to the collapse of that Ministerial, see Hopewell (n 119) 81. The G-33 is a large coalition of developing countries led by India that also emerged at the Cancun Ministerial. In contrast to the G-21, its objective is 'to limit the degree of market opening required of developing countries' in the area of agriculture, see ibid 87. For more information about these coalitions, see also Narlikar, *International Trade and Developing Countries: Bargaining Coalitions in the GATT & WTO* (n 117) 177–95.

[199] Hopewell (n 119) 98.

[200] See, eg, the position of the states in the G-33 in Rorden Wilkinson, Erin Hannah, and James Scott, 'The WTO in Bali: What MC9 Means for the Doha Development Agenda and Why It Matters' (2014) 35 Third World Quarterly 1032, 1042–43.

[201] Rodríguez Mendoza and Wilke (n 132) 299.

[202] Joost Pauwelyn, 'The Sutherland Report: A Missed Opportunity for Genuine Debate on Trade, Globalization and Reforming the WTO' (2005) 8 Journal of International Economic Law 329, 336.

[203] Amendment of the TRIPS Agreement, WT/L/641 (6 December 2005). Note, however, that the amendment did not enter into force until 23 January 2017.

[204] Protocol of Amendment to insert the WTO Trade Facilitation Agreement into Annex 1A of the WTO Agreement, WT/L/940 (27 November 2014). It entered into force on 22 February 2017.

[205] Howse (n 173) 22. The Package, which is composed of six Ministerial Decisions on agriculture, cotton, and issues related to least-developed countries, is outlined in the Nairobi Ministerial Declaration, WTO Doc WT/MIN(15)/DEC (19 December 2015).

[206] European Union, Concept Paper on WTO Modernisation, 18 September 2018, 2, available at <https://trade.ec.europa.eu/doclib/docs/2018/september/tradoc_157331.pdf>.

Despite widespread acknowledgment that the WTO has a 'consensus problem',[207] its Members have been reluctant to abandon this decision-making method. If anything, the WTO's commitment to consensus has intensified over time.[208] Article IX:1 of the WTO Agreement allows for a vote if consensus cannot be reached, but this mechanism has never been used.[209] Even decisions that expressly require a vote under the WTO Agreement, such as authoritative interpretations, are now generally considered to require consensus.[210] This has meant that in addition to being unable to negotiate new rules, the Members have been incapable of engaging with their existing agreements.[211] As a result, power was slowly siphoned away from the Membership and towards the WTO Appellate Body—an issue discussed in the next section.

Dingweth suggests that the democracy discourse surrounding the WTO's consensus procedure may account for the Members' unwillingness to vote.[212] After all, at the height of this discourse in 2000, Moore made repeated promises that the WTO would never abandon consensus decision-making, stating that 'the consensus principle . . . is not negotiable'[213] and '[c]onsensus . . . is required before any agreement can approved and this will not change'.[214] This appears to have created a sense amongst the Members that the WTO's use of consensus decision-making was somehow sacred. A study conducted in 2001 by the South Centre—an organization composed of states in Africa, Asia, and Latin America—found that '[e]ven after considering the disadvantages of the consensus principle, in terms of depriving developing countries to exploit their majority', most states in the South saw the WTO's consensus procedure as 'both necessary and non-negotiable'.[215]

2.4 The Rise of the Appellate Body

Amid the political paralysis, the WTO Appellate Body (AB) emerged as one of the institution's most powerful organs. As Howse reflected on the WTO's first two

[207] See, eg, Peter Sutherland and others, *The Future of the WTO: Addressing Institutional Challenges in the New Millennium* (World Trade Organization 2005) 64.

[208] Ehlermann and Ehring (n 34) 510–12.

[209] Jennifer Hillman, 'Three Approaches to Fixing the World Trade Organization's Appellate Body: The Good, the Bad and the Ugly?' [2018] Institute of International Economic Law Issue Brief 12. See also Alex Ansong, 'Democracy in the World Trade Organization: Are Some Members More Equal Than Others?' (2017) 14 International Organizations Law Review 154, 156.

[210] Isabelle Van Damme, 'Treaty Interpretation by the WTO Appellate Body' (2010) 21 European Journal of International Law 605, 612.

[211] Howse (n 173) 28–29.

[212] Klaus Dingwerth, 'Democracy' in Klaus Dingwerth and Clara Weinhardt (eds), *The Language of World Trade Politics: Unpacking the Terms of Trade* (1st edn, Routledge 2018) 91–93.

[213] Moore (n 182).

[214] Mike Moore, 'Moore Urges Trade Package for Poorest Countries' (13 April 2000) <https://www.wto.org/english/news_e/spmm_e/spmm27_e.htm>.

[215] Amrita Narlikar, 'WTO Decision-Making and Developing Countries' (2001) 11 South Centre Working Paper.

decades of existence in 2016: 'if we turn from the political and diplomatic setting to the dispute settlement system of the WTO, we see a judicial branch in full evolution through this entire period, entertaining hundreds of claims and producing a vast jurisprudential *acquis*.'[216] The WTO's main consensus procedure played a significant role in this story. In particular, the almost complete breakdown of the WTO as a negotiating forum caused a greater reliance on the dispute settlement system among the Members.[217] But the rise of the AB was also facilitated through two other consensus principles: negative consensus and judicial consensus. These are discussed in turn.

During the Uruguay Round, the US pushed for the WTO to have a judicialized dispute settlement mechanism.[218] Although the GATT 1947 had a dispute settlement procedure, consensus was required at every step of the process. This meant that states could block both the formation of a panel as well as the adoption of its report.[219] In contrast, the WTO's dispute settlement mechanism was 'given teeth',[220] with disputes to be settled at first instance by panels, followed by appeals to the AB. Under the new system, the referral of disputes to this process, the adoption of reports, and the authorization of retaliation by the Dispute Settlement Body (DSB) could only be blocked via 'negative consensus'. That is, rather than giving some states a de facto veto over every turn of the process, all steps would be taken unless there was a consensus not to.[221]

Unlike the positive consensus provisions, the negative consensus rule in the Dispute Settlement Understanding (DSU) was not simply intended to make decision-making difficult; it was designed to make it effectively impossible. This reading of the negative consensus rule is supported by statements by former GATT and WTO Directors-General. In 1994, for example, GATT Director-General Peter Sutherland described the negative consensus rule as 'perhaps the most significant change'[222] to come out of the Uruguay Round because it would enable dispute settlement to become 'speedy and *automatic*'.[223] In 1998, WTO Director-General Renato Ruggiero was even more explicit, stating '[t]he new system for the settlement of disputes among States has . . . made it *practically impossible* to block the adoption of decisions'.[224]

216 Howse (n 173) 10.

217 Richard H Steinberg, 'The Impending Dejudicialization of the WTO Dispute Settlement System?' (2018) 112 American Society for International Law Proceedings 316.

218 Hopewell (n 119) 57.

219 Nitsan Chorev, 'The Institutional Project of Neo-Liberal Globalism: The Case of the WTO' (2005) 34 Theory and Society 317, 330.

220 Hopewell (n 119) 58.

221 Chorev (n 219) 331.

222 'Sutherland Dismisses Fears that the World Trade Organization Will Infringe Sovereignty as Unfounded' (n 171) 7.

223 ibid [emphasis added].

224 Renato Ruggiero, 'Address to the University of Trieste MIB—School of Management' (22 September 1998) <https://www.wto.org/english/news_e/sprr_e/triest_e.htm> [emphasis added].

Given the improbability that all WTO Members, including the disputing parties, would reach a consensus not to establish a panel, adopt the panel's report, or authorize a remedy, Flett describes the phrase 'decides by consensus' in the relevant provisions of the DSU as 'redundant verbiage'.[225] In his view, '[t]he only explanation for the presence of this language is that it is designed to obfuscate, or at least facilitate the adoption of a revolutionary rule by using familiar language (the language of consensus)'.[226] Or, put in another way, the negative consensus rule in the DSU Agreement may be seen as another instance of the idea of 'consensus' being mobilized to lend authority to the institutional architecture of the multilateral trade regime—this time, in relation to its newly judicialized dispute settlement system. It is perhaps for this reason that, in 2016, former Director-General Pascal Lamy described the negative consensus rule as '*l'astuce diplomatique*'[227] ('the diplomatic trick') that allowed the multilateral trade regime to cross 'the Rubicon of supranationality',[228] ensuring that WTO law would be 'much more biting than that prevailing in the rest of the international system'.[229]

Despite this 'trick', the drafters of the Uruguay Agreements clearly intended the Members to retain some political control over the AB. Article IX:2 of the WTO Agreement, for example, gives them the 'exclusive authority to adopt interpretations' of the Uruguay Agreements. Yet, as noted above, a preference for consensus decision-making in this area has precluded the Membership from ever doing so.[230] This created what some scholars described as a 'constitutional flaw'[231] within the WTO system. For unlike in national systems that adhere to the principle of 'separation of powers', there was no effective legislative check on the decisions of the WTO's judicial branch.[232]

At the same time, the AB made a number of procedural decisions that enabled it to become an independent and effective judiciary.[233] One such decision was using consensus decision-making itself. This was set out in the AB's Working Procedures, which provided that '[t]he Appellate Body and its divisions shall make every effort to take their decisions by consensus'.[234] 'Consensus' was then defined in a similar

[225] James Flett, 'From the Green Room to the Court Room (And Back): Judicial Clarification of Ambiguity in WTO Law and the Effects on Subsequent Negotiations' (2011) 1 Oñati Socio-Legal Series 1, 9.

[226] ibid.

[227] Pascal Lamy, 'L'Organisation Mondiale Du Commerce et Le Droit' (18 January 2016) <https://academiesciencesmoralesetpolitiques.fr/2016/01/18/lorganisation-mondiale-du-commerce-et-le-droit/>.

[228] ibid: 'le Rubicon de la supranationalité'.

[229] ibid: 'C'est ainsi que le droit de l'OMC est devenu beaucoup plus mordant que celui prévalant dans le reste du système international.'

[230] Howse (n 173) 28.

[231] Steinberg (n 217) 318.

[232] ibid.

[233] See, generally, Gregory Shaffer, Manfred Elsig, and Sergio Puig, 'The Extensive (but Fragile) Authority of the WTO Appellate Body' (2016) 79 Law and Contemporary Problems 237.

[234] Working Procedures for Appellate Review, No WT/AB/WP/6 (16 August 2010), 3:2.

fashion to the WTO Agreement—'a decision is deemed to be made by consensus if no Member formally objects to it'.[235] According to Shaffer, Elsig, and Puig, the AB took this principle very seriously, often striving to provide a consensus-based report even in cases when disagreement amongst the members existed.[236] Nonetheless, in contrast to the Membership, the AB would occasionally abandon consensus. As Ruiz Fabri explains, '[j]udicial consensus is not the same as political consensus . . . A judicial body in charge of a case cannot decide not to decide'.[237] When an AB member did deliver a separate opinion, they did so anonymously in accordance with Article 17(11) of the DSU.

In the view of some scholars, the AB's decision to operate through consensus was essential to the consolidation of its authority.[238] First, like the negative consensus rule, it gave the AB's procedure an air of familiarity to the WTO Membership and resonated with existing institutional ideas around consensus and legitimacy.[239] Second, it helped to enhance the appearance of independence and impartiality in the AB's reports.[240] Third, the AB's use of consensus decision-making left its decisions less open to non-compliance by reducing the sense that there could have been an alternative outcome.[241] As former AB member David Unterhalter put it, '[t]he decisions of the AB yield *singular answers*'.[242]

The Membership's inability to reach either positive or negative consensus, combined with the success of the AB's own consensus-based approach, saw the WTO transform from a member-driven organization into a 'judiciocracy', or, as Howse described it in 2016, a system of 'global governance by judiciary'.[243] Even before the collapse of the Doha Round negotiations in 2008, scholars had begun to raise concerns about the democratic implications of global trade governance falling into the hands of seven AB members. In 2001, for example, Barfield wrote that 'the imbalance between the ineffective rulemaking procedures and the highly efficient judicial mechanisms will increasingly pressure the panels and the AB to "create" law, raising intractable questions of democratic legitimacy'.[244] Some states in the global South also began to worry that the AB's use of judicial consensus might prevent their views from being adequately taken into account in the formation of WTO

235 See the 'Definition' section in ibid.

236 Shaffer, Elsig, and Puig (n 233) 253. See also Meredith Kolsky Lewis, 'The Lack of Dissent in WTO Dispute Settlement' (2006) 9 Journal of International Economic Law 895, 905.

237 Hélène Ruiz Fabri, 'The WTO Appellate Body or Judicial Power Unleashed: Sketches from the Procedural Side of the Story' (2017) 27 European Journal of International Law 1075, 1078.

238 See, eg, Shaffer, Elsig, and Puig (n 233) 253.

239 Lewis (n 236) 916.

240 Shaffer, Elsig, and Puig (n 234) 254.

241 Lewis (n 236) 905–06.

242 David Unterhalter, 'Farewell Speech' (22 January 2014) <https://www.wto.org/english/tratop_e/dispu_e/unterhalterspeech_e.htm> [emphasis added].

243 Howse (n 173).

244 Claude E Barfield, 'Free Trade, Sovereignty, Democracy: The Future of the World Trade Organization' (2001) 2 Chicago Journal of International Law 403, 408.

law. In 2002, for example, the WTO Least Developed Countries Group criticized the 'stifling' and 'sanitized' nature of the AB's consensus-based approach, arguing that 'dissenting judgments may bring to the fore usually unheard concerns which may in the long run shape the evolution of the system'.[245]

WTO representatives explained away the rise of the AB and its use of judicial consensus through another discourse of 'equality', 'legitimacy', and 'democracy'—this time, mainly with reference to the principle of the 'rule of law'. In 2000, for example, Director-General Moore drew a connection between the WTO's judicialized dispute settlement system, the rule of law, and inter-state equality, stating:

> If the WTO did not exist, people would be . . . crying out for a mechanism that helps governments avoid coming to blows over trade disputes. That is what the WTO is . . . We uphold the rule of law. The alternative is the law of the jungle, where might makes right and the little guy doesn't get a look in.[246]

As time went on, the AB members also contributed to this narrative, sometimes explicitly referencing the idea of 'democracy'. In his farewell address in 2012, for example, AB member Shotaro Oshima said the following:

> The truth is, when an AB report is issued, there is no winner or loser among the parties, because the only winner is the dispute settlement process of the WTO . . . It is a victory for the rule of law . . . [which] is the *essence of democracy*.[247]

As part of their praise of the WTO's dispute settlement system, some AB members singled out their use of judicial consensus. In 2014, for example, former AB member Unterhalter spoke at length about the AB's 'legitimacy and authority'[248] and congratulated the AB members for their 'shared desire to come up with an answer that . . . reflects consensual positions'.[249] For a long time, these discourses helped to maintain the AB's authority, enabling it to become seen as the 'jewel in the crown of the WTO'[250] system, rather than a usurper of political power. However, as we will see in Chapter 6, the imbalance between the WTO's judicial and political branches would eventually draw the ire of the US, prompting it to take a number of decisions that would plunge the future of the WTO into uncertainty.

[245] Negotiations on the Dispute Settlement Understanding: Proposal by the LDC Group, WTO Doc TN/DS/W/17 (9 October 2002), 2. For commentary, see Lewis (n 237) 925–26.

[246] Mike Moore, 'The Backlash against Globalization?' (26 October 2000) <https://www.wto.org/english/news_e/spmm_e/spmm39_e.htm>.

[247] Shotaro Oshima, 'Farewell Speech' (13 June 2012) 3–4 <https://www.wto.org/english/news_e/news12_e/speech_shotaro_e.doc> [emphasis added].

[248] Unterhalter (n 242).

[249] ibid.

[250] Pascal Lamy quoted in World Trade Organisation, 'WTO Disputes Reach 400 Mark' (Press Release, 2009) <https://www.wto.org/english/news_e/pres09_e/pr578_e.htm>.

2.5 Conclusion: Consensus and the Authority of the Multilateral Trade Regime

This chapter examined the GATT/WTO's claim to operate by consensus. It revealed that, when articulated as a procedure, the meaning of consensus has not been stable. In the 1960s and 1970s, 'consensus decision-making' encompassed both the GATT's 'sense of the meeting' procedure and UNCTAD's 'conciliation' procedure. Even within the multilateral trade regime, the meaning of consensus changed. Whereas under the GATT framework it referred to a process of decision-making that could be potentially concluded 'when those who do not agree either keep quiet . . . or are so few or so small in terms of their interest in the issue that their agreement is not regarded . . . as essential',[251] in the WTO it came to mean one that could only be concluded when '*no* Member, present at the meeting . . . formally objects to the proposed decision'.[252] The term 'consensus' also came to describe the AB's method of decision-making and the automatic procedures associated with the WTO's dispute settlement system, despite the differences between those procedures and the WTO's principal method of consensus decision-making.

Throughout these shifts and divergences in meaning, however, consensus has consistently operated as a technique of authorization and deauthorization. When the global North's rhetorical push for consensus began in the 1960s and 1970s, consensus was used to describe what the NIEO was not, helping to delegitimize its vision of international law and unsettle the claim that it would be more democratic than the existing system. At around the same time, consensus came to refer to the GATT's 'sense of the meeting' procedure, bolstering the authority of that framework by imbuing it with an air of equality and inclusivity. In the move to the WTO, the use of the term 'consensus' in relation to the negative consensus rule helped to normalize the automaticity of the new trade organization's dispute settlement system. In the wake of the global South's disappointment with the outcome of the Uruguay Round, WTO representatives mobilized a democratic discourse around the Members' use of consensus decision-making to explain away the decision-making difficulties the institution was encountering and claim the WTO was 'the most democratic international body in existence today'.[253] When the AB emerged as one of the WTO's most powerful organs, that body's 'desire to come up with an answer that . . . reflects consensual positions' was linked to its 'legitimacy and authority'[254] and portrayed as a victory for the 'rule of law'. In sum, over the history of the multilateral trade regime, the idea of consensus has repeatedly functioned to stabilize the authority of the GATT/WTO and the organs contained therein.

[251] Patterson (n 162) 184.
[252] WTO Agreement (n 153) fn 1 [emphasis added].
[253] Moore (n 191) 47.
[254] Unterhalter (n 242).

In my account, the success of consensus as a technique of authorization across these different contexts lay in its ability to gesture towards a profound, yet unfixed and unquantifiable, level of agreement. On the one hand, by purporting to seek a high level of agreement, the idea of consensus lent itself to ideas of equality and inclusivity. This helped to boost the democratic credentials of the GATT/WTO at times when inter-state equality or political/judicial imbalance had become heightened issues. On the other hand, by not fixing the number of participants that needed to agree affirmatively with a decision for it to qualify as consensus, the idea proved flexible enough to be applied to a range of different procedures, from the GATT's weighted 'sense of the meeting' procedure to the idea of a decision being taken automatically unless there is a lack of formal objection on a proposal not to take that decision (i.e. the negative consensus rule). This flexibility meant that the idea of consensus could be invoked even when the mode of decision-making to which it was being applied actually worked to entrench inequality between states or asymmetry between political and judicial branches.

Perhaps even more significantly, the idea of consensus also proved flexible enough to describe some outcomes and not others, depending on the claimant's position in terms of wealth and geopolitical power. Whereas the widely supported NIEO could be portrayed by states in the global North as the antithesis of consensus, the Uruguay Agreements continued to carry a consensual status long after many states in the South voiced their discontent. In the following chapter, I analyse in closer detail the idea that the Uruguay Round negotiations were concluded by consensus. In doing so, I move away from the various procedures that carry the name 'consensus' in the GATT/WTO and instead focus on the effects that flow from the claim that something *is* a 'consensus decision' within the multilateral trade regime.

3
The Uruguay Round Consensus and Economic Normativity

3.1 Introduction

In the previous chapter, I explored how the claim to operate according to something called 'consensus decision-making' helped to shore up the authority of the General Agreement on Tariffs and Trade (GATT) and World Trade Organization (WTO) by enabling their representatives to wrap those institutions in discourses of 'equality', 'legitimacy', and 'democracy'. In this chapter, I now consider the authorizing work that consensus has performed in the multilateral trade regime when presented as a finalized state of agreement. To do this, I return to the Uruguay Round of multilateral trade negotiations, which lasted from 1986 until 1993 and culminated in the agreement to establish the WTO. Through a critical discourse analysis of speeches and statements made by states and representatives of the GATT/WTO, I examine the narratives that emerged from the fact that those negotiations were concluded through the GATT's consensus procedure. I argue that the claim that the final outcome of the Uruguay Round negotiations represented an 'international consensus' not only reinforced the authority of the WTO by enabling an origin story of unity and agreement to form around it, but also helped to authorize discourses proclaiming the triumph of free-market capitalism by contributing to the sense that there were no longer any alternatives or opposition left.

The chapter is in three sections. The first section begins with an account of how the consensual status of the Uruguay Agreements played into mythmaking around the WTO in the 1990s and 2000s. It then examines the way the Uruguay Round consensus interacted with, and lent authority to, other post-Cold War discourses. Drawing on insights from queer theory, I also consider how this discursive mingling helped to deauthorize alternative economic ideas and practices. The second section of the chapter turns to resistance to the claim that the Uruguay Agreements represented an international consensus from both within and outside the WTO, as well as the difficulties different actors encountered when seeking to dislodge the consensus narrative that had formed around the WTO system. In the final section of the chapter, I trace the eventual decline of the Uruguay Round consensus discourse by sketching how WTO Director-General

Consensus in International Law. Claerwen O'Hara, Oxford University Press. © Claerwen O'Hara 2026.
DOI: 10.1093/9780198948643.003.0003

Pascal Lamy attempted to shift to a 'Geneva Consensus' discourse in the early 2010s.

3.2 The Discursive Effects of the Uruguay Round Consensus

3.2.1 The Uruguay Round Consensus and Mythmaking around the WTO

In modern times, origin stories have become crucial to mythmaking. As Peter Fitzpatrick writes, 'an obsession with origins is perhaps the most obvious substitute for the mythically transcendent'.[1] If we cannot rely on the divine to understand an object, we use an account of its origins to make claims about its essence.[2] In the case of the WTO, institutional representatives constructed an origin story around the use of consensus decision-making during the Uruguay Round of multilateral trade negotiations. In particular, they emphasized the fact that those negotiations concluded on 15 December 1993 with more than 120 states having reached consensus on several draft trade agreements, including one establishing the WTO.[3] Indeed, in the WTO's early years, it became commonplace for its representatives to attach the term 'consensus-based' to their descriptions of the new trade system. In the 1990s, WTO Director-General Renato Ruggiero regularly referred to the WTO as 'a framework of *consensus-based* trade rules which is now almost universal',[4] 'a system of *consensus-based* rules that could embrace all of the world's economies',[5] and a 'system [that] has brought together 132 countries under shared international rules, *agreed by consensus*'.[6] When Mike Moore became Director-General in 1999, he continued to emphasize the WTO's consensual origins, describing it as a 'system of *consensus-based* multilateral trade rules'.[7]

The ability of so many states to arrive at such a far-reaching 'consensus' does sound impressive. And to some extent it was. However, it did not mean that all of the parties affirmatively supported the bargain struck. While the terms 'unanimity' and 'consensus' are often used interchangeably, even by representatives of

1 Peter Fitzpatrick, *The Mythology of Modern Law* (Routledge 1992) 48.

2 ibid. See also Hilary Charlesworth, 'The Travels of Human Rights: The UNESCO Human Rights Exhibition 1950–1953' in Sundhya Pahuja and Shane Chalmers (eds), *Routledge Handbook of International Law and the Humanities* (Routledge 2021) 188.

3 Craig VanGrasstek, *The History and Future of the World Trade Organization* (World Trade Organization 2013) 39–80.

4 Renato Ruggiero, 'Address to the Second Summit of the Americas' (18 April 1998) <https://www.wto.org/english/news_e/sprr_e/santia_e.htm>.

5 Renato Ruggiero, 'From Vision to Reality: The Multilateral Trading System at Fifty' (26 February 1998) <https://www.wto.org/english/news_e/sprr_e/sanjos_e.htm>.

6 Renato Ruggiero, 'Opening Statement, Geneva Ministerial' (1998) <https://www.wto.org/english/thewto_e/minist_e/min98_e/anniv_e/dg_e.htm>.

7 See, eg, Mike Moore, 'Global Health Policy' (2000) 356 The Lancet 680.

the GATT/WTO,[8] these two decision-making methods are distinct. Unanimity requires an affirmative vote from all parties.[9] In contrast, in the GATT, a consensus was generally considered to have been reached when no party formally objected to the proposed decision.[10] This meant that, as a matter of procedure, the Uruguay Round accord was a 'consensus' not because all of the parties had agreed, but because none of them had formally disagreed. This distinction is far from inconsequential. As we saw in the previous chapter, by shifting the focus from agreement to lack of disagreement and dispensing with formal voting rules, the GATT's consensus procedure tended to function as an informal system of weighted voting.[11] During the Uruguay Round, the weighted nature of this decision-making procedure was exacerbated through the use of small gatherings known as Green Room meetings and coercive tactics on the part of the United States (US) and European Community (EC).[12] As a result, the agreements that emerged from the Uruguay Round were tipped in favour of the global North.

The outcome of the Uruguay Round was also shaped by a rise in corporate power. Although corporate lobbies had long had an influence on GATT negotiations, particularly since the 1970s,[13] their role in the lead-up to and during the Uruguay Round was unprecedented.[14] In the 1980s, powerful corporate lobby groups emerged in the US, United Kingdom (UK), and other states in the global North, which placed significant pressure on their governments to pursue trade agreements in areas such as services, intellectual property, and investment.[15] Once the Uruguay Round was under way, these lobby groups advised Northern delegations on the negotiating texts and drafted principles to serve as the blueprint for the new trade agreements.[16] Alessandrini writes that the level of involvement of the

[8] See, eg, Alan Wolff, 'International Cooperation Must Balance Freedom of Action and Respect for Others' (13 September 2019) <https://www.wto.org/english/news_e/news19_e/ddgaw_13sep19_e.htm>.

[9] Alex Ansong, 'Democracy in the World Trade Organization: Are Some Members More Equal Than Others?' (2017) 14 International Organizations Law Review 154, 157.

[10] The WTO Agreement defines consensus as when 'no Member, present at the meeting when the decision is taken, formally objects to the proposed decision', see Marrakesh Agreement Establishing the World Trade Organization, 1994, 1867 UNTS 154, fn 1. Article IX:1 suggests that consensus decision-making in the GATT operated under a similar definition, providing: 'the WTO shall continue the practice of decision-making by consensus followed under GATT 1947.' However, note that there was some uncertainty in the GATT framework about whether a consensus could be declared when a small number of states formally objected to the proposed decision, see Section 2.3.1 in Chapter 2 of this book.

[11] Asif H Qureshi, *The World Trade Organization: Implementing International Trade Norms* (Manchester University Press 1996) 6.

[12] See Section 2.2.3 in Chapter 2 of this book.

[13] Andrew Lang, *World Trade Law After Neoliberalism: Re-Imagining the Global Economic Order* (Oxford University Press 2011) 230.

[14] Donatella Alessandrini, *Developing Countries and the Multilateral Trade Regime: The Failure and Promize of the WTO's Development Mission* (Hart Publishing 2010) 106.

[15] John Croome, *Reshaping the World Trading System: A History of the Uruguay Round* (World Trade Organization 1995) 122.

[16] On the role of corporate actors with respect to trade in services negotiations, see Jane Kelsey, *Serving Whose Interests? The Political Economy of Trade in Services Agreements* (Routledge-Cavendish

corporate sector in the Uruguay Round 'signalled the entry of a new actor in the international arena'.[17] While the negotiations continued to be conducted officially between states, corporate lobby groups were able to take advantage of the weighted nature of the GATT's consensus procedure to influence the drafting of the Uruguay Agreements.

In relation to the Trade-Related Aspects of Intellectual Property Rights[18] (TRIPS) Agreement, for example, lobby groups from the US, Europe, and Japan came together to form a shadow 'private-sector consensus'[19] on trade and intellectual property.[20] According to Drahos and Braithwaite, this enabled them to capture the negotiating position of the Quad,[21] which then went on to drive their agenda and crush any 'resistance of developing countries . . . through trade power'.[22] Consequently, in addition to being imbalanced on a North–South axis, the Uruguay Agreements reflected the neoliberal orientation prevailing in corporate and government circles in states such as the US and UK at the time.[23]

Nonetheless, both the asymmetry of the Uruguay Round negotiations and the particularity of the resulting agreements began to be obscured from view the moment a final consensus had been proclaimed. This was due, in part, to the murky nature of the GATT's consensus procedure itself. As Kennedy writes about consensus decision-making: 'Because consensus produces no actual recorded vote . . . all that is seen is the institutional output.'[24] As a result, 'the institution seems to speak as a whole, losing the individuated voices of its members'.[25] This process was also helped along by WTO representatives, who began reframing the Uruguay Round consensus as an instance of complete and unforced agreement. This can be seen in Director-General Mike Moore's account of the WTO system in 2002: 'The WTO is not imposed on countries . . . No country is forced to sign our agreements. Each and every one of the WTO's rules is negotiated by Member governments

2008) 76–82. On corporate actors in the context of intellectual property, see Peter Drahos and John Braithwaite, *Information Feudalism: Who Owns the Knowledge Economy?* (Earthscan 2002) 122–28.

[17] Alessandrini (n 14) 106.

[18] Agreement on Trade-Related Aspects of Intellectual Property Rights, Marrakesh Agreement Establishing the World Trade Organization, Annex 1C, opened for signature 15 April 1994, 1869 UNTS 299 (entered into force 1 January 1995).

[19] Edmund Pratt, quoted in Drahos and Braithwaite (n 16) 122.

[20] Intellectual Property Committee (US), Keidanren (Japan), Union of Industrial and Employers' Confederations of Europe (UNICE), *Basic Framework of GATT Provisions on Intellectual Property: Statement of Views of the European, Japanese and United States Business Communities* (June 1988).

[21] Drahos and Braithwaite (n 16) 128. The 'Quad' refers to the US, EC, Canada, and Japan. See Section 2.2.3 of Chapter 2 in this book.

[22] ibid 12.

[23] For a discussion of the term 'neoliberalism' and the way I am using it in this book, see Section 2.2.3 of Chapter 2.

[24] David Kennedy, 'The Move to Institutions' in Jan Klabbers (ed), *International Organizations* (2nd edn, Routledge 2016) 134.

[25] ibid.

and agreed by consensus.'[26] While it is the case that states must ratify the Uruguay Agreements in order to be bound, Moore's suggestion that the WTO's *consensual origins* meant that Members had actively agreed to 'each and every one' of its rules evokes the concept of unanimity more than it does the WTO's own definition of consensus, which is based around a lack of objection.[27] Through this slight re-framing, the consensus decisions underpinning the Uruguay Agreements began to appear more like unanimous ones, allowing them to trade on the positive connotations of unanimity, without having resulted from the same procedural stringency.

Combined with the discourse of democracy that had already started to form around consensus decision-making by that time,[28] this (mis)representation of the consensual origins of the WTO provided fertile ground for mythmaking. In particular, it allowed the birth of the WTO to be retold as a tale of international unity, in which the global North and South had finally arrived at a collective vision for global trade. Reflecting on the Uruguay Round years in 1996, for example, Director-General Ruggiero declared the 'death of the North-South divide'[29] in global trade relations, describing it as 'an event as significant as the demolition of the Berlin Wall'.[30] That same year, Ruggiero also stated that the 'new unity of developing and developed countries inside a single system will be credited as the greatest achievement of the multilateral system'.[31] Scholars put forward a similar narrative. In 2003, for example, Ford argued that during the Uruguay Round, '[d]eveloped and developing country traders redefined the boundaries of Self and Other to establish a shared identity as multilateral traders'.[32]

This newfound North–South unity was understood not in terms of pressure or even compromise during the Uruguay Round negotiations, but rather as a result of a worldwide embrace of free-market values—a trend that will be discussed in more detail in the following section. Thus Ruggiero attributed the end of the North–South divide to 'the embrace of market-opening and liberalization policies in countries at all levels of development'.[33] Likewise, in 1999, Director-General Moore linked the 'changing dynamic of North-South relations' to 'the economic revolution which ha[d] been unfolding in much of the developing world', whereby '[c]ountries in Latin America, Asia, and now Africa [had] moved . . . towards a

[26] Mike Moore, 'Democracy, Development and the WTO' (26 March 2002) <https://www.wto.org/english/news_e/spmm_e/spmm82_e.htm>.

[27] See WTO Agreement (n 10), fn 1.

[28] For an account of the democratic discourse surrounding the WTO's consensus procedure, see Section 2.3.2 in Chapter 2 of this book.

[29] Renato Ruggiero, 'The Road Ahead: International Trade Policy in the Era of the WTO' (28 May 1996) <https://www.wto.org/english/news_e/pres96_e/pr049_e.htm>.

[30] ibid.

[31] Renato Ruggiero, 'Trading towards Peace' (12 November 1996) <https://www.wto.org/english/news_e/pres96_e/pr058_e.htm>.

[32] Jane Ford, *A Social Theory of the WTO: Trading Cultures* (Palgrave Macmillan 2003) 117.

[33] Ruggiero (n 29).

world of freer markets and more open, rules-based trade.'[34] This was also Ford's view: 'during the Uruguay Round, many developing countries ... adopted a free trade stance ... [This was] important in constituting developing countries' new identities and a "super-" rather than "multi-"lateral culture in the WTO regime.'[35] Notably absent in many of these accounts were the structural adjustment programmes that had been coercively imposed on many states in the South in the 1980s and early 1990s under the rubric of another consensus—the 'Washington Consensus'—which had often been the cause of the 'economic revolutions' of which they spoke. The Washington Consensus is discussed in more detail below.

Instead, as is common in origin stories, the claim of worldwide economic consensus was situated within a larger narrative of progress.[36] In this case, it was one that began with the creation of the GATT in 1947. In this narrative, the US and the other early signatories to the GATT were portrayed as 'visionaries', who understood the virtues of free trade and open markets. But, for more than four decades, their vision had been resisted by other groups of states, including the Socialist Bloc and the global South in its insistence on the establishment of a New International Economic Order (NIEO) in the 1960s and 1970s.[37] Then, so the story went, at the end of the twentieth century, these previously recalcitrant states finally saw the light and agreed to a new trade system underpinned by free-market values. An example of this narrative can be seen in US President Bill Clinton's speech at the 1998 WTO Ministerial Meeting in Geneva, which celebrated the fiftieth anniversary of the multilateral trade system:

> And so, at mid-century, a farsighted generation of leaders ... embraced the revolutionary idea that freedom—free democracies, free markets, the free flow of ideas, the free movement of people—would be the surest route to the greatest prosperity for all ... In the fullness of time, they have been proven *spectacularly right* ... A trading community that began with 23 member nations now embraces 132 economies, and 31 more are working to join.[38]

In this statement, we catch a glimpse of a historiography that emerged in international law following the fall of the Berlin Wall and the collapse of the Soviet Union, in which 'events after 1990 were read as the fulfilment of a destiny prefigured

[34] Mike Moore, 'The WTO: The Challenge Ahead' (1 July 1999) <https://www.wto.org/english/news_e/spmm_e/spmm01_e.htm>.

[35] Ford (n 32) 117.

[36] On the relationship between origin stories and progress narratives, see eg Charlesworth (n 2) 188.

[37] For more on the New International Economic Order (NIEO), see Section 2.2.2 in Chapter 2 of this book.

[38] Bill Clinton, 'Statement, Geneva Ministerial' (18 May 1998) <https://www.wto.org/english/thewto_e/minist_e/min98_e/anniv_e/clinton_e.htm> [emphasis added].

for international law and institutions in 1945'.[39] According to Craven, Pahuja, and Simpson, this historiography had two effects. First, it performed an authorizing function. Craven, Pahuja, and Simpson write that '[m]uch as the nineteenth-century historiographies of international law authorized an imperial international law but located the "origin" of the state system in 1648', a key effect of this historiography 'has been to author and authorise a new international law coinciding with a period of US dominance, which finds its origins in 1945'.[40] Second, it had the effect of recasting the Cold War 'as a period of legal stasis, or a "hiatus" between two highpoints of legal utopianism'.[41] This, in turn, worked to erase a great deal of what happened in between the 1940s and 1990s, including Third World and Soviet deployments of international law.[42]

As a strand of this historiography, the presentation of the WTO system as the fulfilment of a mid-century vision produced similar effects. Although there were notable differences between the 'embedded liberalism' that guided the GATT system and the WTO's more neoliberal approach to trade,[43] the tale of continuity and progress that we see in Clinton's speech lent authority to the new, US-dominated trade organization by imbuing it with a sense of destiny. The claim that the Uruguay Round consensus proved that the GATT's founders were 'spectacularly right' also helped to invalidate other approaches to the economy and trade that had been proposed during the twentieth century. After all, embedded within that claim was a sub-narrative, in which the Socialist Bloc and the proponents of the NIEO 'had been fundamentally misguided in their view of history and development'.[44]

The narratives of unity and destiny that formed around the WTO's consensual origins helped to naturalize the Uruguay Agreements and their underlying neoliberal orientation. By portraying the WTO system as the result of a preordained worldwide agreement, rather than coercive tactics, Green Room meetings, and corporate lobbying, it began to appear 'normal' or like 'common sense'.[45] Eventually, WTO law would become 'a very stable—perhaps even boring—area of international law';[46] all the while the WTO remained one of the most intrusive international institutions in the world.[47] All the talk about the North and

[39] Matthew Craven, Sundhya Pahuja, and Gerry Simpson, 'Reading and Unreading a Historiography of Hiatus' in Matthew Craven, Sundhya Pahuja, and Gerry Simpson (eds), *International Law and the Cold War* (Cambridge University Press 2019) 2.

[40] ibid 3.

[41] ibid 2.

[42] ibid 3.

[43] See generally, Lang (n 13).

[44] Nils Gilman, 'The New International Economic Order: A Reintroduction' (2015) 6 Humanity 1, 8, discussing how the NIEO was viewed by the 'new "post-historical" consensus in favor of "free trade" that consolidated by the late 1980s among mainstream economists in the north'.

[45] On the way the Uruguay Round consensus was portrayed as 'the triumph of reason on both the developed and developing countries' part' see Alessandrini (n 14) 128.

[46] Rachel Brewster, 'The Trump Administration and the Future of the WTO' (2018) 44 The Yale Journal of International Law Online 6, 7.

[47] BS Chimni, 'International Institutions Today: An Imperial Global State in the Making' (2004) 15 European Journal of International Law 1, 7–8.

South being unified within a single system and the GATT model having finally triumphed also helped to foreclose other ways of imagining global trade governance. As we saw in the previous chapter, there was a time when the United Nations Conference on Trade and Development (UNCTAD) acted as 'a genuine counterweight to GATT, presenting an alternative institutional arrangement to facilitate global trade'.[48] After the Uruguay Round consensus and the discourses of international agreement that followed, the WTO came to be treated as the only body for governing global trade by states and activists alike.[49] This saw UNCTAD slowly fade into irrelevance, its role largely reduced to producing reports on topics relating to trade and development.[50]

3.2.2 Projecting Outwards: The Uruguay Round Consensus and the End of History

The effects of the discourse of worldwide unity emanating from the Uruguay Round consensus were not limited to mythmaking around the WTO. From quite early on, the Uruguay Round consensus discourse began to blend with, and lend authority to, other post-Cold War discourses. For as we saw in the previous chapter, the Uruguay Round had taken place against the backdrop of a rapidly shifting political landscape. As Dunkely writes, '[t]he Uruguay Round agreement came at a time of momentous world-wide change—the end of the Cold War, the collapse of the Soviet Union, the political triumph of capitalism, the ascendancy of free market economics, . . . and the apparent dissolution of socialist, or even social democratic, alternatives'.[51]

These historic events were both constitutive of and constituted by a thick layer of discourse which Susan Marks calls 'liberal millenarianism'.[52] This discourse proclaimed that with the end of the Cold War, there was now a 'worldwide consensus in favour of liberalism, including not just [free-market] capitalism but liberal democracy as well'.[53] The seeds of this discourse had been sown in the 1980s, with the rise of neoliberalism and claims from figures such as UK Prime Minister Margaret Thatcher that there was 'no alternative' to free-market capitalism.[54] When the

[48] Michael Strange, 'Discursivity of Global Governance: Vestiges of "'Democracy'" in the World Trade Organization' (2011) 36 Alternatives: Global, Local, Political 240, 250.

[49] ibid.

[50] Kristen Hopewell, *Breaking the WTO: How Emerging Powers Disrupted the Neoliberal Project* (Stanford University Press 2016) 65.

[51] Graham Dunkley, *The Free Trade Adventure: The WTO, the Uruguay Round, and Globalism—A Critique* (Zed Books 2000) 8.

[52] Susan Marks, 'The End of History? Reflections on Some International Legal Theses' (1997) 3 European Journal of International Law 449.

[53] ibid 451.

[54] See eg, Margaret Thatcher, 'Speech to Conservative Women's Conference' (21 May 1980) <https://www.margaretthatcher.org/document/104368>. For commentary, see Bradley W Bateman, 'There Are

Berlin Wall fell, this sense of inevitability hit new heights, as reflected by Francis Fukuyama's well-known thesis that the spread of free-market capitalism and liberal democracy in the late 1980s and early 1990s not only signalled 'the end of the Cold War ... but the end of history as such'.[55]

The Uruguay Round consensus—reinterpreted by institutional representatives as something more akin to unanimity—became a lightning rod for this discourse. After all, the idea of more than 120 states reaching consensus on a new (neo)liberal trade system was arguably greater evidence of the claim that there was now a '*worldwide* consensus in favour of liberalism' than the fall of the Berlin Wall. As a result, the liberal millenarian discourse was rapidly taken up by the multilateral trade regime's representatives. In 1994, for example, GATT Director-General Peter Sutherland summed up the Uruguay Round consensus in the following terms:

> On 15 December 1993 the world changed. Maybe not as dramatically as the moment when the Berlin Wall fell, but then unlike that very necessary demolition job, the success of the Uruguay Round was a work of construction ... Put simply, governments came to the conclusion that the notion of a new world order was not merely attractive but absolutely vital.[56]

Sutherland went on to clarify that the 'new world order' to which he was referring was not the global South's NIEO, with its vision of international democracy and socialist globalization, but rather one underpinned by '[liberal, domestic] democratic and free-market principles'.[57] In this speech, we see Sutherland set the tone for many WTO speeches to come by portraying the Uruguay Round consensus as the product of a larger political and economic consensus that was sweeping the globe in the post-Cold War era. Echoing Fukuyama, Sutherland saw this new worldwide agreement as not only encompassing free-market principles, but liberal democracy as well. As such, he suggested that the Uruguay Round consensus signalled something bigger than the birth of a new trade regime; it was the beginning of a 'new world order'.

In the years that followed, WTO officials continued to represent the legal consensus reached on the Uruguay Agreements as evidence of a larger, ideological consensus. At times, this discourse was more modest and specifically tied to the

Many Alternatives: Margaret Thatcher in the History of Economic Thought' (2002) 24 Journal of the History of Economic Thought 307.

[55] Francis Fukuyama, 'The End of History?' (1989) 16 The National Interest 3, 4.

[56] Peter Sutherland, 'Global Trade—The Next Challenge: Address to the World Economic Forum' (GATT Press Release, 28 January 1994).

[57] ibid. On the way in which states in the global South tend to invoke the idea of 'democracy' in international law in the context of inter-state equality, whereas states in the global North tend to focus on domestic democracy, see Hilary Charlesworth, 'International Legal Encounters with Democracy' (2017) 8 Global Policy 34.

WTO's free-trade agenda. In 1998, for example, Director-General Ruggiero declared that '[t]he success of the WTO was the result—not the cause—of a broadening international consensus about the value of trade liberalization'.[58] Likewise, on another occasion that same year, Ruggiero stated that there was 'a strengthening consensus that open trade offers the best available path to growth and modernization'.[59] Similar statements were made in the context of shifting North–South trade relations, as outlined in the previous section.

At other times, this discourse would spill over into broader claims about the triumph of free-market capitalism in the post-Cold War era. In 1998, for example, Ruggiero declared that '[t]he end of the Cold War meant the end of any pretence of a viable competition between centrally-planned and market-based systems'.[60] In 2001, Director-General Moore went further, describing 'Marxist economics' as the 'cruellest hoax of the last century' and noting that '[n]o one seriously considers this an option any longer'.[61] Some WTO Members toed a similar line. At the 1998 Ministerial Meeting in Geneva, for example, US President Clinton reminded the audience that they were living in 'a moment when . . . the argument over which is better—free enterprise or state socialism—ha[d] been won . . . [and] people on every continent seek to join the free market system'.[62] Similarly, in his opening statement at the 1999 Ministerial Conference in Seattle, the Singaporean Minister for Trade and Industry, George Young-Boon Yeo, declared that '[f]or over two billion human beings living in the former centrally-planned economies and in the developing world, the age of ideology is over. They look now to the global market for a better life.'[63]

Occasionally, these claims would go even further, encompassing the global turn to liberal democracy as well. In his 1998 speech, for example, Clinton triumphantly told WTO Members that 'for the first time in human history, a majority of the world's people live under governments of their own choosing'.[64] Likewise, in 1999, Director-General Moore said:

> We ought also to celebrate that there has never been a time in the history of our species where more people have enjoyed freedom in the polling place and the market place . . . Freedom and democracy is now the only valid revolution . . .

[58] Renato Ruggiero, 'The Next 50 Years: Challenges and Opportunities for the Multilateral Trading System' (*Hamburg*, 11 June 1998) <https://www.wto.org/english/news_e/sprr_e/hambur_e.htm>.

[59] Renato Ruggiero, 'The Multilateral Trading System at Fifty' (*United Kingdom*, 16 January 1998) <https://www.wto.org/english/news_e/sprr_e/london_e.htm>.

[60] Ruggiero (n 58).

[61] Mike Moore, 'Promoting Openness, Fairness and Predictability in International Trade for the Benefit of Humanity' (8 June 2001) <https://www.wto.org/english/news_e/spmm_e/spmm64_e.htm>.

[62] Clinton (n 38).

[63] George Young-Boon Yeo, 'Singapore Statement, Seattle Ministerial' (30 November 1999), WTO Doc WT/MIN(99)/ST/1.

[64] Clinton (n 38).

> These values now find a consensus of support from practically every part of the world.[65]

Just when it seemed like these statements no longer had much to do with the Uruguay Round consensus or the WTO, their authors would link them back. In the same 1999 speech, for example, Moore drew a connection between the trade liberalization agenda of the Uruguay Agreements and the spread of democracy in the post-Cold War era by claiming that '[e]conomic freedom cannot be separated from political freedom. They are each other's guarantor'.[66]

Following on from this purported link between democracy and globalized neoliberal capitalism, proponents of the Uruguay Round consensus narrative suggested that the outcome of the Uruguay Round represented not only the views of governments and experts, but also the will of 'the people'. On separate occasions, for example, both Ruggiero and Moore claimed that '[t]he Berlin Wall fell because millions of people rebelled not only against the loss of their political freedom, but against the loss of their material and economic freedom as well'.[67]

According to proponents of this narrative, the reason why both governments and their constituencies were now united in their support for globalized neoliberal capitalism was because there was no other option. Echoing Margaret Thatcher's slogan 'there is no alternative' or 'TINA',[68] Ruggiero asked in 1998, '[w]hy does this consensus [on trade liberalization] exist? Because the history of the latter half of this century has taught us that there is really no rational alternative.'[69] On another occasion, he also said, '[t]he need is not to discuss whether globalization is a good thing, but to ask . . . "what would be the alternative?"'.[70] Sometimes, these claims went further, portraying the WTO's brand of globalization as an inevitable force that could not be undone. In 1999, for example, Moore stated, '[g]lobalization is with us; it cannot be uninvented'.[71] In another speech that same year, he also declared, '[g]lobalization is not going away'.[72] In a similar vein, US President Clinton

[65] Moore (n 34).

[66] ibid. For an overview of the argument that free trade is democracy-enhancing, see Robert Howse, 'How to Begin to Think About the "Democratic Deficit" at the WTO' in Stefan Griller (ed), *International Economic Governance and Non-Economic Concerns: New Challenges for the International Legal Order* (Springer 2003).

[67] Ruggiero (n 58); Mike Moore, 'Challenges for the Global Trading System in the New Millennium' (Washington, DC, 28 September 1999) <https://www.wto.org/englIsh/news_e/spmm_e/spmm08_e.htm>.

[68] In the 1980s, UK Prime Minister Margaret Thatcher often used the phrase 'there is no alternative' in relation to neoliberal economics, for an overview see Bateman (n 54) 310.

[69] Ruggiero (n 58).

[70] Renato Ruggiero, 'An Enabling Environment for Development: The Contribution of the Multilateral Trading System: Address to ECOSOC' (2 July 1997) <https://www.wto.org/english/news_e/sprr_e/ecosoc_e.htm>.

[71] Moore (n 34).

[72] Mike Moore, 'Executive Session of the Senate Finance Committee' (28 September 1999) <https://www.wto.org/english/news_e/spmm_e/spmm09_e.htm>.

told attendees at the 1998 Geneva Ministerial, '[g]lobalization is not a policy choice—it is a fact'.[73]

The blending of liberal millenarianism and the Uruguay Round consensus discourse no doubt helped to consolidate the WTO's authority even further by heightening the sense that the new trade regime was inevitable. But perhaps even more potently, this discursive fusion also enabled the Uruguay Round consensus to stabilize and reinforce the larger 'End of History' narrative by anchoring it in legal authority. Whereas the claim that there was now a worldwide consensus on (neo)liberalism was previously only an inference based on regime change, shifting geopolitics, and the iconic imagery of the tumbling Berlin Wall, proponents of the liberal millenarian discourse now had a more concrete example of such a consensus. For on 15 December 1993, more than 120 states had arrived at a consensus on a new trade regime that would be underpinned by neoliberal values and which would be known (at the behest of the US[74]) as the '*World* Trade Organization'. What is more, this moment was not just a 'consensus' because the GATT Secretariat liked this term or because some states felt that it was one; it was a 'consensus' because the longstanding practice of the GATT deemed it to be such.

By grounding and authorizing claims that the world had now settled on its final economic form, the Uruguay Round consensus helped to reinforce the hegemony of globalized neoliberal capitalism. Marxist theorist Antonio Gramsci used the term 'hegemony' to describe 'the process by which a ruling class naturalizes its domination by installing the presuppositions of its own worldviews as the common sense of society as a whole'.[75] Writing in the 1920s and 1930s, Gramsci argued the modern capitalist state was not only held in place by coercive forces but also through the mass internalization of ideas favourable to capitalist relations of production.[76] In Gramsci's account, those ideas were disseminated through the 'intellectual and moral leadership'[77] of families, schools, law courts, and the media, all of which he loosely called 'civil society', until they eventually came to appear like the only reasonable ideas that could exist. In the 1980s and 1990s, a new, globalized, neoliberal form of capitalism underwent a similar process, as we can see in the various claims from political and academic figures that there could be 'no alternative' to that model. And while there were many discursive and material forces that facilitated this process, the discourses emanating from the Uruguay Round consensus played their part by infusing such claims with an air of legal authority and objectivity.

[73] Clinton (n 38).

[74] VanGrasstek (n 3) 67.

[75] Nancy Fraser, *The Old Is Dying and the New Cannot Be Born: From Progressive Neoliberalism to Trump and Beyond* (Verso 2019) 12, summarizing Gramsci's concept of 'hegemony'.

[76] See generally, Antonio Gramsci, *Selections from the Prison Notebooks* (Quentin Hoare and Geoffrey Nowell Smith eds, 2014 edn, International Publishers 1971).

[77] ibid 57.

The result was not only the strengthening of one economic imaginary, but also the deauthorization and even erasure of alternative economic ideas and practices. Howse and Langille point out that, in terms of its legal architecture, the new WTO system actually still allowed some room for domestic pluralism.[78] Yet, as the world's economic, political, and legal voices seemed to fall into alignment, the notion of a world with diverse economic models became increasingly unthinkable. Queer theorists have long been sensitive to the way this kind of 'lining up' of voices can work to foreclose difference. Eve Kosofsky Sedgwick even had a term for it—'Christmas effects'.[79] This is because Sedgwick considered Christmas to be a time in the US when all of the institutions—religion, state, capital, ideology, domesticity—'line up with each other so neatly once a year' to speak with 'one voice', creating a discursive monolith in which 'everything means the same thing'.[80] In this hegemonic moment, there is no space for subjects or practices that do not conform to the dominant narrative, making Christmas a depressing and alienating time for many. Sedgwick used the idea of 'Christmas effects' to reflect on the way the alignment of gender, sex, and sexuality under heteronormativity can erase diversity and contrasted this 'lockstep of unanimity' with the 'open mesh of possibilities' embraced by queer theory.[81]

Sara Ahmed makes a similar point in her book *Queer Phenomenology: Orientations, Objects, Others*—in her case in relation to the 'lining up' of images, rather than discourses. Ahmed presents us with a memory she has of entering a resort dining room, in which 'table after table, couple after couple, [took] the same form: one man sitting by one woman'.[82] While this scene was a familiar one, Ahmed describes herself as 'shocked' in that moment by the alignment and repetition, whereby each table presented the same form of heterosexual sociality, asking '[h]ow is it possible, with all that is possible, that the same form is repeated again and again?'[83] Entering the room with her lesbian partner, Ahmed felt as if she were in '[t]he wrong kind of couple', and she reflects on how "[b]eing out of line can be uncomfortable'.[84] Ahmed uses this memory to argue that people are not born straight but rather become straight through a 'field of heterosexual objects', which help to bring them 'into line' with heteronormative expectations.[85] Like the lining up of institutions at Christmastime or tables of heterosexual couples at a resort, the alignment and repetition of voices proclaiming the triumph of free-market values

[78] Robert Howse and Joanna Langille, 'Continuity and Change in the World Trade Organization: Pluralism Past, Present, and Future' (2023) 117 American Journal of International Law 1.

[79] Eve Kosofsky Sedgwick, *Tendencies* (Duke University Press 1993) 5.

[80] ibid 5–6.

[81] ibid 6–8.

[82] Sara Ahmed, *Queer Phenomenology: Orientations, Objects, Others* (Duke University Press 2006) 82.

[83] ibid.

[84] ibid.

[85] ibid 79–92.

through the fusion of the Uruguay Round consensus and the 'End of History' narratives functioned as an economic 'straightening device',[86] helping to block the possibility of economic diversity from the horizon.

This is not to say that, in the aftermath of the Cold War, other economic practices and imaginaries ceased to exist in the world. Writing in 1996, at the height of the combined liberal millenarian–Uruguay Round consensus discourse, Gibson-Graham sought 'to queer' the global economy by reading it for 'difference rather than dominance'.[87] This led them to point out that there were (and still are) a 'great variety of noncaptialist practices',[88] from hunting, fishing, and gathering to gift-giving, housework, and co-operative exchange. Likewise, Rancière draws our attention to the 'surplus subjects'—that is, 'the multitude of individuals and peoples'[89] who were rendered invisible and unsayable by the consensual logic of the immediate post-Cold War era but who nevertheless continued to exist within those societies.[90] Indeed, and as we shall see in the following section, the WTO would come face-to-face with some of these 'surplus subjects' in the late 1990s. Rather, the intermingling of the Uruguay Round consensus and the End of History narrative helped to secure globalized neoliberal capitalism as a 'hegemonized *discourse*',[91] whose primary assault was on 'the anti-capitalist *imagination*'.[92] While economic alternatives may not have actually been displaced, they rapidly began to disappear from view, such that, for many, it became easier 'to imagine the thoroughgoing deterioration of the earth . . . than the breakdown of late capitalism'.[93]

3.3 Resistance and Hegemony

3.3.1 Encountering Resistance from Within

Part of the reason why the institutional rhetoric around the Uruguay Round consensus may have been asserted so strongly, especially in the late 1990s, was because the WTO was in fact encountering a counter-narrative from both within and

[86] Ahmed uses the term 'straightening devices' to describe the mechanisms that enforce heteronormativity and other dominant norms, see Ahmed (n 82).

[87] JK Gibson-Graham, *The End of Capitalism (As We Knew It): A Feminist Critique of Political Economy* (2nd edn, University of Minnesota Press 2006). Gibson-Graham later described this book as an attempt to 'queer the economy', which involved a practice of 'reading for difference rather than dominance' in JK Gibson-Graham, *A Postcapitalist Politics* (University of Minnesota Press 2006) xxxi–xxxii.

[88] Gibson-Graham, *A Postcapitalist Politics* (n 87) xxxii.

[89] Jacques Rancière, *Dissensus: On Politics and Aesthetics* (Steven Concoran tr, Continuum International Publishing Group 2010) 102.

[90] Jacques Rancière, *Disagreement: Politics and Philosophy* (Julie Rose tr, University of Minnesota Press 1999) 26.

[91] JK Gibson-Graham, 'Queer(y)Ing Capitalism in and out of the Classroom' (1999) 23 Journal of Geography in Higher Education 80, 82 [emphasis added].

[92] Gibson-Graham, *The End of Capitalism* (n 87) 3 [emphasis added].

[93] Fredric Jameson, *The Seeds of Time* (Columbia University Press, 1994), quoted in ibid ix.

outside the institution. Inside the WTO, states in the global South challenged the idea that the Uruguay Round consensus had come about as a result of a shared North–South vision for the global economy. In 1998, for example, at the same fiftieth anniversary event in Geneva at which US President Clinton had spoken breathlessly about the triumph of free-market capitalism and the foresight of the GATT's founders, South African President Nelson Mandela and Cuban President Fidel Castro also delivered speeches. In these speeches, they outlined their dismay with the asymmetrical outcome of the Uruguay Round negotiations. Mandela said the following:

> We must be frank in our assessment of the outcome of the Uruguay Round. The developing countries were not able to ensure that the rules accommodated their realities. For understandable reasons it was mainly the preoccupations and problems of the advanced industrial economies that shaped the agreement.[94]

Castro was even more direct: 'The United States obtained practically everything it wanted with the agreements leading to the establishment of the WTO ... The Third World countries have been losing everything.'[95] Both also expressed doubt about the neoliberal orientation underpinning the Uruguay Agreements. In Castro's case, this was explicit:

> Despite so much euphoria no one can be sure of how long the United States economic system, ruled by the blind laws of the market economy, will be able to prevent a financial meltdown ... The problem is that now a big crisis would go global and have unforeseeable consequences.[96]

Castro thus urged WTO Members to 'turn this organization into an instrument of the struggle for a more just and better world.'[97] Mandela's critique of the economic principles underpinning the WTO was more muted. While he reaffirmed 'that the building of a multilateral rules-based system [was] fundamentally correct',[98] he questioned the particular logic of the WTO system, noting the widening 'gap between rich and poor'[99] and the distressing level of 'poverty, homelessness and unemployment [that] ... the world now knows.'[100] In this way, Mandela highlighted how, despite all the talk of economic sameness, the neoliberal orientation

[94] Nelson Mandela, 'Statement, Geneva Ministerial' (19 May 1998) <https://www.wto.org/english/thewto_e/minist_e/min98_e/anniv_e/mandela_e.htm>.
[95] Fidel Castro, 'Cuba Statement, Geneva Ministerial' (1998) <https://www.wto.org/english/thewto_e/minist_e/min98_e/anniv_e/castro_e.htm>.
[96] ibid.
[97] Mandela (n 94).
[98] ibid.
[99] ibid.
[100] ibid.

embedded in the WTO was not resulting in a homogenization of life-worlds across the globe, but instead having profoundly uneven impacts on different regions and communities.[101]

In response to such criticisms, however, WTO representatives and states in the global North simply fell back on the authority of the Uruguay Round consensus, which, as mentioned above, had been reinterpreted within some institutional circles as something close to unanimity. As Howse documents, every time states from the South raised concerns about the Uruguay Agreements, they were simply 'reminded that they had "voluntarily" consented to the deal'.[102] Spurred on by the euphoria of liberal millenarianism, WTO representatives were also able to reframe such statements of discontent as statements of *support* for the new trade system. In a speech following the 50th anniversary event, for example, Director-General Ruggiero gave the following account of those proceedings:

> Three weeks ago in Geneva we marked the 50th anniversary of the multilateral trading system . . . [N]ot a single speaker questioned the validity of multilateral trade or of the WTO. From President Clinton to President Castro, Prime Minister Blair to President Mandela . . . all saw this system as indispensable to growth and stability in our interdependent world; even if each one had a different perspective on success and failure, reflecting different backgrounds and historical experiences.[103]

Ruggiero's account of Castro and Mandela's speeches seems almost absurd. After all, both had appeared to question the validity of the system as it currently stood. Moreover, Castro's speech in particular served as a reminder that neither the Third World project nor the 'spectre of Marx' had yet been fully conjured away.[104] Nonetheless, these details did not seem to matter to representatives of the WTO. What was important was that both Castro and Mandela spoke about the WTO as if were *the* forum for dealing with matters relating to global trade, thereby inadvertently restabilizing the institution and reinforcing the idea that it was the product of a worldwide consensus.[105] As such, their words were not only powerless against the Uruguay Round consensus discourse; they became constitutive of it.

[101] On the unevenness of capitalist development generally, see Ntina Tzouvala, *Capitalism as Civilization: A History of International Law* (Cambridge University Press 2020) 4. For this argument in relation to international trade and investment law specifically, see Ntina Tzouvala, 'Book Review: World Trade and Investment Law Reimagined: A Progressive Agenda for an Inclusive Globalization' (2020) 31 European Journal of International Law 1166.

[102] Robert Howse, 'The World Trade Organization 20 Years On: Global Governance by Judiciary' (2016) 27 European Journal of International Law 9, 21.

[103] Ruggiero (n 58).

[104] On the way in which Fukuyama's End of History thesis may be read as an attempt to conjure away the spectre of Marx, see Jacques Derrida, *Specters of Marx: The State of the Debt, the Work of Mourning and the New International* (Peggy Kamuf tr, Routledge 1994).

[105] Strange (n 48) 249–50, discussing the WTO's emergence as the 'natural' body for global trade governance and the way modes of resistance centred on the WTO can reinforce that status.

Perhaps understanding the discursive monolith they were up against, states in the South began to express their discontent in different ways. One way was through consensus decision-making itself. At the 1999 Seattle Ministerial Conference, states in the South refused to join in a consensus to launch a new round, citing the Northern states' use of weighted tactics similar to those employed during the Uruguay Round, such as exclusive Green Room meetings. Although the WTO Membership eventually agreed to a new round at the Doha Ministerial in 2001, the Doha Round itself was characterized by a profound lack of agreement between the North and South. Cho explains that this was because the Doha Round—also known as the 'Doha *Development* Round' in apparent 'acknowledgement that the WTO system "owed something to developing countries"'[106]—was seen by the South as an opportunity 'to redeem the unbalanced deal that it had suffered as a result of the Uruguay Round'.[107] When this was not forthcoming, those negotiations quickly descended into a prolonged standoff between the North and South, effectively collapsing in 2008 and officially being put to rest in 2015.

But, for a long time, even this sustained 'political dissensus'[108] did not undo the WTO or the sense that it was underpinned by a worldwide consensus. In 2010, for example, two years after the Doha Round had collapsed and with the world in the throes of a financial crisis eerily similar to the one Castro had warned of, the WTO's fifth Director-General, Pascal Lamy, still proudly described the WTO as a system underpinned by 'a simultaneous consensus on the virtues of opening up trade . . . [and] the existence of tested multilateral trade rules'.[109] Lamy also attributed the WTO's relative stability during the Global Financial Crisis (GFC)[110] to this underlying consensus, claiming that it had enabled the institution to 'avoid the suicidal protectionist wave that we feared two years ago'.[111]

The ability of the Uruguay Round consensus to overshadow the years of disagreement that followed again seems to lie in the opaque nature of the WTO's consensus procedure, in which only a *lack* of (formal) disagreement, and not disagreement itself, is officialized. As a result, this method of decision-making works to elevate instances of consensus, while simultaneously downplaying and concealing moments of dissent. As Strange writes, 'consensus in the WTO is utilized to displace dissensus from the formal arena, limiting the extent to which it may be expressed beyond the informal, and low-visibility, domain of international diplomacy'.[112] Or, put in another way, the WTO's consensus procedure establishes what

[106] Sungjoon Cho, 'The Demise of Development in the Doha Round Negotiations' (2010) 45 Texas International Law Journal 573, 589, quoting Finger (2009).
[107] ibid 577.
[108] Howse (n 102) 23.
[109] Pascal Lamy, 'Crisis Is Opportunity to Restore Coherence in Global Economic Governance' (8 December 2010) <https://www.wto.org/english/news_e/sppl_e/sppl181_e.htm>.
[110] On the WTO's relative stability during the GFC, see Brewster (n 46) 2–3.
[111] Lamy (n 109).
[112] Michael Strange, *Writing Global Trade Governance: Discourse and the WTO* (Routledge, 2014) 75.

feminist and queer theorists would describe as a 'public/private divide',[113] in which instances of (apparent) agreement are given full access to the public sphere and different and dissenting viewpoints are cast into the WTO's 'closet'. The Uruguay Round's success could thus remain the WTO's formal, outward story, whereas for many years the Doha Round's failure could be seen as an informal and internal matter—a point of institutional embarrassment, but not a wholesale displacement of the WTO's consensus-based origin story.

3.3.2 Encountering Resistance from the Outside

In the late 1990s, the WTO also began to encounter resistance from outside its walls. This resistance formed part of a larger 'anti-' or 'alter-globalization' movement,[114] which had begun to emerge in the mid-1990s—even before the WTO had officially opened its doors. On 1 January 1994, for example, around two weeks after the Uruguay Round had concluded and three and a half months before the Uruguay Agreements were signed,[115] the Zapatista Army of National Liberation announced its presence with a twelve-day armed uprising in the state of Chiapas in Mexico. This uprising coincided with the date on which the North American Free Trade Agreement came into effect.[116] A predominantly Indigenous movement, the Zapatistas declared war not only on the Mexican state, but also on globalized neoliberalism itself.[117]

In October that same year, on the other side of the world in Madrid, protesters descended on the annual joint meeting of the International Monetary Fund (IMF) and World Bank. These protesters were enraged by something known as the 'Washington Consensus'. The term 'Washington Consensus' was coined by British economist John Williamson in 1989 to denote ten policy prescriptions promoted by the IMF, World Bank, and US Treasury in the 1980s and early 1990s as the standard 'reform' package.[118] These policy prescriptions, which included

[113] For an overview of queer and feminist perspectives on the 'public/private divide' see Michael Warner, *Publics and Counterpublics* (Zone Books 2005). On how this divide plays into international law, see Hilary Charlesworth and Christine Chinkin, *The Boundaries of International Law: A Feminist Analysis* (Manchester University Press 2016) 56–59; Dianne Otto, 'Fearless Speech: A Portrait of UN Typist Shirley Hazzard', *Portraits of Women in International Law* (Oxford University Press 2023).

[114] This movement was often described as the 'anti-globalization' movement in the media, but participants tended to prefer the term 'alter-globalization' because they were not necessarily opposed to greater connection between different parts of the world; their primary concern was with the neoliberal form that that connection took.

[115] The Uruguay Agreements were signed on 15 April 1994 in Marrakesh.

[116] Naomi Klein, 'Farewell to the "End of History": Organization and Vision in Anti-Corporate Movements' (2002) 38 Socialist Register 1, 4.

[117] ibid. For more on the Zapatistas, see Alex Khasnabish, *Zapatistas: Rebellion from the Grassroots to the Global* (Zed Books 2010).

[118] John Williamson, 'A Short History of the Washington Consensus' (2009) 15 Law and Business Review of the Americas 7.

macroeconomic reforms such as privatization, deregulation, and trade liberalization, were often coercively imposed on states in the global South via draconian structural adjustment programmes (SAPs). Like the Uruguay Round consensus discourse, the Washington Consensus functioned as an economic 'straightening device', working to foreclose economic ideas and practices that did not conform to the dominant economic philosophy in the US at the time. As Kapoor writes of the SAPs, '[t]hrough a queer lens this all looks like an exercise in economic *straightening*, aimed at disciplining, punishing and exorcizing'[119] the Third World for its economic 'abnormality'. It was against this backdrop that protesters interrupted World Bank President Lewis Preston's opening speech at the 1994 Madrid meeting by unfurling a banner behind him that read 'World Bank Murderer', and dropping fake dollar bills from the ceiling.[120]

In the years that followed, these alter-globalization protests spread 'like a brushfire'.[121] Similar protests took place in Auckland, Vancouver, Manila, Birmingham, London, Geneva, Kuala Lumpur, and Cologne against international bodies such as the G7 and the Asia Pacific Economic Cooperation.[122] While the protests were decentralized and unpredictable, they were also, as Klein writes, 'intricately linked to one another'[123]—a vast, interconnected 'network of "hubs and spokes"'.[124]

It was not long before the alter-globalization movement turned its sights on the nascent WTO. Even before the so-called Battle of Seattle, WTO meetings had started to attract protesters. At the 1998 Geneva Ministerial at which Clinton, Castro, and Mandela had spoken, around 5,000 activists from all over the world converged on the city, arguing that the WTO's free trade agenda 'despoils the environment and enslaves dispossessed peoples'.[125] Over the same few days, the recently launched 'Joint Action Forum of Indian People Against the WTO and Anti-People Policies' organized an anti-WTO rally of approximately 200,000 people in Hyderabad, India.[126] But rising community discontent with the WTO became front-page news in 1999, when its Ministerial Conference in Seattle was engulfed by protests of around 40,000 people, many of them coming from other US states

[119] Ilan Kapoor, 'The Queer Third World' (2015) 36 Third World Quarterly 1611, 1616.

[120] Kate Bedford, *Developing Partnerships: Gender, Sexuality, and the Reformed World Bank* (University of Minnesota Press 2009) 2.

[121] Roger Keil, 'From Los Angeles to Seattle: World City Protests and the New Global Resistance' in Benjamin Shephard and Ronald Hayduk (eds), *From ACT UP to the WTO: Urban Protest and Community Building in the Era of Globalization* (Verso 2002) 333.

[122] Klein (n 116) 5.

[123] ibid 4.

[124] ibid 5.

[125] Patrick Lane, 'Time for Another Round' *The Economist* (3 October 1998) <https://www.economist.com/special-report/1998/10/01/time-for-another-round>. On the number of protesters involved in the 1998 Geneva protest, see 'Thousands Attend Geneva Anti-Globalization Protest' *Institute for Agriculture and Trade Policy News* (25 June 2000) <https://www.iatp.org/news/thousands-attend-geneva-anti-globalization-protest>.

[126] Rahul Rao, *Third World Protest: Between Home and the World* (Oxford University Press 2010) 161.

and countries.[127] These protests blocked thousands of delegates from attending the opening meeting[128] and, in combination with the internal actions of representatives from the global South, are widely considered to have brought about the failure to launch a new round of trade negotiations at the Seattle Ministerial.[129]

A central concern of the 1999 Seattle protests was the threat the WTO posed to democracy.[130] In contrast to institutional claims that the Uruguay Round consensus represented the will of 'the people', the protesters complained that the WTO had come about without their consent. This is unsurprising, given that, in most jurisdictions, the Uruguay Agreements had been subject to little democratic scrutiny. As Petersmann observes, 'many national parliaments in WTO member countries ratified the 25,000 pages of the Uruguay Round Agreements within a few hours without proper parliamentary review and transparent discussion'.[131] Moreover, and in opposition to the narrative that free markets and free societies were interlinked, the protesters expressed concern that the WTO would continue to undermine domestic democracy due to its neoliberal orientation. This was because the new global trade regime not only extended its reach into a range of policy areas previously belonging to the domestic sphere, but also brought with it a compulsory and binding dispute settlement system in which 'only protectionist measures, never neo-liberal practices, could be contested'.[132] During the Seattle protests, these concerns were summed up by a giant banner, hung from a crane over the city, with two arrows pointing in different directions, one with the word 'democracy' on it and the other with the word 'WTO'.[133]

Despite being part of a wider backlash against globalized neoliberal capitalism which had already been playing out in various locations around the world since the mid-1990s, the energy, scale, and effectiveness of the 1999 Seattle protests took many by surprise. After all, they sat uneasily with the dominant discourse of the time, which claimed that everyone was on board with the new neoliberal world order. Kauffman writes, '[t]o the political mainstream, the clashes in Seattle seemed

[127] John Burgess and Steven Pearlstein, 'Protests Delay WTO Opening: Seattle Police Use Tear Gas; Mayor Declares a Curfew' *The Washington Post* (1 December 1999) <https://www.washingtonpost.com/wp-srv/WPcap/1999-12/01/089r-120199-idx.html>.

[128] ibid.

[129] Quinn Slobodian, '20 Years After Seattle, the Clash of Globalizations Rages On' *The Nation* (29 November 2019) <https://www.thenation.com/article/activism/seattle-trade-globalization/>.

[130] Quinn Slobodian, *Globalists: The End of Empire and the Birth of Neoliberalism* (Harvard University Press 2018): 'The old foe of "majoritarianism" returned as people claimed "that the present inter-governmental arrangement is 'undemocratic'"'.

[131] Ernst-Ulrich Petersmann, 'Human Rights and International Economic Law in the 21st Century: The Need to Clarify Their Interrelationships' (2001) 4 Journal of International Economic Law 3, 27.

[132] Nitsan Chorev, 'The Institutional Project of Neo-Liberal Globalism: The Case of the WTO' (2005) 34 Theory and Society 317, 318.

[133] Klaus Dingwerth, 'Democracy' in Klaus Dingwerth and Clara Weinhardt (eds), *The Language of World Trade Politics: Unpacking the Terms of Trade* (1st edn, Routledge 2018).

to materialize from nowhere. According to conventional wisdom[,] ... after all, the left ... had virtually disappeared.'[134]

WTO representatives initially responded to these protests by reaffirming that the WTO was underpinned by a worldwide consensus on globalized neoliberal capitalism; it was just that some segments of the population had not yet been caught up. As Director-General Ruggiero put it in 1998:

> It would be a sad irony if, at a time when there has never been a broader awareness among governments and elites about the benefits of trade, openness and integration, we found a widening gap between these governments and the publics they serve. We cannot allow this gap to open.[135]

Following the 'Battle of Seattle' in 1999, the WTO's response took on a more aggressive tone, with Director-General Moore no longer portraying the protesters as uninformed masses but rather as the foolish enemies of an End of History that had already taken place.[136] This can be seen in the following statement made by Moore in 2002: 'Globalization works. And it isn't going away ... While freedom and capitalism are under threat—from disaffected terrorists to *anti-globalist extremists*—they remain the only valid socio-economic systems world-wide since the collapse of the Soviet Bloc.'[137] Sometimes, the popular discontent was even used in a way to reaffirm the idea that the world had reached its final political and economic form. In 1999, for example, Moore framed the protests as a by-product of the demise of ideological alternatives, stating, '[i]n the absence of other "isms" to vent frustration upon, globalism is the only "ism" left.'[138]

The alter-globalization movement came to see that it could not overcome the combined Uruguay Round consensus–liberal millenarian narrative by fighting it directly. As activist and member of the Council of Canadians Maude Barlow observed, '[w]e are up against a boulder. We can't remove it.'[139] They also quickly learnt that, like the words of representatives from the global South, their protests could inadvertently work to restabilize both the WTO and the overall sense that 'globalism was the only "ism" left', thereby not only leaving the boulder in its place, but also propping it up and securing it in position.[140]

[134] LA Kauffman, 'A Short History of Radical Renewal' in Benjamin Shephard and Ronald Hayduk (eds), *From ACT UP to the WTO: Urban Protest and Community Building in the Era of Globalization* (Verso 2002) 35.

[135] Ruggiero (n 58) 50.

[136] On the way anti-WTO protesters were portrayed 'as naive and unaware of the inevitable realities of the modern world', see Strange (n 48) 250.

[137] Mike Moore, 'Globalization: The Impact of the Doha Development Agenda on the Free Market Process' (2002) <https://www.wto.org/english/news_e/spmm_e/spmm77_e.htm> [emphasis added].

[138] Moore (n 34) [emphasis added].

[139] Quoted in Klein (n 116) 7.

[140] Gibson-Graham explains that '[w]hen theorists [or activists] depict patriarchy, or racism, or compulsory heterosexuality, or capitalist hegemony they are not only delineating a formation they hope to

The alter-globalization movement changed course. It decided that it was time to 'stop screaming about what it [was] against and start articulating what [it was] for'.[141] One way in which this was carried out was by setting up the World Social Forum—an annual meeting for activists and civil society groups from around the globe to discuss social and economic alternatives to globalized neoliberalism, the first of which took place in Porto Alegre in Brazil in 2001 under the slogan 'Another World Is Possible'.[142] The aim of such meetings was not to find an alternative overarching ideology through which to 'wrest control'[143] from institutions such as the WTO. After all, in the view of activists like Naomi Klein and Maude Barlow, recognizing that there was a boulder blocking their path did not mean constructing another boulder; it meant finding creative and diverse ways 'to go underneath [the boulder], to go around it and over it'.[144] In this regard, despite often using a non-voting method of decision-making known as 'consensus' themselves,[145] the alter-globalization movement actively resisted arriving at a singular, substantive consensus in the way the WTO claimed to have done.[146]

Instead, embracing the Zapatista slogans of a 'world with multiple worlds within it'[147] and 'one no and many yeses',[148] participants in the alter-globalization movement sought to 'queer'[149] the social and economic landscape by 'asserting and creating multiple other ways of being in the world'.[150] This included setting up autonomous zones of counterpower, and bringing together a broad coalition of workers, youth, women, queers, immigrants, people of colour, and Indigenous groups.[151] Their aim was to produce 'not a blueprint for some utopian new world,

see destabilized or replaced. They are also generating a representation of the social world and endowing it with performative force. To the extent that this representation becomes influential it may contribute to the hegemony of a "hegemonic formation", see Gibson-Graham, *The End of Capitalism* (n 87) xxxix.

141 Klein (n 116) 1.
142 ibid.
143 Gibson-Graham, *A Postcapitalist Politics* (n 87) xx.
144 Klein (n 116) 7.
145 Geoffrey Pleyers, *Alter-Globalization: Becoming Actors in the Global Age* (Polity Press 2010) 80.
146 Klein (n 116) 4, noting that they avoided 'forced consensus and laboured manifestos'.
147 ibid 13. This is also sometimes expressed as 'a world where many worlds fit', see Levi Gahman, 'Building "A World Where Many Worlds Fit": Indigenous Autonomy, Mutual Aid, and an (Anti-Capitalist) Moral Economy of the (Rebel) Peasant' in Jessica Duncan and Megan Bailey (eds), *Sustainable Food Futures: Multidisciplinary Solutions* (Routledge 2017). The idea of a world of multiple worlds is discussed further in Chapter 7 of this book.
148 Klein (n 116) 4.
149 On the way in which this pursuit of economic diversity can be considered 'queer' see Gibson-Graham (n 91). See also, Jamie Heckert, 'Intimacy with Strangers/Intimacy with Self: Queer Experiences of Social Research' in Kath Browne and Catherine J Nash (eds), *Queer Methods and Methodologies Intersecting Queer Theories and Social Science Research* (Routledge 2016) 45, discussing the resonances between the Zapatistas' commitment to multiple worlds and queer theory.
150 Michal Osterweil, 'Place-Based Globalists: Rethinking the Global in the Alternative Globalization Movement' [2004] Unpublished paper, Department of Anthropology, University of North Carolina, Chapel Hill 8.
151 Klein (n 116) 4; Keil (n 121) 333.

but a plan to protect the possibility of many worlds'.[152] It was to embrace an idea of both society and the economy as 'a rich and prolific disarray'.[153]

In this way, the alter-globalization movement, or at least segments thereof, staged what Rancière would call a 'dissensus'.[154] In the work of Rancière, 'dissensus' means something different to the way it was used above in the context of the Doha Round. It is not simply persistent disagreement in a consensus decision-making process. Rather, for Rancière, to enact a dissensus means to insert a division into society's 'common sense' by creating 'a dispute over what is given and about the frame within which we see something as given'.[155] It occurs when the 'surplus' or 'uncounted' subjects—'the part of those that has no part'[156] in a society—enter onto the political stage and bring about a 'contradiction of two worlds in a single world: the world where they are and the world where they are not'.[157] Through this process, people and things that had been hitherto invisible or unsayable under the consensus order start to become seen and heard, disrupting what had previously seemed like a 'happy circle between law and fact'.[158] By appearing to assert 'we're here, we're not capitalist, get used to it',[159] just as Queer Nation had declared 'we're here, we're queer' before them,[160] the alter-globalization movement brought about such a contradiction of worlds: the one in which history had ended, and the one in which it had not.[161]

In some ways, this strategy proved a success. By the mid-2000s, few were talking about the End of History any more. Perhaps this was simply because history itself had continued to march forward, throwing up events like 9/11 and the War on Terror that followed. But in the view of scholars such as Osterweil, the alter-globalization movement, and, in particular, localized segments such as the Zapatistas, did help to rob the post-Cold War consensus order 'of its monopoly and singular definitions of time, space and value, thereby destroying [or at least

[152] Klein (n 116) 13.
[153] Gibson-Graham, *The End of Capitalism* (n 87) xxxix.
[154] Rancière (n 89).
[155] ibid 69.
[156] ibid 70.
[157] Rancière (n 90) 27.
[158] Rancière (n 89) 102.
[159] Gibson-Graham use this slogan to capture those embracing the idea that 'the economic world is already queer', see Gibson-Graham (n 91) 84. On the way the alter-globalization movement embodied this idea, see Gibson-Graham, *A Postcapitalist Politics* (n 87) xix–xxii.
[160] Queer Nation was a queer activist organization founded by members of ACT UP in 1990 in New York City. Gibson-Graham's use of the slogan 'we're here, we're not capitalist, get used to it' is based on the Queer Nation slogan, 'we're here, we're queer, get used to it'. On the links between the alter-globalization movement and queer activist organizations like Queer Nation and ACT UP, see generally Benjamin Shephard and Ronald Hayduk (eds), *From ACT UP to the WTO: Urban Protest and Community Building in the Era of Globalization* (Verso 2002). On the way Queer Nation's slogan resonates with the thought of Rancière, see Samuel A Chambers, 'A Queer Politics of the Democratic Miscount' (2009) 8 Borderlands.
[161] Klein writes that, for her, the first World Social Forum represented 'the end of The End of History', see Klein (n 116) 1.

fraying] its hegemony'.[162] Some international economic organizations also made attempts at reform in response to these community attitudes. In 1998, for example, World Bank Chief Economist Joseph Stiglitz acknowledged that 'the Washington consensus [had] not provide[d] the answer' and stated that the Bank was adopting a 'post-Washington consensus agenda'.[163] As part of this new agenda, the Bank began focusing on issues such as gender, good governance, and the rule of law as key priorities.[164] The extent to which this new approach represented a departure from, or simply an adjustment of, the Washington consensus model is debatable.[165] Nevertheless, the Bank tried to distance itself from it and, in 2004, World Bank President James Wolfensohn declared that 'the Washington Consensus ha[d] been dead for years'.[166]

As liberal millenarianism receded into history and institutions like the World Bank fled from the 'damaged brand name'[167] of the Washington Consensus, for a long time the Uruguay Round consensus retained its mythical status. While the scope of the discourse surrounding it shrunk and claims about it being linked to a general spread of democracy and free-market capitalism dropped off, WTO representatives maintained that, at the very least, it represented a worldwide commitment to the WTO system. Director-General Lamy stated in 2008 that '[t]he establishment of the WTO at the conclusion of the Uruguay Round . . . was a signal that the majority of the countries in the world wanted a wide a far-reaching global trade body to promote . . . trade rules—in goods, services and intellectual property'.[168]

In the view of representatives of the WTO, few had come to regret this commitment. In 2005, for example, WTO Director-General Supachai Panitchpakdi said, 'ten years after its foundation, the WTO has never been more relevant and more important'.[169] He then went on to note that despite the WTO having been a subject of 'controversy' during its first decade, the world had nonetheless 'learned that there [was] no alternative to the global trading system in international commerce'.[170] Likewise, in 2008, Lamy noted: 'today everyone agrees that the Uruguay Round increased world income by several hundreds of billions of dollars, and

[162] Osterweil (n 150) 8.

[163] Joseph E Stiglitz, 'Keynote Address: More Instruments and Broader Goals: Moving Toward the Post-Washington Consensus' [1998] Villa Borsig Workshop Series.

[164] Rahul Rao, 'Global Homocapitalism' (2015) 194 Radical Philosophy 38, 39.

[165] Bedford (n 120) xiv.

[166] James Wolfensohn, 'Opening Remarks at the Shanghai Conference on Scaling Up Poverty Reduction (26 May 2004)' in Andrew Kircher (ed), *Voice for the World's Poor: Selected Speeches and Writings of World Bank President James D. Wolfensohn, 1995-2005* (The World Bank 2005) 475.

[167] John Williamson, 'From Reform Agenda to Damaged Brand Name: A Short History of the Washington Consensus and Suggestions for What to Do Next' (2003) 40 Finance and Development 10.

[168] Pascal Lamy, 'Negotiations Can Find Compromise on the Safeguards Issue' (13 December 2008) <https://www.wto.org/english/news_e/sppl_e/sppl98_e.htm>.

[169] Supachai Panitchpakdi, 'The WTO after 10 Years: The Lessons Learned and the Challenges Ahead' (11 March 2005) <https://www.wto.org/english/news_e/spsp_e/spsp35_e.htm>.

[170] ibid.

that the establishment of the WTO . . . marked an important advance in world governance.'[171]

Arguably, the persistence of this discourse was linked to the legal status of both the Uruguay Round consensus and the agreements it produced. A political claim of consensus is often fleeting and its contours difficult to define. It is difficult to say how many people or states in the 1990s were really committed to liberal democracy and globalized capitalism or when that trend began and how long it lasted. A legal claim of consensus, on the other hand, is much easier to pin down. The Uruguay Round negotiations not only produced instances of 'consensus' between states under well-established practices of the GATT, culminating with a grand final consensus on the identifiable date of 15 December 1993, but they also resulted in 25,000 pages of agreements that set out the substance of those consensus decisions, and which were subsequently signed and ratified by those states. While the GATT's consensus procedure may have been a highly slippery method of international decision-making, such results are more certain than a floating claim of political consensus. This gave WTO representatives something tangible to hold on to that proponents of some of the other post-Cold War consensus discourses never had.

Through their conversion into binding treaty law and the institutional form of the WTO, the consensus decisions reached during the Uruguay Round could also become frozen in time; locked in place through the 'stickiness' of international law.[172] Even once it was no longer fashionable to talk euphorically about the triumph of free-market capitalism, the WTO system still existed, churning away according to a neoliberal script set down in the mid-1990s. As a result, the consensus discourse surrounding the WTO was able to outlast the political and economic context from which it had emerged.

3.4 Trading Consensuses: Pascal Lamy and the 'Geneva Consensus'

Despite the ability of the Uruguay Round consensus discourse to outlive the End of History narrative with which it had once been so intimate, in the 2010s that discourse too began to crack. This was partly due to the ongoing failure of the Doha Round negotiations, which had effectively been on 'life support'[173] since their breakdown in 2008 and would remain that way until their abandonment in 2015. The *Financial Times* described this as 'a death scene so drawn-out it would have

[171] Pascal Lamy, 'Speech to the European Parliament Committee on International Trade' (29 May 2008) <https://www.wto.org/english/news_e/sppl_e/sppl90_e.htm> [emphasis added].

[172] On the idea that law, including international law, works 'to create stickiness on social relations', see Wouter G Werner, 'Regulating Speed: Social Acceleration, and International Law' in Moshe Hirsch and Andrew Lang (eds), *Research Handbook on the Sociology of International Law* (Edward Elgar Publishing 2018) 93.

[173] 'The Doha Round Finally Dies a Merciful Death' *Financial Times* (21 December 2015) <https://www.ft.com/content/9cb1ab9e-a7e2-11e5-955c-1e1d6de94879>.

done credit to a Victorian melodrama' and denounced the Doha Round as 'one of the longest-running farces in global policymaking'.[174] Against this backdrop, and with greater temporal distance from the Uruguay Round, it became harder for WTO representatives to maintain that the system was underpinned by an international consensus, even if they still had the Uruguay Agreements to attempt to prove it.

The early 2010s also saw a new wave of anti-neoliberal sentiment as the world grappled with the fallout from the GFC, expressing itself through movements such as Occupy Wall Street in 2011.[175] While the WTO was less of a direct target for these movements than it had been for the alter-globalization movement of the 1990s and early 2000s, the protesters' opposition to globalized neoliberal capitalism added further pressure to its already flailing worldwide consensus narrative. As we shall see in Chapter 6, in the mid-2010s, the WTO would encounter discontent from the right side of politics as well.[176]

Before these tensions hit boiling point, however, WTO Director-General Pascal Lamy made a last-ditch effort to inject a sense of consensus into the institution. He did so by creating a new consensus narrative, built around something called the 'Geneva Consensus'. Lamy first coined this term in 2005, as part of his bid to become Director-General.[177] He subsequently referred to the 'Geneva Consensus' in a number of speeches during his time in that role.[178] It was not until 2013, however, when the WTO was in serious need of reinvigoration, that Lamy properly fleshed out the idea in his book, *The Geneva Consensus: Making Trade Work for All*.[179]

Unlike the Uruguay Round consensus, Lamy's Geneva Consensus was not a legal consensus. It did not refer to any consensus decision reached by the Members under the WTO's decision-making rules. After all, during Lamy's eight years as Director-General, WTO Members could reach consensus on very little.[180] Rather, like the Washington Consensus or claims about a worldwide consensus on liberalism, it was based on inference. As Lamy put it in 2005, when he was first introducing the term to the WTO General Council, 'I believe that we share this view, on what one might call "a Geneva consensus", of some sort'.[181] By the time of his 2013 book, Lamy described the Geneva Consensus as an approach to trade

[174] ibid.

[175] For an overview of the Occupy Movement, see Noam Chomsky, *Occupy* (Penguin 2012).

[176] Slobodian (n 129).

[177] Pascal Lamy, 'Statement, WTO Director-General Selection Process' (26 January 2005) <https://www.wto.org/english/thewto_e/dg_e/stat_lamy_e.htm>.

[178] See eg, Pascal Lamy, 'It's Time for a New "Geneva Consensus" on Making Trade Work for Development' (30 October 2006) <https://www.wto.org/english/news_e/sppl_e/sppl45_e.htm>.

[179] Pascal Lamy, *The Geneva Consensus: Making Trade Work for All* (Cambridge University Press 2013).

[180] For more about decision-making deadlock during this period, see Section 2.3.2 of Chapter 2 of this book.

[181] Lamy (n 177).

governance that had been guiding the WTO and other Geneva-based institutions 'in recent years'.[182]

According to Lamy, at its core, the Geneva Consensus was about 'humanizing globalization and establishing further justice and equity'.[183] In his view, this meant 'making trade work for development',[184] 'dealing with the imbalances created between winners and losers from trade opening',[185] and recognizing the interrelationship between WTO law and human rights.[186] It was not, however, a rejection of the WTO system or the Uruguay Round consensus discourse that had long surrounded it. As we saw earlier, Lamy had himself embraced a pared-back version of the Uruguay Round consensus discourse during his time as Director-General. Instead, Lamy positioned the Geneva Consensus against the much-maligned *Washington* Consensus. In a speech Lamy delivered in 2006, for example, he said: 'I agree with others that we have passed the time of the Washington Consensus. It is time for a new consensus. Call it "Geneva consensus", if you like.'[187] For Lamy, the Geneva Consensus would respond to the failings of the Washington Consensus by emphasizing not only structural reforms, but also development, human rights, and states' 'capacity to better address the costs of, and better distribute the benefits of, trade opening'.[188]

Based on this account, it may seem as if the WTO had undergone, or was about to undergo, significant reform. This was not the case. In Lamy's view, the existing WTO system already aligned with his vision of 'humanized globalization'. This can be seen in Lamy's account of human rights and trade. For Lamy, human rights and WTO rules were 'mutually supportive'[189] because they were 'based on the same values—individual freedom and responsibility, non-discrimination, rule of law and welfare through peaceful co-operation among individuals'.[190] Since its creation, the WTO had worked to further human rights by 'putting in place rules to regulate trade flows and remove trade distortions',[191] thereby spreading open and just trade around the world. This, in turn, had helped to 'polis[h] and softe[n] the most barbarous mores'.[192] In Lamy's account, global trade had also facilitated

[182] Lamy (n 179) 17–18.
[183] Lamy, quoted in Slobodian (n 130) 276.
[184] Lamy (n 178).
[185] Lamy (n 179) 16.
[186] ibid: Chapter 11; Pascal Lamy, 'Trade and Human Rights Go Hand in Hand' (26 September 2010) <https://www.wto.org/english/news_e/sppl_e/sppl172_e.htm>.
[187] Lamy (n 178).
[188] Lamy (n 179) 17.
[189] ibid 148.
[190] ibid. On the way Lamy's views on trade and human rights reflected a long history of neoliberal thinkers espousing a connection between free market economics and human rights, see Jessica Whyte, *The Morals of the Market: Human Rights and the Rise of Neoliberalism* (Verso 2019) 28.
[191] Lamy (n 179) 147.
[192] ibid. Lamy was quoting French Enlightenment philosopher Montesquieu, who argued that commerce can have a civilizing and pacifying effect on society. On the way Montesquieu's 'doux commerce' theory provided a bridge between human rights and neoliberal thought, see Whyte (n 190) 57.

compliance with human rights law by providing 'the instrument most commonly adopted by developed countries to put pressure on states violating human rights'.[193] He pointed out that states in the global North often used trade measures to enforce human rights law, 'either as a carrot, in the form of the offer of greater trading opportunities, or as a stick, through the imposition of restrictions, such as embargoes'.[194]

In fact, for Lamy, a significant component of the Geneva Consensus was simply recognizing that the WTO could not do much more than it was already doing. After all, '[t]he WTO [was] not a development agency'[195] or a human rights body; its 'core role [was] trade opening'.[196] As such, while the WTO certainly needed to spend more time coordinating its efforts with other institutions, it could only play a small part in the larger project of 'humanizing globalization'.[197] The rest would fall to 'other actors on the international economic policy scene, such as the UN family, the Bretton Woods institutions and regional development banks',[198] as well as national governments. It was for this reason that Lamy called it the *Geneva* Consensus: 'this city is home to both the WTO and the United Nations and embodies the very idea of a society of nations working together towards a shared goal.'[199]

In other words, as Slobodian writes, 'the WTO sought to add new rhetoric without changing the basic structure of the organization'.[200] In some ways, Lamy's Geneva Consensus discourse was simply a weaker version of the Uruguay Round consensus discourse in new clothes. The language of 'democracy' had been replaced by that of 'human rights' and the relevant consensus had been shrunk down from the 'world' to international bodies and delegations located in Geneva. But it was ultimately still the same story about the virtues of trade liberalization and the WTO being underpinned by a sense of unity and agreement. It was just that now this discourse was not directly connected to an instance of legal consensus.

It could also be argued that the Uruguay Round consensus had always been the Geneva Consensus in disguise. As Dunkley wrote in 2000, years before Lamy first used the term, '[i]n the case of the Free Trade Adventure, we could speak of a "Geneva consensus", and the Uruguay Round was cast in this mould',[201] noting that '[t]he current free trade debate has been virtually dominated by an "elite consensus", i.e. amongst governments, business, bureaucrats and Free Trade economists'[202]

[193] Lamy (n 179) 148.
[194] ibid 149.
[195] Lamy (n 178).
[196] Lamy (n 179) 17.
[197] ibid 1.
[198] ibid 17.
[199] ibid viii.
[200] Slobodian (n 130) 276.
[201] Dunkley (n 51) 17.
[202] ibid.

located in Geneva. Put in another way, Lamy's Geneva Consensus discourse was perhaps an admission that WTO's consensus narrative had never really been about all WTO Members and their constituencies being on board. The legal consensus reached during the Uruguay Round had simply lent authority to something decided by a small circle of trade policy insiders. Now, faced with a persistent lack of legal consensus in the Doha Round, Lamy was prepared to drop references to the WTO Membership and the institution's consensus procedure altogether and construct a new consensus narrative instead.

Pascal Lamy's Geneva Consensus discourse never became as prominent as the Uruguay Round consensus discourse and, ultimately, it had little impact on the trajectory of the WTO. Perhaps it helped to paper over the almost complete breakdown of the WTO's political branch for a little longer. It may have also appeased some of the WTO's opponents through its emphasis on human rights. Yet, as we will see in Chapter 6, the Geneva Consensus did little to counter the growing sense that the narratives of ideological consensus surrounding the WTO did not match the reality on the ground.

3.5 Conclusion: Consensus and the Stabilization of Economic Normativity

This chapter explored the relationship between the WTO and a number of intersecting consensus narratives. This story it told is instructive to the overarching argument of this book on multiple fronts. First, just as the previous chapter demonstrated that it is not always useful to think about consensus in international law as a specific procedure, this chapter showed that it can be unhelpful to conceive of consensus as a quantifiable state of agreement. In this chapter, we met multiple claims of consensus—the Uruguay Round consensus, the Washington Consensus, the Geneva Consensus, and the post-Cold War claim that there existed a 'worldwide consensus in favour of liberalism'. These claims of consensus were presented as international agreements. Yet, in most cases, the agreement proved immeasurable, intangible, even illusory, once placed under scrutiny; a mirage that blurred and receded from view the moment one stared directly at it. Its subjects could not be counted and its contours could not be defined.

The Uruguay Round consensus was, to some extent, different. Unlike the Washington Consensus, the Geneva Consensus, and the claim that there was a worldwide consensus in favour of liberalism, it had a procedural 'backstory' rooted in the GATT's longstanding practice of consensus decision-making. The agreements that emerged from the Uruguay Round negotiations were also written down, had the binding status of treaty law, and gave rise to the institutional form of the WTO. This not only gave proponents of the claim that the outcome of the

Uruguay Round represented an international consensus something to hold onto but also imbued that claim with an air of objectivity. In this regard, the Uruguay Round consensus reveals how the practices and rituals of international law can work to stabilize a consensus claim. Nevertheless, even in the case of the Uruguay Round consensus, the nature and extent of the final agreement cannot be measured. While statements from states in the global South in the aftermath of the Round suggest that it was by no means complete, the absence of a voting record means that the number of states that affirmatively agreed with the final outcome remains unknown.

Second, this chapter sketched how, when presented as a state of agreement, consensus in international law can operate as a potent authorizing device. The claim that the WTO system was the product of consensus helped to reinforce the authority of the WTO by allowing a myth of unity and destiny to grow up around it. The presentation of the outcome of the Uruguay Round as a worldwide economic consensus also worked to ground and authorize post-Cold War discourses proclaiming the triumph of free-market capitalism. In my argument, these effects are again attributable to the gesture that consensus makes towards a widespread, yet unfixed and unquantifiable, level of agreement. In this case, the immeasurability of the agreement worked to conceal the difference and dissent that lay beneath the consensus claim. This is because, unlike a majority opinion, a claim of consensus does not produce an identifiable minority. Although it is generally acknowledged that consensus does not mean that *all* parties affirmatively agreed, this blurring of numbers makes it difficult to describe the gap that exists between a consensus agreement and a complete agreement, helping to paper over divergent views. Combined with the purportedly largescale nature of the agreement, the result was the projection of visions of unity and homogeneity onto the world.

Third, this chapter illustrated the historical specificity of consensus as a technique of authorization. Just as the previous chapter sketched how the turn to consensus by international institutions such as the GATT took place against the backdrop of demands for a more democratic international legal order in the 1960s and 1970s, this chapter showed how the discourses surrounding the Uruguay Round consensus were shaped by the historical context of the post-Cold War period. The euphoria surrounding the collapse of the Soviet Union and the fall of the Berlin Wall both reinforced and was reinforced by the sense of worldwide agreement emanating from the claim that more than 120 states had reached consensus on a new trade organization. This enabled the authorizing work of the Uruguay Round consensus to extend far beyond the authority of the multilateral trade regime itself, encompassing larger regimes of economic normativity.

In the following two chapters, I turn away from the WTO to consider how the idea of consensus has performed in a very different institutional setting: the European Court of Human Rights. Replicating the structure of the chapters on the

GATT/WTO, I begin by considering how the European Court of Human Rights' claim to base its decisions on consensus has interacted with the authority of the European human rights system (Chapter 4). I then turn to the authorizing work performed by the European Court of Human Rights' claims about the existence or non-existence of a European consensus on a particular matter through a case study on sexuality rights (Chapter 5).

4

European Consensus and the Authority of the European Court of Human Rights

4.1 Introduction

In the 1970s, at around the same time that consensus was becoming a popular method of decision-making in international organizations, the European Court of Human Rights (ECtHR; the Court) created a method of treaty interpretation that would later become known as 'European consensus'. Under this interpretative method, the ECtHR undertakes a comparative analysis of the laws and practices of the Member States of the Council of Europe in order to determine whether they would support a particular reading of the European Convention on Human Rights (ECHR). This chapter examines the relationship between the ECtHR's claim to base its decisions on a 'European consensus' and the Court's authority.

As with consensus decision-making in the multilateral trade regime, the chapter locates the emergence of 'European consensus' as a technique of authorization in a particular history. It describes how the ECtHR began using a comparative method of interpretation following a period of social and political upheaval in Western Europe in the 1960s and 1970s. During that period, the ideas underpinning the ECHR had come under challenge and new social movements were signalling a desire for an international law that better reflected their views and values. In my argument, the ECtHR's turn to comparative reasoning helped to shore up the authority of the European human rights system by providing the Court with a way to 'update' the ECHR, while also allowing it to appear to engage with European views and values in the process of doing so. These features of the ECtHR's use of comparative analysis, along with it gradually acquiring the name 'European consensus', resulted in this interpretive approach becoming associated with discourses of 'progress', 'public voice', and, later, 'democracy' as well, helping to establish a positive reputation for the ECtHR. Yet, as in the multilateral trade regime, these discourses did not always sit easily with the reality of the decision-making procedure they described. For the Court's concept of European consensus neither gave the Member States and their constituencies an opportunity for direct input into the ECtHR's decision-making process nor consistently operated as an effective vehicle of legal change.

This chapter begins by sketching the historical context in which the interpretive method that would become 'European consensus' first emerged. It then turns to

Consensus in International Law. Claerwen O'Hara, Oxford University Press. © Claerwen O'Hara 2026.
DOI: 10.1093/9780198948643.003.0004

the ECtHR's use of comparative analysis in its decisions in the 1970s and early 1980s, exploring both how this new interpretive method operated and the public, academic, and governmental responses to it. Following this, the chapter examines how the ECtHR's comparative method developed over the 1980s and 1990s, from its acquisition of the name 'European consensus' to the discourses of 'progress' and 'public voice' that came to surround it. The final part of the chapter explores the work that the ECtHR's use of European consensus has done since the European human rights system underwent significant changes in 1998, paying close attention to its increasing association with a discourse of 'democracy' in the early twenty-first century.

4.2 The Road to European Consensus: 1948–1975

4.2.1 Background: The European Human Rights System

The European Convention on Human Rights[1] is an international human rights treaty that opened for signature in 1950 and came into operation in 1953. It was drafted within the Council of Europe (CoE)—an international organization founded by Belgium, Denmark, France, Ireland, Italy, Luxembourg, the Netherlands, Norway, Sweden, and the United Kingdom (UK) in 1949,[2] whose stated aims are to foster greater unity between the Member States and realize human rights.[3] In its original form, the ECHR set out thirteen civil and political rights that the Contracting Parties agreed to protect within their jurisdictions. To interpret and enforce these rights, the ECHR established a European Commission of Human Rights (the Commission) and a European Court of Human Rights.[4] Up until its abolition in 1998, the Commission was responsible for assessing the admissibility of individual complaints made under the ECHR. If the Commission found a case to be well-founded, it would then launch a case in the Court on an individual's behalf. The Commission came into existence in 1954; the Court in 1959, when a required eight Members of the CoE had accepted its optional jurisdiction.[5] Both the Court and Commission sat in Strasbourg, France. When referring to these bodies collectively, I will describe them as the 'Strasbourg organs'.

[1] European Convention on Human Rights and Fundamental Freedoms, as amended by Protocols Nos 11 and 14, opened for signature 4 November 1950, ETS 5 (entered into force 3 September 1953) ('ECHR').

[2] Statute of the Council of Europe, 87 UNTS 103 (5 May 1949) ('CoE Statute').

[3] ibid, Article 1(a) and (b).

[4] ECHR (n 1), Article 19. For the original version, see European Court of Human Rights, 'Official original text', *Collections*, <https://www.echr.coe.int/Documents/Archives_1950_Convention_ENG.pdf>.

[5] Mikael Rask Madsen, 'The European Court of Human Rights: From the Cold War to the Brighton Declaration and Backlash' in Karen J Alter and Laurence R Helfer (eds), *International Court Authority* (Oxford University Press 2018) 247.

Many portray the ECHR, and the CoE more generally, as a response to the horrors of the Second World War and the Holocaust.[6] After all, it was in the midst of the War, in 1942, that British Prime Minister Winston Churchill first called for the establishment of a 'Council of Europe . . . with a high court to adjust disputes'[7] as a way to 'prevent renewed aggression and the preparation of future wars'.[8] The ECHR and CoE are also frequently understood to be a product of the Cold War.[9] Madsen, for example, writes that 'the rapid drafting of the ECHR reflected a growing fear of . . . Soviet imperial expansionism into Western Europe'.[10] In this context, the ECHR was seen as a way to create a 'club of Western European countries that . . . were like-minded when it came to the protection of liberal European democracy'.[11]

However, historian Marco Duranti argues that 'communism and fascism were not the only targets that the founders of the European human rights system had in their sights'.[12] In his account, another significant, but lesser-known, influence on the drafting of the ECHR was the rise of socialist politics in Western Europe. In the immediate aftermath of the War, left-wing parties had formed government in a number of Western European countries, including the United Kingdom (UK), France, Belgium, and the Netherlands.[13] Members of opposition parties, church leaders, and property owners in these countries were concerned that 'ever-expanding state bureaucracies . . . placed at the disposal of socialist governments backed by left-wing parliamentary majorities'[14] would infringe their rights and freedoms. Duranti contends that it was primarily these groups, and not the socialist governments that were in power at the time, who pushed for a European human rights system, as a way to keep the 'tyranny of the majority' in check.[15]

Indeed, the Congress of Europe, which was held in the Hague in 1948 and set the blueprint of the ECHR, was not state-based.[16] Rather, delegates from all over Europe were invited by the International Committee of the Movements for European Unity

[6] See, eg, Thomas Buergenthal, 'International Law and the Holocaust' in Michael J Bazyler and Roger P Alford (eds), *Holocaust Restitution: Perspectives on the Litigation and Its Legacy* (New York University Press 2006) 24.

[7] Winston Churchill, 'A Four Year Plan For England' (*Broadcast from London over the BBC*, 21 March 1943) <http://www.ibiblio.org/pha/policy/1943/1943-03-21a.html>.

[8] ibid.

[9] See, eg, Mikael Rask Madsen, 'From Cold War Instrument to Supreme European Court: The European Court of Human Rights at the Crossroads of International and National Law and Politics' (2007) 32 Law and Social Inquiry 137.

[10] ibid 140.

[11] ibid.

[12] Marco Duranti, *The Conservative Human Rights Revolution: European Identity, Transnational Politics, and the Origins of the European Convention* (Oxford University Press 2017) 3.

[13] In the UK, the Labour Party was elected in 1945; in Belgium, the Belgian Socialist Party in 1945; in the Netherlands, the Labour Party in 1945; and in France, the French Section of the Workers' International in 1947.

[14] Duranti (n 12) 7.

[15] ibid 5.

[16] ibid 100.

in their personal capacity.[17] This meant that those who attended the Congress and devised the ECHR did not necessarily represent the positions of their governments. In fact, at the persuasion of the British Labour Party, a number of socialist governments boycotted the conference.[18] In their place, members of opposition parties took a leading role. David Maxwell Fyfe, for example, who was a prosecutor in the Nuremburg Trials and a Conservative Member of Parliament (MP) in the UK, advocated forcefully for the creation of a European charter of human rights at the Congress[19] and is now considered one of the ECHR's 'founding fathers'.[20] Churchill was also the honorary chair of the Congress of Europe, despite being the Leader of the Opposition in the UK at the time.[21] While the resolutions produced by the Congress of Europe had no legal force, they set in motion a process that would eventually lead to the establishment of the European human rights system.[22]

What appealed to figures such as Maxwell Fyfe about the proposed ECHR was the prospect of creating a 'European high court empowered to overrule the decisions of national executives, judiciaries, and legislatures'.[23] In Maxwell Fyfe's view, such a court was necessary to prevent European countries falling prey to totalitarianism, which, following the economist Friedrich von Hayek,[24] he believed could emerge from 'within democratic movements and persist even after the fall of authoritarian regimes'.[25] In contrast, many on the European left at the time opposed a judicialized European human rights system, denouncing the proposal as 'undemocratic' due to its potential to override the will of the national majority.[26]

Maxwell Fyfe, Churchill, and other early proponents of the ECHR also saw in the proposed human rights system an opportunity to create a Western European legal order based on a nostalgic mix of Christian and liberal values.[27] Duranti writes that, for them, '[l]ooking forward meant looking back—way back—beyond the death and destruction of the recent past'[28] to 'a mythical Christian Europe of a bygone age'.[29] At the same time, these figures wished to re-create an imagined

[17] ibid.
[18] ibid 105.
[19] ibid 219–220.
[20] Ed Bates, *The Evolution of the European Convention on Human Rights: From Its Inception to the Creation of a Permanent Court of Human Rights* (Oxford University Press 2010) 52.
[21] Duranti (n 12) 101.
[22] ibid 358.
[23] ibid 7.
[24] On the influence of Hayek's *Road to Serfdom* (George Routledge and Sons, 1944) on Maxwell Fyfe and the European human rights project, see ibid 221–23. On the influence of Hayek's work on human rights thinking more generally, see Jessica Whyte, *The Morals of the Market: Human Rights and the Rise of Neoliberalism* (Verso 2019).
[25] Duranti (n 12) 5.
[26] ibid.
[27] ibid 350.
[28] ibid 96. See also Samuel Moyn, *Christian Human Rights* (University of Pennsylvania Press 2015) 99; Samuel Moyn, *The Last Utopia: Human Rights in History* (Harvard University Press 2010) 77–78.
[29] Duranti (n 12) 96.

nineteenth-century golden age when Europe was, in their view, a thriving civilization based on the rule of law, free trade, and property rights.[30] This mixed vision for Europe is reflected in the 1949 Statute of the Council of Europe, which combines references to spirituality and liberalism in its Preamble by describing the Member States' 'devotion to the spiritual and moral values which are . . . the true source of individual freedom, political liberty and the rule of law'.[31] It also shines through the text of the ECHR, which not only contains multiple references to 'morals',[32] but also, in a departure from the 1948 Universal Declaration of Human Rights,[33] protects almost no social and economic rights.[34]

The European human rights system did not initially have the influence some had hoped for. Concerned that a supranational court would be used by its opponents to prevent the implementation of its socialist economic programme, the post-war British Labour government successfully campaigned for both the ECtHR's jurisdiction and the right of individual petition to be optional.[35] This, in turn, saw some of the CoE's largest Member States fail to sign up to the ECtHR's jurisdiction for several decades. The UK, for example, did not accept the optional clauses on individual petition and ECtHR jurisdiction until 1966, despite the British Conservative Party under Churchill returning to government in 1951. France also refused to ratify the ECHR or accept the ECtHR's jurisdiction until 1974, and did not accept the right of individual petition until 1981.[36] In both cases, scholars have attributed this delay to the wave of decolonial movements that were taking place across the British and French Empires between the late 1940s and 1970s and concerns in the UK and France that the European human rights system could be used as a 'political weapon by "colonial" agitators'.[37]

Reluctance to accept the ECtHR's jurisdiction prompted the Strasbourg organs to move cautiously in their early years so as to secure the trust of the Member States.[38] Between 1955 and 1975, for example, the Commission found that only 127 of the 6,847 individual complaints it received were admissible.[39] The Court delivered even fewer judgments during this period. Before 1974, it had decided only

[30] ibid 215.

[31] CoE Statute (n 2), Preamble.

[32] For example, ECtHR judges must be of 'high moral character', see Article 21(1) of the ECHR (n 1). This requirement was originally contained in Article 39(3). The ECHR also permits the Member States to limit several rights 'for the protection of . . . morals', see Articles 8(2), 10(2) and 11(2), Ibid.

[33] UN Doc UNGAR 217A(III) (10 December 1948).

[34] Duranti (n 12) 218.

[35] ibid 4.

[36] Madsen (n 9) 145. However, note that both the United Kingdom and France were still heavily involved with the Court in its early years, holding the presidency of the Court in turn until the end of the 1960s, ibid 148.

[37] AW Brian Simpson, *Human Rights and the End of Empire: Britain and the Genesis of the European Convention* (Oxford University Press 2001) 299. For a discussion of the relationship between France, the ECHR and decolonization, see also Madsen (n 9) 145.

[38] Bates (n 20) 217.

[39] These figures are derived from Tables 6.3 and 6.4 in ibid 192, 240.

nine cases on the merits.[40] Though the Strasbourg organs' restrained approach did eventually help to win the confidence of some CoE Member States,[41] it also meant that, prior to the 1970s, many Europeans had never heard of the ECtHR.[42] As a result, the European human rights system enjoyed little authority in Western Europe in the first two decades of its existence. In 1971, at a human rights conference hosted by the CoE, law professor Pierre-Henri Prélot captured the ECHR's limited influence with a metaphor: 'after the great initial blaze, the fire has from then on been smouldering beneath the ashes.'[43]

4.2.2 'A Newly Emerging Consensus': Sørensen's 1975 Proposal

In 1975, Max Sørensen delivered a speech at the Fourth International Colloquy on the European Convention on Human Rights entitled 'Do the Rights Set Forth in the European Convention on Human Rights in 1950 Have the Same Significance in 1975?'[44] At the time, Sørensen was the former President of the European Commission on Human Rights and a judge of the European Court of Justice in Luxembourg. He would go on to become a judge of the ECtHR in Strasbourg five years later.[45] In his speech, Sørensen answered the question posed in his title by arguing that the ECHR 'ha[d] preserved its initial significance'.[46] This was so despite significant changes that had occurred in Europe since the drafting of the ECHR and the 'cautious' approach the Strasbourg organs had taken up until that point, which he believed could be explained, in part, 'by the fact that recognition of their powers . . . is optional'.[47]

If the European human rights system were to continue to retain its relevance, however, Sørensen was of the view that the ECtHR would need to use what he called 'evolutive interpretation'.[48] That is, it would need to interpret the ECHR as a 'living legal instrument',[49] capable of keeping 'pace with progress in national legal institutions and standards'.[50] Sørensen believed that he could already see

[40] ibid 257.
[41] ibid 261.
[42] Chris Moores, *Civil Liberties and Human Rights in Twentieth-Century Britain* (Cambridge University Press 2017) 137.
[43] Pierre-Henri Prélot, Parliamentary Conference on Human Rights, (Vienna 18–20 October 1971), quoted in Bates (n 20) 172.
[44] Max Sørensen, 'Do the Rights Set Forth in the European Convention on Human Rights In 1950 Have the Same Significance in 1975?', *Proceedings of the Fourth Annual International Colloquy about the European Convention on Human Rights* (Ministry of Foreign Affairs of Italy and the Secretariat General of the Council of Europe 1975).
[45] Council of Europe, *The Conscience of Europe: 50 Years of the European Court of Human Rights* (Third Millennium Publishing Limited 2010) 125.
[46] Sørensen (n 44) 86.
[47] ibid 94.
[48] ibid 88.
[49] ibid 106.
[50] ibid 94.

glimmers of this approach in the Strasbourg organs' decisions. But his speech is now known for its suggestion that one way for the ECtHR to interpret the ECHR 'evolutively' would be by looking for '*a newly emerging consensus*'[51] in the law and practice of the CoE Member States.[52] Sørensen was quick to assure his audience that did not mean that the ECtHR should 'promote social reform'.[53] Rather, in his view, the ECtHR could use consensus-based interpretation as a way to 'bring States which are lagging behind into line with a general trend in ideas and institutions in Europe'.[54] What would be important in this respect was ensuring that the relevant developments were 'sufficiently widespread and not limited to a few states'.[55] The principle that Sørensen outlined in this speech would eventually go on to become a method of interpretation used by the ECtHR known as 'European consensus'.

Delivered two months after Henry Kissinger's 'Global Consensus and Economic Development' speech in the United Nations General Assembly and against the backdrop of the widespread uptake of consensus decision-making in international organizations,[56] Sørensen's 'consensus'-based proposal might have been influenced by developments taking place in international law at that time. After all, Sørensen had a background in public international law and has been described as 'nothing if not a classical international lawyer'.[57] However, the legal principle that he outlined was different to the consensus procedures being used in international organizations. First, it was envisaged as a method of treaty interpretation, rather than a method of decision-making between states.[58] Second, it was explicitly tied to the idea of legal 'evolution'. Third, Sørensen's notion of an 'emerging consensus' seemed to allow for more overt dissent than the idea of 'no formal objection' that came to underpin consensus decision-making, since it was specifically aimed at bringing states 'lagging behind into line with a general trend'.

In seeking to understand why Sørensen put forward this proposal when he did, scholars have tended to emphasize institutional changes that were taking place in the CoE at that time. Bates, for example, observes that 'Sørensen was speaking at a remarkable time for Strasbourg'[59] because, between 1966 and 1974, several CoE Member States, including the UK, France, Switzerland, and Italy, had either

[51] Ibid 106 [emphasis added].

[52] See Ed Bates, 'Consensus in the Legitimacy-Building Era of the European Court of Human Rights' in Panos Kapotas and Vassilis P Tzevelekos (eds), *Building Consensus on European Consensus: Judicial Interpretation of Human Rights in Europe and Beyond* (Cambridge University Press 2019) 51.

[53] Sørensen (n 44) 106.

[54] ibid.

[55] ibid 94.

[56] See Section 2.2 in Chapter 2 of this book.

[57] Eirik Bjorge, *The Evolutionary Interpretation of Treaties* (Oxford University Press 2014) 12.

[58] In this regard, the principle outlined by Sørensen was legally more akin to the principle that a treaty should be interpreted in light of 'any subsequent practice in the application of the treaty' contained in Article 31(3)(b) of the Vienna Convention on the Law of Treaties, see Ineta Ziemele, 'European Consensus and International Law', *The European Convention on Human Rights and General International Law* (Oxford University Press 2018) 28–29.

[59] Bates (n 52) 51.

ratified the ECHR or accepted the ECtHR's jurisdiction.[60] According to Bates, this signalled that '[i]t was time for the Court to play a bigger role',[61] leading to proposals for it to adopt a more constitutional approach to interpretation, such as that of Sørensen. In my view, however, it is also important to look to the broader social and political context. For as Sørensen himself noted, 'far-reaching political, economic and social changes' had occurred in Western Europe between the drafting of the ECHR and his speech in 1975, including 'radical demographic change'.[62] More specifically, in the 1960s, a growing number of young adults, increasing rates of university attendance, and dissatisfaction with the Cold War *status quo* had combined to produce a new language of dissent aimed at the institutions and assumptions of the post-war years.[63] This saw social movements spring up across Western Europe, contesting not only the capitalist state, but 'norms of the nuclear family, traditional gender roles and moral conformism'[64] as well.

The unrest came to a head in 1968, when Western Europe was swept by a tidal wave of protests, pushing some parts of the region to the brink of revolution.[65] The best known of these protests was the May 1968 uprising in France, which began with student occupations of universities and culminated with widespread violence in the streets, the seizure of public buildings,[66] and a nation-wide general strike of around 10 million people.[67] That same year, there were student protests in West Berlin,[68] large-scale marches in Northern Ireland,[69] and the so-called hot autumn in Italy in which workers, joined by students and members of the non-parliamentary left, staged a series of large strikes and occupations, bringing Italian production to a near standstill.[70] Though the year 1968 drew to a close with many of the protests and rebellions having been suppressed, the radical politics that had risen to the surface did not end there. Instead, they continued well into the 1970s,

[60] ibid.

[61] ibid.

[62] Sørensen (n 44) 86.

[63] Jeremi Suri, *Power and Protest: Global Revolution and the Rise of Detente* (Harvard University Press 2003) 88.

[64] Robert Gildea and James Mark, 'Introduction' in Robert Gildea, James Mark, and Anette Warring (eds), *Europe's 1968: Voices of Revolt* (Oxford University Press 2013) 1.

[65] See generally Robert Gildea, James Mark, and Anette Warring (eds), *Europe's 1968: Voices of Revolt* (Oxford University Press 2013).

[66] See, eg, Kate Bredeson, 'L'Entrée Libre à L'Ex-Théâtre de France: The Occupation of the Odéon and the Revolutionary Culture of the French Stage' in Julian Jackson, Anna-Louise Milne, and James S Williams (eds), *May 68: Rethinking France's Last Revolution* (Palgrave Macmillan 2011).

[67] Alissa J Rubin, 'May 1968: A Month of Revolution Pushed France Into the Modern World' *New York Times* (5 May 2018) <https://www.nytimes.com/2018/05/05/world/europe/france-may-1968-revolution.html>. See also Kristin Ross, *May '68 and Its Afterlives* (The University of Chicago Press 2002) 58.

[68] Richard Vinen, *The Long '68: Radical Protest and Its Enemies* (Allen Lane 2018) Chapter 6.

[69] See generally, Simon Prince, *Northern Ireland's '68: Civil Rights, Global Revolt and the Origins of the Troubles* (Irish Academic Press 2007).

[70] Rebecca Clifford, Robert Gildea, and James Mark, 'Awakenings' in Robert Gildea, James Mark, and Anette Warring (eds), *Europe's 1968: Voices of Revolt* (Oxford University Press 2013) 22.

giving birth to the gay liberation movement, the women's liberation movement, the prisoners' rights movement, and Eurocommunism.

The social and political upheavals of the 1960s and 1970s posed a challenge to the already flailing authority of the European human rights system in a number of ways.[71] First, the new social movements sat uneasily with the ECHR's vision of democracy. For although the potency of the ECtHR had been dampened by its optional jurisdiction, the ECHR was still founded on the idea that rights and freedoms were better protected by a legal institution that existed outside of democracy.[72] Conversely, social movements in the 1960s and 1970s believed that Western Europe needed more, rather than less, democracy. Whereas the post-war socialists had been concerned about the impact of a supranational court on domestic parliaments, activists in this period were suspicious of all forms of hierarchy and institutional authority, including those associated with representative democracy.[73] This saw demands for greater participation in all forms of social, economic, and political life,[74] and many begin experimenting with models of direct and participatory democracy instead.[75] Across Western Europe, workers' councils and open assemblies emerged and social movements started using decision-making methods based on non-voting, which they called 'consensus decision-making'.[76] However, unlike in international organizations, their use of consensus decision-making was often paired with a resistance to arriving at a singular, overarching vision, with participants emphasizing diversity and plurality alongside the goal of reaching consensus.[77] According to Maeckelbergh, these practices would end up influencing the mode of consensus decision-making adopted by the alter-globalization in the 1990s,[78] as descrin the previous chapter.

In addition to their demands for greater democracy, the new social movements put forward an alternative understanding of morality and social justice to that underpinning the European human rights system. As we saw above, the drafting of the ECHR was influenced by Christian-inspired ideas of morality.[79] Once the European human rights system was up and running, this vision of morality

[71] Writing on the history of human rights in the West more generally, Moyn argues, 'In 1968, human rights were in crisis, because their partisans had not found a way to ally themselves with an exploding wave of popular movements', see Moyn, *The Last Utopia* (n 28) 171.

[72] Marco Duranti, 'The Strasbourg Court Is Anti-Democratic, Just as Its Founders Intended' (*OpenDemocracy*, 13 July 2013) <https://www.opendemocracy.net/en/opendemocracyuk/strasbourg-court-is-anti-democratic-just-as-its-founders-intended/>.

[73] Ben Mercer, *Student Revolt in 1968: France, Italy and West Germany* (Cambridge University Press 2020) 130.

[74] Hagen Schulz-Forberg, 'Claiming Democracy: The Paris 1968 May Revolts in the Mass Media and Their European Dimensions' (2009) 31 Cuadernos de Historia Contemporánea 27, 45.

[75] Marianne Maeckelbergh, 'The Road to Democracy: The Political Legacy of "1968"' (2011) 56 International Review of Social History 301, 310–12.

[76] ibid 310.

[77] ibid 302.

[78] ibid 316.

[79] Duranti (n 12) 96; Moyn, *Christian Human Rights* (n 28) 99.

continued to be reflected in the Strasbourg organs' decisions. Over the 1950s and 1960s, for example, several applications were lodged with the Commission challenging the criminalization of homosexual acts. Most of these originated in West Germany and pertained to Article 175 of the German Criminal Code—a far-reaching Nazi-era law that prohibited not only 'unnatural fornication between men' but also any 'lewd act' between males.[80] The Commission dismissed all of these applications as inadmissible on the grounds of being 'manifestly ill-founded'. While this was characteristic of the Commission's approach at that time, Johnson finds the Commission's willingness to dismiss challenges to Nazi-era legislation surprising, especially 'when one considers that . . . the Convention was conceived as a direct response to fascism'.[81] It is arguable, however, that the Commission's stance was influenced by the Christian-inspired moral imaginary underpinning the ECHR, which did not envisage the protection of 'sexual deviants'. After all, in some of its decisions, the Commission was quite explicit about its view that 'the Convention allow[ed] a High Contracting Party to punish homosexuality'.[82]

In contrast, the social movements of the 1960s and 1970s rejected moral conformism and were highly sceptical of the use of law as a way to impose personal morality on the people. By the late 1960s, students all over Western Europe were engaged in what has been described as a 'sexual revolution', in which they cast off long-standing moral codes relating to marriage, reproduction, and promiscuity and embraced the idea of sexual freedom instead.[83] As the 1960s turned into the 1970s and the gay and women's liberation movements got under way, existing moral regimes concerning heterosexuality and gender came under challenge as well.[84] This led to multiple law reform campaigns to bring down repressive laws inspired by past regimes of morality, such as those criminalizing abortion, homosexuality, and sex work.[85]

In the late 1960s, Member States began raising concerns about the gap that was emerging between the values underpinning the CoE and those of the new social movements. In 1969, for example, Austrian Chancellor Josef Klaus told the Parliamentary Assembly of the Council of Europe (PACE): 'If there is a great European sore which all of us have caused in some way or other, it is this: for

[80] Although the original prohibition on homosexuality was introduced in 1871, it was drastically extended in 1935 by the Nazis, see Paul Johnson, *Homosexuality and the European Court of Human Rights* (Routledge 2013) 22.

[81] ibid 28.

[82] *X v Federal Republic of Germany*, App No. 530/59 Eur Commn HR (4 January 1960) 194.

[83] Dagmar Herzog, *Sexuality in Europe: A Twentieth-Century History* (Cambridge University Press 2012) 133–46. See also Gert Hekma and Alain Giami, *Sexual Revolutions* (Palgrave Macmillan 2014).

[84] See generally, Massimo Prearo, 'The 1970s Moment in Sexual Politics' in Julian Jackson, Anna-Louise Milne, and James S Williams (eds), *May 68: Rethinking France's Last Revolution* (Palgrave Macmillan 2011).

[85] On these law reform campaigns see, Herzog (n 83) 152–60; Nikolaos Papadogiannis and Sebastian Gehrig, '"The Personal Is Political": Sexuality, Gender and the Left in Europe During the 1970s' (2015) 22 European Review of History 1, 3.

various reasons we have not done enough in our countries to engage our young people.'[86] Klaus called on the Member States to 'bridge the gap between the generations', lest the divisions that had emerged compromise 'the eternal ideal of Europe [and] ... our mission to safeguard Western civilization'.[87] Sentiments such as these saw the PACE establish a European Youth Foundation and a European Youth Centre that same year as a way to give a voice to young people within the CoE.[88]

In the 1970s, legal scholars began arguing that the Strasbourg organs themselves needed to do more to engage the European public. In 1973, for example, Beddard wrote that now that the Court and Commission had 'won the confidence of the European States', it was time for them to come out from 'behind their procedural barricade' and establish 'themselves not only as the conscience and watchdog of Europe but as a source of help and respite for its citizens'.[89] In 1974, Dowrick went even further, asserting that the ECHR 'must be developed to satisfy the moral sense of the newer generations and this could best be done by enabling the Court to evolve a dynamic "jurisprudence"'.[90] And it was in this context that Sørensen delivered his 1975 speech, arguing not only that the ECHR should be capable of 'evolving', but also that this be carried out through an engagement with the views and values of Western Europe via the principle of 'consensus'.

4.3 The European Court of Human Rights' Turn to Comparative Reasoning

4.3.1 The Court's Comparative Decisions of the Mid-1970s

In the years following Sørensen's speech, the Strasbourg organs began using comparative reasoning in their decisions. However, they did not immediately do so in the 'evolutive' way outlined by Sørensen. Instead, the ECtHR established the two other ways in which it now uses European consensus. First, in the case of *Engel and Others v the Netherlands*[91] (1976), the ECtHR established a link between comparative reasoning and the principle of 'autonomous interpretation', which holds that the terms in the ECHR are to be understood from a European, rather than

[86] Josef Klaus, Chancellor of the Federal Republic of Austria, Speech to the Parliamentary Assembly of the Council of Europe (2 October 1969), <http://www.assembly.coe.int/nw/xml/Speeches/Speech-XML2HTML-EN.asp?SpeechID=114&a1=0&p2=0&lang=EN>.

[87] ibid.

[88] See 'Our Context, History & Background', *European Youth Foundation*, Council of Europe, <https://www.coe.int/en/web/european-youth-foundation/history>.

[89] Ralph Beddard, *Human Rights and Europe: A Study of The Machinery of Human Rights Protection of the Council of Europe* (Sweet & Maxwell 1973) 98.

[90] FE Dowrick, 'Juristic Activity in the Council of Europe—25th Year' (1974) 23 International and Comparative Law Quarterly 610, 624.

[91] App Nos 5100/71; 5101/71; 5102/71; 5354/72; 5370/72, Eur Ct HR (8 June 1976) ('*Engel*').

national, perspective.[92] *Engel* arose from a complaint by a number of conscripted soldiers serving in the Netherlands armed forces that the imposition of penalties by military courts for military offences had violated their right to a fair trial under Article 6 of the ECHR. In response, the Netherlands argued that Article 6 did not apply because it was limited to 'civil rights and obligations' and 'criminal charges' and, under Dutch law, military penalties were classified as 'disciplinary' offences. The ECtHR rejected this argument, holding that it would be the 'common denominator of the respective legislation of the various contracting parties'[93] that would determine the meaning of Convention-based concepts such as 'criminal charge', rather than the domestic law of the state concerned. This led the ECtHR to conclude that some of the charges in question constituted 'criminal charges' for the purposes of Article 6 of the ECHR.

Second, in *Handyside v the United Kingdom*[94] (1976), the ECtHR established a link between comparative reasoning and the width of the 'margin of appreciation', which refers to the 'latitude of deference or error'[95] that the Court will afford the Member States in their implementation of the ECHR. In particular, the ECtHR determined that the existence of different approaches between the Member States would produce a wide margin of appreciation, whereas a common European position was more likely to result in a narrower margin.[96] *Handyside* concerned the conviction of a proprietor of a publishing company under the Obscene Publications Acts 1969/1964 (UK) for the publication of *The Little Red School Book*—a book intended for persons aged 12–18, which contained, amongst other things, information about sex.[97] The applicant complained that his conviction violated his right to freedom of expression under Article 10 of the ECHR. However, the ECtHR found that the impugned law and the actions taken against the applicant fell within the exception in Article 10(2) relating to the 'protection of morals'.[98] In arriving at this conclusion, the ECtHR held that states enjoy a wide margin of appreciation with respect to laws designed to safeguard morality since there was no 'uniform European conception of morals . . . especially in our era which is characterized by a rapid and far-reaching evolution of opinions'.[99]

[92] Bates (n 20) 323. See also George Letsas, 'The Truth in Autonomous Concepts: How to Interpret the ECHR' (2000) 15 European Journal of International Law 279.

[93] *Engel* (n 91) [82].

[94] App No 5493/72 Eur Ct HR (7 December 1976) ('*Handyside*').

[95] Howard Charles Yourow, *Margin of Appreciation Doctrine in the Dynamics of European Human Rights* (Brill 1996) 13. Note that the Court had already established a connection between comparative reasoning and the margin of appreciation in *Case "Relating to Certain Aspects of the Laws on the Use of Languages in Education in Belgium" v Belgium (Merits)*, App Nos 1474/62; 1677/62; 1691/62; 1769/63; 1994/63; 2126/64, Eur Ct HR (23 July 1968) (The '*Belgian Linguistics' case No. 2*). However, it considerably developed that connection in *Handyside* (n 94).

[96] On how the ECtHR's use of comparative reasoning interacts with the margin of appreciation, see Kanstantsin Dzehtsiarou, *European Consensus and the Legitimacy of the European Court of Human Rights* (Cambridge University Press 2015) 132–37.

[97] *Handyside* (n 94) [9]–[15].

[98] ibid [45]–[46].

[99] ibid [48].

Although these two cases are now considered important from a doctrinal perspective, they did little to capture the imagination of the European public at the time. In particular, the ECtHR's willingness to allow the UK's suppression of sexual speech to stand in *Handyside* only confirmed to some onlookers that it was 'a conservative interpreter of human rights'.[100] Perhaps owing to such impressions of the ECtHR, at around this time, European activists began creating their own international 'tribunals' to address their social justice concerns in Western Europe. Although the practice of using 'people's tribunals'—that is, civil society initiatives which assert a 'popular jurisdiction' that operates outside of both the state and international institutions[101]—had existed in Western Europe since the mid-1960s, they had mainly focused on issues in other regions, such as American war crimes in Vietnam[102] and political repression in Latin America.[103] However, in the 1970s, these tribunals began focusing on issues closer to home. In 1976, for example, a group of feminists organized the International Tribunal on Crimes Against Women in Brussels to address 'gendered crimes'.[104] While the International Tribunal on Crimes Against Women was international in focus, many of its participants came from Western Europe.[105] Then, in 1978, the Third International Russell Tribunal was convened with the explicit purpose of addressing infringements of civil liberties in West Germany.[106]

The extent to which these people's tribunals replicated an international court or strayed into the ECHR's jurisdiction varied. The International Tribunal on Crimes Against Women, truer to '*la pensée '68*', was not based around the individual or the state, the latter being denounced as 'man-made'.[107] Instead, the Tribunal was envisaged as an opportunity for 'women', as a collective, to indict 'patriarchy' as a whole.[108] There was no panel of judges and no expert witnesses,

[100] Rob Watts, *Criminalizing Dissent: The Liberal State and the Problem of Legitimacy* (Routledge 2020) 120, discussing the views of Dinah Shelton (1999).

[101] Dianne Otto, 'Impunity in a Different Register: People's Tribunals and Questions of Judgment, Law, and Responsibility' in Karen Engle, Zinaida Miller, and DM Davis (eds), *Anti-Impunity and the Human Rights Agenda* (Cambridge University Press 2016) 316.

[102] The First Russell Tribunal, convened in 1966 and 1967 by philosophers Bertrand Russell and Jean-Paul Sartre, concerned war crimes committed in Vietnam by the United States, see Tor Krever, 'Remembering the Russell Tribunal' (2017) 5 London Review of International Law 483.

[103] The Second Russell Tribunal, which ran from 1973 to 1976, addressed political repression in Chile, Brazil, and other parts of Latin America, see Andrew Byrnes and Gabrielle Simm, 'International Peoples' Tribunals: Their Nature, Practice and Significance' in Andrew Byrnes and Gabrielle Simm (eds), *Peoples' Tribunals and International Law* (Cambridge University Press 2018) 12.

[104] Dianne Otto, 'Beyond Legal Justice: Some Personal Reflections on People's Tribunals, Listening and Responsibility' (2017) 5 London Review of International Law 225, 227.

[105] Gabrielle Simm, 'Peoples' Tribunals, Women's Courts and International Crimes of Sexual Violence' in Andrew Byrnes and Gabrielle Simm (eds), *Peoples' Tribunals and International Law* (Cambridge University Press 2018) 69.

[106] Hugh Mosley, 'Third International Russell Tribunal on Civil Liberties in West Germany' (1978) 14 New German Critique 178, 178.

[107] Diana Russell and Nicole Van de Ven, *Crimes against Women: Proceedings of the International Tribunal* (Les Femmes 1976) 7.

[108] Otto (n 101) 305–06.

with the organizers preferring their analyses to be 'informed by feelings, not just intellect'.[109] Moreover, it sought to expose 'crimes' unrecognized by any legal system at the time.[110] Some of these crimes, such as 'forced motherhood', overlapped with matters before the Commission, which had a complaint regarding West Germany's restrictions on abortion pending at the time.[111] Others fell outside of the ECHR's civil and political jurisdiction, such as the lack of wages for housework.[112]

The Third Russell Tribunal was more formal in its 'doing of law'.[113] It collected evidence, selected international 'jurors', and invited state authorities to present a defence.[114] It also adopted a 'civil-rights model'[115] and considered a number of matters that were similar to those that had previously come before the European human rights system, including the oppression of communists[116] and gay discrimination[117] in West Germany. Yet, despite their differences, both the International Tribunal on Crimes Against Women and the Third Russell Tribunal can be seen as expressing a desire to 'democratize' international law in Europe by giving 'the people' an opportunity to speak in its name.[118]

It is unclear whether the ECtHR took any notice of these initiatives. But they may have had some influence on the trajectory of its interpretive approach. For three weeks after the Third Russell Tribunal concluded its first hearings in early April 1978, the ECtHR handed down its landmark decision in *Tyrer v The United Kingdom*,[119] in which, for the first time, it used comparative reasoning in the 'evolutive' manner proposed by Sørensen. In doing so, the ECtHR would set in motion a transformation of the European human rights system's reputation, whereby the 'conservative, Cold War origins of the convention were forgotten'[120] and the Court began to take on a 'progressive', even 'democratic', aura.

[109] Russell and Van de Ven (n 107) 220.
[110] Otto (n 101) 306.
[111] In 1975, an application was lodged with the Commission concerning the criminalization of abortion in West Germany. In 1977, the Commission rejected the claim, see *Bruggemann and Scheuten v Federal Republic of Germany*, App No 6959/75, Eur Ct HR (12 July 1977).
[112] Otto (n 101) 306.
[113] ibid 295.
[114] Craig Griffiths, 'Gay Activism in Modell Deutschland' (2015) 22 European Review of History 60, 66.
[115] ibid 71.
[116] The Third Russell Tribunal was primarily set up to hear testimony about the practice of *Berufsverbot* ('job ban')—a government program of loyalty checks which excluded 'radicals' (mainly communists) from government jobs, see Mosley (n 106) 178; Griffiths (n 114) 61.
[117] On the inclusion of gay discrimination in the Third Russell Tribunal, see Griffiths (n 114) 61.
[118] On the 'democratic impulse these tribunals often embody', see Craig Borowiak, 'The World Tribunal on Iraq: Citizens' Tribunals and the Struggle for Accountability' (2008) 30 New Political Science 161, 165.
[119] App No 5856/72, 26 Eur Ct HR (25 April 1978) ('*Tyrer*').
[120] Moyn, *The Last Utopia* (n 28) 81.

4.3.2 The Landmark Decisions of *Tyrer*, *Marckx*, and *Dudgeon*

The case of *Tyrer v the United Kingdom* concerned the use of birching (a form of whipping) as a state-sanctioned punishment in the Isle of Man. The applicant, who had received 'three strokes of the birch ... on his bare buttock'[121] as a criminal punishment for assault, submitted a complaint under the ECHR arguing, amongst other things, that the birching had infringed his right to freedom from degrading treatment under Article 3.[122] In a now famous passage, the ECtHR stated that 'the Convention is a living instrument which . . . must be interpreted in the light of present-day conditions'.[123] As such, it could not 'but be influenced by the developments and commonly accepted standards in the penal policy of the member States of the Council of Europe in this field'.[124] The ECtHR then went on to note that 'in the great majority of the member States', 'judicial corporal punishment is not, it appears, used and, indeed, in some of them, has never existed in modern times'.[125] On the basis of this common ground, the ECtHR held that the use of birching in the Isle of Man constituted degrading treatment and thus a violation of Article 3 of the ECHR.

The ECtHR quickly followed up its decision in *Tyrer* with two more 'living instrument' judgments. The first occurred in *Marckx v Belgium* (1979),[126] which arose from a complaint by Paula Marckx, an unmarried Belgian woman, and her infant daughter Alexandra. Their complaint related to Belgian family law, which automatically recognized married mothers as the parent of a child by virtue of their name being on the birth certificate but required unmarried mothers to undergo a legal process in order to formally 'adopt' their child. It also concerned Belgian intestacy law, which afforded children born out of wedlock fewer inheritance rights even if the child's maternal affiliation had been recognized via the aforementioned adoption procedure. The ECtHR held that the laws in question breached the right to respect for family life (Article 8), the right to non-discrimination in conjunction with the right to respect for family life (Article 8 and Article 14), and the right to non-discrimination in conjunction with the right to property (Article 14 and Article 1 of Protocol 1). In arriving at this decision, the ECtHR stated that although 'at the time when the Convention ... was drafted, it was regarded as permissible and normal in many European countries to draw a distinction in this area between the "illegitimate" and the "legitimate" family', the 'Convention must be interpreted in the light of present-day conditions'.[127] In this regard, the ECtHR held that it

[121] Graham Zellick, 'Corporal Punishment in the Isle of Man' (1978) 27 International and Comparative Law Quarterly 665, 665.
[122] The applicant also made arguments in relation to Articles 1, 8, 13, and 14 of the ECHR, see *Tyrer* (n 119) [19].
[123] ibid [31].
[124] ibid.
[125] ibid [38].
[126] App No 6833/74, Eur Ct HR (13 June 1979) ('*Marckx*').
[127] ibid [41].

could not 'but be struck by the fact that the domestic law of the great majority of the member States of the Council of Europe ha[d] evolved and [was] continuing to evolve, in company with the relevant international instruments, towards full juridical recognition of the maxim "mater semper certa est" ["the mother is always certain"]'.[128]

The second occurred in *Dudgeon v United Kingdom* (1981),[129] which concerned a challenge to the criminal prohibition of both 'buggery' and acts of 'gross indecency' between men in Northern Ireland by Jeff Dudgeon, a gay activist living in Belfast.[130] The ECtHR held that the impugned laws violated Dudgeon's right to private life under Article 8 of the ECHR. Again, this was largely due to the ECtHR's identification of a new European position:

> As compared with the era when that legislation was enacted, there is now a better understanding, and in consequence an increased tolerance, of homosexual behaviour to the extent that in the great majority of the member States of the Council of Europe it is no longer considered to be necessary or appropriate to treat homosexual practices of the kind now in question as in themselves a matter to which the sanctions of the criminal law should be applied.[131]

On the basis of this new Western European trend, the ECtHR held that '[i]t cannot be maintained . . . that there is a "pressing social need" to make such acts criminal offences'[132] and thus that the impugned law could not be justified under the public moral exception contained in Article 8(2).

The comparative method established by the ECtHR in *Tyrer*, *Marckx*, and *Dudgeon* was highly discretionary. The ECtHR did not set a clear threshold for the level of agreement or common practice required before it would apply an 'evolutive' interpretation. It did not even undertake any form of 'open census' of the number of states involved in the trends upon which it was relying.[133] Instead, the ECtHR simply referred to the 'great majority' of Member States having adopted a particular legal approach.[134] In *Dudgeon*, the ECtHR also claimed that there was now a 'better understanding, and in consequence an increased tolerance, of homosexual behaviour' in Western Europe without providing any evidence in support of this shift in public opinion other than the aforementioned legal trend.

[128] ibid.
[129] App No 7525/76, 25 Eur Ct HR (22 October 1981) ('*Dudgeon*').
[130] ibid [13].
[131] ibid [60].
[132] ibid.
[133] See Robert Wintemute, *Sexual Orientation and Human Rights: The United States Constitution, the European Convention, and the Canadian Charter* (Clarendon Press 1995) 137.
[134] Luzius Wildhaber, Arnaldur Hjartarson, and Stephen Donnelly, 'No Consensus on Consensus? The Practice of the European Court of Human Rights' (2013) 33 Human Rights Law Journal 248, 249.

In *Marckx*, the ECtHR was more specific about 'the relevant international instruments' upon which it was relying, citing both the Convention on the Establishment of Maternal Affiliation of Natural Children (1962) and the Convention on the Legal Status of Children born out of Wedlock (1975).[135] However, as the ECtHR itself acknowledged, at the time, both treaties had only been ratified by four CoE Member States.[136] The ECtHR did not consider this to be a problem, stating that there was 'no reason to attribute the currently small number of Contracting States to a refusal to admit equality between "illegitimate" and "legitimate" children'.[137] In fact, in its view, the mere existence of these two treaties evinced 'a clear measure of common ground in this area amongst modern societies'.[138] In this reasoning, the ECtHR seemed to make it clear that what would constitute a common European position under its new interpretive approach would ultimately be a matter for the Court, rather than something to be determined by a set standard.

Nevertheless, Bates writes that 'the rather rudimentary approach adopted by the Court . . . did not seem to particularly tarnish its reputation or credibility, at least not at the time'.[139] Rather, it was these comparative judgements of the late 1970s and early 1980s that helped to *establish* the authority of the ECtHR.[140] Indeed, over the following decade, the number of complaints submitted under the ECHR skyrocketed.[141] In 1981, for example, the Commission received 404 applications. In 1993, the number had increased to 2,037.[142] By the mid-1980s, public interest in the European human rights system had reached such heights that one of the ECtHR judges commented, 'it would now be politically impossible in most countries to withdraw from the Convention, as it has captured the minds of the public to a great extent'.[143]

This was partly the result of a surge in human rights discourse that was taking place in Western Europe and North America at around the around the same time.[144] As Samuel Moyn documents, the term 'human rights' appeared with increasing frequency in British and American newspapers from the year 1977 onwards,[145] reflecting a rising enthusiasm for human rights law in general throughout

135 *Marckx* (n 126) [41].
136 ibid.
137 ibid.
138 ibid.
139 Bates (n 52) 56.
140 Bates writes, 'arguably, it was the judgments of the late 1970s, . . . along with other famous cases from the early-to-mid 1980s, which helped establish Strasbourg's reputation', ibid. In his view, 'resort to the consensus principle, that is, common European standards, by the Strasbourg institutions was an important, indeed necessary, feature of the success story of the period up to Protocol 11 (although obviously not the only one)', ibid 45.
141 Moyn, *The Last Utopia* (n 28) 80.
142 Paul Johnson, *Going to Strasbourg: An Oral History of Sexual Orientation Discrimination and the European Convention on Human Rights* (Oxford University Press 2016) 45.
143 Brian Walsh (1987), quoted in Bates (n 52) 56.
144 See generally, Moyn, *The Last Utopia* (n 28).
145 ibid 231 Appendix 1: '"Human Rights" in Anglo-American News, with 1977 breakthrough'.

the West.[146] But growing public interest in the European human rights system also appears to have been linked to the ECtHR's judgments in *Tyrer*, *Marckx*, and *Dudgeon*.[147] After all, as Madsen writes, those judgments seemed to reflect 'socio-political developments of the more permissive and less patriarchal society that was taking form in many European countries'.[148] In *Tyrer*, we appear to see a shift in thinking around the use of state-sanctioned violence; in *Marckx* and *Dudgeon*, we can see the influence of the women's liberation and gay liberation movements of the 1970s.[149]

This reflection of contemporary values was key to the success of the ECtHR's new interpretive approach. On the one hand, it gave onlookers the impression that the ECtHR was 'extremely progressive'.[150] Combined with the ECtHR's references to 'evolution' and the ECHR as a 'living instrument', this led many to take the view that the ECtHR would continue to interpret the ECHR in a progressive way. Writing on the ECtHR's *Tyrer* and *Marckx* decisions in 1980, for example, Drzemczewski commented that its approach to treaty interpretation now emphasized 'the evolutive, dynamic and progressive elements' of European legal standards so as to ensure that European human rights law would 'keep pace with social and legal advances'.[151]

On the other hand, the ECtHR's reflection of contemporary values gave Europeans the impression that their views and values were now not only being registered in Strasbourg but were also capable of shaping European human rights law. A 1981 article in the *Guardian* newspaper, for example, summarized the ECtHR's judgment in *Dudgeon* in the following two sentences:

> The ruling said that homosexuality was 'an essentially private manifestation of the human personality'. Since the existing law was enacted in Northern Ireland

[146] For an account of how this 'breakthrough' of human rights in the US and Western Europe pushed activists in the UK towards the ECHR, see Moores (n 42) 224.

[147] Writing in 1978, for example, Zellick noted that *Tyrer* had 'aroused more interest in the United Kingdom than any other decision of the Court', see Zellick (n 121) 665. Likewise, Goldhaber considers the Court's judgment in *Dudgeon* to have 'help[ed] establish the court in the public imagination', see Michael D Goldhaber, *A People's History of the European Court of Human Rights* (Rutgers University Press 2007) 33. The Belgian public were also highly engaged by the *Marckx* case, with Paula Marckx even being voted Belgium's Woman of the Year in 1980 by *Libelle* magazine, the main Flemish weekly, see ibid 21.

[148] Madsen (n 5) 252. Likewise, Bates observes that these decisions 'reflected the social revolution of the 1960s and changes in attitudes concerning matters such as illegitimacy', see Bates (n 20) 357. Goldhaber also writes that decisions such as *Marckx* 'reflected the spirit of [the] day', Goldhaber (n 147) 19.

[149] Philip Girard, 'The Protection of the Rights of Homosexuals under the International Law of Human Rights: European Perspectives' [1986] *Canadian Human Rights Yearbook* 3, 18.

[150] Laurence R Helfer, 'Lesbian and Gay Rights as Human Rights: Strategies for a United Europe' (1991) 32 Virginia Journal of International Law 157, 173, describing the impression left by *Dudgeon*. See also Wintemute (n 133) 133, 139.

[151] Andrew Drzemczewski, 'The Sui Generis Nature of the European Convention on Human Rights' (1980) 29 International and Comparative Law Quarterly 54, 62.

a considerably better understanding and an increased tolerance of homosexual behaviour had been achieved.[152]

Here, we see the outcome of that case being attributed almost entirely to the 'achievement' of shifting community values.

At the same time, by engaging with legal standards and state practice, the ECtHR did not appear to go over the heads of the Member States in establishing this new 'European ethos'[153] either. As O'Donnell commented in 1982, the ECtHR's judgments in *Tyrer*, *Marckx*, and *Dudgeon* seemed to carry with them 'the weight of legal tradition of the entire European system'.[154] This worked to imbue those judgments with a sense of objectivity and deference to the Member States notwithstanding the discretionary nature of the ECtHR's new interpretive approach.[155] As a result, the Member States seemed to accept the ECtHR's use of comparative reasoning. While the cases of *Tyrer*, *Marckx*, and *Dudgeon* generated controversy in the UK and Belgium,[156] both governments eventually implemented the ECtHR's decisions.[157] In the years that followed, the Member States also continued to renew their acceptances of the Convention's optional clauses and, in 1985, passed a resolution reaffirming their commitment to the ECHR.[158]

Together with the public enthusiasm for the ECtHR, this governmental support meant that, by the mid-1980s, the Court enjoyed considerable authority within Western Europe. In 1986, at a conference on International Courts and the Protection of Human Rights in the US, a former Registrar of the ECtHR, Heribert Golsong, told his audience, '[t]he Court acts with great authority; in Western Europe, it is perceived as the preeminent authority over those matters usually covered by the catalogues of civil rights and freedoms in national constitutions'.[159]

[152] Anne McHardy, 'Ban on Homosexual Acts Denies Rights' *The Guardian* (23 October 1981).

[153] For the argument that European consensus relies on an idea of a 'pan-European ethos', see Jens T Theilen, *European Consensus Between Strategy and Principle: The Uses of Vertically Comparative Legal Reasoning in Regional Human Rights Adjudication* (Nomos 2021) 119–26.

[154] Thomas A O'Donnell, 'The Margin of Appreciation Doctrine: Standards in the Jurisprudence of the European Court of Human Rights' (1982) 4 Human Rights Quarterly 474, 480.

[155] Theilen argues that the Court's use of comparative reasoning can be seen as a 'compromise' between 'incremental development' and respect for the 'States parties' democratic processes', see Theilen (n 153) 402–03.

[156] Zellick describes the *Tyrer* judgment as having 'provoked more comment hostile to the Court and the Convention than any other', Zellick (n 121) 665. Likewise, *Dudgeon* caused uproar amongst some religious conservatives in Northern Ireland, see Goldhaber (n 147) 39.

[157] Note, however, that it took Belgium until 1987 to implement the *Marckx* judgment, see Goldhaber (n 147) 21. Also note that the UK implemented the judgment in *Tyrer* by simply informing the Isle of Man that 'the United Kingdom Government took the view that judicial corporal punishment in the Isle of Man must now be held to be in breach of the [ECHR]', see David Bonner, 'The Beginning of the End for Corporal Punishment?' (1979) 42 Modern Law Review 580, 582–83. By contrast, the UK government swiftly implemented *Dudgeon* by passing the Homosexual Offences (Northern Ireland) Order 1982 (UK) the following year.

[158] Bates (n 20) 401 and 426.

[159] Heribert I Golsong, 'The European Commission of Human Rights' (1987) 2 Connecticut Journal of International Law 285, 285. Golsong went on to discuss cases such as *Marckx*, which 'gave the

4.4 The Birth of 'European Consensus'

4.4.1 European Consensus in the 1980s and 1990s: A 'Formula' for Progress

Over the 1980s and 1990s, the ECtHR continued to develop its use of comparative reasoning as a method of treaty interpretation. Most notably, it began using the term 'consensus' to describe it. While both the Commission and legal scholars had been using the term 'consensus' in this context since the late 1970s and early 1980s, respectively,[160] the Court itself did not use this term until 1989.[161] Moreover, even once it did start using the word 'consensus' with increasing frequency in the 1990s,[162] it did so alongside a variety of other phrases, such as 'common ground between the Contracting States'[163] and 'common European standard'.[164] Nevertheless, the ECtHR's embrace of the language of 'consensus' in the final decade of the twentieth century led some scholars to begin calling it 'European consensus'.[165] And it was through this interaction between scholarship and case law that this interpretive method acquired the name by which it is known today: 'European consensus'.[166] In attainting this name, the ECtHR's use of comparative analysis came to seem as if it were founded on a single, coherent concept.[167]

During this period, the ECtHR also began to look to sources beyond law and public opinion as part of its consensus inquiry. In particular, it started to engage with the opinions of scientists, medical professionals, and other experts. This trend had its origins in some of the Commission's decisions in the 1970s. In *X v Federal*

impression that the Court was on the way to developing a firm theory of interpreting the Convention in a dynamic manner', see ibid 291.

160 For an early example of the Commission using this term, see *X v United Kingdom* App No 7215/75, Eur Commn HR (Report) (12 October 1978) [146]. For an early example of a scholar using it, see O'Donnell (n 53) 479–84.

161 See *Soering v United Kingdom*, App No 14038/88, 161 Eur Ct HR (7 July 1989) [102]. However, even then, the Court was quoting Amnesty International's amicus brief.

162 See, eg, *B v France*, App No 13343/87, Eur Ct HR (25 March 1992) [48]; *X, Y and Z v United Kingdom*, App No 21830/93, Eur Ct HR (22 April 1997) [39]; *Sheffield and Horsham v United Kingdom*, App Nos 22985/93 and 23390/94, Eur Ct HR (30 July 1998) [55].

163 See, eg, *Cossey v United Kingdom*, App No 10843/84, Eur Ct HR (27 September 1990) [40].

164 See, eg, *X, Y and Z v United Kingdom* (n 162) [44].

165 For an early use of the term 'European consensus' see Laurence R Helfer, 'Finding a Consensus on Equality: The Homosexual Age of Consent and the European Convention on Human Rights' (1990) 65 New York University Law Review 1044, 1045–46.

166 On the role that scholars have played in cementing the language of 'European consensus', see Jaroslav Větrovský, 'Determining the Content of the European Consensus Concept: The Hidden Role of Language' in Panos Kapotas and Vassilis P Tzevelekos (eds), *Building Consensus on European Consensus: Judicial Interpretation of Human Rights in Europe and Beyond* (Cambridge University Press 2019) 121.

167 Větrovský writes that 'the terminological shift consisting in replacing a variety of expressions used by the ECtHR [European Court of Human Rights] by a single "overarching" term discloses (or possibly generates) an important aspect that all investigations into the concept probably have in common: the EuC [European consensus] concept is considered to be *one thing*...', ibid 121–22.

Republic of Germany (1975),[168] for example, the Commission made reference to 'various concording analyses . . . of psychologists, sociologists and specialists in social protection'[169] with respect to homosexual behaviour. But the Court itself began to rely on expertise in the 1980s and 1990s in the context of a number of cases concerning the right of transgender people to change the sex recorded in their birth certificates.[170] In these cases, the ECtHR repeatedly stressed that it would have regard 'to scientific and social developments'[171] alongside comparative legal analysis, and, in some of its decisions, devoted considerable attention to the state of 'medico-scientific' knowledge concerning the 'the essential nature of transsexualism'.[172]

As a result of this approach, by the early 1990s, scholars such as Helfer had begun claiming that the ECtHR relied on 'three distinct factors as evidence of consensus':[173] (1) legal consensus, as derived from European domestic law, regional legislation, and international treaties; (2) European public consensus; and (3) expert consensus.[174] Through this categorization, the ECtHR interpretive method began to take on the appearance of an objective, almost scientific, formula for determining whether European human rights standards had 'evolved', imbuing it with further authority.[175]

At the same time, the ECtHR remained firmly in control over its European consensus inquiry. It continued to be elusive about key details, such as the percentage of the Member States required to follow a particular approach before it would achieve legal consensus status and the weight to be accorded to different sources of consensus.[176] In the 1980s and 1990s, the ECtHR also exercised considerable discretion as to when the idea of European consensus would be relevant. In the case of *Johnston and Others v Ireland* (1986),[177] for example, which concerned Ireland's prohibition on divorce, the ECtHR rejected the applicants' argument that due to 'social developments' the ECHR should now be read to include a right to divorce.[178] The ECtHR stated that it could not 'by means of an evolutive interpretation, derive from these instruments a right that was not included therein at the outset'.[179] In support of this point, the ECtHR pointed to the Convention's *travaux*

[168] App No 5935/72, Eur Commn HR (30 September 1975).
[169] ibid 56.
[170] Wildhaber, Hjartarson, and Donnelly (n 134) 253.
[171] See, eg, *Rees v United Kingdom*, App No 9532/81, Eur Ct HR (17 October 1986) [47]; *Cossey* (n 163) [40]; *Sheffield and Horsham* (n 162) [60].
[172] See, eg, *Sheffield and Horsham* (n 162) [56]–[57].
[173] Laurence R Helfer, 'Consensus, Coherence and the European Convention on Human Rights' (1993) 26 Cornell International Law Journal 133, 139.
[174] Helfer first made this argument in 1990, see Helfer (n 165) 1056–57.
[175] On the relationship between categorization and legal authority, see Shaunnagh Dorsett and Shaun McVeigh, *Jurisdiction* (Routledge-Cavendish 2012) 71–76.
[176] Helfer (n 173) 140.
[177] App No 9697/82, Eur Ct HR (18 December 1986).
[178] ibid [53].
[179] ibid.

préparatoires, which 'disclose[d] no intention to include ... any guarantee of a right to have the ties of marriage dissolved by divorce'.[180] This originalist approach contrasted with the ECtHR's willingness to use European consensus to 'update' the ECHR with respect to illegitimacy in the earlier case of *Marckx*.[181] It should also be noted that, prior to 1998, the ECtHR comparative research was primarily based on the judges' own personal knowledge of their national law, supplemented by submissions from non-governmental organizations (NGOs).[182]

The combination of the ECtHR's discretion and the sources of 'consensus' upon which it was relying meant that, despite gradually becoming known as '*European* consensus', this interpretive method was skewed towards the perspective of a professional elite—namely, that of national judges, lawmakers, scientific experts, medical professionals, and, above all else, the judges on the Court itself. While social views continued to be a factor in the ECtHR's inquiry into the existence of a consensus, their force was diluted by its reliance on law and, increasingly, expertise as well. Moreover, the substantial discretion exercised by the ECtHR over this interpretive method meant that its findings of consensus, including those of social consensus, were often shaped by the views of the judges themselves.[183]

This orientation towards judicial and scientific knowledge affected both the pace and shape of the changes being generated by the ECtHR's use of European consensus. By the 1990s, it had become apparent that European consensus was a slow way of bringing about legal 'evolution'.[184] In *X v United Kingdom* (1978),[185] for example, the Commission had rejected a challenge to the UK's higher age of consent for homosexual sex, partly on the grounds there was 'a consensus among most European countries that legislation controlling homosexual behaviour [was] necessary'.[186] It would then take almost twenty years and several more challenges before the Commission found, on the basis of a European consensus, that a different age of consent for homosexual males breached the ECHR, in the 1997 case of *Sutherland v United Kingdom*.[187] Similarly, it took more than fifteen years and many applications between the 1986 case of *Rees v United Kingdom*[188] and the

[180] ibid [52].

[181] On the inconsistency between *Johnston and Others* and *Marckx*, see Kathleen Dillon, 'Divorce and Remarriage as Human Rights: The Irish Constitution and the European Convention on Human Rights at Odds in Johnston v. Ireland' (1989) 22 Cornell International Law Journal 63, 85–86.

[182] Dzehtsiarou (n 96) 82–85.

[183] On the way in which the ECtHR's consensus analysis produces 'knowledge of reality in ways that are relational to, and dependent upon, the interests (in the most general sense) of those who "apply" it', see Paul Johnson, 'Sociology and the European Court of Human Rights' (2014) 62 *The Sociological Review* 547, 553.

[184] See, eg, Goldhaber (n 147) 46; Anna van der Vleuten, 'Transnational LGBTI Activism and the European Courts: Constructing the Idea of Europe' in Philip M Ayoub and David Paternotte (eds), *LGBT Activism and the Making of Europe: A Rainbow Europe?* (Palgrave Macmillan 2014) 135–37.

[185] *X v United Kingdom* (n 168).

[186] ibid [146].

[187] App No 25186/94, Eur Commn HR (1 July 1997). The Court later confirmed this decision in *SL v Austria*, App No 45330/99, Eur Ct HR (9 January 2003).

[188] *Rees* (n 171).

2002 case of *Christine Goodwin v United Kingdom*[189] for the ECtHR to recognize the right of post-operative transgender people in the UK to legally change their gender via consensus-based reasoning.[190]

Some scholars have suggested that these delays were simply the result of the ECtHR seeking out the position of 'a substantial majority of majorities'[191] in Europe, which would be a difficult threshold to reach at the best of times, let alone in the context of minority rights.[192] Yet, when we look closely at some of the lines of cases in which the process of legal 'evolution' has been slowest, we find that the delays were partly caused by the ECtHR's practice of waiting for changes in expert opinion, which, as Dzehtsiarou points out, is perhaps an even harder goal to reach.[193]

In particular, a lack of 'noteworthy scientific developments'[194] regarding the precise 'causes of the condition of transsexualism'[195] weighed heavily in the ECtHR's reasoning for not recognizing the right of transgender people to legally change their gender prior to 2002. Take *Sheffield and Horsham v United Kingdom* (1998),[196] for example. In that case, the ECtHR emphasized that 'the applicants [had] not shown that since [its previous judgment on this matter] . . . there [had] been any findings in the area of medical science which settle[d] conclusively the doubts concerning the causes of the condition of transsexualism'.[197] In relation to the expert evidence that the applicants had adduced, it said: '[w]hile Professor Gooren's research into the role of the brain in conditioning transsexualism may be seen as an important contribution to the debate in this area . . . it cannot be said that his views enjoy the universal support of the medico-scientific profession'.[198] This lack of 'universal' scientific agreement, along with the fact that twenty-three of the thirty-seven Member States surveyed legally permitted birth certificate changes for transgender people—a number considered worthy of an 'evolutive' interpretation by some of the dissenting judges[199]—led the majority to conclude that they

[189] App No 28957/95, Eur Ct HR (11 July 2002).

[190] This outcome was largely achieved by the Court switching the focus of its consensus analysis away from 'a common European approach to the resolution of the legal and practical problems posed' to 'a continuing international trend in favour not only of increased social acceptance of transsexuals but of legal recognition of the new sexual identity of post-operative transsexuals', ibid [84]. For a critique of this change in focus, see Jeffrey A Brauch, 'The Dangerous Search for an Elusive Consensus: What the Supreme Court Should Learn from the European Court of Human Rights' (2009) 52 Howard Law Journal 277, 284–85.

[191] Wintemute (n 133) 137.

[192] See, eg, Eric Heinze, 'Sexual Orientation and International Law: A Study in the Manufacture of Cross-Cultural Sensitivity' (2001) 22 Michigan Journal of International Law 283, 288–90.

[193] Dzehtsiarou (n 96) 56: 'The nature of expert evidence, whereby different experts promote different views, makes the attainment of such consensus difficult, if not impossible, in most cases.'

[194] *Sheffield and Horsham* (n 162) [55].

[195] Ibid. See also *Cossey* (n 163) [40].

[196] *Sheffield and Horsham* (n 162).

[197] ibid [56].

[198] ibid.

[199] Joint Partly Dissenting Opinion of Judges Bernhardt, Thór Vilhjálmsson, Spielmann, Palm, Wildhaber, Makarczyk, and Voicu.

should not depart from the ECtHR's previous judgments.[200] This was so despite their acknowledgement that '[e]ven if there [had] been no significant scientific developments . . . it [was] nevertheless the case that there [was] an increased social acceptance of transsexualism'.[201] Here we see that rather than being the result of majoritarian prejudice, the ECtHR's delay in recognizing transgender rights was driven, in large measure, by scientific and judicial doubt.

In addition to affecting the speed of legal 'evolution', the ECtHR's reliance on expertise as part of its search for a European consensus had an impact on the substance of its decisions. When the ECtHR finally recognized the right of transgender people to change their gender legally in *Christine Goodwin* (2002), for example, it did so partly on the basis of an increasing 'acceptance of the condition of gender identity disorder by the medical professions and health authorities within Contracting States'.[202] In the view of some scholars, this finding only reinforced the medicalized and pathologized transgender subject that had already begun to emerge from the ECtHR's previous judgments on the matter,[203] rendering the overall outcome 'bittersweet'.[204] Similar outcomes will be explored in relation to the ECtHR's case law on sexuality in the following chapter.

4.4.2 Perceptions of the ECtHR and European Consensus in the Twilight of the Twentieth Century

Yet, even as the temporal and normative effects of the ECtHR's use of European consensus started to become clear, this interpretive method continued to be viewed in a positive light within the academic literature. Some scholars expressed frustration at the ECtHR's opaque and somewhat inconsistent way of deploying European consensus.[205] In 1987, for example, Yourow wrote, '[e]specially vexing in any attempt to uncover the meaning of the consensus factor is the consistently unsubstantiated nature of the Court's pronouncements'.[206] Likewise, in 1993, Helfer criticized 'the ambiguity in the tribunals' current consensus methodology'.[207] Nevertheless, support for European consensus generally remained high among

[200] *Sheffield and Horsham* (n 162) [57]–[58].

[201] ibid [60].

[202] *Christine Goodwin* (n 189) [100].

[203] Damian A Gonzalez-Salzberg, *Sexuality and Transsexuality under the European Convention on Human Rights: A Queer Reading of Human Rights Law* (Hart Publishing 2019) 43.

[204] Sara Bengtson, Damian A Gonzalez-Salzberg, and Paul Johnson, 'Christine Goodwin v the United Kingdom' in Loveday Hodson and Troy Lavers (eds), *Feminist Judgments in International Law* (Hart Publishing 2019) 176.

[205] Wildhaber, Hjartarson, and Donnelly (n 134) 249: 'The opacity and lack of guidance, which was characteristic of the old Court, angered some of the earlier academic writers visibly.'

[206] Howard Charles Yourow, 'Margin of Appreciation Doctrine in the Dynamics of European Human Rights Jurisprudence' (1987) 3 Connecticut Journal of International Law 111, 158.

[207] Helfer (n 173) 135.

legal commentators in the final decades of the twentieth century, with those critical of the ECtHR's methodology simply urging it to adopt a more coherent and precise approach so as to maintain the legitimacy of what they saw as an important interpretive method.[208] Benvenisti summarized the academic position in 1999 as follows: 'The ECHR's consensus doctrine enjoys considerable support among legal commentators. The supporters, while critical of the vague process of identifying consensus . . . choose to highlight its bright side.'[209]

The 'bright side' which scholars sought to highlight again hinged on the twin narratives of 'progress' and 'public voice' that we met in the previous section. In 1990, for example, Helfer praised the ECtHR's interpretive method of European consensus for allowing it to 'expand the protection which the Convention provides to individuals throughout Europe and to interpret the Convention as a modern document which is responsive to progressive European conditions and attitudes'.[210] Here, we not only see the idea that, through its search for a European consensus, the ECtHR was able to engage with European public opinion, but also the view that this process was inherently linked to 'progress' and an expansion of rights under the ECHR.

In the twilight of the twentieth century, applicants under the ECHR also tended to see the ECtHR in a 'progressive' and even 'democratic' light. Hugo Greenhalgh, a gay activist and applicant under the ECHR in 1993, has reflected that 'at the time, the European Court of Human Rights seemed to offer a future model of democracy and freedom where rights were recognized and equality was enshrined'. He continued, 'it represented hope for us . . . [It] seemed this amazing, wonderful, shiny, beacon of equality and modernity.'[211] What is more, Greenhalgh believed that if his case had progressed to the ECtHR,[212] it would have succeeded because there was an 'emerging European consensus on "gay rights"'[213] at that time: 'We would have won the case in Strasbourg . . . Society was on the cusp of change, not just in the UK but across Europe as well.'[214] Greenhalgh was not alone in his understanding of the importance of the Court's use of European consensus to

[208] See, eg, ibid.

[209] Eyal Benvenisti, 'Margin of Appreciation, Consensus, and Universal Standards' (1999) 31 New York University Journal of International Law and Politics 843, 851.

[210] Helfer (n 165) 1056. However, note that there is a contrasting view, which praises European consensus for enabling the ECtHR to develop its case law 'only incrementally'. For a summary of this position, see Theilen (n 153) 344–45.

[211] Hugo Greenhalgh, quoted in Johnson (n 142) 95–96.

[212] In 1993, Hugo Greenhalgh submitted an application under the ECHR, along with Ralph Wilde and William Parry, regarding the UK's higher age of consent for male homosexual acts, which was twenty-one years at the time, see *Wilde, Greenhalgh and Parry v United Kingdom*, App No 22382/93, Eur Commn HR (19 January 1995). In 1994, the UK Parliament reduced the age of consent for male homosexual sex to eighteen years. While this was still a different age to age of consent for heterosexual sex, the Commission regarded this reform to have resolved the matter complained of and struck the application off its list of cases in 1995.

[213] Johnson (n 142) 187.

[214] Greenhalgh, quoted in ibid.

the outcome of ECHR cases. Through a series of interviews with former lesbian, gay, and bisexual applicants under the ECHR, Johnson found that applicants' expectations about the likely success of their application were often shaped by the ECtHR's European consensus inquiry and the idea 'that the broader social and political relations of European societies determine the outcome of complaints to Strasbourg rather than a strict "moral" interpretation of the rights and freedoms contained in the Convention'.[215]

This sense of political engagement and forward momentum seemed to drive applicants to use the ECtHR not only to resolve their discrete human rights grievances, but also as a forum through which to bring about social and legal change. In his interviews, Johnson found that '[o]ne of the most common aspirations' amongst applicants under the ECHR was 'a desire to change the *law* in ways that will have widespread benefit for other individuals . . . [as well as] an ambition to achieve broader *social* change'.[216] Similar impressions of European consensus and change also motivated activist lawyers and NGOs to invest time and resources in ECHR cases. Since the late 1970s, NGOs had become increasingly involved in the European human rights system cases by representing applicants, providing support for the litigation, and, from 1983, when the ECtHR amended its rules of procedure to allow third party participation,[217] submitting amicus briefs.[218] Over the 1980s and 1990s, it became commonplace for NGOs to make submissions to the ECtHR about what constitutes a European consensus on an issue in their amicus briefs,[219] with the aim of altering the Court's case law.[220]

The embrace of the European human rights system by individuals and NGOs seeking to bring about change at the turn of the century meant that the ECtHR was using the idea of European consensus to resolve politically charged issues with increasing frequency. The result was a 'juridifcation' of politics, in which European public debate was increasingly being simulated through a discretionary method of judicial interpretation rather than taking place within local decision-making structures. While this may not have been the ECtHR's intention, the transfer of political questions to the European judicial arena caused concern in some of the CoE Member States and, in particular, the UK, which had been the subject of a

[215] ibid.

[216] ibid 178 [emphasis in the original].

[217] The ECtHR amended then Rule 37(2) of the Rules of Court in 1983 to allow third party participation both by States or any other person. For commentary, see Rachel A Cichowski, 'Civil Society and the European Court of Human Rights' in Jonas Christoffersen and Mikael Rask Madsen (eds), *The European Court of Human Rights between Law and Politics* (Oxford University Press 2011) 87.

[218] See generally ibid.

[219] Nicole Bürli, 'Amicus Curiae as a Means to Reinforce the Legitimacy of the European Court of Human Rights' in Spyridon Flogaitis, Tom Zwart, and Julie Fraser (eds), *The European Court of Human Rights and its Discontents: Turning Criticism into Strength* (Edward Elgar Publishing 2013) 137–42.

[220] See, eg, the description by Robert Wintemute, an academic and activist lawyer, of what has motivated him to submit European consensus-focused amicus briefs on behalf of NGOs over the years in Johnson (n 142) 169.

large number of the Court's 'evolutive' decisions. As early as 1985, commentators in the UK worried that 'the Court and the Commission ... [were] being drawn into making political judgments seen by many as the province of democratically elected parliament'.[221] Yet, like the other CoE Member States, the UK government generally seemed to tolerate this situation, implementing the ECtHR's decisions and renewing its acceptance of the optional clauses.[222] In a testament to the ECtHR's authority during this period, the UK also joined the other Member States in ratifying Protocol 11[223] in the mid-1990s, thereby helping to transform the ECHR into a 'quasi-constitutional' system.[224] This transformation is described in the following section.

4.5 European Consensus in the Post-1998 European Court of Human Rights

4.5.1 Protocol 11

On 1 November 1998, Protocol 11 came into force, which not only replaced both the Commission and Court with a new single, permanent Court, but also rendered the ECtHR's jurisdiction compulsory.[225] The immediate catalyst for these reforms had been the expansion of the CoE's membership eastward following the fall of the Berlin Wall.[226] The sharp rise in signatories to the ECHR, combined with the ever-increasing popularity of the European human rights system, caused the number of applications made under the ECHR to soar further. As we saw earlier, in 1993, the Commission registered 2,037 applications. By 1997, the annual figure had more than doubled to 4,750.[227] The merger of the Commission and the Court was thus envisaged as a way to streamline ECHR cases and reduce pressure on the system. However, other aspects of Protocol 11, such as the decision to make the 'new' Court's jurisdiction compulsory, seem to have simply been the result of the Member States' enthusiasm for the European human rights system. Or, at least,

[221] *The Daily Telegraph* (1985), cited in Ed Bates, 'The UK and Strasbourg: A Strained Relationship—The Long View' in Katja S Ziegler, Elizabeth Wicks, and Loveday Hodson (eds), *The UK and European Human Rights: A Strained Relationship?* (Hart Publishing 2015) 47.

[222] ibid 48.

[223] Protocol 11 to the European Convention for the Protection of Human Rights and Fundamental Freedoms, Restructuring the Control Machinery Established Thereby, opened for signature 11 May 1994, ETS 155 (entered into force 1 November 1998).

[224] On the 'quasi-constitutional' nature of the European human rights system, Protocol 11, and the complex relationship between the UK government and the Court, see Bates (n 20) 436–40.

[225] Protocol 11 (n 223).

[226] Jeffrey A Brauch, 'The Margin of Appreciation and the Jurisprudence of the European Court of Human Rights: Threat to the Rule of Law' (2005) 11 Columbia Journal of European Law 113, 114.

[227] European Court of Human Rights, *Annual Report 2001* (Registry of the European Court of Human Rights 2002) 9.

some of the ECtHR judges interpreted them to indicate as much. In 1996, President of the Court Rolv Ryssdal described the drafting of Protocol 11 as evidence that the Member States were now 'sufficiently mature . . . to commit themselves fully to an international judicial system of human rights protection'.[228]

During the negotiations on Protocol 11, some Member States had expressed concerns about the democratic implications of the removal of the optional clauses. In particular, the UK had worried that by abolishing the Member States' right to review the ECtHR's jurisdiction, they might be giving up an important 'democratic safeguard'.[229] But, in contrast to what happened in the early 1950s, such concerns were quickly brushed aside and, before long, all of the Member States had ratified Protocol 11.[230] In the view of some scholars, this signalled an implicit approval of the ECtHR's use of European consensus.[231]

4.5.2 European Consensus after Protocol 11 and the Emergence of a Democratic Discourse

In the 'new' ECtHR, European consensus underwent a number of additional changes. Most notably, and perhaps in recognition of the ECHR's expanded membership, from the year 2000 onwards, the Court itself began using the term '*European* consensus' (instead of simply referring to a 'consensus').[232] The post-1998 Court also made changes to the way it conducted its comparative research. In particular, it established a Research Division composed of ten full-time lawyers within its Registry to prepare comparative law reports.[233] These reports were and continue to be confidential and inaccessible to the general public.[234] But, over time, the ECtHR adopted the practice of providing a summary of the research in its judgments.[235] To some scholars, this represented a marked improvement in the ECtHR's consensus methodology.[236] However, to this day, the ECtHR has never defined 'European consensus' or provided clear guidance about the number of Member States required to follow a particular law or practice before it will be said to have achieved consensus status.[237] Moreover, the ECtHR's approach has

[228] Rolv Ryssdal, 'The Coming of Age of the ECHR' (1996) 1 European Human Rights Law Review 18, 22.
[229] Bates (n 221) 49.
[230] Bates (n 20) 460.
[231] See, eg, Thomas Kleinlein, 'Consensus and Contestability: The ECtHR and the Combined Potential of European Consensus and Procedural Rationality Control' (2017) 29 European Journal of International Law 871, 883.
[232] *Marlow v United Kingdom*, App No 42015/98, Eur Ct HR (5 December 2000).
[233] Dzehtsiarou (n 96) 86–88.
[234] ibid 88.
[235] ibid.
[236] See, eg, Wildhaber, Hjartarson, and Donnelly (n 134) 249, 257; Dzehtsiarou (n 96) 4, 82.
[237] Panos Kapotas and Vassilis P Tzevelekos, 'How (Difficult Is It) to Build Consensus on (European) Consensus?' in Panos Kapotas and Vassilis P Tzevelekos (eds), *Building Consensus on European*

continued to vary, with it sometimes accepting a very 'thin' majority as a consensus,[238] and at other times requiring larger numbers.[239]

It is also noteworthy that the comparative reports produced by the ECtHR's Research Division have tended to be based on a sample of Member States' laws, rather than those of all the Member States. In 2013, Wildhaber, Hjartarson, and Donnelly found that this meant that the post-1998 ECtHR's consensus analysis was often grounded in the practice of less than 60 per cent of the Member States, and sometimes much less.[240] In addition to rendering the ECtHR's interpretive method even more discretionary, this use of sampling arguably introduced a new power dynamic into its European consensus inquiry. This is because some of the most commonly cited reasons for the ECtHR's use of sampling are the Research Division's limited resources,[241] and a lack of readily available information about some Member States' laws.[242] From this, one can infer that the ECtHR may be more likely to include Member States in its samples whose laws are easily accessible, available in dominant languages, and the subject of scholarly research, thereby creating an implicit bias in favour of wealthy, Western European states.[243]

Despite these issues, a new discourse of 'democracy' began to form around the ECtHR's use of European consensus as a method of interpretation in the post-1998 era. As we have seen, there were already traces of this discourse in the early 1990s, with scholars depicting European consensus as a vehicle of 'public voice' and applicants occasionally using the language of 'democracy' to describe the Court itself. But from the late 1990s onwards, the connection between European consensus and democracy became more explicit, particularly within the academic literature. In the first few articles in which this occurred, the authors tended to be critical of the ECtHR's 'democratic' approach. In 1999, for example, Benvenisti argued that while European consensus reflected 'a respect of sovereignty, of the notion of subsidiarity, and of national democracy' due to its emphasis on the Member States' laws and practices, it ultimately 'prevented the Court from fulfilling the crucial task of becoming the external guardian against the tyranny by majorities'.[244]

Consensus: Judicial Interpretation of Human Rights in Europe and Beyond (Cambridge University Press 2019) 9–10.

[238] See, eg, *Oliari and Others v Italy*, App Nos 18766/11 and 36030/11, Eur Ct HR (31 July 2015) [178].

[239] See, eg, *Stübing v Germany*, App No 43547/08, Eur Ct HR (12 April 2012) [61]. These cases are discussed in more detail in Chapter 5 of this book.

[240] Wildhaber, Hjartarson, and Donnelly (n 134) 258.

[241] Vassilis P Tzevelekos and Kanstantsin Dzehtsiarou, 'International Custom Making and the ECtHR's European Consensus Method of Interpretation' (2016) 16 European Yearbook of Human Rights 313.

[242] Judge Bîrsan quoted in Dzehtsiarou (n 96) 103.

[243] For this argument in the context of customary international law and the global South, see George Rodrigo Bandeira Galindo and César Yip, 'Customary International Law and the Third World: Do Not Step on the Grass' (2017) 16 Chinese Journal of International Law 251, 258–60. On the similarities between European consensus and customary international law, see Tzevelekos and Dzehtsiarou (n 241).

[244] Benvenisti (n 209) 852.

This argument echoed that of the ECHR's founding figures when they put forward the idea of a supranational human rights court in the aftermath of the Second World War.

By the mid-2000s, however, the tone of the conversation began to change. In 2006, Koch and Vedsted-Hansen argued that the fact that the ECtHR's 'evolutive' approach to interpretation was anchored in 'sources of law which are under the current influence by democratically legitimised bodies such as domestic legislatures'[245] was a reason why it did not pose a threat to democracy in Europe. In 2012, Petkova went further, describing European consensus as a form of 'democratic constitutionalism',[246] in which the ECtHR established a 'dialogical node'[247] with its constituency by enabling the Member States to act as its 'pollsters'.[248] Likewise, in 2015, Dzehtsiarou contended that European consensus was a tool used by the ECtHR to 'engage in dialogue with the Contracting Parties'[249] and inform itself about their 'democratic preferences'.[250] In his view, this 'offer[ed] some democratic legitimation to the choices made by the ECtHR'.[251] For although '[a] decision supported by European consensus cannot claim the same level of democratic legitimacy as the decision of a directly elected parliament, . . . it brings the ECtHR closer to people'.[252] To many of these scholars, the democratic credentials of European consensus were important precisely because of the ECtHR's position outside of national democratic structures. Jens Theilen summarizes their position as follows: European consensus is justified because it purportedly 'mitigates the lack of democratic control available at the transnational level'.[253]

The democratic perception of European consensus was not confined to academic circles. Judges on the Court also made similar statements. In a 2017 speech, for example, Judge Paulo Pinto de Albuquerque said:

> From the seminal formulation of the European consensus in *Tyrer* emanates a vision of an [sic] *deliberative, international democracy* in which a majority or representative proportion of the Contracting Parties to the Convention is considered to speak in the name of all and thus is entitled to impose its will on other Parties.[254]

[245] Ida Elisabeth Koch and Jens Vedsted-Hansen, 'International Human Rights and National Legislatures—Conflict or Balance?' (2006) 75 Nordic Journal of International Law 3, 12.
[246] See, eg, Bilyana Petkova, 'The Notion of Consensus as a Route to Democratic Adjudication?' (2012) 14 Cambridge Yearbook of European Legal Studies 663.
[247] ibid 675.
[248] ibid 692.
[249] Dzehtsiarou (n 96) 157.
[250] ibid 170.
[251] ibid 211.
[252] ibid.
[253] Theilen (n 153) 118.
[254] Paulo Pinto de Albuquerque, 'Is the ECHR Facing an Existential Crisis?' *Speech delivered at the Mansfield College, Oxford* (28 April 2017) <https://www.law.ox.ac.uk/sites/files/oxlaw/pinto_openin

One reason for the rise of this democratic discourse, particularly in the 2010s, may have been that a counter-narrative had been brewing in the UK and a number of other Member States. The thrust of this counter-narrative was that the ECtHR was using its living instrument approach to 'legislate' for Europe and the Member States no longer had any 'democratic override' short of withdrawing from the ECHR altogether.[255] As we will see in Chapter 6, such concerns would eventually lead to a 'backlash' against the ECtHR and demands that it show greater deference to national decisions.[256] In an attempt to restabilize the authority of the European human rights system, judges and academic supporters of the ECHR appear to have latched on to European consensus as a way to demonstrate a democratic link between the ECtHR and the people. Judge Pinto de Albuquerque's description of the Court's use of European consensus as a form of 'deliberative, international democracy', for example, appeared in a speech entitled 'Is the ECHR Facing an Existential Crisis?', in which he spoke at length about the growing criticism of the Court in the UK.[257] Likewise, in the book in which he describes European consensus as a tool of democratic dialogue, Dzehtsiarou opens with the question '[h]as the European Court of Human Rights . . . lost its legitimacy?' and states that his book's overall argument 'is that European consensus can enhance the legitimacy of the ECtHR' against the backdrop of 'recent fierce attacks'.[258]

Yet, the problem with the democratic account of European consensus is that it overlooks the fact that neither the Member States nor their constituencies actually have a direct say over the outcome of the ECtHR's consensus inquiry. Despite Judge Pinto de Albuquerque's reference to a representative proportion of Member States being 'entitled to impose its will on other Parties' and the term 'consensus' exuding 'the virtues of discussion and consultation',[259] what constitutes a 'European consensus' is ultimately something constructed by the ECtHR. The ECtHR's comparative approach to interpretation might thus be seen as an instance of 'post-politics', as described by theorists such as Chantal Mouffe and Jacques Rancière, in which political problems are converted into technical or moral problems[260]—in this

g_presentation_2017.pdf> [emphasis added]. Judge Pinto de Albuquerque also made this statement in his partly dissenting opinion in *Muršić v Croatia*, App No 7334/13, Eur Ct HR (20 October 2016) [20].

[255] On this trend in the UK, see Bates (n 221). On this trend in the Netherlands, see BM Oomen, 'A Serious Case of Strasbourg-Bashing? An Evaluation of the Debates on the Legitimacy of the European Court of Human Rights in the Netherlands' (2016) 20 International Journal of Human Rights 407.

[256] See, eg, the Brighton Declaration (2012) and the Copenhagen Declaration (2018), discussed in Section 6.3 of Chapter 6. See also Protocol No. 15 Amending the Convention for the Protection of Human Rights and Fundamental Freedoms, opened for signature 24 June 2013, CETS 213, 2013 (entered into force 1 August 2021).

[257] Pinto de Albuquerque (n 254) .

[258] Dzehtsiarou (n 96) 1.

[259] Jacques Rancière, *Chronicles of Consensual Times* (Steven Corcoran tr, Continuum International Publishing Group 2010) 1.

[260] Chantal Mouffe, *On the Political* (Routledge 2005); Jacques Rancière, *Dissensus: On Politics and Aesthetics* (Steven Concoran tr, Continuum International Publishing Group 2010) 71, 100.

case 'human rights' problems—to be resolved by legal and scientific experts capable of finding a 'rational consensus' for society.[261] In this way, as in the General Agreement on Tariffs and Trade (GATT) and World Trade Organization (WTO), the democratic discourse that came to surround the ECtHR's use of consensus did not necessarily align with the operational reality of the decision-making method that it described.

4.6 Conclusion: Consensus and the Authority of the European Human Rights System

This chapter has shown that, in different international legal and institutional contexts, the term 'consensus' can refer to very different methods of decision-making. Although Sørensen's 1975 suggestion that the ECtHR embrace the idea of consensus came at a time when consensus decision-making was becoming a popular procedure in international organizations, the decision-making process that emerged from his proposal was distinct. It was neither based around non-voting (as in the GATT's 'sense of the meeting' procedure) nor discussions between representatives of states (as in the UN Conference on Trade and Development's conciliation procedure). It was not even based around the Court's judges writing a single decision (as in the WTO Appellate Body's practice of judicial consensus). Rather, 'European consensus' came to describe a method of judicial interpretation based on the ECtHR undertaking a comparative analysis of law, social views, and expertise in the CoE Member States.

Despite these differences, the ECtHR's claim to base some of its decisions on the idea of consensus produced similar effects to consensus decision-making in the GATT/WTO. Most notably, it helped to shore up the authority of the ECtHR against a backdrop of shifting social values and democratic mistrust by enabling it to 'update' the ECHR, while also appearing to engage with European views and values in the process of doing so. These features of European consensus resulted in the ECtHR's interpretive approach becoming associated with discourses of 'progress', 'public voice', and, eventually, 'democracy', prompting individuals and NGOs to turn to the European human rights system as a forum through which to bring about social and legal change and paving the way for the Member States to expand and reinforce the European human rights system. Yet, when we look closely, European consensus has been neither particularly progressive nor democratic. Instead, it was and continues to be a highly discretionary method of judicial

[261] For an overview of the idea of 'post-politics' see Japhy Wilson and Erik Swyngedouw, 'Seeds of Dystopia: Post-Politics and the Return of the Political' in Japhy Wilson and Erik Swyngedouw (eds), *The Post-Political and Its Discontents: Spaces of Depoliticization, Spectres of Radical Politics* (Edinburgh Scholarship 2014).

interpretation that privileges the perspective of certain actors over others. As a vehicle of legal evolution, it can also take decades to generate change.

What are we to make of the dissonance between the expectations and discourses surrounding European consensus and its operational reality? In my argument, this tension is again rooted in the gesture that the idea of consensus makes towards an unfixed, yet seemingly profound, level of agreement. Although the ECtHR sometimes substitutes the word 'consensus' with other phrases, such as 'the great majority of Member States' or 'a common European standard', its use of comparative reasoning has always revolved around this gesture. That is, the ECtHR has always claimed to look for laws and practices that are widespread in Europe, but has never set an exact threshold for doing so. This has had two effects. On the one hand, the ECtHR's claim to seek out a purportedly high level of agreement has lent itself to democratic discourses. On the other hand, by blurring the numbers and sources upon which it relies, the ECtHR has created a process of decision-making that can replicate and sometimes even exacerbate underlying power relations—whether they be those between judge and citizen, medical expert and queer, or wealthy state and poor state.

Some scholars have suggested that the ECtHR could easily 'fix' its use of European consensus by defining it or setting a more precise threshold.[262] Yet, to do so may well be to deprive the ECtHR's interpretive method of its consensual quality. For if the ECtHR were to state the exact percentage of Member States or people required to establish a 'consensus', it would no longer be looking for a 'consensus', but rather a 'simple majority', 'supermajority', or 'unanimity'. This, in turn, could undo the democratic and progressive allure of its interpretive method by clarifying the boundaries of inclusion/exclusion, as well as the possibilities for change. Viewed in this way, it is perhaps unsurprising that the ECtHR has not adopted such a course of action. As Wildhaber, Hjartarson, and Donnelly write, '[i]t appears that the Court is hoping to keep the concept fuzzy enough to avoid the consequences of adopting one particular theory'[263] as to what 'European consensus' is or should be, lest it compromise the authority it has come to enjoy as a result of this interpretive method.[264] However, as we will see in Chapter 6, the gap between perception and reality with respect to the ECtHR's use of European consensus would become a contributing factor in some of the contestation surrounding the European human rights system today.

[262] See, eg, Dzehtsiarou (n 96) 207–08.

[263] Wildhaber, Hjartarson, and Donnelly (n 134) 249. See also Kapotas and Tzevelekos (n 237) 10.

[264] For the argument that the Court sees its authority as rooted in the European public opinion, see Or Bassok, 'The European Consensus Doctrine and the ECtHR Quest for Public Confidence' in Panos Kapotas and Vassilis P Tzevelekos (eds), *Building Consensus on European Consensus: Judicial Interpretation of Human Rights in Europe and Beyond* (Cambridge University Press 2019).

5
European Consensus and Sexual Normativity

5.1 Introduction

In the previous chapter, I explored how the European Court of Human Rights' (ECtHR) claim to base its decisions on a 'European consensus' helped to reinforce the authority of the European human rights system by giving it an air of 'progress' and 'democracy'. In this chapter, I now consider the authorizing work performed by the ECtHR's substantive claims about the existence or non-existence of a European consensus. This is carried out through an analysis of the ECtHR's case law relating to sexuality, using a queer theoretical lens. The ECtHR's use of European consensus has played a prominent role in its decisions relating to sexuality rights under the European Convention on Human Rights (ECHR). In particular, since the case of *Dudgeon v United Kingdom* (1981), it has been a central element in the ECtHR's recognition of sexuality and relationship rights for lesbian, gay, bisexual, transgender, and intersex (LGBTI) people, from the right to homosexual sex to the right to same-sex relationship recognition. Scholars and LGBTI activists alike have welcomed these decisions, pointing to the ways in which an accumulation of rights has benefited the European queer community. Yet, as I argue in this chapter, by routinely grounding its decisions relating to sexuality in the idea of 'consensus', the ECtHR has worked to author and authorize narrow constructions of sexuality and Europeanness, closing off spaces for alterity. As a result, the ECtHR's claims of European consensus have operated to uphold and sustain the dominant sexual order, even in those cases in which they have led to the recognition of new rights for LGBTI people.

The chapter begins with an overview of the Strasbourg organs' use of European consensus in their decisions relating to sexuality rights, demonstrating how this interpretive method became a central element in the ECtHR's recognition of rights for LGBTI people. The chapter then turns to the work that the ECtHR's claims of European consensus have done in the context of sexuality rights. First, it examines the exclusionary effects of the ECtHR's claims of European consensus in relation to marginalized sexualities that exist outside of the 'LGBTI' acronym, such as sadomasochism and consensual adult incest. Second, it explores how the ECtHR's claims of European consensus have operated as a regulatory device over queer

Consensus in International Law. Claerwen O'Hara, Oxford University Press. © Claerwen O'Hara 2026.
DOI: 10.1093/9780198948643.003.0005

sexualities within that acronym by enabling it to reinforce narrow ideas about what constitutes 'sexual orientation' or 'the family'. Third, the chapter assesses the way in which the ECtHR's claims of European consensus have lent authority to an idea of Europe as inherently 'gay-friendly', contributing to the co-option of queer lives in pursuit of political agendas.

5.2 European Consensus and Sexuality Rights: An Overview

'European consensus' has been described as a 'hallmark' of the Strasbourg organs' case law relating to sexuality rights.[1] The Strasbourg organs began using comparative reasoning in their adjudication of sexuality rights claims in the mid-1970s, when the ECtHR's use of European consensus as a method of treaty interpretation was first taking shape. At that time, however, it was primarily used as a way to reject such claims. This occurred on the basis of both the existence and the non-existence of a common European standard. In *Handyside v United Kingdom* (1976),[2] for example, the ECtHR held that the United Kingdom's (UK) ban on a sexually 'obscene' book did not violate the ECHR due to there being *no* 'uniform European conception of morals'.[3] By contrast, in *X v United Kingdom* (1978),[4] the European Commission of Human Rights (the Commission) held that the UK's different age of consent for male homosexual relations did not breach the ECHR partly because there *was* 'a consensus among most European countries that legislation controlling homosexual behaviour is necessary'.[5]

This all changed in 1981 with the case of *Dudgeon v United Kingdom*,[6] when, for the first time in a sexuality-related case, the ECtHR used the idea of European consensus in connection with its 'living instrument' approach. As discussed in the previous chapter, the ECtHR's 'living instrument' approach refers to its interpretation of the ECHR 'in the light of present-day conditions'.[7] The ECtHR is more likely to apply a new or 'evolutive' interpretation to the text of the ECHR when it can identify a common European approach in support of it. *Dudgeon* arose from a challenge to the criminalization of homosexuality in Northern Ireland. In a departure from the Commission's previous decisions relating to homosexuality, the ECtHR held that Northern Ireland's criminal prohibition on homosexual practices violated the right to private life under Article 8 of the ECHR. This was due, in large measure, to the ECtHR's finding that 'in the great majority of the member

1 Paul Johnson, *Homosexuality and the European Court of Human Rights* (Routledge 2013) 25.
2 App No 5493/72 Eur Ct HR (7 December 1976).
3 ibid [48].
4 App No 7215/75, Eur Comm'n HR (Report) (12 October 1978).
5 ibid [146].
6 App No 7525/76, 25 Eur Ct HR (22 October 1981).
7 *Tyrer v United Kingdom*, App No 5856/72, 26 Eur Ct HR (25 April 1978) [31].

States . . . it [was] no longer considered to be necessary or appropriate to treat homosexual practices . . . as in themselves a matter to which the sanctions of the criminal law should be applied'.[8]

Since *Dudgeon*, the ECtHR has recognized a range of other sexuality rights for LGBTI people through its identification of a European consensus, from an equal age of consent for homosexual relations[9] to relationship recognition for same-sex couples.[10] However, this journey has not been straightforward. Before producing these apparent successes, comparative reasoning was often the main basis upon which the Strasbourg organs rejected the same claims. A lack of European consensus also continues to be one of the principal reasons the ECtHR gives for its denial of certain sexuality and relationship rights under the ECHR, from the right to consensual adult incest[11] to the right to same-sex marriage.[12]

Nonetheless, scholars and activists have generally narrated the gradual accumulation of sexuality and relationship rights for LGBTI people via the ECtHR's use of European consensus as a story of progress. Throughout the literature, the ECtHR's use of European consensus in sexuality-related cases is presented as a tale of forward momentum, whereby European human rights law is depicted as moving ever closer to a 'better' future in which queer people will one day be full subjects under the ECHR.[13] This can be seen in the characterization of the ECtHR's case law concerning LGBTI rights in terms of 'successes' and 'setbacks',[14] as well as in claims that it is only a matter of time before the ECtHR will inevitably recognize a right to same-sex marriage through its identification of a new European consensus.[15] This sense of progressive development has led scholars and activists alike to support the ECtHR's use of European consensus in cases relating to sexuality.[16] However, the focus on 'progress' and rights accumulation obscures the way the ECtHR's claims of European consensus have worked to authorize discourses that regulate, erase,

[8] ibid [60].

[9] *S.L. v Austria*, App No 45330/99, Eur Ct HR (9 January 2003).

[10] *Oliari and Others v Italy*, App Nos 18766/11 and 36030/11, Eur Ct HR (31 July 2015).

[11] *Stübing v Germany*, App No 43547/08, Eur Ct HR (12 April 2012).

[12] See, eg, *Chapin and Charpentier v France*, App No 40183/07, Eur Ct HR (9 June 2016). For commentary, see Loveday Hodson, 'The European Court of Human Rights and Same-Sex Marriage: Incompatible Bedfellows?' (2025) 47 Journal of Social Welfare and Family Law 69.

[13] Francesca Romana Ammaturo, 'The Right to a Privilege? Homonormativity and the Recognition of Same-Sex Couples in Europe' (2014) 23 Social & Legal Studies 175.

[14] ibid.

[15] See, eg, Amaury A Reyes-Torres, 'Oliari v. Italy: The First Step to Equal Marriage in Europe?' (*Jurist*, 17 August 2015) <https://www.jurist.org/commentary/2015/08/Amaury-Reyes-Torres-Equal-Marriage/>; Giuseppe Zago, 'Oliari and Others v. Italy: A Stepping Stone Towards Full Legal Recognition of Same-Sex Relationships in Europe' (*Strasbourg Observers*, 16 September 2015) <https://strasbourgobservers.com/2015/09/16/oliari-and-others-v-italy-a-stepping-stone-towards-full-legal-recognition-of-same-sex-relationships-in-europe/>.

[16] See, eg, Laurence R Helfer, 'Finding a Consensus on Equality: The Homosexual Age of Consent and the European Convention on Human Rights' (1990) 65 New York University Law Review 1044, 1056.

and co-opt sexual difference. In what follows, I explore these effects through a queer reading of a selection of Strasbourg cases relating to sexuality.

5.3 The Marginalization of Sexualities Outside the European Consensus

At the height of the sexual revolution in Europe in the 1960s, theorists and activists emphasized the links between different sexual subaltern groups. The term 'sexual subaltern', coined by Ratna Kapur, describes all people who are marginalized on account of their sexual identities and/or practices.[17] Sexual subalterns in the occupied Sorbonne in Paris in May 1968, for example, were influenced by the ideas of Lars Ullerstam, who argued that all 'sexual deviations', including homosexuality, incest, exhibitionism, paedophilia, and sadism, were 'fully legitimate methods of satisfying the sexual urge'.[18] Accordingly, the students established the *Comité d'Action Pédérastique Révolutionnaire* (Committee of Revolutionary Pederastic Action), which claimed to stand for the emancipation of all 'sexual minorities', not just homosexuals.[19] Even once organizations were founded all over Europe in the 1970s under the banner of 'gay liberation', many of those organizations continued to show solidarity with other 'repressed' sexual groups.[20]

As sexual subalterns began to turn to the ECtHR in the 1980s and 1990s, however, a clear distinction emerged between (respectable) gay and lesbian people, who were gradually transformed into rights-bearing subjects, and other sexual subalterns, who were not. The ECtHR's use of European consensus played a role in producing this distinction. In *Dudgeon*, for example, the ECtHR's claim about there being a new European standard was confined to 'an increased tolerance . . . of homosexual behaviour'[21] within the Member States of the Council of Europe (CoE), rather than an increasing European openness to sexual freedom more generally. Consequently, the ECtHR went on to hold that the right to respect for private life under Article 8 of the ECHR demanded only the decriminalization of 'private homosexual relations between adult males capable of valid consent',[22] rather than of *all* consensual adult sexual relations.[23]

[17] Ratna Kapur, 'Post-Colonial Economies of Desire: Legal Representations of the Sexual Subaltern' (2001) 78 Denver University Law Review 855.

[18] Lars Ullerstam, quoted in Michael Sibalis, '"And What Then about 'Our' Problem?"—Gay Liberation in the Occupied Sorbonne in May 1968' in Julian Jackson, Anna-Louize Milne, and James S Williams (eds), *May 68: Rethinking France's Last Revolution* (Palgrave Macmillan 2011) 126.

[19] Michael Sibalis, 'The Gay Liberation Movement in France' in Gert Hekma and Alain Giami (eds), *Sexual Revolutions* (Palgrave Macmillan 2014) 190.

[20] David Paternotte, Gert Hekma, and Alain Giami, 'Pedophilia, Homosexuality and Gay and Lesbian Activism', *Sexual Revolutions* (Palgrave Macmillan 2014) 264.

[21] *Dudgeon* (n 6) [60].

[22] ibid [61].

[23] Michele Grigolo, 'Sexualities and the ECHR: Introducing the Universal Sexual Legal Subject' (2003) 14 European Journal of International Law 1023.

The narrow parameters of the ECtHR's decision in *Dudgeon* meant that when the Court came to address the prosecution and imprisonment of three men for engaging in group sadomasochistic sex in *Laskey, Jaggard and Brown v the United Kingdom* (1997),[24] it was able to find that no violation of Article 8 of the ECHR had occurred. This was so despite it accepting that the activities in question 'were consensual and ... conducted ... for no apparent purpose other than the achievement of sexual gratification',[25] as well as that they 'did not lead to any instances of infection, permanent injury or the need for medical attention'.[26] In *Laskey*, the ECtHR did not expressly ground its judgment in the idea of European consensus, instead finding the law permissible under the 'public health' exception contained in Article 8(2). However, Brems suggests that the ECtHR's decision to depart from *Dudgeon* was likely influenced by the fact that, in its view, 'the European consensus to decriminalize homosexual behaviour [did] not extend to sadomasochistic activities'.[27] This reading of *Laskey* is supported by a later case, *Pay v United Kingdom* (2008),[28] in which the ECtHR made reference to changing social attitudes towards the practice of sadomasochism.[29]

The ECtHR's use of European consensus as an interpretive method has also worked to exclude sexualities not captured by the LGBTI acronym from protection under the ECHR on a more explicit basis. This can be seen in *Stübing v Germany* (2012),[30] which concerned the criminalization of consensual adult incest in Germany. The applicant in *Stübing* had been convicted and sentenced to a term of imprisonment for conducting a consensual sexual relationship with his adult sister. He lodged a complaint with the ECtHR, in which, citing *Dudgeon*, he argued that Germany's criminal prohibition on sexual intercourse between siblings of the opposite sex violated his right to private life under Article 8. To determine whether this breach had occurred, the ECtHR undertook a comparative analysis. Although it found that there was no common European standard on whether consensual adult incest should be criminalized,[31] the ECtHR established that there

[24] App Nos 21627/93, 21628/93, and 21974/93, Eur Ct HR (19 February 1997).

[25] ibid [8].

[26] ibid.

[27] Eva Brems, 'The Margin of Appreciation Doctrine of the European Court of Human Rights: Accommodating Diversity within Europe' in David Forsythe and Patrice McMahon (eds), *Human Rights and Diversity: Area Studies Revisited* (University of Nebraska Press 2003) 81, 103. For further commentary on the ECtHR's case law relating to sadomasochism more generally, see Alexandra C Grolimund, 'Sadomasochism at the European Court of Human Rights: Rights to Sex and Drawing the Line between Privacy and Public Interest' in Tamsin Phillipa Paige and Claerwen O'Hara (eds), *Queer Encounters with International Law: Lives, Communities, Subjectivities* (Routledge 2024) 127; Giovanna Gilleri, *Sex, Gender and International Human Rights Law: Contesting Binaries* (Routledge 2023) Chapter 6.

[28] App No 32792/05, Eur Ct HR (16 September 2008).

[29] ibid 13. *Pay v United Kingdom* concerned the dismissal of an employee for his engagement in bondage, discipline, dominance and submission, and sadomasochism (BDSM). In that case, the ECtHR also found no violation of the ECHR.

[30] *Stübing* (n 11).

[31] ibid [61]. However, the ECtHR held that there was no trend towards decriminalization of incest either.

was 'a broad consensus . . . that sexual relationships between siblings are neither accepted by the legal order nor by society as a whole'.[32] On the basis of these mixed results, the ECtHR held 'that the domestic authorities enjoy[ed] a wide margin of appreciation in determining how to confront incestuous relationships between consenting adults'[33] and thus found no breach of Article 8.[34]

It is tempting to suggest that the distinction that arose between (respectable) gay and lesbian subjects and other sexual subalterns under the ECHR was simply the result of the ECtHR basing its decisions on the views and values of a majority of Europeans as part of its search for a European consensus. After all, this legal trend maps onto a larger socio-political trend in which gay and lesbian people have gradually become more accepted within Europe, whereas other sexual subalterns have not. In 1984, for example, Gayle Rubin argued that a 'sex hierarchy'[35] had developed in Western society, with the monogamous heterosexual at the top, gay and lesbian people somewhere in the middle depending on their level of promiscuity, and 'the most despised sexual castes',[36] including transsexuals, sex workers, sadomasochists, and those who engage in intra-familial and inter-generational sex, at the bottom.[37] That Rubin's sex hierarchy is mirrored in the ECtHR decisions in *Dudgeon*, *Laskey*, and *Stübing* could be taken to indicate that those decisions were a reflection of popular opinion. It is with this majoritarian understanding of European consensus in mind that scholars such as Benvenisti and Brauch are critical of the Court's interpretive method.[38] In their view, European consensus can work to make social acceptance a pre-condition of human rights, thereby exposing unpopular minority groups to the 'tyranny of the majority' and undermining the very purpose of human rights law.[39]

However, as we saw in the previous chapter, the ECtHR's use of European consensus in its decisions does not involve a popular referendum on who is entitled to human rights. Rather, it is a discretionary method of judicial interpretation, which is often based on a number of different factors, including legal trends, expert opinion, and social views.[40] Further, to the extent that the ECtHR does rely

[32] ibid.

[33] ibid.

[34] ibid [67].

[35] Gayle Rubin, 'Thinking Sex: Notes for a Radical Theory of the Politics of Sexuality' in Guy Parker and Peter Aggleton (eds), *Culture, Society and Sexuality: A Reader* (University College London Press 1999) 153 (originally published in 1984).

[36] ibid 151.

[37] In her overview of the 'sex hierarchy', Rubin does not explicitly list incest. However, elsewhere in her essay, she discusses taboos and criminal prohibitions against incest alongside her discussion of other marginalized sexualities, see ibid 151, 159.

[38] Eyal Benvenisti, 'Margin of Appreciation, Consensus, and Universal Standards' (1999) 31 New York University Journal of International Law and Politics 843, 851–52; Jeffrey A Brauch, 'The Dangerous Search for an Elusive Consensus: What the Supreme Court Should Learn from the European Court of Human Rights' (2009) 52 Howard Law Journal 277, 288–90.

[39] Benvenisti (n 38) 851–52; Brauch (n 38) 288–90.

[40] Helfer (n 16) 1056–57.

on European social views, its findings either tend to be inferred from the state of domestic law in Europe or constructed by the judges themselves. This can be seen in the ECtHR's decision in *Stübing*, in which its finding that there was 'a broad consensus' that sexual relationships between siblings are not accepted by European society was primarily based on the fact that none of the Member States allowed siblings to get married.[41] Yet, as Gonzalez-Salzberg points out, if the ECtHR had conflated sex and marriage in this way in the context of homosexuality, it would never have arrived at the decision that it did in *Dudgeon*, since no Member State at the time allowed for same-sex marriage.[42] As such, Gonzalez-Salzberg opines that 'perhaps, it was the Court's own revulsion towards the violation of the incest taboo which allowed it to reach the decision to validate the domestic criminalization.'[43]

Nevertheless, by claiming to ground its decisions in the views and values of 'Europe', the ECtHR helped to lend authority to the distinction that had emerged between (respectable) gay and lesbian people and other sexual subalterns. Take *Laskey*, for example. In the absence of similar statements to those that we find in *Dudgeon* about there being an increased 'understanding' and 'tolerance' in Europe in relation to the sexual activity in question, the ECtHR's judgment not only reinforced the idea that sadomasochistic homosexual sex was different to, and less worthy of protection than, non-sadomasochistic homosexual sex, but also implicitly projected that distinction back onto the standards of Europe, making it appear to be 'normal' and like European 'common sense'.

The authorizing effect of European consensus with respect to the distinction between (respectable) gay and lesbian people and other sexual subalterns is even more pronounced in *Stübing*, where the ECtHR actually used the language of 'consensus'. For although the term 'consensus' does not mean a 'complete agreement' in either the ECtHR's usage of the term or its everyday meaning, linguistically it leaves little room for dissent. Unlike the word 'majority', which has 'minority' as its counterpart, it is difficult to describe the space that exists between a 'general agreement' and a 'complete agreement'. This allows a discursive slippage to occur, whereby a claim of 'consensus' can begin to appear like a claim of 'unanimity', despite the two being conceptually distinct. Accordingly, when the ECtHR invokes the idea of a 'European consensus', it can appear to speak on behalf of everyone in European society. This can have a totalizing effect, whereby alternative viewpoints and ways of being are not simply marginalized but erased. It can push public discourses from a conception of 'us and them' to an idea of 'everyone' in which the 'other' no longer exists.

[41] *Stübing* (n 11) [61].
[42] Damian A Gonzalez-Salzberg, *Sexuality and Transsexuality under the European Convention on Human Rights: A Queer Reading of Human Rights Law* (Hart Publishing 2019) 77.
[43] ibid.

This effect can be illuminated through a reading of the ECtHR's decision in *Stübing* through the lens of Rancière's concept of the 'surplus subjects'. For Rancière, 'surplus subjects' are those who are 'uncounted' within a particular society; 'the part of those who have no part'.[44] They exist outside of what he calls the 'police order', which is 'the allocation of ways of doing, ways of being, ways of saying'.[45] In other words, the 'surplus subjects' are those who are invisible or unsayable within a particular society; they are the ones that '*are not*'.[46] Rancière does not apply the concept of 'surplus subjects' to sexual subalterns, instead using 'the poor of ancient times, the third estate, the modern proletariat'[47] as examples. However, Chambers argues that Rancière's notion of the 'surplus subjects' resonates with Judith Butler's concept of 'unintelligibility',[48] which they apply in the context of sexual and gender norms.[49] According to Butler, to be unintelligible is to exist so far beyond the regimes of sexual and gender normativity that you are rendered 'illegible',[50] such that even when you speak you 'find that your language is hollow, [and] . . . no recognition is forthcoming'.[51]

The practitioner of incest has long dwelled amongst the uncounted or unintelligible. As Butler writes, incest is widely considered to be 'a sexual irregularity that is terrifying, repulsive, unthinkable'.[52] In his submissions to the ECtHR, the applicant in *Stübing* seemed to acknowledge that his relationship with his adult sister could not be visible or sayable, stating that they 'had constantly avoided drawing public attention to themselves'[53] and explaining that their relationship had only come into 'the public eye' because welfare officers had reported the incidents.[54] In other words, he suggested that, had he not become entangled in the legal system, his intention was to remain unnoticed and uncounted within European society. And yet, via a series of legal events, and a sense of injustice, the applicant had been propelled onto the fringes of visibility and now stood before the ECtHR claiming his rights.

According to Rancière, such an assertion of rights on the part of the uncounted can be precisely what creates a rupture in the police order, allowing politics to break through. By acting as subjects with rights, surplus subjects can stage what

[44] Jacques Rancière, *Dissensus: On Politics and Aesthetics* (Steven Concoran tr, Continuum International Publishing Group 2010) 70.
[45] Jacques Rancière, *Disagreement: Politics and Philosophy* (Julie Rose tr, University of Minnesota Press 1999) 29.
[46] ibid 26.
[47] ibid 9.
[48] Judith Butler, *Undoing Gender* (Routledge 2004).
[49] Samuel A Chambers, 'A Queer Politics of the Democratic Miscount' (2009) 8 Borderlands 3–4.
[50] Butler (n 48) 27.
[51] ibid 30.
[52] ibid 157.
[53] *Stübing* (n 11) [41].
[54] Patrick Stübing, 'Application No. 43547/08: Stübing vs Federal Republic of Germany', Submission in *Stübing v Germany*, 14 January 2011, 13 (on file with author).

Rancière calls a 'dissensus',[55] whereby they bring about '[t]he contradiction of two worlds in a single world: the world where they are and the world where they are not'.[56] This dissensus can cut through the police order by inserting a division into society's '"common sense": a dispute over what is given and about the frame within which we see something as given'.[57]

On Rancière's account, the police order will attempt to prevent a dissensus from erupting by reasserting 'that there is but a single reality'.[58] This is a process that he calls 'consensus':

> Consensus means much more than the reasonable idea and practice of settling political conflicts by forms of negotiation and agreement . . . It means the attempt to get rid of politics by ousting the surplus subjects . . . Consensus means closing the spaces of dissensus by plugging the intervals and patching over the possible gaps between appearance and reality or law and fact.[59]

In *Stübing*, the ECtHR's claim of European consensus operated in a similar way to Rancière's understanding of 'consensus'. At the moment that the applicant was stepping into the realm of visibility and sayability by asserting his rights under the ECHR, the ECtHR used the idea of a European consensus to close the sexual boundaries of European society once more. This can be seen in the ECtHR's assertion that there existed 'a *broad consensus* . . . that sexual relationships between siblings are neither accepted by the legal order nor by *society as a whole*'.[60] As noted above, this finding was largely based on the lack of availability of marriage for adult siblings throughout Europe. The ECtHR also provided a breakdown of the Member States' different legal positions on incest, thereby demonstrating that there was in fact no complete agreement on the matter. Nevertheless, through its references to 'broad consensus' and 'society as a whole', the ECtHR helped to erase practitioners of incest from European life altogether. For they were not part of the 'everyone' on whose behalf this 'broad consensus' seemingly spoke. And there is no space for them within a society that, in their absence, could be designated as 'whole'.

The impact of the ECtHR's consensus claim in *Stübing* can perhaps be seen in the illegibility of the incest practitioner following that decision.[61] In the aftermath of the case, few commentators came to defend the rights of the incestuous

[55] Rancière (n 44) 69.
[56] Rancière (n 45) 27.
[57] Rancière (n 44) 69.
[58] Jacques Rancière, *Chronicles of Consensual Times* (Steven Corcoran tr, Continuum International Publishing Group 2010) ix.
[59] Rancière (n 44) 71–72.
[60] *Stübing* (n 11) [61] [emphasis added].
[61] For a discussion of the illegibility of sexual subalterns, see Ratna Kapur, *Gender, Alterity and Human Rights: Freedom in a Fishbowl* (Edward Elgar Publishing 2018) 55–79.

family.[62] This was so despite the applicant having been imprisoned on multiple occasions for his consensual relationship with his sister and evidence that he had been physically attacked while in detention.[63] In several case commentaries, the author also makes reference to something called the 'yuck factor'—a feeling that one supposedly experiences when thinking about incest.[64] This again recalls Rancière's writing on the 'surplus subjects', whom he contends are doomed to be cast as animals who cannot speak but instead only make noises 'expressing pleasure or pain'.[65] In these case commentaries, we see practitioners of incest reduced to an animal-like existence in which they are a cause of human repulsion, rather than equals with their own views and voices. It is arguable that the dismissive, if not outright hostile, tone of these commentaries was influenced by the force of the ECtHR's consensus claim in *Stübing*, which not only found the incest-practising 'other' to be lacking in rights, but also authorized the idea that they belonged outside of European society altogether. As such, for sexual subalterns who do not fall neatly into the LGBTI acronym, the ECtHR's use of European consensus has been far from inclusionary and progressive. Rather, it has been a cause of their legal exclusion from the ECHR and a contributing factor in their continued marginalization within, and even discursive erasure from, the idea of 'Europe' more broadly.

5.4 The Regulation of Sexualities Within the European Consensus

In addition to authorizing sexual discourses that exclude and erase some sexual subalterns, the ECtHR's claims of European consensus have operated as a regulatory device over those sexualities within its sphere of inclusion. In particular, its claims of consensus have functioned to regulate and discipline modes of same-sex desire and family-making by lending authority to narrow ideas about what constitutes 'sexual orientation' or 'the family'. Legal and human rights discourses can have a constitutive and normative effect without engaging in consensus claims.

[62] Compared to the number of commentaries that appear in response to the Court's decisions on LGB rights, only a few were generated by its judgment in *Stübing*. See Marko Milanovic, 'Incest in the European Court' (*EJIL: Talk!*, 15 April 2012) <https://www.ejiltalk.org/incest-in-the-european-court/>; Daniel Sokol, 'What's So Wrong with Incest? The Case of Stübing v Germany' (*UK Human Rights Blog*, 15 April 2012) <https://ukhumanrightsblog.com/2012/04/15/whats-so-wrong-with-incest-the-case-of-stubing-v-germany/>; JR Spencer, 'Incest and Article 8 of the European Convention on Human Rights' (2013) 72 Cambridge Law Journal 5; see eg Karen Jane Dyer, 'The Need to Re-Evaluate Incest in the Age of Assisted Reproductive Techniques: Stübing v Germany' (2012) 42 Family Law 1144; James A Roffee, 'No Consensus on Incest? Criminalization and Compatibility with the European Convention on Human Rights' (2014) 14 Human Rights Law Review 541. While some of these pieces take issue with the Court's reasoning in *Stübing*, none of them expressly argue that it came to the wrong decision.

[63] *Stübing* (n 11) [11].

[64] See, eg, Milanovic (n 62); Sokol (n 62); Spencer (n 62).

[65] Rancière (n 45) 22.

Indeed, some queer legal theorists have shown that the ECtHR's case law on sexuality rights has functioned to construct a narrowly defined 'homosexual legal subject' through legal technologies other than European consensus.[66] In this section, I argue that through its claims of European consensus, the ECtHR has lent additional force to such discourses. This is due not only to the totalizing effect that a consensus claim can have by appearing to speak on behalf of 'everyone', but also the ECtHR's use of different sources of consensus—legal, public, and expert. By combining comparative legal reasoning with ideas of scientific and social consensus, I assert that the ECtHR's consensus claims take on a greater appearance of 'truth'.

In making this argument, I am drawing on Foucault's account of modern power, in which law and disciplines, such as science, medicine, and sociology, come together to form a 'common matrix'[67] through which knowledges and truths are then produced.[68] This view of Foucault's writings is not universally accepted. Hunt and Wickham, for example, contend that Foucault 'expels' law from modern power relations, supplanting it with disciplinary power instead.[69] However, I agree with Golder and Fitzpatrick's reading of Foucault, in which they see law and disciplinary power as having an interdependent relationship.[70] Pointing to Foucault's references to the 'scientifico-juridical complex', 'epistemological-juridical formation', and 'juridico-anthropological logic',[71] Golder and Fizpatrick argue that, in Foucault's account of modernity, law comes to exist in a 'perpetual hyphenation, reliant in some measure upon "the scientific", "the epistemological", and "the anthropological" to give it some purchase'.[72] This tendency can be observed in the ECtHR's claims of European consensus, which lend authority to the sexual constructions it (re)produces through its creation of a combined socio-scientifico-legal discourse.

In the following two subsections, I explore how the Strasbourg organs' use of European consensus has authorized ideas and assumptions that regulate sexual alterity through two examples: (1) the construction of 'the homosexual' in cases relating to the age of consent and (2) the construction of 'the same-sex family' in cases concerning relationship and adoption rights. I trace how the Strasbourg organs' understanding of these concepts changed over time through their use of European consensus as a method of interpretation, eventually leading to the recognition of new rights for LGBTI people. Despite these changes, I illustrate how

[66] See, eg, Grigolo (n 23); Gonzalez-Salzberg (n 42).

[67] Michel Foucault, *Discipline and Punish: The Birth of the Prison* (Alan Sheridan tr, Penguin 1991) 23.

[68] Michel Foucault, *The History of Sexuality Vol 1: An Introduction* (Robert Hurley tr, Pantheon 1980); Foucault (n 67).

[69] Alan Hunt and Gary Wickham, *Foucault and Law: Towards a Sociology of Law as Governance* (Pluto Press 1994).

[70] Ben Golder and Peter Fitzpatrick, *Foucault's Law* (Routledge-Cavendish 2009).

[71] Foucault (n 67) 19–28.

[72] Golder and Fitzpatrick (n 70) 60.

the Strasbourg organs' claims of consensus have continued to constrain the queer subject and uphold the heteronormative order through the discourses they have helped to authorize.

5.4.1 Constructing 'The Homosexual'

In the mid-1970s, prior to the ECtHR's 1981 decision in *Dudgeon*, the European Commission of Human Rights used comparative reasoning to reject a number of applications challenging laws that provided for a higher age of consent for male homosexual relations as compared with heterosexual and female homosexual relations. In these decisions, the Commission's use of comparative reasoning (re)produced a particular ontological understanding of 'the homosexual male', in which he was constructed as a danger to young people.[73] This can be seen in *X v Federal Republic of Germany* (1975),[74] in which the applicant argued that the higher age of consent for homosexual sex under Article 175 of the German Criminal Code violated his right to private life under Article 8 and right to non-discrimination under Article 14 of the ECHR. On the basis of comparative reasoning, the Commission found the application to be manifestly ill-founded and thus inadmissible.

In relation to Article 8, the Commission held that the purpose underlying West Germany's law—'to prevent homosexual acts with adults having an unfortunate influence on the development of heterosexual tendencies in minors'[75]—was justified under the exception of 'protecting the rights of others' in Article 8(2). In arriving at this conclusion, the Commission relied on the existence of a common European standard in favour of the protection of children, noting that 'the need to protect the rights of children and adolescents . . . [was] broadly admitted in a large number of member states'.[76] While the Commission acknowledged that the extent of the risk posed to adolescents by exposure to homosexuality remained 'a subject of controversy',[77] it held that the Member States enjoyed some discretion as to the specificities of their law in this area. This was due to a *lack* of a common European standard with respect to the precise age of consent for male homosexual relations, whereby '[s]ome states [had] fixed [the homosexual age of consent] at 16 and others at 21'.[78]

With respect to the applicant's complaint regarding the right to non-discrimination under Article 14, the Commission held that the difference in treatment between male and female homosexual relations was reasonable because

[73] Johnson (n 1) 36.
[74] App No 5935/72, Eur Commn HR (30 September 1975).
[75] ibid 54.
[76] ibid 55.
[77] ibid 54.
[78] ibid 55.

the West German government's assertion that 'masculine homosexuality' posed a 'specific social danger'[79] was supported by 'various concording analyses . . . of psychologists, sociologists and specialists in social protection'.[80] In particular, the Commission was influenced by a number of studies which found that 'masculine homosexuals often constitute[d] a distinct socio-cultural group with a clear tendency to proselytise adolescents'.[81]

In this case, we see the Commission's use of comparative reasoning import an understanding of homosexual men as 'a class of human beings who share distinctive traits'.[82] They were constructed as 'sexual predators' with a propensity to prey on adolescents.[83] In this regard, 'the male homosexual' was understood not merely as an 'aberrant' but rather as a 'species',[84] with specific behavioural tendencies. At the same time, however, the understanding of sexuality reproduced in this case allowed for a certain level of fluidity by maintaining that adolescents were vulnerable to 'sexual corruption' through exposure to homosexual sex.

In addition to importing these sexual constructions, the Commission's use of comparative analysis lent authority to them. This was due to the 'multi-layered'[85] nature of the Commission's analysis, whereby it not only considered legal and social standards in Europe, but also engaged with expert studies provided by the government of West Germany. While the Commission did not frame these studies as 'expert consensus', its use of the term 'concording analyses' and failure to mention any alternative expert account gave its reliance on them the semblance of an expert consensus claim. In this regard, this case may be seen as an early example of the Commission using the idea of expert consensus to construct sexuality through a scientific account, or, to use Foucault's terminology, a '*scientia sexualis*'[86]—a technique that would become more pronounced in later cases. By combining claims of social and legal consensus with an appeal to expertise, the Commission was able to twist law and disciplinary knowledge into a single web of intelligibility. This helped to authorize its construction of the homosexual male by allowing it to take on a greater appearance of 'truth'.

More than two decades later, in *Sutherland v United Kingdom* (1997),[87] the Commission recognized a right to an equal age of consent for male homosexual relations. This was largely due to 'major changes . . . [having taken place] in professional opinions—particularly in the medical profession'[88] regarding the age at

[79] ibid 56.
[80] ibid.
[81] ibid.
[82] Johnson (n 1) 36.
[83] ibid.
[84] Foucault (n 68) 43.
[85] Eszter Polgari, 'European Consensus: A Conservative and a Dynamic Force in European Human Rights Jurisprudence' (2018) 12 Vienna Journal on International Constitutional Law 59, 72.
[86] Foucault (n 68) Pt 3.
[87] App No 25186/94, Eur Comm'n HR (1 July 1997).
[88] ibid [59].

which sexual orientation becomes 'fixed'. The Commission found that the medical community now believed that 'sexual orientation was usually established before the age of puberty in both boys and girls' and 'fixed by the age of 18'.[89] As such, there was little point in trying to protect adolescents from exposure to homosexual sex. In addition, the Commission found that there was a new legal consensus in Europe whereby 'equality of treatment in respect of the age of consent [was] now recognized by the great majority of Member States'.[90] In light of this medico-legal consensus, the Commission held that there was no longer any 'reasonable and objective justification for maintaining a different age of consent for homosexual and heterosexual acts'.[91] It therefore found that the impugned law violated the right to private life under Article 8 of the ECHR, in conjunction with the right to non-discrimination basis of 'sexual orientation' under Article 14.

The ECtHR later confirmed this decision in the case of *S.L. v Austria* (2003),[92] which concerned Austria's higher age of consent for male homosexual relations. In *S.L.*, the ECtHR found that there was an 'ever growing European consensus to apply equal ages of consent for heterosexual, lesbian and homosexual relations'[93] and that 'the vast majority of experts . . . [now believed] that sexual orientation was in most cases established before the age of puberty'.[94] Consequently, it agreed with the Commission that a different age of consent for male homosexual relations violated the right to respect for private life under Article 8, together with the right to non-discrimination under Article 14 of the ECHR.

In *Sutherland* and *SL.*, the Strasbourg organs' claims of European consensus introduced a strong essentialist narrative into European human rights law, in which sexual orientation was understood as an immutable characteristic that becomes 'fixed' at a certain age. In both cases, this narrative was again given force through the Strasbourg organs' combination of legal and expert consensus, enabling law and disciplinary power to fuse and reinforce one another. In *S.L.*, it was also bolstered by the ECtHR's language of consensus, in which it referred to 'ever growing European consensus' and 'the vast majority of experts', imbuing its account of sexuality with a sense of pervasiveness. Indeed, the essentialist ontology introduced by these decisions now enjoys such authority in Strasbourg case law that it seems only an expert account to the contrary could displace it. In *Bayev and Others v Russia* (2017),[95] for example, the ECtHR stated that Russia would need to produce 'science-based evidence that one's sexual orientation or identity is

[89] ibid.
[90] ibid [60].
[91] ibid [64].
[92] *SL* (n 9).
[93] ibid [42].
[94] ibid [43].
[95] App nos 67667/09, 44092/12, and 56717/12, Eur Ct HR (13 November 2017).

susceptible to change under external influence'[96] if it were to establish that its ban on 'homosexual propaganda' were reasonable.

The authority of the essentialist narrative produced in *Sutherland* also seems to have had what Judith Butler calls a 'performative effect'[97] on applicants. Following the Commission's decision in *Sutherland,* the applicant in *S.L.* articulated his sexual orientation as a stable characteristic, telling the ECtHR that '[a]t the age of fifteen he was *sure* of his homosexuality'.[98] This effectively replicated the applicant's submission in *Sutherland* that, from his early teenage years, he had 'felt *sure* that his sexual orientation was homosexual'.[99] While essentialist narratives had been deployed by applicants in earlier cases,[100] the striking similarity between these two accounts suggests that the applicant in *S.L.* may have been influenced by the applicant's success in *Sutherland* and, in particular, the validation of his essentialist narrative through the Commission's expert consensus claim. This is not to say that he, or subsequent applicants using similar sexual accounts, necessarily deployed essentialism as a conscious strategy. Rather, as Johnson, following Butler, argues, they may have simply reoriented their speech to make their claims intelligible in this new discursive landscape.[101]

The turn to essentialism on the part of both the Strasbourg organs and queer applicants no doubt played an important role in bringing an end to Europe's unequal consent laws, as well as other discriminatory laws later down the track. And yet, it has also operated to limit the very many dimensions along which sexuality may be expressed.[102] This is because, by constructing 'sexual orientation' as an unchangeable predisposition towards either heterosexuality or homosexuality, the Strasbourg organs' decisions in *Sutherland* and *S.L.* worked to erase fluid and non-binary experiences of sexuality, as well as sexualities that are not defined by the 'gender object of choice'.[103] In doing so, these decisions may have paved the way for the dismissive approach taken by the Strasbourg organs towards sexualities that do not fit neatly into the homosexual/heterosexual binary,[104] as we saw earlier with regard to sadomasochism and incest. Furthermore, rather than breaking down the heteronormative social order, the essentialism that now pervades Strasbourg case law arguably helps to uphold and sustain it. I am using the term 'heteronormative'

[96] ibid [78].

[97] Judith Butler, *Notes Toward a Performative Theory of Assembly* (Harvard University Press 2015) 61.

[98] *S.L.* (n 9) [9] [emphasis added].

[99] *Sutherland* (n 87) [17] [emphasis added].

[100] See, eg, *Dudgeon v United Kingdom* (n 6); *Norris v Ireland*, App No 10581/83, Eur Ct HR (26 October 1988).

[101] Johnson (n 3) 49, citing Judith Butler, *Excitable Speech: A Politics of the Performative* (Routledge 1997).

[102] Eve Kosofsky Sedgwick, *Epistemology of the Closet* (1st edn, University of California Press 2008) 8.

[103] ibid.

[104] Gonzalez-Salzberg (n 42) 92.

here to refer a worldview which promotes heterosexuality as the normal or preferred sexual orientation. According to Grigolo, the essentialist perspective can reinforce heteronormativity by naturalizing the binary within which the 'other' (i.e. the homosexual) is defined.[105] This, in turn, works to confirm and stabilize the position of the dominant category (i.e. the heterosexual).[106]

This overall outcome went against what some queer activists had hoped for from the age of consent debates in Europe. In 1994, for example, Peter Tatchell—a member of the queer activist group OutRage![107]—wrote an opinion piece in the British newspaper *The Independent* arguing that '[t]he age of consent debate [was] largely about the extent to which our society is prepared officially to sanction sexual diversity'.[108] He saw the UK's unequal consent law as 'symptomatic of a wider social homophobia which rejects erotic pluralism and demands conformity to exclusive heterosexuality' and called for a 'change from a hetero-centric culture to a sexually pluralistic one' so that '[e]veryone [could] feel free to express their queer desires'.[109] In contrast, the Strasbourg organs' claims of European consensus in *Sutherland* and *S.L.* worked to regulate sexual difference and reinforce the dominant sexual order, notwithstanding the role they ultimately played in expanding the rights of LGBTI subjects.

5.4.2 Constructing 'the Same-Sex Family'

The Strasbourg organs' claims of European consensus have also authorized normative ideas about relationships and family, which have similarly functioned to regulate alterity. Originally, this came in the form of the ECtHR using the idea of European consensus to maintain a strictly heterosexual definition of 'family'. This can be seen in *Mata Estevez v Spain* (2001),[110] which concerned the refusal to grant a survivor's pension to the applicant following the death of his male partner on the grounds that they had not been married. At that time, marriage was not available for same-sex partners in Spain. The applicant complained, inter alia, that this amounted to discriminatory treatment infringing his right to family life and thus

[105] Grigolo (n 23) 1025.
[106] ibid.
[107] For more on this group and its activism around the UK's age of consent laws in the 1990s, see Ian Lucas, *OutRage! An Oral History* (Cassell 1998). On the age of consent debate in the UK more generally, see Matthew Waites, *The Age of Consent: Young People, Sexuality and Citizenship* (Palgrave Macmillan 2005).
[108] Peter Tatchell, 'A Gayer Place than You Think: If Homosexuals Were Afforded Equal Rights, Bizexuality Would Be the Norm in Britain, Argues Peter Tatchell' *Independent* (24 January 1994) <https://www.independent.co.uk/voices/a-gayer-place-than-you-think-if-homosexuals-were-afforded-equal-rights-bizexuality-would-be-the-norm-in-britain-argues-peter-tatchell-1402224.html?r=67833>.
[109] ibid.
[110] App No 56501/00, Eur Ct HR (10 May 2001).

constituted a breach of Article 8, taken together with Article 14 of the ECHR. In response, the ECtHR relied on a lack of European consensus to find that same-sex couples did not come within the scope of 'family life' under Article 8. It said:

> despite the growing tendency in a number of European States towards the legal and judicial recognition of stable *de facto* partnerships between homosexuals, this is, given the existence of little common ground between the Contracting States, an area in which they still enjoy a wide margin of appreciation . . . Accordingly, the applicant's relationship with his late partner does not fall within Article 8 in so far as that provision protects the right to respect for family life.[111]

The ECtHR thus found this aspect of his application to be inadmissible. At around the same time, the ECtHR also used a lack of European consensus to cast doubt on 'the homosexual family' in the context of parenting. In *Fretté v France* (2002),[112] which concerned the denial to a single gay man of an authorization to adopt a child, the ECtHR held there was no European consensus on adoption by homosexual people across all three sources of consensus. In relation to legal and public consensus, the ECtHR found that '[a]lthough most of the Contracting States do not expressly prohibit homosexuals from adopting where single persons may adopt, it is not possible to find in the legal and social orders of the Contracting States uniform principles on these social issues'.[113] With regard to expert consensus, the ECtHR held that 'the scientific community . . . [was] divided over the possible consequences of a child being adopted by one or more homosexual parent'.[114] On the basis of this broad lack of European consensus, the ECtHR afforded France a wide margin of appreciation and thus found no violation of Article 8, together with Article 14 of the ECHR.

In both *Mata Estevez* and *Fretté*, the authorizing work of the ECtHR's claims of European consensus lay in the absence of consensus. Narrow ideas about 'the family' were authorized through a lack of legal and/or scientific certainty, which enabled the ECtHR to default to a heterosexual worldview. Stone argues that this was achieved in *Fretté* through the ECtHR's implicit reliance on the 'precautionary principle', which holds that precautionary measures should be employed when there is scientific uncertainty about whether a particular activity is harmful.[115] On this reading, the ECtHR was able to draw on the suggestion of harm to children to give weight to a heteronormative understanding of parenting, despite the lack of

111 ibid 4.
112 App No 36515/97, Eur Ct HR (26 February 2002).
113 ibid [41].
114 ibid [42].
115 Thomas Willoughby Stone, 'Margin of Appreciation Gone Awry: The European Court of Human Rights' Implicit Use of the Precautionary Principle in Frette v. France to Backtrack on Protection from Discrimination on the Basis of Sexual Orientation' (2003) 3 Connecticut Public Interest Law Journal 271.

consensus on the matter. Moreover, by grounding this possibility of harm in the views of the 'scientific community', the ECtHR imbued this perspective on parenting with an air of objectivity.

By the late 2000s, the ECtHR's approach towards the notion of 'family' had begun to change. In *EB v France* (2008),[116] for example, the ECtHR reversed its position with respect to individual gay and lesbian adoption rights. However, the ECtHR did not use the idea of a European consensus in that case—an inconsistent move for which it has been criticized.[117] Two years later, in *Schalk and Kopf v Austria* (2010),[118] the ECtHR also redefined 'family life' under Article 8 of the ECHR, and this time it did so on the basis of a European consensus.[119] *Schalk* concerned an application challenging the lack of same-sex marriage or other form of same-sex relationship recognition in Austria. In that case, the ECtHR held that due to a 'rapid evolution of social attitudes towards same-sex couples',[120] it now considered 'a *cohabiting* same-sex couple living in a *stable de facto partnership*'[121] to constitute 'family' within the meaning of Article 8. Although the ECtHR later dropped the requirement of 'cohabitation' in *Valliantos and Others v Greece* (2013),[122] the definition of 'family life' produced in *Schalk* otherwise persists in European human rights law today insofar as it is limited to same-sex couples in a 'stable committed relationship'.[123]

A number of commentators have described the Court's new definition of 'family' in *Schalk* as a 'victory' for LGBTI rights,[124] with some even suggesting it signalled a move away from heteronormativity.[125] However, like the account of sexuality produced in *Sutherland* and *S.L.*, the ECtHR's construction of 'family' in *Schalk* still works to uphold the heteronormative order. This is because heteronormativity is an 'ideological composite',[126] which asserts 'normal' and 'valid' ways

[116] App No 43546/02, Eur Ct HR (22 January 2008).

[117] See, eg, Johnson (n 1) 79; Junko Nozawa, 'Drawing the Line: Same-Sex Adoption and the Jurisprudence of the ECtHR on the Application of the European Consensus Standard under Article 14' (2013) 29 Merkourios Utrecht Journal of International and European Law 66; Kathleen A Doty, 'From Fretté to E.B: The European Court of Human Rights on Gay and Lesbian Adoption' (2009) 18 Law & Sexuality 121.

[118] App No 30141/04, Eur Ct HR (24 June 2010).

[119] Recall that the Court uses European to define autonomous concepts in the ECHR, such as 'family life'.

[120] *Schalk* (n 118) [93].

[121] ibid [94] [emphasis added].

[122] App Nos 29381/09 and 32684/09, Eur Ct HR (7 November 2013).

[123] *Oliari and Others v Italy* (n 10) [65], [169].

[124] See, eg, Jens M Scherpe, 'Same-Sex Couples Have Family Life' (2010) 69 Cambridge Law Journal 463, 464.

[125] Antonis Paschalides & Co LLC, '"New Families"? The Case of Schalk and Kopf v Austria on Same-Sex Unions and the Current Legal Situation of Cyprus' (30 January 2013) <https://www.paschalides.com/articles/family-law/124-new-families-the-case-of-schalk-and-kopf-v-austria-on-same-sex-unions-and-the-current-legal-situation-of-cyprus>.

[126] Ramona Faith Oswald, Libby Balter Blume, and Stephen R Marks, 'Decentering Heteronormativity: A Proposal for Family Studies' in Vern L Bengtson and others (eds), *Sourcebook of Family Theories and Methods: An Interactive Approach* (Thousand Oaks 2005) 144.

of being which extend beyond heterosexuality alone, but which have heterosexuality at their core, including adherence to the model of the monogamous nuclear family. Through its emphasis on stability, fidelity, and domesticity, the ECtHR's definition of 'family' lent authority to values aligned with heteronormativity, notwithstanding its inclusion of same-sex couples. While the ECtHR did not invoke expertise in this case, it lent weight to these values through its blanket reference to European 'social attitudes', which made it appear as if everyone or almost everyone in Europe understood the family through this lens.

The changed meaning of 'family' in *Schalk* must also be read alongside the overall outcome of that case, in which the ECtHR held that the ECHR did not protect a right to same-sex marriage or other form of relationship recognition. This was largely due to a lack of legal consensus on both matters. In relation to marriage, the ECtHR found that there was no European consensus because '[a]t present no more than six out of forty-seven Convention States allow same-sex marriage'.[127] With respect to other forms of recognition, the ECtHR held that while there was an 'emerging European consensus towards legal recognition of same-sex couples', there was 'not yet a majority of States providing for [such] . . . recognition'.[128] Consequently, the ECtHR cast the matter as 'one of evolving rights with no established consensus, where States . . . enjoy a margin of appreciation'.[129] Since its judgment in *Schalk*, the ECtHR has gone on to recognize a right to legal recognition for same-sex couples in *Oliari and Others v Italy* (2015) due to 'a thin majority of CoE States . . . [having] legislated in favour of such recognition'.[130] However, the ECtHR has maintained that the right to marry under Article 12 does not apply to same-sex couples, partly because of a continued lack of European consensus.[131]

Through its decision in *Schalk*, and its subsequent case law, the ECtHR helped to cultivate a politics of 'homonormativity'.[132] Lisa Duggan coins the term 'homonormativity' to describe 'a politics that does not contest dominant heteronormative assumptions and institutions, but upholds and sustains them, while promising the possibility of a . . .depoliticized gay culture anchored in domesticity and consumption'.[133] By referring to 'evolving rights' and an 'emerging consensus' in cases such as *Schalk* and *Oliari*, the ECtHR created a sense of forward momentum, making it seem as if same-sex relationship recognition, and ultimately same-sex marriage, were just around the corner. This, in turn, appears to have encouraged queer applicants to focus their energy on pursuing these rights, sometimes to the detriment of other political causes. Through this process, the

[127] *Schalk* (n 118) [58].
[128] ibid [105].
[129] ibid.
[130] *Oliari and Others v Italy* (n 10) [178].
[131] ibid [192]; *Chapin and Charpentier v France* (n 12) [36].
[132] Lisa Duggan, *The Twilight of Equality? Neoliberalism, Cultural Politics, and the Attack on Democracy* (Beacon Press 2003).
[133] ibid 50.

European queer community has become further and further aligned with heteronormative values, or at least the ECtHR has interpreted their behaviour to indicate as much. In *Bayev and Others v Russia* (2017), the ECtHR observed that 'far from being opposed to family values—many persons belonging to sexual minorities manifest allegiance to the institutions of marriage, parenthood and adoption, as evidenced by the steady flow of applications to the Court from members of the LGBT community who wish to have access to them'.[134]

And yet, through its claim to base its decisions on a European consensus, the ECtHR has continued to withhold the right to marriage from LGBTI people. In other words, it has encouraged same-sex couples to perform marriage-like relationships to qualify as 'family' and acquire certain relationship rights, while simultaneously preserving heterosexual privilege under the ECHR by excluding them from the right to marriage itself.[135] As such, despite the ECtHR's understanding of 'family' having changed over time through its use of European consensus, it continues to uphold the dominant sexual order.

5.5 European Consensus and European Identity

The ECtHR's claims of European consensus have also played a role in shaping the identity of Europe itself. More specifically, through its use of European consensus in sexuality-related cases, the ECtHR has lent authority to an idea of Europe as inherently 'gay-friendly'. This reflexive aspect of European consensus has likely resulted in some benefits for the queer community. However, the sense of ownership that it has fostered over LGBTI rights can also lead to queer lives being co-opted for other political agendas. Indeed, as I show in this section, Europe's 'gay-friendly' identity has, on occasion, resulted in LGBTI people being instrumentalized in the promotion of Europe's moral and cultural superiority vis-à-vis the rest of the world.

Francesca Ammaturo argues that, in Europe, over 'the last four decades[,] there has been the emergence of a fundamentally (neo)liberal consensus on the necessity of ensuring equal rights and protection . . . to LGBTQI persons'.[136] She contends that this has led to the development of 'a European identity [of] being intrinsically "queer-friendly"',[137] built upon an idea of European sexual exceptionalism. Ammaturo points to various examples in support of this, including a statement issued by the President of the European Council declaring that protection against 'discrimination on the basis of gender and sexual orientation . . . is something that *distinguishes* Europe from many other parts of the world'.[138] While Ammaturo does

[134] *Bayev* (n 95) [67].
[135] Ammaturo (n 13) 4–5.
[136] Francesca Romana Ammaturo, *European Sexual Citizenship: Human Rights, Bodies and Identities* (Palgrave Macmillan 2017) 28.
[137] ibid 4.
[138] Van Rompuy quoted in ibid 58 [emphasis added].

not specifically connect this new European 'consensus' and the sense of regional identity that it has produced to the ECtHR's interpretive method of 'European consensus', she does link it to the ECtHR's judgments.[139] In particular, Ammaturo argues that the ECtHR, as the self-proclaimed 'conscience of Europe', has played an important role in fostering a notion of 'European citizenship' built upon a respect for LGBTI rights.[140]

In my argument, however, the ECtHR's claims of European consensus have played an important role in the construction of this regional identity. This is because, in the majority of its decisions recognizing new sexuality and relationship rights for LGBTI people, the ECtHR has directly attributed this outcome to the work of 'Europe' through its concept of European consensus—whether it be the work of European social attitudes, or the work of European lawmakers and scientists. As such, with each decision, the ECtHR provides Europe with a reflection of itself as the creator of LGBTI rights, thereby inscribing these rights into Europe's very identity. In more recent decisions, the ECtHR has also begun weaving together its various findings of European consensus in sexuality-related cases to form one overarching European consensus in support of LGBTI rights. In doing so, the ECtHR has helped to frame its recognition of various LGBTI rights as a tale of European character development, rather than as separate legal events.

This can be seen in *Alekseyev v Russia* (2010),[141] in which the ECtHR held that a ban on gay pride marches in Moscow violated the right to freedom of assembly under Article 11 of the ECHR, taken together with the right to non-discrimination under Article 14. In response to the Russian government's argument that 'there was no consensus . . . as to the extent to which homosexuality was accepted in each country',[142] the ECtHR compiled decades of its case law to demonstrate the existence of a strong European consensus in favour of LGBTI rights. While the ECtHR acknowledged that there remained some LGBTI-related issues on which 'no European consensus had been reached',[143] it stated that:

> There [was] ample case-law reflecting a long-standing European consensus on such matters as abolition of criminal liability for homosexual relations between adults[,] . . . homosexuals' access to service in the armed forces[,] . . . the granting of parental rights[,] . . . equality in tax matters and the right to succeed to the deceased partner's tenancy[;] . . . more recent examples include equal ages of consent under criminal law for heterosexual and homosexual acts.[144]

[139] ibid 4.
[140] ibid 64.
[141] App Nos 4916/07, 25924/08, and 14599/09, Eur Ct HR (21 October 2010).
[142] ibid [61].
[143] ibid [83].
[144] ibid.

By linking together its different findings of European consensus over the years, the ECtHR was able to project a single 'gay-friendly' identity onto Europe. Later in the case, the ECtHR lent further authority to this idea through its claim of European consensus in relation to the specific issue of gay pride marches. On this point, the ECtHR held that '[t]here [was] no ambiguity about the other member States' recognition of the right of individuals to openly identify themselves as gay, lesbian or any other sexual minority, and to promote their rights and freedoms'.[145] This reference to there being 'no ambiguity' about other Member States' position on LGBTI rights not only reinforced the idea that Europe is inherently 'gay-friendly', but also cast doubt on the 'Europeanness' of any Member State that would dare ban a gay pride march—in this case, Russia.

In *Alekseyev*, we thus catch a glimpse into the complexities of Europe's 'gay-friendly' identity, which, like the ECtHR claims of European consensus, does not necessarily reflect the position of all CoE Member States. As Ammaturo writes, the ECtHR not only plays a 'crucial role in portraying Europe as a tolerant, open and respectful continent for LGBTQI persons' but also in 'identifying intolerant and homo- and transphobic "others" both within and outside its borders'.[146] Ammaturo situates *Alekseyev* in the context of a wider dispute over LGBTI rights in the CoE, in which it may be seen as a prelude to the 'outright confrontation between "Europe" and Russia'[147] that occurred in 2012–13 in response to Russia's introduction of an 'anti-homosexual propaganda' bill. In this dispute, some Western European politicians went so far as stating that, if Russia could not respect LGBTI rights, it should withdraw from the CoE altogether.[148] The ECtHR's decision in *Alekseyev* may have contributed to Russia's increasing isolation within the CoE through the totalizing effect of its consensus claim. For just like the practitioner of incest or the family that does not adhere to long-term monogamy, Russia found itself to no longer be part of the 'Europe' on whose behalf the consensus spoke.

In this Europe–Russia confrontation, we begin to see how, through the idea of a 'gay-friendly' European identity, queer people can be deployed for political ends. 'Europe' was able to use LGBTI rights to lay claim to a moral exceptionalism on matters of sexual freedom and human rights.[149] This was so even though, as we saw above, some Western European states still discipline people for engaging in sexual practices that diverge from the norm, such as consensual incest and sadomasochism. While taking this stance on LGBTI rights may have given Europe political currency,[150] it ultimately did little to assist the Russian queer community. As Ammaturo argues, Europe's fierce condemnation of Russia's LGBTI rights record

[145] ibid [84].
[146] Ammaturo (n 136) 63.
[147] ibid.
[148] See eg Dutch politician Sophie in 't Veld cited in ibid 62.
[149] ibid 58.
[150] ibid 49.

only reinforced a perception in Russia that same-sex desire is a Western construct.[151] Indeed, since the dispute between Europe and Russia over LGBTI rights, there has been an increase in violent and oppressive measures towards queer people in Russia.[152] This trend is discussed further in the next chapter.

Jasbir Puar coins the term 'homonationalism' to describe the instrumentalization of LGBTI rights for nationalist agendas.[153] Building on Foucault's claim that 'the legitimization of the modern couple is complicit with, rather than working against'[154] modes of social regulation and surveillance, Puar argues that LGBTI subjects are deployed—and, indeed, can sometimes deploy themselves—to justify racist, Islamophobic, imperialistic, and militaristic polices.[155] This takes place through an overarching narrative of 'progress' and 'modernity', in which '"acceptance" and "tolerance" for gay and lesbian subjects have become a barometer by which the right to and capacity for national sovereignty is evaluated'.[156] Although Puar acknowledges that similar trends exist in Europe,[157] her work focuses on the US post-9/11, in which the War on Terror and other oppressive 'anti-terrorist' measures were partly justified by a need to confront 'Muslim homophobia'.

Puar's concept of homonationalism has been applied in the context of Europe's 'gay-friendly' regional identity[158]—in this case, what we may call a 'homoregionalism'. In a similar manner to the US, Europe's view of itself as inherently respectful of LGBTI rights has resulted in queer lives being co-opted in the promotion of Europe's cultural and moral superiority. In addition to Europe's confrontation with Russia, this can be seen in the moral panic over 'migrant homophobia' that occurred in the wake of the European 'refugee crisis' in 2015, in which anti-migrant and Islamophobic discourses were mobilized through expressions of concern for the welfare of European LGBTI communities and a need to maintain Europe's 'gay-friendly' culture.[159] In 2016, Hungarian Prime Minister Viktor Orbán

[151] ibid 62.

[152] ibid. In 2018, for example, Russia used these laws to ban its largest gay website: 'Russia Bans Popular LGBT Website for "Propaganda of Nontraditional Sexual Relations"' *The Moscow Times* (30 March 2018) <https://themoscowtimes.com/news/russia-bans-popular-lgbt-website-propaganda-nontraditional-sexual-relations-61007>.

[153] Jasbir K Puar, *Terrorist Assemblages: Homonationalism in Queer Times* (2nd edn, Duke University Press 2017).

[154] Foucault, cited in ibid 39.

[155] Puar (n 153).

[156] Jasbir K Puar, 'Rethinking Homonationalism' (2013) 45 International Journal of Middle East Studies 336, 336.

[157] Puar (n 153) 11.

[158] See eg, Ammaturo (n 136); Thomas Spijkerboer, 'Gender, Sexuality, Asylum and European Human Rights' (2018) 29 Law and Critique 221.

[159] Jin Haritaworn, 'Wounded Subjects: Sexual Exceptionalism and the Moral Panic on "Migrant Homophobia" in Germany' in Encarnacion Gutierrez Rodriguez and Manuela Boatcă Costa Sérgio (eds), *Decolonizing European Sociology: Transdisciplinary Approaches* (Routledge 2010); Marjoleine Zieck, 'The European Refugee Crisis from a Vantage Point of View' (2016) 45 Netherlands Journal of Legal Philosophy 3, 4; Spijkerboer (n 158).

even went as far saying that accepting Syrian refugees also meant 'importing ... homophobia',[160] notwithstanding his government's own anti-queer policies.[161] In these examples, we can see Europe's 'gay-friendly' identity being deployed in a way that not only paints Europe as culturally superior, but also demonizes the Muslim 'other'.[162]

In my argument, the ECtHR's claims of European consensus are complicit in the instrumentalization of queer bodies in the pursuit of such political agendas. By attributing almost all its decisions recognizing sexuality rights to 'Europe', the ECtHR has fostered a sense of European ownership over LGBTI rights and, along with them, the subjects of those rights. Dzehtsiarou acknowledges that European consensus has this potential, writing that '[t]hrough consensus, the Contracting Parties can influence the interpretation of the Convention, and perhaps this creates a sense of common ownership of the Convention case-law'.[163] In his view, this can enhance the legitimacy of the ECtHR by creating avenues for participation in its human rights adjudication.[164] Yet, this sense of 'common ownership' can also be harmful, especially when the rights over which ownership is claimed are not 'common' but instead relate to a specific group of people, as in the case of LGBTI rights. Such a sense of possession can lead to queer people being co-opted in the pursuit of a European politics in which they may want no part. The ECtHR's claims of European consensus also appear to be implicated in the various exclusions that have been justified through the rhetoric of LGBTI rights. This is because, by mobilizing the notion of a regional 'consensus', the ECtHR has fostered a sense of a closed community. It has created an idea of a single 'Europe', built upon the values of sameness and agreement.[165] In doing so, it has helped to shut off spaces for difference and push the 'other' out, whether it be the incest-practising 'other' or the refugee 'other'.

[160] Kai Diekmann, 'Hungary's Prime Minister Says Accepting Syrian Refugees "Also Means Importing Terrorism, Criminalism Anti-Semitism and Homophobia"' *Business Insider* (Online, 25 February 2016) <https://www.businessinsider.com.au/viktor-orban-interview-refugee-migrant-hungary-2016-2?r=US&IR=T>.

[161] For an overview of these policies, see Hadley Z Renkin and Victor Trofimov, 'The Global Dialectics of Homonationalism and Homophobia' (2023) 27 Sexuality & Culture 1987, 1987–88.

[162] For a more thorough examination of how 'representational tropes associated with civilizational hierarchies ... shine through in how the 'European' of European consensus is conceptualized', see Jens T Theilen, 'Civilizational Hierarchies and the Notion of "Europe" in the European Convention on Human Rights' (2025) 36 European Journal of International Law 135.

[163] Kanstantsin Dzehtsiarou, *European Consensus and the Legitimacy of the European Court of Human Rights* (Cambridge University Press 2015) 7.

[164] ibid 6–7.

[165] On the homogenizing effects of European consensus, see Jens T Theilen, *European Consensus Between Strategy and Principle: The Uses of Vertically Comparative Legal Reasoning in Regional Human Rights Adjudication* (Nomos 2021) 135–36. On the way the ideas of homogeneity and like-mindedness associated with European consensus help to reinforce an idea of 'Europe and the Rest', see Theilen (n 162) 135–38.

5.6 Conclusion: Consensus Claims and the Ousting of Difference

When understood as a state of agreement, the nature and extent of a 'European consensus' is difficult to pin down. Although the ECtHR tends to provide a breakdown of the Member States' different legal positions, it often shifts the number of Member States required to have a particular law before it will identify a legal consensus, as well as the inferences it is prepared to draw from a given legal trend. Recall, for example, the weight the Court attached to the lack of availability of marriage for siblings in *Stübing*, as compared to the lack of availability of marriage for same-sex partners in *Dudgeon*. The ECtHR's claims of social and expert consensus are even more vague, with it often making references to 'social attitudes'[166] or the views of 'the scientific community',[167] without explaining who or how many hold the positions that it identifies.

Nevertheless, the ECtHR's claims about the existence or non-existence of a European consensus have lent considerable authority to the constructions of sexuality and Europeanness produced in its decisions. This is partly due to the unfixed, and sometimes unquantifiable, nature of a consensus claim. Unlike unanimity, a claim of consensus does not mean a complete agreement; it almost always entails some exclusion.[168] And yet, unlike a claim of majority opinion, which has the idea of a minority opinion as its counterpart, a claim of consensus affords little discursive space to those who do not conform to the dominant position. As a result, when the ECtHR invokes the idea of a European consensus, it can appear to speak on behalf of 'everyone' in European society. This can have a totalizing effect, whereby alternative views and ways of being are not simply marginalized but erased. The authorizing effect of the ECtHR's claims of European consensus is also the result of its use of different sources of consensus—legal, public, and expert. By combining comparative legal reasoning with ideas of science and social views, the ECtHR has enabled law and disciplinary power to fuse and reinforce one another, helping its constructions to take on a greater appearance of 'truth'.

In this chapter, I focused on these effects in the context of sexual difference. I showed how the ECtHR's claims of European consensus have functioned to regulate, discipline, and co-opt some sexual subalterns, while ousting others from the idea of 'Europe' altogether. However, in the final section, we caught a glimpse of how the tension between the ECtHR's claims of European consensus and alterity has also extended beyond the experiences of sexual subalterns. In particular, the ECtHR's claims about the existence or non-existence of a regional consensus have helped to authorize a narrow European identity that allows little space for

166 *Schalk* (n 118) [93].
167 *Fretté* (n 112) [42].
168 Chantal Mouffe, *The Democratic Paradox* (Verso 2000) 104.

difference, whether it be Russian difference or the difference associated with Muslim refugees. In the following chapter, I explore the way in which the idea of consensus has played into difficulties facing both the ECtHR and the World Trade Organization. As part of this exploration, I consider how the gap between the singular European identity constructed by the ECtHR's consensus claims and the diverse reality on the ground has contributed to some of the 'backlash' that the European human rights system is experiencing today.

6
Consensus and Crisis in the World Trade Organization and European Court of Human Rights

6.1 Introduction

So far, this book has provided an account of how the idea of consensus has functioned as technique of authorization in the General Agreement on Tariffs and Trade (GATT)/World Trade Organization (WTO) and European Court of Human Rights (ECtHR). First, in Chapters 2 and 4, it described how both institutions' claim to base their decisions on a consensus worked to imbue their practices with an air of 'legitimacy' and 'democracy', helping to ward off counter-visions of international law that claimed to be more democratic than the existing system, and contributing to the sense that the GATT/WTO and ECtHR were the most appropriate institutions to govern or adjudicate in their respective areas. Second, in Chapters 3 and 5, it described how the two institutions' practice of grounding their substantive decisions in the notion of consensus lent authority to both those decisions and their underlying worldviews by concealing different and dissenting viewpoints, enabling the legal regimes associated with both institutions to appear normal and like 'common sense'. In both cases, I argued that these effects stemmed from the gesture that the idea of consensus makes towards a widespread, yet unfixed, level of agreement. This gestrure holds out the promise of attending to many different perspectives, conjuring ideas of representation and public 'voice', while at the same time giving little visibility to any differences between those perspectives in the end product, making things seem more settled than they are. Throughout these chapters, I also demonstrated that, by never setting a precise threshold for that agreement, the idea of consensus has proven flexible enough to be applied to a range of decision-making practices and outcomes, including ones that sit uneasily with the discourses of democracy and sameness that it generates. This tension has meant that the authorizing work performed by the idea of consensus has not been straightforward, but at once both potent and precarious.

Since the 2010s, both the WTO and the ECtHR have experienced renewed challenges to their authority—this time, from the political right—leading to shifts and difficulties in the way that they function. In the WTO, the most prominent

Consensus in International Law. Claerwen O'Hara, Oxford University Press. © Claerwen O'Hara 2026.
DOI: 10.1093/9780198948643.003.0006

example of this has been the US' unilateral decision to paralyze the Appellate Body in 2019, leaving the institution 'dejudicialised'.[1] The ECtHR's challenges have centred on contestation and 'backlash' from several Member States of the Council of Europe, leading to measures aimed at reeling in the Court's power. In this chapter, I re-describe these periods of institutional turbulence through the lens of each institution's use of consensus. I argue that by helping to build their authority on visions of representation and homogeneity that did not always match the reality on the ground, the idea of consensus in the WTO and the ECtHR has contributed to some of the problems they face today.

This chapter is in three sections. The first section considers how practices and discourses of consensus in the WTO contributed to the Appellate Body impasse of 2017–19. The second section explores the role of European consensus in some of the recent backlash against the ECtHR. The third section discusses the difficulties both institutions now face in resolving their respective crises and reflects on the importance of difference and dissent for generating new ideas and ways of thinking.

6.2 The World Trade Organization's Appellate Body Impasse

In 2017, the United States (US), under the first Trump Administration, began blocking consensus on all appointments to the WTO Appellate Body (AB)—a quasi-judicial body of seven standing members that heard appeals from panels on disputes under WTO law. This policy was not entirely new. For reasons outlined further below, under the Obama Administration, the US refused to renominate American AB member Hillman in 2011 and blocked the reappointment of Korean AB member Chang in 2016.[2] However, as Brewster writes, 'the Trump administration's policy of blocking *all Appellate Body nominees*, regardless of judicial philosophy, [was] a categorical change'.[3] Indeed, it would eventually result in the AB losing its quorum of three in December 2019, rendering it inoperative.[4] The WTO's use of consensus decision-making is at the heart of this story. Most notably, it was the procedure that gave the US an effective veto over AB appointments,[5]

[1] For this term, see Richard H Steinberg, 'The Impending Dejudicialization of the WTO Dispute Settlement System?' (2018) 112 American Society for International Law Proceedings 316.

[2] Jeffrey L Dunoff and Mark Pollack, 'The Judicial Trilemma' (2017) 111 American Journal of International Law 225, 268.

[3] Rachel Brewster, 'The Trump Administration and the Future of the WTO' (2018) 44 The Yale Journal of International Law Online 6, 8–9 [emphasis in the original].

[4] The AB requires a quorum of three, see Understanding on Rules and Procedures Governing the Settlement of Disputes 1994, 1869 UNTS 299 (DSU), Article 17:1. On 11 December 2019, its membership fell to one. However, two AB members stayed on until June 2020 to complete a report.

[5] Decisions on the appointment of AB members must be taken 'by consensus', see Article 2:4 of the DSU, ibid.

enabling it to destroy the WTO's judicial branch contrary to the will of most the other Members.[6] But the idea of consensus also contributed to these events in other, more complex ways. In the following two subsections, I describe how the gap between discourse and reality with respect to the WTO's consensus claims helped to create the conditions in which the AB impasse took place.

6.2.1 Consensus Decision-Making in the WTO and Ideas of Democracy

As described in Chapter 2, in the transition from the GATT to the WTO, the operation of consensus decision-making in the multilateral trade regime changed. Whereas under the GATT framework, consensus decision-making had primarily functioned as an informal method of weighted decision-making, in the WTO, it brought political decision-making to a near standstill.[7] This change was the result of a combination of legal and political factors, including the codification of the consensus procedure in the WTO Agreement,[8] the global South's dismay at the asymmetrical outcome of the Uruguay Round, and a gradual re-conceptualization of the WTO's consensus procedure as non-negotiable through an institutional discourse of 'democracy'.[9] Over time, this breakdown of political decision-making prompted a greater reliance on the WTO's dispute settlement system as a substitute for negotiations,[10] transforming the WTO from a purportedly 'Member-driven' organization into one in which the WTO AB was the primary 'engine of global economic governance'.[11] From its early days, the AB adopted the practice of taking its own decisions by consensus.[12] Together with the AB's rise to power, this saw judicial consensus effectively replace political consensus as the basis for many decisions coming out of the WTO.

[6] On the way no other Member appeared to support 'the politically motivated US blocking of the filling of AB vacancies', see Ernst-Ulrich Petersmann, 'How Should WTO Members React to Their WTO Crises?' [2019] World Trade Review 1.

[7] Steinberg (n 1) 317–18. Note, however, that some decisions have come into being over the WTO's lifetime, such as Agreement on Trade Facilitation, WTO Doc WT/L/931, 2014. For more details, see Chapter 2. Political decision-making also continued to occur to some extent through an opaque network of WTO committees, see Andrew Lang and Joanne Scott, 'The Hidden World of WTO Governance' (2009) 20 The European Journal of International Law 575.

[8] 1994, 1867 UNTS 154 ('WTO Agreement'), Article IX:1.

[9] See Section 2.3 of Chapter 2.

[10] Steinberg (n 1) 317–18.

[11] Robert Howse, 'The World Trade Organization 20 Years On: Global Governance by Judiciary' (2016) 27 European Journal of International Law 9, 75. See also Rajesh Babu, 'Decision Making in the WTO: From Negotiated Law-Making to Judicial Law- Making' in Julien Chaisse and Tsai-Yu Lin (eds), *International Economic Law and Governance* (Oxford University Press 2016).

[12] Hélène Ruiz Fabri, 'The WTO Appellate Body or Judicial Power Unleashed: Sketches from the Procedural Side of the Story' (2017) 27 European Journal of International Law 1075. For more details, see Chapter 2.

On one level, this change was not particularly significant. Writing on the shift from the diplomatic decision-making of the GATT to the scientific and judicialized world of the WTO, Knox and Kotiaho highlight the deep continuities between the two models, including the fact that '*both* [were] structured in such a way as to be radically opaque to forms of popular political mobilization'.[13] While Knox and Kotiaho's analysis is focused on the way in which the GATT's diplomacy was itself a form of expertise with its 'own internal codes and practices that are highly inaccessible to those not trained in them',[14] their observations can equally be applied to the operation of consensus decision-making in the multilateral trade regime. In both institutional settings, the idea of consensus worked to obscure the inner workings of global trade governance by blurring the decision-makers behind a given decision.[15] The nature of those inner workings simply shifted: instead of a small group of state diplomats and corporate lobbyists taking or influencing decisions of worldwide significance behind the smokescreen of consensus, it was now a small group of (quasi) judges doing so.[16]

From the perspective of the US, however, the effective replacement of political consensus with judicial consensus was a significant shift. It meant that the US—the architect of the WTO and its most dominant Member—was no longer in control of global trade governance or the consensus narrative being produced around it. This became a problem for the US when the AB's reports did not reflect its interests. In 2006, for example, the US was infuriated by a report in which the AB found that the US' use of 'zeroing'[17] to calculate anti-dumping duties was inconsistent with WTO law.[18] In response, the US 'took the uncommon step of circulating detailed critiques of the decision to WTO Members'.[19] At that time, however, the Doha Round was still on foot and so the US also sought to resolve its grievances by placing the issue of 'zeroing' on the Doha Round negotiating agenda, arguing that the matter 'should not be left to dispute settlement'.[20]

[13] Robert Knox and Paavo Kotiaho, 'Beyond Competing Liberalisms: The World Trade Organization as Class Project' (2014) 23 Social & Legal Studies 426, 430.

[14] ibid.

[15] On the lack of transparency created by the AB's consensus-based approach, see Meredith Kolsky Lewis, 'The Lack of Dissent in WTO Dispute Settlement' (2006) 9 Journal of International Economic Law 895, 925. See also Mitsuo Matsushita, 'Reflections on the Functioning of the Appellate Body', *A History of Law and Lawyers in the GATT/WTO: The Development of the Rule of Law in the Multilateral Trading System* (Cambridge University Press 2015) 556, reflecting on how the absence of dissent in the Appellate Body contributed to the 'impression of secretiveness' that lingers around WTO procedure.

[16] On the continuities between political and judicial consensus, see Lewis (n 15) 916: 'many of the Appellate Body's procedures, and the overall emphasis on consensus, make sense given that the DSU was replacing a system that relied entirely on consensus'.

[17] 'Zeroing' is 'the failure to count in negative dumping transactions in determining the anti-dumping duty', see Howse (n 11) 71.

[18] WTO, *United States—Laws, Regulations and Methodology for Calculating Dumping Margins (Zeroing)—Report of the Appellate Body*, WT/DS294/AB/R (18 April 2006).

[19] Jeanne J Grimmett, *WTO Dispute Settlement: Status of U.S. Compliance in Pending Cases* (US Congressional Research Service 2011) 61, fn 313.

[20] US, Offsets for Non-Dumped Comparisons, Negotiating Group on Rules, TN/RL/W/208, 5 June 2007, 2, available at <http://www.jmcti.org/2000round/com/doha/tn/rl/tn_rl_w_208.pdf>.

Following the effective collapse of the Doha Round in 2008, the US changed tack. It began interfering with AB appointments, partly as a way to disrupt that body's consensus-based approach. In 2011, for example, the Obama Administration opposed the reappointment of US AB member Jennifer Hillman, allegedly due to her lack of dissenting opinions.[21] The Office of the US Trade Representative (USTR) then put forward the names of candidates whom it believed were more likely to dissent.[22] Even if the US could not control the outcome of the AB's reports, it at least seemed determined to inject a different, more US-friendly narrative into them.[23] In 2016, the US also attempted to pierce the AB's veil of consensus by blocking the reappointment of South Korean member Seung Wha Chang.[24] The US based its opposition to Chang's appointment on the quality of the reports on which he had participated, thereby attempting to single out an individual AB member for his judicial style.[25] In response, the other AB members sent a letter to the WTO Dispute Settlement Body arguing that, due to their use of consensus, no case could be considered 'the result of a decision by one AB Member'.[26] These events, including the AB's attempts to resist the US' interference through reference to their consensus procedure, set the scene for the Trump Administration's decision to block consensus on *all* AB nominees from 2017 onwards.

In addition to affecting the US' dominance over WTO decision-making, the institution's transformation into a 'judiocracy' was harder to reconcile with the democratic discourses that representatives had deployed around the WTO's use of consensus decision-making over the years. In insisting that the WTO's use of consensus decision-making between its Members was a 'fundamental democratic guarantee'[27] in the 1990s and 2000s, for example, both Directors-General Renato Ruggiero and Mike Moore had often referred to governmental decision-making and national democratic processes as well. In 1998, Ruggiero described the WTO as 'a system which operates by consensus, *with all decisions approved by each government and ratified by each national parliament*'.[28] Likewise, in 1999, Moore

[21] Dunoff and Pollack (n 2) 268.

[22] Inside US Trade, 'For Appellate Body Candidates, USTR Prioritised Willingness To Dissent' *World Trade Online* (7 September 2011) <https://insidetrade.com/daily-news/appellate-body-candidates-ustr-prioritised-willingness-dissent>.

[23] On the US' promotion of dissenting opinions in the WTO dispute settlement system, see Manfred Elsig and Mark Pollack, 'Agents, Trustees, and International Courts: The Politics of Judicial Appointment at the World Trade Organization' (2014) 20 European Journal of International Relations 391, 409.

[24] Dunoff and Pollack (n 2) 268.

[25] ibid 269.

[26] Quoted in Raj Bhala, 'Chaos: Recent Developments in International Trade Law at the Multilateral, Regional, and U.S. Levels' [2018] Recent Developments in the Law: University of Kansas School of Law 5.

[27] Mike Moore, 'The WTO Is Back On Track for Trade and Development' (16 February 2000) <https://www.wto.org/english/news_e/spmm_e/spmm24_e.htm>.

[28] Renato Ruggiero, 'The Future of the World Trading System' (15 April 1998) <https://www.wto.org/english/news_e/sprr_e/bergen_e.htm> [emphasis added].

said, '[o]ur mission is to enhance the independence of the sovereign state through agreements reached by *the consensus of our Member governments, agreed by their parliamentary process*.'[29] Now, in a system in which most trade decisions were the product of judicial consensus, there was no longer the same purported link back to the 'will of the people'. As discussed in Chapter 2, even before the collapse of the Doha Round, commentators had begun worrying about 'the imbalance between the ineffective rulemaking procedures and the highly efficient judicial mechanisms' in the WTO, noting that the AB's power raised 'intractable questions of democratic legitimacy'.[30]

During the AB impasse, the US appeared to draw discursively on these existing democratic concerns. It described the AB as 'unaccountable'[31] and 'activist',[32] and stressed that WTO 'dispute settlement that goes beyond existing rules has not been approved by Members and does not have democratic legitimacy or support'.[33] In speeches before the UN General Assembly (UNGA), US President Trump also denounced 'mammoth multinational trade deals, [and] unaccountable international tribunals'[34] and told the world, 'if you want democracy, hold on to your sovereignty'.[35] In making these assertions, the Trump Administration seemed to echo not only scholars' concerns about the AB's rise to power, but also the language put forward by the alter-globalization movement in the 1990s. As Slobodian wrote of Trump's WTO-related speeches in 2018, '[f]or those of us who came of age in the 1990s, there was an eerie sense of déjà vu. Then, too, there were protests against global institutions insulated from democratic decision-making.'[36] By creating a link between the AB impasse and longstanding unease surrounding the WTO's democratic credentials, the Trump Administration may have helped to lend credibility to its actions, at least in the eyes of some segments of its domestic population.

In official trade documents and meetings, the Trump Administration fleshed out its democratic rhetoric with more technical complaints about the AB having

[29] Mike Moore, 'Trade for Development—The Way Ahead' (14 September 1999) <https://www.wto.org/english/news_e/spmm_e/spmm04_e.htm> [emphasis added].

[30] Claude E Barfield, 'Free Trade, Sovereignty, Democracy: The Future of the World Trade Organization' (2001) 2 Chicago Journal of International Law 403, 408.

[31] United States Trade Representative, Trade Policy Agenda of the President of the United States (2019) 26.

[32] ibid.

[33] Dennis Shea, 'Statement by Deputy U.S. Trade Representative and U.S. Permanent Representative to the WTO, WTO General Council' (*US Mission to International Organizations in Geneva*, 8 May 2018) <https://geneva.usmission.gov/2018/05/08/ambassador-dennis-sheas-statement-at-the-wto-general-council/>.

[34] Address by Mr Donald Trump, President of the United States of America, UN GAOR, 72nd sess, 3rd plen mtg, Agenda Item 110, UN Doc A/72/PV.3 (19 September 2017), 14.

[35] Address by Mr Donald Trump, President of the United States of America, UN GAOR, 74th sess, 3rd plen mtg, Agenda Item 8, UN Doc A/74/PV.3 (24 September 2019), 11.

[36] Quinn Slobodian, 'Trump, Populists and the Rise of Right-Wing Globalization' *New York Times* (22 October 2018) <https://www.nytimes.com/2018/10/22/opinion/trump-far-right-populists-globalization.html>.

overstepped its role.[37] In its 2018 Trade Policy Agenda, for example, the Trump Administration connected its policy of blocking AB appointments to concerns about that body's failure to complete reports within the 90-day time limit, its use of precedent and *obiter dicta*, its members' tendency to stay on after the expiration of their terms, and, most importantly, the AB's alleged practice of 'judicial overreach'.[38] Absent from the US' specific complaints, however, was any mention of the WTO's consensus procedure, notwithstanding the role that it had played in facilitating the AB's rise and locking the US and other WTO Members out of global trade governance. This contrasted with the interpretation of the issue by the organization itself, whose representatives tended to place the Members' use of consensus decision-making at the centre of the AB impasse. In September 2019, for example, WTO Deputy Director-General Alan Wolff framed the institution's troubles in the following terms: '[t]he basic problem is not the appellate body. [It] is rule-making in the WTO. If you need consensus to make a rule, that's very difficult to achieve'.[39]

As between the US and the WTO, this divergence is perhaps unsurprising. After all, the WTO's consensus procedure was the tool enabling the US to attack the AB and reassert control over the institution. Why, in this context, would the US raise concerns about consensus decision-making? Moreover, even with its propensity for political stalemate, the WTO's consensus procedure has still tended to favour the US over other WTO Members. This is because the Uruguay Agreements are themselves tilted towards the interests of the global North and the consensus procedure can be used as a veto power to preserve that imbalance. Consider, for example, the deadlock over a widely backed proposal put forward by South Africa and India in 2020 to temporarily waive intellectual property protections for COVID-19 vaccines and other medical technologies.[40] Before changing its position in 2021,[41] the US, along with the UK, the EU, and a handful of other wealthy states, relied on the WTO's practice of taking decisions on waivers by consensus to block the proposal, thereby 'privileging the monopoly rights of their powerful pharmaceutical corporations over the global effort to protect public health during a pandemic'.[42]

[37] On the oddly technical nature of these complaints, see Rémi Bachand, 'What's Behind the WTO Crisis? A Marxist Analysis' (2020) 31 European Journal of International Law 857, 860–61.

[38] United States Trade Representative, Trade Policy Agenda of the President of the United States (2018), 22–28.

[39] Alan Wolff quoted in Bo Seo, 'WTO Urges Australia to Look Beyond Regional Trade' *Australian Financial Review* (23 September 2019) <https://www.afr.com/politics/federal/wto-urges-australia-to-look-beyond-regional-trade-20190919-p52sy2>.

[40] Communication from India and South Africa, Waiver from Certain Provisions of the TRIPS Agreement for the Prevention, Containment and Treatment of COVID-19, Council for Trade-Related Aspects of Intellectual Property Rights, WTO Doc IP/C/W/669 (2 October 2020).

[41] In May 2021, the US finally agreed to back a waiver but warned that the 'negotiations will take time given the consensus-based nature of the institution and the complexity of the issues involved', see 'Statement from Ambassador Katherine Tai on the Covid-19 Trips Waiver' (*Office of the United States Trade Representative*, 5 May 2021) <https://ustr.gov/about-us/policy-offices/press-office/press-releases/2021/may/statement-ambassador-katherine-tai-covid-19-trips-waiver>.

[42] Anne Orford, 'Broken Bargains' (*London Review of Books Blog*, 5 May 2021) <https://www.lrb.co.uk/blog/2021/may/broken-bargains>.

However, the US' refusal to take aim at consensus decision-making also points to another way in which this method of decision-making played into the AB impasse: through the Members' unwavering attachment to it. For what rendered the AB impasse an 'impasse' was not only the US' opposition to AB appointments but also the WTO Membership's unwillingness to abandon consensus decision-making in order to save the body once described as the 'jewel in the crown'[43] of the WTO system. Not all commentators believed that it would have been legally possible for the Members to vote on the appointment of AB members.[44] This is because such decisions are governed by Article 2:4 of the Dispute Settlement Understanding, which only mentions 'consensus'. Nonetheless, during the AB impasse, several scholars argued that the Membership could legally turn to such a vote by resorting to the general voting mechanism contained in Article IX:1 of the WTO Agreement.[45] To clarify the legality of this move, they asserted, WTO Members could also, by a two-thirds majority vote, adopt an authoritative interpretation in support of it under Article IX:2. But even with this advice, no WTO Member requested a vote. This was so, despite a total of 119 Members coming together in December 2019, just before the AB's demise, to call for the vacancies to be filled.[46]

Some scholars have attributed the Members' reluctance to even attempt a vote on AB appointments to fears that the US would withdraw from the WTO if they did so.[47] After all, President Trump had threatened such a US withdrawal in 2018.[48] However, the discourse of the other WTO Members tells a more complex story. For during the AB impasse, several Members also went out of their way to issue statements in support of consensus decision-making. At the 2017 Buenos Aires Ministerial, Argentina stated that it continued 'to believe in the consensus route, which is fundamental for reaching legitimate decisions that we can all call our own'.[49] In May 2019, China said that while the WTO was facing an 'unprecedented existential crisis',[50] any reform must 'follow the practice of decision-making by consensus'[51] and be pursued on 'equal footing'.[52] That same month, at the Ministerial

[43] Pascal Lamy quoted in 'WTO Disputes Reach 400 Mark', 6 November 2009, https://www.wto.org/english/news_e/pres09_e/pr578_e.htm.

[44] See, eg, Tetyana Payosova, Gary Clyde Hufbauer, and J Jeffrey Schott, 'The Dispute Settlement Crisis in the World Trade Organization: Causes and Cures' (2018) 18–5 Policy Brief: Peterson Institute for International Economics 11.

[45] Jennifer Hillman, 'Three Approaches to Fixing the World Trade Organization's Appellate Body: The Good, the Bad and the Ugly?' [2018] Institute of International Economic Law Issue Brief; Pieter Jan Kuijper, 'From the Board: The US Attack on the WTO Appellate Body' (2018) 45 Legal Issues of Economic Integration 1; Petersmann (n 6).

[46] Afghanistan et al., Appellate Body Appointments, WT/DSB/W/609/Rev.15, 6 December 2019.

[47] See, eg, Payosova, Hufbauer and Schott(n 44) 11.

[48] E Helmore, 'Trump: US will quit World Trade Organization unless it "shapes up"', *The Guardian*, 31 August 2018, <https://www.theguardian.com/us-news/2018/aug/30/trump-world-trade-organization-tariffs-stock-market>.

[49] Statement by President Macri, Buenos Aires Ministerial, WT/MIN(17)/75, 10 December 2017.

[50] China, Proposal on WTO Reform, WT/GC/W/773, 13 May 2019 [1.10].

[51] ibid [1.6].

[52] ibid.

Meeting of Developing Countries in New Delhi, India's Commerce Minister described the WTO's use of consensus decision-making as 'too valuable to lose'.[53] Following that meeting, seventeen states from the South issued a joint statement asserting that '[m]ultilateral avenues, based on consensus, remain the most effective means to achieve inclusive development-oriented outcomes'.[54]

These statements reveal that the association between consensus and ideas of 'equality', 'legitimacy', and (implicitly) 'democracy' still persisted in the WTO right up until the AB's demise. This was so, despite the US using the WTO's consensus procedure in a way that would destroy the dispute settlement system that many Members claimed they wanted to retain, and years of political paralysis before that. Almost as striking as what these statements said, however, was who said them. Almost all of the Members actively advocating for the preservation of the consensus procedure during the AB impasse were from the global South, representing a reversal of the geopolitical positions in the 1960s and 1970s, when it had mainly been states in the global North and GATT representatives championing consensus decision-making.

An unwillingness to let go of the idea of consensus in the WTO on the part of some states in the South has also played into attempts to revive the institution's negotiating function. Since 2017, some Members have endeavoured to move away from the WTO's 'single undertaking' principle by making a greater use of 'plurilateral negotiations'—that is, negotiations amongst a subset of the WTO's membership. More specifically, there have been multiple 'Joint Statement Initiatives' (JSIs), which are statements of intent to negotiate new rules or collaborate on new areas by groups of Members, on topics such as e-commerce, services, and investment facilitation.[55] While there are doubts around how any binding agreements that come out of this process will be legally incorporated into the WTO system, given the requirement that plurilateral agreements be adopted by the consensus of all the Members before they can be added to Annex 4,[56] some commentators see in this shift a pathway for renewing the WTO's political branch.[57]

However, there has been substantial opposition to the WTO's turn to plurilateralism, particularly amongst larger states in the global South, such as India and South Africa.[58] This is partly due to the fact that many of the JSIs are focused

[53] India Press Information Bureau, 'WTO Ministerial Meeting of Developing Countries Concludes in New Delhi Today', 14 May 2019,<https://pib.gov.in/PressReleasePage.aspx?PRID=1571972>.

[54] India et al, Outcome of the WTO Ministerial Meeting of Developing Countries, WT/L/1062, 27 May 2019 [5].

[55] Shamel Azmeh, 'Developing Countries and Joint Statement Initiatives at the WTO: Damned If You Join, Damned If You Don't?' (2024) 55 Development and Change 349, 383–87.

[56] WTO Agreement (n 8) Art X.9. For a discussion of the legal issues, see Jane Kelsey, 'The Illegitimacy of Joint Statement Initiatives and Their Systemic Implications for the WTO' (2022) 55 Journal of International Economic Law 2.

[57] James Bacchus, 'The Future of the WTO: Multilateral or Plurilateral?' (*CATO Institute*, 25 May 2023) <https://www.cato.org/policy-analysis/future-wto>.

[58] Azmeh (n 55) 387.

on projects that are of particular interest to states in the global North, such as investment facilitation.[59] But these states' opposition to the plurilateral turn in the WTO also seems to be the result of the WTO's longstanding emphasis on consensus. In an interview conducted by Shamel Azmeh, for example, one representative of a Member opposed to the JSIs said:

> We have been saying, if it is about the numbers, then we can say the same thing about the G90 proposal on special and differential treatment. Because we have the numbers of developing countries that are fully behind the proposal, but you have refused any discussion or outcome on that matter. So, it is not necessarily the number of countries that are participating in any initiative. It is about respecting the underpinning principles of the WTO. *We agreed that we will make decisions by consensus . . . The fact that we have the numbers does not mean that an issue enjoys consensus in the WTO.* And of course, if we have a rules-based multilateral trading system, we need to respect the rules of the system.[60]

Here, we see that after decades of being told that the global South's projects cannot succeed in the multilateral trade regime, despite enjoying far-reaching support, because they do not represent an international 'consensus', some states in the South are now resentful of any shift that does not appear to hold states in the North to the same standard.

In this regard, the crisis in the WTO can be understood, at least in part, as a consequence of the dissonance that has emerged between the operation of the WTO's consensus procedure, which had rendered global trade governance not only opaque and unaccountable but also increasingly dysfunctional, and the discourses that were constructed around it, which have depicted it as good and democratic, and, therefore, something that should never be abandoned. It is unclear whether states in the South have now internalized the democratic discourse surrounding consensus decision-making, are frustrated by attempts on the part of the global North to flip the script when it suits them, or are simply deploying these discourses themselves in furtherance of their own interests.[61] But whatever their motives, the result is the same. While the idea that all Members must always reach consensus is wreaking havoc in the WTO, there is substantial resistance to moving away from that idea—a resistance that is often articulated through longstanding institutional discourses about the benefits of consensus decision-making. And, as a result,

[59] ibid 377.

[60] Quoted anonymously in ibid 387–88 [emphasis added].

[61] This may be particularly so for 'emerging powers' such as China and India, which have each acquired the economic clout to use the consensus procedure as a 'veto' power on their own. In 2014, for example, India 'vetoed' the Trade Facilitation Agreement until it won the right to continue its food subsidy programme, see Mitsuo Matsushita and others, *The World Trade Organization: Law, Practice, and Policy* (3rd edn, Oxford University Press 2015) 298.

the WTO finds itself unable to act, stuck between the dysfunction of consensus decision-making and its lingering democratic allure.

6.2.2 The WTO and Discourses of Economic Sameness

The AB impasse must also be seen in light of the substantive claims of consensus regarding the multilateral trade regime. In particular, it should be considered within the context of the discourse of ideological consensus that was constructed around the conclusion of the Uruguay Round negotiations in the mid-1990s, which claimed that the consensus of more than 120 states on the establishment of the WTO, as well as several other trade agreements, was evidence of a worldwide agreement on the virtues of trade liberalization and the necessity of globalized neoliberal capitalism more generally. As we saw in Chapter 3, this discourse was resisted both inside the WTO by states in the global South, as well as outside of the institution in the form of the alter-globalization movement. But, for a long time, that resistance and the counter-narratives it put forward could barely be heard over the dominant consensus discourse, which was stabilized in law through the existence of the Uruguay Round Agreements.[62]

During the AB impasse, the US, under the first Trump Administration, attacked the Uruguay Round consensus narrative. In his 2019 speech before the UNGA, President Trump declared that '[g]lobalism [had] exerted a religious pull over past leaders, causing them to ignore their own national interests'.[63] He went on to imagine a future that would allow greater space for national difference, stating, '[t]he future does not belong to globalists. The future belongs to patriots. The future belongs to sovereign and independent nations who protect their citizens, respect their neighbors, and honor *the differences that make each country special and unique*.'[64] This 'anti-globalist' stance contrasted starkly with the discourse of the US in the 1990s, when US President Clinton had agreed with WTO representatives that globalization was 'not a policy choice' but 'a fact'.[65]

The discursive shift in the US was partly driven by economic causes. In particular, it should be seen in light of another event that had coincided with the collapse of the Doha Round—the Global Financial Crisis (GFC). The GFC, which had its roots in the US' subprime mortgage market, was not directly connected to the WTO. Nevertheless, it caused immense economic suffering in both the US and around the world, leading to a growing disillusionment with the global economic

[62] See Section 3.3 of Chapter 3.
[63] Address by Mr Donald Trump (n 35).
[64] ibid [emphasis added].
[65] Bill Clinton, 'Statement, Geneva Ministerial' (18 May 1998) <https://www.wto.org/english/thewto_e/minist_e/min98_e/anniv_e/clinton_e.htm>.

system more generally.[66] Furthermore, for some regions in the US, such as the 'Rust Belt',[67] this economic suffering came on top of decades of economic decline as a result of the globalized trading system, which had seen US manufacturing jobs move offshore.[68] During his campaign for the US presidency, Trump not only gave a voice to this economic pain but also wove it into a populist narrative in which 'globalist elites' had betrayed the working people.[69] Speaking before a crowd in Pittsburgh in June 2016, for example, Trump said the following:

> Our politicians have aggressively pursued a policy of globalization, moving our jobs, our wealth and our factories to Mexico and overseas. Globalization has made the financial elite, who donate to politicians, very, very wealthy ... [I]t has left millions of our workers with nothing but poverty and heartache.[70]

This economic narrative proved highly successful at the polls and Trump's denunciation of 'globalism' in the UNGA in 2019 may be seen as a continuation of it.

The US' turn towards a rhetoric that celebrates 'patriotism' and national 'difference' can also be seen as a reaction against the claim that there was no alternative to globalized neoliberalism, which the Uruguay Round consensus had helped to authorize. This is because that claim had not actually displaced alternative political views or identities; it had simply suppressed them. As a result, throughout the world, there was a growing appetite for leaders who could 'provide people with some form of hope, with a belief that things could be different'.[71] In his election campaign, Trump did just this. At the same rally in Pittsburgh in 2016, he told his audience, '[o]n trade, on immigration, on foreign policy, we are going to put America first again ... We are going to embrace the possibilities of change, but real change ... It's time to believe in the future.'[72] Here, we see Trump challenge the idea that the End of History had taken place by calling on his audience to 'believe in the future' once again. Moreover, he claimed to offer 'real change' by promising to

[66] On the GFC and the anti-neoliberal sentiment that emerged in its wake, see Nancy Fraser, *The Old Is Dying and the New Cannot Be Born: From Progressive Neoliberalism to Trump and Beyond* (Verso 2019) 24–26; Chantal Mouffe, *For a Left Populism* (Verso 2018) 18–19.

[67] The 'Rust Belt' refers to a region of the Northeastern and Midwestern United States that was once a manufacturing hub but has been experiencing economic decline since the early 1980s.

[68] Fraser (n 66) 21–24.

[69] Following Laclau and Mouffe, I am using the term 'populist' here to describe 'a discursive strategy of constructing a political frontier dividing society into two camps and calling for the mobilization of the "underdog" against "those in power"', see Mouffe (n 66) 10–11, drawing on Ernesto Laclau in *On Populist Reason* (Verso 2005).

[70] 'Donald Trump's Speech on Trade' *Time* (28 June 2016) <https://time.com/4386335/donald-trump-trade-speech-transcript/>. On the populist nature of such speeches and how they relate to the AB impasse, see Imogen Saunders, 'Populism, Backlash and the Ongoing Use of the World Trade Organization Dispute Settlement System: State Responses to the Appellate Body Crisis' (2021) 35 Maryland Journal of International Law 172.

[71] Chantal Mouffe, *On the Political* (Routledge 2005) 71.

[72] 'Donald Trump's Speech on Trade' (n 70).

put 'America first'. After years of being told that there was no other way, this future-oriented nationalist rhetoric likely struck a chord with some parts of the American population. As Chantal Mouffe wrote in 2005 on the rise of a similar nationalist populism in Europe:

> In a context where the dominant discourse proclaims that there is no alternative to the current neo-liberal form of globalization and that we should accept its dictats, it is not surprising that a growing number of people are listening to those who proclaim that alternatives do exist and that they will give back to the people the power to decide.[73]

The first Trump Administration did not live up to this promise. In fact, it is debatable whether the first Trump Administration even brought about any major economic shift. Gruszczynski and Lawrence, for example, argue that, at least domestically, that Administration left many existing power structures in place and retained a neoliberal agenda (albeit in a more localized form).[74] However, in going against the rest of the WTO Membership and unilaterally destroying the AB via the WTO's consensus procedure, the first Trump Administration could at least lay claim to disrupting the globalist consensus narrative and defanging the institution that had once been at the heart of it.

And yet, despite all its rhetoric about respect for national difference, the US' attack on the AB also appears to have been driven by the failure of another state to conform to the WTO's consensus narrative: China. For when China joined the WTO in 2001, there had been expectation that it would join in the consensus allegedly underpinning that institution and move towards a more free market economy. This can be seen in US President Bill Clinton's speech on the China Trade Bill in 2000, in which he declared that '[b]y joining the W.T.O., China [was] . . . agreeing to import one of democracy's most cherished values: economic freedom.'[75] Instead of following this path, however, China developed its own model of state capitalism, based around state-owned enterprises (SOEs).[76] This led to economic success. By 2009, China had become the world's largest exporter of goods.[77] China's economic rise not only threatened the economic dominance of the global North, but also sat uneasily with previous suggestions from WTO Directors-General that there could be 'no alternative' to US-style capitalism.[78]

[73] Mouffe (n 71) 70.

[74] See generally, Lukasz Gruszczynski and Jessica Lawrence, 'Trump, International Trade and Populism', *Netherlands Yearbook of International Law 2018* (TMC Asser Press 2019).

[75] Bill Clinton, 'Speech on China Trade Bill' (*Johns Hopkins University*, 9 March 2000) <https://www.iatp.org/sites/default/files/Full_Text_of_Clintons_Speech_on_China_Trade_Bi.htm>.

[76] Mark Wu, 'The "China, Inc." Challenge to Global Trade Governance' (2016) 57 Harvard International Law Journal 261.

[77] 'China Becomes World's No. 1 Exporter, Passing Germany' *New York Times* (10 January 2010) <https://www.nytimes.com/2010/01/11/business/global/11chinatrade.html>.

[78] For a detailed description of these suggestions, see Chapter 3.

By the mid-2010s, China's economic heterodoxy had become a major concern for US and European policymakers.[79] In both these regions, there was a sense that 'China ha[d] reneged on an implicit promise'[80] by failing to comply with the consensus vision established at the end of the Uruguay Round. Following the election of Donald Trump in 2016, the US became increasingly vocal about this sense of betrayal. In 2019, for example, President Trump said the following in his address to the UNGA:

> In 2001, China was admitted to the World Trade Organization. Our leaders then argued that this decision would compel China to liberalise its economy . . . Two decades later, this theory has been tested and proven completely wrong. Not only has China declined to adopt promised reforms, it has embraced an economic model dependent on massive market barriers, heavy state subsidies, currency manipulation, product dumping, forced technology transfers, and the theft of intellectual property and also trade secrets on a grand scale.[81]

The US also became more active about its discontent. In 2018, for example, the first Trump Administration imposed tariffs on China with the aim of forcing it to abandon what the US considered to be unfair trade practices and intellectual property theft[82]—a policy that has found renewed force under the second Trump Administration.[83] But even more importantly for the purposes of the story being told here, the US launched its attack against the WTO AB, which it considered to have played a helping hand in China's ability to maintain a different economic model. This can be seen in the Trump Administration's 2019 Trade Policy Agenda, which states, 'China has no fear of WTO dispute settlement, even as it continues

[79] Dani Rodrik, 'The WTO Has Become Dysfunctional' *Financial Times* (5 August 2018) <https://www.ft.com/content/c2beedfe-964d-11e8-95f8-8640db9060a7>.

[80] Andrew Lang, 'Heterodox Market Orders in the Global Trade System' in Alvaro Santos, Chantal Thomas, and David Trubek (eds), *World Trade and Investment Law Reimagined: A Progressive Agenda For An Inclusive Globalization* (Anthem Press 2019) 83.

[81] Address by Mr Donald Trump (2019) (n 35).

[82] Anna Swanson, 'Trump's Trade War With China Is Officially Underway' *New York Times* (5 July 2018) <https://www.nytimes.com/2018/07/05/business/china-us-trade-war-trump-tariffs.html>.For commentary, see Andrew Lang, 'Protectionism's Many Faces' (2018) 44 The Yale Journal of International Law Online 54.

[83] In April 2025, the US increased tariffs on China to 125 per cent, see Modifying Reciprocal Tariff Rates to Reflect Trading Partner Retaliation and Alignment, Executive Order, White House (9 April 2025), available at: <https://www.whitehouse.gov/presidential-actions/2025/04/modifying-reciprocal-tariff-rates-to-reflect-trading-partner-retaliation-and-alignment/>. This formed part of a wider policy in which the second Trump Administration has sought to impose '"reciprocal" tariffs on virtually the entire globe', see Nicholas Lamp, 'What President Trump's "Reciprocal" Tariffs Mean for International (Trade) Law' (*EJIL: Talk!*, 30 April 2025) <https://www.ejiltalk.org/what-president-trumps-reciprocal-tariffs-mean-for-international-trade-law/>. However, the threatened tariff on China is by far the largest. At the time of writing, the tariff increase has been postponed and the policy remains in flux, see 'Donald Trump Extends China's 145pc Tariff Deadline for Another 90 Days' *ABC News* (12 August 2025) <https://www.abc.net.au/news/2025-08-12/donald-trump-extends-tariff-truce-with-china/105640320>.

to embrace a state-led, mercantilist approach to the economy and trade that is fundamentally incompatible with the open, market-based approach expressly envisioned and followed by other WTO Members'.[84] That document also claims: 'the Chinese government is eager to draw upon the judicial activists at the WTO to protect its economic system.'[85]

These statements suggest that the US' decision to block appointments to the AB was not only an expression of non-conformity with the WTO's consensus narrative on the part of the US; it was also an attempt to push back against China's non-conformity. Viewed from this angle, the AB impasse can be seen as a contradictory response from a state wishing to throw off the shackles of a past consensus narrative, while still subsumed by the logic of that same narrative. And so, the WTO again finds itself trapped—in this case, between lingering post-Cold War discourses of global homogeneity and the failure of those discourses to meet the world.

6.3 Backlash Against the European Court of Human Rights

Since the late 2000s, the ECtHR has been the subject of a political 'backlash' from a number of Council of Europe (CoE) Member States, including the United Kingdom (UK), the Netherlands, Denmark, Switzerland, Türkiye, and, before it left the CoE in 2022, Russia.[86] European consensus has been a significant feature of this backlash, albeit in different and sometimes implicit ways. As discussed further below, in Western liberal democracies such as the UK and Denmark, much of the discontent has centred on the ECtHR's use of European consensus to interpret the European Convention on Human Rights[87] (ECHR) 'evolutively', which critics

[84] United States Trade Representative (n 31), 26.

[85] ibid. On this point about judicial activism, the US was particularly critical of the AB's reports finding that China's SOEs would only constitute 'public bodies' for the purposes of determining a subsidy if they possessed governmental authority, see, eg, WTO, *United States—Definitive Anti-Dumping and Countervailing Duties on Certain Products from China—Report of the Appellate Body*, WT/DS379/AB/R (11 March 2011) [317]. The Trump Administration considered this interpretation as not only another instance of judicial overreach, but also a weakening of the WTO's free-market orientation. The Office of the USTR stated in a 2020 report, 'The WTO was created by and for market economies, but the Appellate Body's public body interpretation . . . favors non-market economies operating through SOEs at the expense of market economies', United States Trade Representative, Report on the Appellate Body of the World Trade Organization (February 2020) 9, available at:<https://ustr.gov/sites/default/files/Report_on_the_Appellate_Body_of_the_World_Trade_Organization.pdf>.

[86] Mikael Rask Madsen, 'Two-Level Politics and the Backlash against International Courts: Evidence from the Politicization of the European Court of Human Rights' (2020) 22 The British Journal of Politics and International Relations. On 15 March 2022, the Government of the Russian Federation informed the Secretary General of its withdrawal from the CoE. That same day, the PACE unanimously adopted an Opinion which considered that the Russian Federation could no longer be a Member State following its invasion of Ukraine. See 'The Russian Federation is excluded from the Council of Europe', *Council of Europe: Newsroom*, 16 March 2022 <https://www.coe.int/en/web/portal/-/the-russian-federation-is-excluded-from-the-council-of-europe#:~:text=In%20an%20extraordinary%20meeting%20this,after%2026%20years%20of%20membership>.

[87] Opened for signature 4 November 1950, ETS 5 (entered into force 3 September 1953).

increasingly view as undemocratic. Prior to its departure from the CoE, the discontent in Russia had more been about the norms the ECtHR's claims of European consensus had generated, particularly in relation to issues such as lesbian, gay, bisexual, transgender, and intersex (LGBTI) rights, which some state and religious figures claimed were a threat to Russian 'traditional values'.[88]

By 2012, discontent in the UK had hit such heights that the UK government convened a CoE meeting to discuss reforms aimed at rebalancing the power between the Court and national institutions.[89] The final text of the Brighton Declaration (2012),[90] as agreed to by all forty-seven Member States at the time, called on the ECtHR to give greater prominence to both the margin of appreciation and the principle of subsidiarity. The 'margin of appreciation' refers to the 'latitude of deference or error'[91] that the ECtHR allows Member States in their implementation of the ECHR. Subsidiarity is 'the principle that, where possible, final decisions should be made nationally'.[92] By emphasizing these two principles, the Brighton Declaration sent a message to the ECtHR that the Member States now wanted it to play a less interventionist role. The following year, in 2013, Protocol 15 was drafted, which inserts both of those principles into the preamble of the ECHR.[93] This Protocol, which entered into force in 2021, is the first amendment in the history of the European human rights system that restricts rather than enhances the authority of the ECtHR.[94]

Following the Brighton Declaration in 2012, the ECtHR adopted a more deferential approach towards the Member States' national law and politics, making reference to the margin of appreciation with greater frequency in its decisions[95] and focusing more on domestic decision-making processes rather than the substance of Member States' laws.[96] By 2014, one Strasbourg

[88] Dmitri Bartenev, 'LGBT Rights in Russia and European Human Rights Standards' in Lauri Mälksoo and Wolfgang Benedek (eds), *Russia and the European Court of Human Rights: The Strasbourg Effect* (Cambridge University Press 2017) 326.

[89] On the 'rebalancing' function of the Brighton Declaration, see Mikael Rask Madsen, 'Rebalancing European Human Rights: Has the Brighton Declaration Engendered a New Deal on Human Rights in Europe?' (2018) 9 Journal of International Dispute Settlement 199.

[90] Brighton Declaration, 20 April 2012, available at <https://www.echr.coe.int/Documents/2012_Brighton_FinalDeclaration_ENG.pdf>.

[91] Howard Charles Yourow, *Margin of Appreciation Doctrine in the Dynamics of European Human Rights* (Brill 1996) 13.

[92] David Cameron, 'Speech Made by the Prime Minister of the United Kingdom to the Parliamentary Assembly of the Council of Europe' (25 January 2012) <http://www.assembly.coe.int/nw/xml/Speeches/Speech-XML2HTML-EN.asp?SpeechID=31&a1=0&p2=0&lang=EN>.

[93] Protocol No. 15 Amending the Convention for the Protection of Human Rights and Fundamental Freedoms, opened for signature 24 June 2013, CETS 213, 2013 (entered into force 1 August 2021), Article 1.

[94] Laurence R Helfer, 'The Burdens and Benefits of Brighton' (*European Society for International Law (ESIL) Reflections*, 8 June 2012) 1 <https://scholarship.law.duke.edu/cgi/viewcontent.cgi?article=5348&context=faculty_scholarship>.

[95] Madsen (n 86).

[96] See generally, Robert Spano, 'The Future of the European Court of Human Rights—Subsidiarity, Process-Based Review and the Rule of Law' (2018) 18 Human Rights Law Review 473.

judge declared that the ECtHR's case law had entered a new era—the 'Age of Subsidiarity'.[97]

Yet, even with this tempered approach, discontent with the ECtHR remained. Consequently, in 2018, the Member States adopted another declaration, the Copenhagen Declaration—this time at the instigation of Denmark.[98] The draft Copenhagen Declaration, as put forward by the Danish government, was more radical than the final outcome. For example, it envisaged a process whereby the Member States could 'discuss the general development of areas of the Court's case law of particular interest to them and, if appropriate, adopt texts expressing their general views'.[99] This proposal was rejected after an outpouring of criticism from non-government organizations (NGOs) concerned about its potential to undermine the ECtHR's independence.[100] The final version of the Copenhagen Declaration instead 'appreciates' the Danish Chairmanship's invitation to a one-off, informal meeting 'where general developments in the jurisprudence of the Court can be discussed'[101] and reiterates the importance of the margin of appreciation and subsidiarity.[102] The Copenhagen Declaration also goes slightly further than the Brighton Declaration by singling out Articles 8–11 of the ECHR (the right to respect for private and family life; freedom of thought, conscience and religion; freedom of expression; and freedom of assembly and association) as areas in which 'there may be a range of different but legitimate solutions which could each be compatible with the Convention depending on the context'.[103]

In the following two subsections, I describe how the ECtHR's claims of European consensus played into the Member States' discontent with the Court by projecting visions of public voice and homogeneity onto Europe that did not always match the reality on the ground.

6.3.1 European Consensus and Ideas of Democracy

In Western European Member States such as the UK, much of the backlash toward the ECtHR has centred on fears that it constitutes a threat to national democracy. This can be seen in a speech made by former British Prime Minister David

[97] Robert Spano, 'Universality or Diversity of Human Rights? Strasbourg in the Age of Subsidiarity' (2014) 14 Human Rights Law Review 487.

[98] Madsen (n 86).

[99] Draft Copenhagen Declaration, 5 February 2018 [41], available at: <https://menneskeret.dk/sites/menneskeret.dk/files/media/dokumenter/nyheder/draft_copenhagen_declaration_05.02.18.pdf>

[100] See, eg, Amnesty International et al., *Joint NGO Response to the Draft Copenhagen Declaration*, 13 February 2018, <https://amnesty.dk/media/3931/joint-ngo-response-to-the-copenhagen-declaration-13-february-2018-with-signatures.pdf>.

[101] Copenhagen Declaration, 13 April 2018, [41], available at: <https://rm.coe.int/copenhagen-declaration/16807b915c>.

[102] ibid [28], [31].

[103] ibid, [28].

Cameron to the Parliamentary Assembly of the Council of Europe (PACE) in 2012, a few months before the Brighton Declaration was adopted. In that speech, Cameron attributed the 'lively debate' going on in the UK concerning the ECtHR to a 'credible democratic anxiety' that it was no longer treating national decisions that had been 'subjected to proper, reasoned, democratic debate' with respect.[104] The term 'European consensus' has not featured prominently in this discourse. Instead, public figures in the UK have tended to either condemn the ECtHR's 'living instrument' approach, which they see as 'the banner under which the Strasbourg court has assumed power to legislate'[105] for the Member States, or lament the fact that 'the margin of appreciation, which allows different interpretations of the Convention, has shrunk, and ... not enough account is being taken of democratic decisions of national parliaments'.[106] In effect, however, the ECtHR's use of European consensus has been at the heart of this critique as it is the interpretive method that the Court uses to 'bring forward a particular human rights issue from the margin of appreciation and trigger evolutive interpretation'.[107]

In the UK, the backlash was sparked by the ECtHR's decision in *Hirst v the United Kingdom (No. 2)* (2005),[108] which held that the UK's blanket ban on prisoner voting violated the right to free elections in Article 3 of Protocol 1 of the ECHR. In that case, the UK government had argued that it should enjoy a wide margin of appreciation because there was no clear European consensus on the matter.[109] At the time, eighteen Member States had no restrictions on prisoner voting, thirteen Member States had a blanket ban similar to that in the UK, and the remaining sixteen had some form of lesser restriction on prisoner voting.[110] The government had also pointed out that the UK's prisoner voting law 'had been adhered to over many years with the explicit approval of Parliament'[111] and that 'the matter had been considered fully by the national courts applying the principles of the Convention under the Human Rights Act'.[112]

The ECtHR did not accept these arguments. While it acknowledged that the UK was 'not alone among Convention countries in depriving all convicted prisoners of the right to vote', it nevertheless found that it was 'a *minority* of Contracting States in which a blanket restriction on the right of convicted prisoners to vote is imposed

[104] Cameron (n 92).
[105] Lord Leonard Hoffman, 'The Universality of Human Rights' (*Judicial Studies Board Annual Lecture*, 19 March 2009) [36] <https://www.judiciary.uk/announcements/speech-by-lord-hoffmann-the-universality-of-human-rights/>.
[106] Cameron (n 92).
[107] Kanstantsin Dzehtsiarou, *European Consensus and the Legitimacy of the European Court of Human Rights* (Cambridge University Press 2015) 24.
[108] App No 74025/01, Eur Ct HR (6 October 2005) ('*Hirst*'). However, note that there had been some public criticism of the Court's 'undemocratic' approach beforehand, see, eg, Hoffman (n 105).
[109] *Hirst* (n 108) [47], [78].
[110] Joint Dissenting Opinion of Judges Wildhaber, Costa, Lorenzen, Kovler, and Jebens in ibid [6].
[111] *Hirst* (n 108) [47].
[112] ibid [48].

or in which there is no provision allowing prisoners to vote'.[113] The ECtHR thus held that although the margin of appreciation was not narrow in this case, it was not 'all-encompassing'[114] either, paving the way for its finding of breach. 'As to the weight to be attached to the position adopted by the legislature and judiciary in the United Kingdom',[115] the ECtHR held that, despite the UK's prisoner voting ban having been discussed by Parliament, there had not been 'any substantive debate by members of the legislature on the continued justification in light of modern-day penal policy and of current human rights standards for maintaining such a general restriction on the right of prisoners to vote'.[116] The ECtHR also noted that the UK's national courts had tended to defer to Parliament on the matter.[117] As such, the ECtHR considered the UK to have fallen short of the proportionality assessment required by Article 3 of Protocol 1 of the ECHR, even within its margin of appreciation.

Some of the dissenting judges on the ECtHR argued that, far from the UK being in 'disharmony with a common European standard', 'the legislation in Europe show[ed] that there [was] little consensus about whether or not prisoners should have the right to vote'.[118] In this connection, they raised a democratic concern with the majority's reasoning:

> [I]t is essential to bear in mind that the Court is not a legislator and should be careful not to assume legislative functions. An "evolutive" or "dynamic" interpretation should have a sufficient basis in changing conditions in the societies of the Contracting States, including an emerging consensus . . . We fail to see that this is so in the present case.[119]

There was little reaction in the UK at the time that *Hirst* was handed down in 2005.[120] It was not until 2010, when enforcement of the ECtHR's judgment became an issue, that controversy erupted.[121] In 2011, the House of Commons

[113] ibid [81] [emphasis added].
[114] ibid [82].
[115] ibid [79].
[116] ibid.
[117] ibid [80].
[118] Joint Dissenting Opinion of Judges Wildhaber, Costa, Lorenzen, and Kovler in ibid [6].
[119] ibid.
[120] Ed Bates, 'The UK and Strasbourg: A Strained Relationship—The Long View' in Katja S Ziegler, Elizabeth Wicks, and Loveday Hodson (eds), *The UK and European Human Rights: A Strained Relationship?* (Hart Publishing 2015) 65.
[121] ibid. In *Greens and MT v United Kingdom*, App Nos 60041/08 and 60054/08, Eur Ct HR (23 November 2010), the Court considered the UK's continued failure to amend legislation imposing a blanket ban on voting in national and European elections for convicted prisoners in detention in the UK following its decision in *Hirst*. The Court applied its 'pilot judgment' procedure and gave the UK government six months from the date the decision becomes final to amend its legislation and remove the blanket ban. For commentary, see Mark Hosking, 'Enforcing the Right to Vote: UK Government Given Deadline to Reinstate Prisoners' Right to Vote' (*Human Rights Law Centre*, 23 November

held a special session to discuss the matter.[122] In that session, some Members of Parliament (MPs) adopted the dissenting judges' view that the ECtHR's application of European consensus had been flawed. They emphasized that '[d]ifferent democracies in Europe take different approaches'[123] and that there was 'no consensus across Europe as to whether those serving custodial sentences should have their right to vote removed'.[124] As such, these MPs considered that the Court had overstepped its role in that decision. Other MPs, however, appeared to question the ECtHR's use of European consensus to intervene in domestic politics altogether, especially in the context of an issue such as the prisoner voting ban, which, they claimed, was the 'settled view of the British people'.[125] These MPs looked back to 'the time of the Tyrer case against Britain in 1978 . . . [when] [t]he judges [had] assumed the powers of legislators'[126] and queried how it had 'come about that we, in a sovereign Parliament, have let these decisions be taken by a kangaroo court in Strasbourg . . . ?'[127]

In the view of some MPs, the 'undemocratic' nature of the ECtHR's interpretive style had also been exacerbated by the architecture of the post-1998 ECHR system. At the same session in the House of Commons, for example, Jack Straw MP, said the following:

> [T]he Strasbourg Court is setting itself up as a supreme court for Europe, with an ever-widening remit . . . Even in countries with supreme courts much more powerful than ours, there is a democratic override of their decisions . . . There is no such democratic override available for decisions of the Strasbourg Court, so . . . we as elected MPs are expected to do the opposite of that in which we believe.[128]

At the end of the House of Commons session, most MPs (234 to 22) voted to defy the ECtHR by leaving the UK's prisoner voting ban in place.[129]

Concerns regarding the democratic threat posed by the ECtHR's interpretive approach extended beyond the UK Parliament. In 2013, for example, Lord Sumption, a judge on the UK Supreme Court, delivered a speech asserting:

2010) <https://www.hrlc.org.au/human-rights-case-summaries/greens-and-mt-v-united-kingdom-2010-echr-1826-23-november-2010>.

[122] United Kingdom, *Parliamentary Debates*, House of Commons, 10 February 2011, <https://hansard.parliament.uk/Commons/2011-02-10/debates/11021059000001/VotingByPrisoners?highlight=living%20instrument#contribution-11021059000488>.
[123] ibid (Denis MacShane MP).
[124] ibid (Stephen Phillips MP).
[125] ibid (Philip Hollobone MP).
[126] ibid (Dominic Raab MP).
[127] ibid (Philip Hollobone MP).
[128] ibid (Jack Straw MP).
[129] ibid.

> [T]he Strasbourg court . . . [claims] that it interprets the Convention in the light of the evolving social conceptions common to the democracies of Europe, so as to keep it up to date. Put like that, it sounds innocuous, indeed desirable. But what it means in practice is that the Strasbourg court develops the Convention by a process of extrapolation or analogy, so as to reflect its own view of what rights are required in a modern democracy.[130]

In this quote, we see Lord Sumption not only criticize the ECtHR for using its concept of European consensus as subterfuge for its own views and values,[131] but also identify that, up until that point, its interpretative approach had seemed 'desirable'. In doing so, he drew attention to the dissonance that developed between the operational reality of European consensus, whereby the Court seemed to 'develop the Convention by a process of extrapolation', and the idea of 'public voice' that had come to surround it.

Before long, even some of the greatest beneficiaries of the ECtHR's claims of European consensus in the UK started to doubt the legitimacy of its approach to interpretation. In the mid-2010s, for example, Jeff Dudgeon—the applicant in the ECtHR's first decision finding that the criminalization of homosexual sex violated the ECHR on the basis of a new common European position[132]—admitted that he 'can be quite critical of the Court today'[133] on account of its interventionist approach, noting 'I'm not sure whether I've got more conservative or it's got a bit more adventurous'.[134]

Democratic concerns relating to the ECtHR resulted in the UK taking a number of actions. In 2012, the UK used its CoE Chairmanship to initiate the Brighton Conference to discuss ways of preventing the Court from 'going over national decisions where it does not need to'.[135] In 2015, UK Prime Minister David Cameron also announced plans to repeal the UK's Human Rights Act 1998 and replace it with a 'British Bill of Rights' as a way to 'break the link' between the European Court of Human Rights and the UK Supreme Court to ensure that the latter remained the 'ultimate arbiter of human rights' in the UK.[136] The following year, Home Secretary Theresa May went even further, calling for a UK withdrawal from

[130] Lord Sumption, 'The Limits of Law' (*27th Sultan Azlan Shah Lecture, Kuala Lumpur*, 20 November 2013) 7–11 <https://www.supremecourt.uk/docs/speech-131120.pdf>.

[131] On the idea that European consensus 'is but a convenient subterfuge for implementing the court's hidden principled decisions', see Eyal Benvenisti, 'Margin of Appreciation, Consensus, and Universal Standards' (1999) 31 New York University Journal of International Law and Politics 843, 852.

[132] See *Dudgeon v United Kingdom*, App No 7525/76, 25 Eur Ct HR (22 October 1981).

[133] Jeff Dudgeon cited in Paul Johnson, *Going to Strasbourg: An Oral History of Sexual Orientation Discrimination and the European Convention on Human Rights* (Oxford University Press 2016) 82.

[134] ibid.

[135] Cameron (n 92).

[136] Nicholas Watt and Rowena Mason, 'Cameron "Committed to Breaking Link with European Court of Human Rights"' *Guardian* (1 June 2015) <https://www.theguardian.com/law/2015/jun/01/david-cameron-european-court-of-human-rights>.

the ECHR.[137] The UK's refusal to implement the ECtHR's decision in *Hirst* also led to a multi-year standoff between the UK and the Court, which only came to an end in 2017 when the CoE accepted the UK's offer to allow a small number of prisoners the right to vote.[138] Though eventually resolved, this period of non-compliance sent shockwaves through the European human rights system. In 2013, for example, the CoE Commissioner for Human Rights, Nils Muižnieks, worried that the UK's defiance on the issue of prisoner voting might spell 'the beginning of the end of the ECHR system' because it 'would send a strong signal' to the other Member States that it was no longer necessary to comply with the Court's judgments.[139]

The UK's criticism of the ECtHR may have also had an impact on other Member States. For over the same period of time, the Netherlands, Switzerland, and Denmark all began to raise similar democratic concerns about the ECtHR. While these concerns were often sparked by specific judgments against those Member States,[140] the discourse surrounding them echoed that circulating in the UK. In the Netherlands, for example, newspaper articles began to run under headlines such as 'The European Court of Human Rights Constitutes a Serious Violation of Democracy'[141] and, in 2011, the Dutch government updated its official human rights policy to include the objective of ensuring that the Court allowed 'more scope for state parties' "margin of appreciation"'.[142] In Switzerland in 2014, former federal judge Martin Schubarth argued that it was 'unacceptable that a small panel of judges, who generally lack the expert knowledge about a legislative authority, handle matters in an undemocratic way instead of the authority itself'[143] and was supported by a number of political parties in advocating for a Swiss withdrawal from the ECHR.[144] In 2017, the Danish Prime Minister raised concerns with CoE Secretary-General, Thorbjørn Jagland, about the ECtHR's 'evolutive' approach to

[137] Theresa May, quoted in Anushka Asthana and Rowena Mason, 'UK Must Leave European Convention on Human Rights, Says Theresa May' *The Guardian* (26 April 2016) <https://www.theguardian.com/politics/2016/apr/25/uk-must-leave-european-convention-on-human-rights-theresa-may-eu-referendum>.

[138] Owen Bowcott, 'Council of Europe Accepts UK Compromise on Prisoner Voting Rights' *Guardian* (8 December 2017) <https://www.theguardian.com/politics/2017/dec/07/council-of-europe-accepts-uk-compromise-on-prisoner-voting-rights>.

[139] Muižnieks quoted in Øyvind Stiansen and Erik Voeten, 'Backlash and Judicial Restraint: Evidence from the European Court of Human Rights' (2020) 64 International Studies Quarterly 770, 772.

[140] For a breakdown of the criticism in different Member States, see Patricia Popelier, Sarah Lambrecht, and Koen Lemmens (eds), *Criticism of the European Court of Human Rights: Shifting the Convention System: Counter-Dynamics at the National and EU Level* (Intersentia 2016).

[141] Thierry Baudet (2010), quoted in BM Oomen, 'A Serious Case of Strasbourg-Bashing? An Evaluation of the Debates on the Legitimacy of the European Court of Human Rights in the Netherlands' (2016) 20 International Journal of Human Rights 407, 414–15.

[142] Dutch Ministry of Foreign Affairs, Responsible for Freedom (2011), available at <https://www.government.nl›policy-notes›2011/08/17>.

[143] Schubarth, quoted in 'ECHR under Pressure on Swiss Anniversary' *Swiss Info* (27 November 2014) <https://www.swissinfo.ch/eng/politics/40-years_echr-under-pressure-on-swiss-anniversary/41132266>.

[144] Oomen (n 141) 408.

interpretation and insisted that the Member States needed a better means to influence the ECtHR's interpretation of the ECHR.[145] This sentiment would later form the basis of Denmark's proposal for a process for the Member States to 'discuss the general development of areas of the Court's case law' in the draft it put forward of the Copenhagen Declaration in 2018.

Despite this contestation, the idea that European consensus somehow injects a democratic element into the ECtHR's case law continues to influence scholarly and institutional discourses. In fact, some of the strongest claims regarding the democratic nature of European consensus came after the Brighton Declaration of 2012.[146] These included ECtHR Judge Paulo Pinto de Albuquerque's description of European consensus as a form of 'deliberative, international democracy'[147] in 2017, and law academic Kanstantsin Dzehtsiarou's claim in 2015 that European consensus 'offer[ed] some democratic legitimation to the choices made by the ECtHR'.[148] Indeed, for Dzehtsiarou, European consensus presented a possible answer to the Member States' desire for greater interaction between the ECtHR and national authorities, as set out in the Brighton Declaration.[149] This is because '[u]nlike [the] margin of appreciation, European consensus is clearly a tool used by the Court to engage in dialogue with the Contracting Parties'.[150] In his view, the ECtHR simply needed to stop applying European consensus in the 'questionable'[151] manner that it had in *Hirst*, where there had been no 'overwhelming consensus'.[152] Views such as these led other scholars to predict that '[w]ith criticism of the Court . . . escalating in a number of states, it is likely that the Court will turn more and more to this method of decision making in an effort to legitimise its judgments' and that European consensus may even 'eventually make its way into a new Protocol to the Convention', alongside the margin of appreciation and the principle of subsidiarity.[153]

[145] Jacques Hartmann, 'A Danish Crusade for the Reform of the European Court of Human Rights' (*EJIL: Talk!*, 14 November 2017) <https://www.ejiltalk.org/a-danish-crusade-for-the-reform-of-the-european-court-of-human-rights/>.

[146] On the connection between the claim that European consensus is legitimacy or democracy-enhancing and the perception that the ECtHR is facing a crisis, see Jens T Theilen, *European Consensus Between Strategy and Principle: The Uses of Vertically Comparative Legal Reasoning in Regional Human Rights Adjudication* (Nomos 2021) 335–37.

[147] Paulo Pinto de Albuquerque, 'Is the ECHR Facing an Existential Crisis?' (*Speech delivered at the Mansfield College, Oxford*, 28 April 2017) <https://www.law.ox.ac.uk/sites/files/oxlaw/pinto_opening_presentation_2017.pdf>.

[148] Dzehtsiarou (n 107) 211.

[149] Brighton Declaration (n 90), Part B 'Interaction between the Court and national authorities'.

[150] Dzehtsiarou (n 107) 157.

[151] ibid 63.

[152] ibid.

[153] Merris Amos, 'Can European Consensus Encourage Acceptance of the European Convention on Human Rights in the United Kingdom?' in Panos Kapotas and Vassilis P Tzevelekos (eds), *Building Consensus on European Consensus Judicial Interpretation of Human Rights in Europe and Beyond* (Cambridge University Press 2019) 259.

The ECtHR has neither turned further towards European consensus in recent years[154] nor have the Member States called for that principle to be enshrined in the ECHR. This is perhaps unsurprising given how explicit some of the condemnation of the ECtHR's practice of interpreting the ECHR in light of 'social conceptions common to the democracies of Europe'[155] has been. Nevertheless, the continuation of the view that comparative analysis can bring 'legitimacy' and 'democracy' to the ECtHR's decisions has meant that European consensus has not disappeared from the Court's case law either. Instead, the ECtHR seems to have taken a more deferential approach towards its use of comparative analysis, whereby it now tends to find that there is *no* European consensus on a particular matter, enabling it to afford the Member State in question a wide margin of appreciation.[156]

While this deferential approach may have quelled some of the immediate criticism the ECtHR would have otherwise received, it has not been without its own consequences. On the one hand, the ease with which the ECtHR has been able to manipulate its use of European consensus to mitigate the Member States' discontent has only served to highlight the way in which the outcome of its comparative inquiry ultimately lies with the judges on the ECtHR, rather than a predictable threshold of people or states. This, in turn, has adversely affected the authority of the ECtHR in the eyes of actors who were otherwise still supportive of it. In response to some of its recent deferential decisions, for example, human rights NGOs have criticized the ECtHR of bending to 'political will'.[157] On the other hand, the continued reliance on European consensus as the basis for the ECtHR's democratic credentials has arguably cut off opportunities for the ECtHR to experiment with more direct modes of communication with the Member States and members of the European public, such as the Danish government's 2018 proposal for the Member States to discuss and express their views on the way that European human rights law was developing[158] or the Inter-American Court of Human Rights' embrace of a more participatory model in which it has become 'normal to give victims the floor to recount their experience and civil society to list their legal arguments or remedies they deem fit during the public hearings'.[159] In this regard, as in the WTO, some of the problems facing the ECtHR seem to lie in the disjuncture that

[154] Peat's data shows a notable drop in the Grand Chamber's use of consensus since 2016, see Daniel Peat, 'The Tyranny of Choice and the Interpretation of Standards: Why the ECtHR Uses Consensus' (2021) 53 New York University Journal of International Law and Politics 381, 423.

[155] Sumption (n 130).

[156] On this trend in the UK, see Amos (n 153).

[157] See, eg, Joint Committee on Human Rights, quoted in ibid 273.

[158] Draft Copenhagen Declaration (n 99) [41].

[159] Ezgi Yildiz, 'Enduring Practices in Changing Circumstances: A Comparison of the European Court of Human Rights and the Inter-American Court of Human Rights' (2020) 34 Temple International and Comparative Law Journal 309, 329. In contrast, the rules and practices of procedure of the ECtHR require applicants to be legally represented and rarely result in applicants or civil society organizations taking the floor during oral hearings.

exists between the democratic discourses surrounding the Court's claims to base its decisions on a European consensus and the operational reality of its interpretive method.

6.3.2 The ECtHR and Ideas of European Sameness

Another concern amongst the CoE Member States has been that the ECtHR's use of European consensus does not allow enough space for local difference. This critique was particularly prominent in Russia prior to its departure from the CoE, which occurred after its invasion of Ukraine in 2022. In 2015, for example, the President of the Russian Constitutional Court demanded that 'the "social and cultural context" of a particular state . . . be taken into account by the ECtHR when using reasoning based on the "European consensus" approach, especially when it deals with issues relating to profound values forming the "moral and cultural code" of a nation'.[160]

To understand this concern, we must recall the homogenizing effect of the ECtHR's use of European consensus. Legally, that interpretive method can have a homogenizing effect by requiring a Member State to conform to the laws or practices adopted by most of them.[161] Discursively, it can have a homogenizing effect by projecting certain views and values onto the identity of 'Europe'.[162] In Chapter 5, I explained how the ECtHR's practice of attributing its decisions recognizing LGBTI rights to the existence of a 'European consensus' had helped to produce a narrowly defined 'gay-friendly' regional identity. This trend also went beyond LGBTI rights. From the early 1990s, there were claims that there was a 'European consensus' on human rights more generally. One example is a speech made by Swedish Prime Minister Carl Bildt before the PACE in 1992:

> There was a time when it was possible to speak about peace and stability in Europe without mentioning freedom, democracy and human rights . . . Those days are gone . . . There is no peace and there is no stability where there is no democracy and no respect for human rights. Today, that is the *European consensus* . . .[163]

[160] Bartenev (n 88) 348, summarizing a 2015 speech by the Chairman of the Russian Constitutional Court, Valery Dmitrievich Zorkin. The original, in Russian, can be accessed at: <www.ksrf.ru/ru/News/Speech/Pages/ViewItem.aspx?ParamId=72>.

[161] Theilen (n 146) 127: 'in most cases in which the ECtHR finds a violation of the Convention will constitute a demand for harmonization: while its judgments technically bind only the parties to the case according to Article 46 (1) ECHR, it is clear that they also have a broader effect.'

[162] ibid 43–44.

[163] Carl Bildt, Prime Minister of Sweden, Speech Made to the Parliamentary Assembly of the Council of Europe (1 October 1992), available at: <http://www.assembly.coe.int/nw/xml/Speeches/Speech-XML2HTML-EN.asp?SpeechID=22> [emphasis added].

Like Europe's 'gay-friendly' identity, this larger human rights-based identity was inflected with a particular set of values. In 2002, for example, Queen Beatrix of the Netherlands addressed the PACE, declaring, 'Europe stands for a particular civilization, with its roots in a common heritage, a shared past, centred on Christian and humanist values that are translated into respect for human rights'.[164] As Jens Theilan points out, this European human rights-friendly identity has also relied on civilizational tropes about Europe being more 'modern' and 'up-to-date' than the non-European 'other'.[165]

The emergence of a 'human rights-friendly' European identity can be traced back to the drafting of the ECHR and figures such as Churchill and Maxwell Fyfe's vision for a post-war Europe.[166] It then gained new force in the late 1970s, when a rediscovery of human rights took place in the West. During the decolonization era, people around the world were using languages of human rights in a variety of ways—to support the cause of national liberation and self-determination, to contest structural racism and imperialism, and to assert demands for a more egalitarian international economic order.[167] As that period came to an end, however, the Euro-American world sought to repossess human rights and naturalize them as a feature of the Western Enlightenment tradition.[168] In this move, human rights were not only reconceived as a 'downsized package of individualist civil and political protections of citizens against states'[169] but also reframed as a product of (Western) European culture. In addition, the claims of figures such as Bildt and Queen Beatrix about the relationship between 'Europe' and human rights in the 1990s and early 2000s were likely fuelled by the post-Cold War context in which they were made and the euphoric sense that liberalism had finally triumphed on the continent.

However, in my view, the ECtHR's claims of European consensus have also played a role in constructing this 'human rights-friendly' European identity.[170] This is because, by repeatedly attributing the development of ECHR rights to European views and practices, the ECtHR's claims of European consensus have worked to inscribe both those rights and the sense of progress surrounding them into Europe's identity—just as described in relation to LGBTI rights in Chapter 5. In the immediate post-Cold War period, the discursive fusion between European

[164] Beatrix, Queen of the Netherlands, Speech to the Parliamentary Assembly of the Council of Europe (25 June 2002) <http://assembly.coe.int/nw/xml/Speeches/Speech-XML2HTML-EN.asp?SpeechID=135>.

[165] Jens T Theilen, 'Civilizational Hierarchies and the Notion of "Europe" in the European Convention on Human Rights' (2025) 36 European Journal of International Law 135.

[166] See Section 4.2.1 of Chapter 4 of this book.

[167] Joseph Slaughter, 'Hijacking Human Rights: Neoliberalism, the New Historiography, and the End of the Third World' (2018) 40 Human Rights Quarterly 735, 756.

[168] ibid 753.

[169] ibid 758.

[170] Theilen also draws this connection, see Theilen (n 165) 132–38.

human rights law and European identity was likely reinforced by the Court's comparative approach gradually becoming known '*European* consensus'.[171]

When Russia joined the CoE in 1996 and ratified the ECHR in 1998, there was an expectation, similar to that which we saw above in relation to China and the WTO, that it would join in this 'European consensus' and undergo a 'human rights-friendly transformation'.[172] Mälksoo describes the prevailing sentiment at the time as follows: 'In case symbolic proof was sought for the fact that the Cold War had indeed ended and a transformation favorable to human rights at the heart of the former Cold War adversary was possible, Russia's ratification of the ECHR in 1998 must have been it.'[173]

In Russia, however, feelings of a loss of identity and independence following the collapse of the Soviet Union and claims that there could now only be one way of being 'European', combined with the economic 'shock therapy' imposed on the country in an attempt to transform its economy into a neoliberal capitalist one,[174] saw it go in a different direction. When Vladimir Putin became President in 2000, he embarked on a nationalist project rooted in anti-Western, religious, and patriarchal values.[175] This was well received domestically, with 'Russia is getting up from its knees' becoming a slogan of growing anti-Western policies and sentiment in the country.[176] As part of his nationalist project, Putin helped to reunify the Russian Orthodox Church—a process that he described as symbolic of 'the rebirth and the reunification of the Russian people itself'.[177]

The rise of the Russian Orthodox Church led to a different understanding of human rights taking hold in Russia to that prevailing in Western Europe. In 2006, for example, the Church adopted the 'Orthodox Declaration on Human Rights and Dignity', which began with a statement that there existed a 'unique Russian civilization'[178] and went on to speak about the importance of harmonizing human rights with religious, moral, and nationalist values:

[171] For one of the earliest uses of the term 'European consensus' see Laurence R Helfer, 'Finding a Consensus on Equality: The Homosexual Age of Consent and the European Convention on Human Rights' (1990) 65 New York University Law Review 1044. For more on the history of the term, see Chapter 4.

[172] Lauri Mälksoo, 'Introduction: Russia, Strasbourg and the Paradox of a Human Rights Backlash' in Benedikt Harzl, Lauri Mälksoo, and Wolfgang Benedek (eds), *Russia and the European Court of Human Rights: The Strasbourg Effect* (Cambridge University Press 2017) 3.

[173] ibid 2.

[174] Naomi Klein, *The Shock Doctrine: The Rise of Disaster Capitalism* (Penguin Press 2008). See also David M Kotz, 'Russia's Financial Crisis: The Failure of Neoliberalism?' *Z Magazine* (January 1999) 28 <http://people.umass.edu/dmkotz/R_Fin_Crisis_99.pdf>.

[175] Oleg Riabov and Tatiana Riabova, 'The Remasculinization of Russia? Gender, Nationalism, and the Legitimation of Power Under Vladimir Putin' (2014) 61 Problems of Post-Communism 23.

[176] Nikita Sleptcov, 'Political Homophobia as a State Strategy in Russia' (2018) 12 Journal of Global Initiatives: Policy, Pedagogy, Perspective 140, 143.

[177] Quoted in Marlène Laruelle, *In the Name of the Nation: Nationalism and Politics in Contemporary Russia* (Palgrave Macmillan 2009) 168.

[178] Quoted in Lauri Mälksoo, 'The Human Rights Concept of the Russian Orthodox Church and Its Patriarch Kirill I: A Critical Appraisal' in Benedek Wolfgang and others (eds), *European Yearbook on Human Rights* (Neuer Wissenschaftlicher Verlag 2013) 404.

> There are values no smaller than human rights. These are faith, morality, the sacred, motherland. Whenever these values come into conflict with the implementation of human rights, the task of the society, state and law is to bring both to harmony.[179]

According to Mälksoo, by putting human rights on the same footing as Russian religious, moral, and nationalist values, the 2006 Orthodox Declaration was an early sign that Russia was not going to join 'the "common European house" and catch up on liberal European values'.[180] By 2010, Western European scholars were lamenting that Russia had become 'increasingly reluctant to learn democracy and human rights'.[181]

Not long after the Orthodox Declaration was issued, Russia adopted a more explicitly anti-Western foreign policy position. In a 2007 speech in Munich, for example, Putin criticized the West, and the US in particular, for its 'monopolistic dominance in global relations'.[182] For Sleptcov, the rise of anti-queer discourses and policies in Russia was closely connected to this shift in Russian foreign policy, as it provided a clear way of creating a sense of national identity that was distinct from Western liberal values[183]—a form of 'heteronationalism'[184] that could stand in opposition to the European 'homoregionalism' we met in Chapter 5.

The different trajectories between the values promoted by the ECtHR and those taking shape in post-Cold War Russia came to a head in the 2010 case of *Alekseyev v Russia*,[185] concerning Moscow's ban on gay pride marches. In its submissions to the ECtHR, Russia argued, inter alia, that gay pride marches were 'banned as a matter of principle' because the promotion of homosexuality was 'incompatible with [Russian] religious doctrines and the moral values of the majority'.[186] As we saw in the previous chapter, the ECtHR did not accept this argument, instead finding a violation of the ECHR on the basis of 'a long-standing European consensus'[187] in favour of both pride marches and LGBTI rights more generally. This outcome generated considerable controversy in Russia.[188] For example, Tatyana Moskalkova, a Member of the State Duma, criticized the Court's judgment in *Alekseyev* as being contrary to 'the norms of morality and ethics . . . [as well as] Russian cultural and religious traditions'.[189]

179 ibid 405.
180 ibid 409.
181 Stephan Parmentier and Katlijn Malfliet (eds), *Russia and the Council of Europe: 10 Years After* (Palgrave Macmillan 2010) 3.
182 Quoted in Sleptcov (n 176) 142.
183 ibid 141.
184 ibid 142.
185 App Nos 4916/07, 25924/08, and 14599/09 (21 October 2010).
186 ibid [78].
187 ibid [83].
188 Bartenev (n 88) 332.
189 Moskalkova, quoted in ibid.

Along with a number of other controversial Strasbourg judgments against Russia, including one directing the Russian government to pay €1.87 billion to the shareholders of the Yukos Oil Company for a breach of property rights in 2014,[190] the fallout from *Alekseyev* prompted a backlash in Russia against the ECtHR. In 2014, Russian President Vladimir Putin publicly indicated that Russia would withdraw from the ECHR if the ECtHR continued to deliver what he described as 'politicised' decisions.[191] In 2015, the Russian Constitutional Court also decided that Strasbourg judgments would be subject to constitutional review before being implemented in Russia—a move that was quickly backed by the Russian legislature.[192] In Mälksoo's view, by redefining the relationship between Russia and the ECtHR in this manner, the Russian Constitutional Court's decision drove home that '[t]he project of Europe's *mission civilisatrice* did not turn out as was envisaged in 1996/1998'.[193]

In the aftermath of the ECtHR's 2010 decision in *Alekseyev*, restrictions on queer people in Russia also worsened. In 2012, for example, the Russian Constitutional Court upheld Moscow's decision to extend its ban on gay pride parades for 100 years.[194] In 2013, a federal Russian 'anti-homosexual propaganda' law was also enacted.[195] The deterioration of queer life-worlds in Russia following the ECtHR's attempt to intervene with a narrative of European consensus coheres with Chantal Mouffe's account of the 'dangers of the consensus model'.[196] In Mouffe's view, 'the absence of an effective pluralism' does not make difference and dissent go away; it simply prevents them from finding effective pathways for expression.[197] As a result, 'when they explode, those antagonisms take extreme forms',[198] sometimes resulting in hate and violence. In Russia, it seems, queer people have become the target of such an explosion.

Russia has not been alone in its resistance to the idea of a standardized European approach to human rights. As Robert Spano, a former judge and president of the

190 *Oao Neftyanaya Kompaniya Yukos v Russia*, App. no. 14902/04, Eur Ct HR (just satisfaction) (31 July 2014).

191 Benedikt Harzl, 'Nativist Ideological Responses to European/Liberal Human Rights Discourses in Contemporary Russia' in Lauri Mälksoo and Wolfgang Benedek (eds), *Russia and the European Court of Human Rights: The Strasbourg Effect* (Cambridge University Press 2017) 365.

192 Lauri Mälksoo, 'Russia's Constitutional Court Defies the European Court of Human Rights: Constitutional Court of the Russian Federation Judgment of 14 July 2015, No 21-П/2015' (2016) 12 European Constitutional Law Review 377, 377.

193 Mälksoo (n 172) 10.

194 'Gay Parades Banned in Moscow for 100 Years' *BBC News* (17 August 2012) <https://www.bbc.com/news/world-europe-19293465>.

195 Paul Johnson, '"Homosexual Propaganda" Laws in the Russian Federation: Are They in Violation of the European Convention on Human Rights?' (2015) 3 Russian Law Journal 37, 44. The federal law replaced a range of similar regional laws that had been passed since 2006, ibid 40–1. Healey describes 2013 as 'Russia's Year of Political Homophobia', see Dan Healey, *Russian Homophobia from Stalin to Sochi* (Bloomsbury Academic 2018) 1.

196 Mouffe (n 71) 69.

197 ibid 82.

198 ibid.

ECtHR, observed in 2014 in relation to all forty-seven Member States' adoption of the Brighton Declaration: 'The unequivocal call for an increased emphasis by the Strasbourg Court on applying a robust and coherent concept of subsidiarity is, by definition, a call for an increased diversity in the protection of human rights.'[199] This sentiment has been particularly notable in the UK. In a 2013 lecture, for example, UK judge Lord Justice Laws emphasized that '[t]here may perfectly properly be different answers to some human rights issues in different States on similar facts. I think the Strasbourg court should recognise this.'[200] In addition, the UK's proposal for a British Bill of Human Rights, which was eventually introduced in 2022 but scrapped the following year, can be seen as reflecting a desire for a more localized version of human rights.[201]

As in Russia, there has also been a rise in anti-queer policies and discourses in the UK in recent years, particularly in relation to transgender people. In 2017, the UK government announced a public consultation on the Gender Recognition Act (GRA) of 2004—the statute the UK introduced to implement the ECtHR's decision in *Christine Goodwin v the UK* (2002),[202] which had held, on the basis of a consensus analysis, that the inability to change one's legal gender on a birth certificate was a violation of Articles 8 and 12 of the ECHR. The consultation on the GRA was sparked by the campaigning of LGBTI groups and medical bodies, who argued that it needed to be updated to decentre the role of psychiatry and other medical expertise in the application process for legal gender recognition by moving to a model of self-identification.[203] Although a majority of respondents were in support of these changes, the UK government ultimately decided against reforming the GRA.[204] Nevertheless, the consultation catalysed what Duffy describes as a 'moral panic' about trans rights and trans inclusion in the UK,[205] led by a coalition of self-proclaimed 'gender critical' feminists and far-right movements, and spurred on by a populist conversative media.[206]

Since then, anti-trans sentiment has found its way into the political and legal establishment, with the UK government blocking a Scottish Bill to introduce self-identification as the basis for legal gender recognition in 2023;[207] the UK Supreme

[199] Spano (n 97) 491.

[200] Lord Justice Laws, 'Lecture III: The Common Law and Europe', *Hamlyn Lectures 2013*, 27 November 2013, 13, available at: <https://www.globalgovernancewatch.org/docLib/20140213_laws-lj-speech-hamlyn-lecture-2013.pdf>.

[201] See Bill of Rights Bill, Parliamentary Bills, UK Parliament, available at: https://bills.parliament.uk/bills/3227.

[202] App No 28957/95, Eur Ct HR (11 July 2002).

[203] Sally Hines, 'Hands towards the Right: UK Gender-Critical Feminism and Right-Wing Coalitions' (2025) 34 Journal of Gender Studies 699, 702.

[204] Sandra Duffy, 'Moral Panics and Legal Projects: Echoes of Section 28 in United Kingdom Transgender Discourse and Law Reform' (2025) 1 Gender and Justice 78, 85–86.

[205] See generally ibid.

[206] See generally Hines (n 203).

[207] Duffy (n 204) 90.

Court ruling in 2025 that, for the purposes of the Equality Act 2010, 'sex' means 'biological sex' and sex is binary;[208] and the UK Equality and Human Rights Commission issuing guidance which prevents trans people from accessing single-sex public spaces.[209] While these changes have not been expressed directly through an anti-European discourse, scholars have drawn connections between shifting attitudes towards gender and queerness in the UK and the country's attempts to assert a national identity in the wake of its departure from the European Union.[210] When considered from this perspective, it is perhaps telling that the group now targeted in the UK acquired their rights through a drawn-out process of litigation in the ECtHR, mediated through the Court's notion of European consensus,[211] rather than a more local process with opportunities for community 'buy-in'. In this regard, the transphobic turn in the UK may represent another instance of Mouffe's contention that a suppression of difference and a negation of the political through the mobilization of the idea of consensus can lead to an 'explosion' of antagonism, sometimes with devastating consequences.[212]

And yet, despite their similar experiences, the UK has not viewed Russia as an ally when it comes to the ECtHR. Indeed, Russia's failure to conform to the European human rights model has formed part of the UK's own discontent with the ECtHR. In 2016, for example, when then-Home Secretary Theresa May was calling for a UK withdrawal from the ECHR, just as Russia had done two years earlier, she said:

> The ECHR can bind the hands of parliament, adds nothing to our prosperity, makes us less secure by preventing the deportation of dangerous foreign nationals—*and does nothing to change the attitudes of governments like Russia's when it comes to human rights.*[213]

This statement suggests that, despite the UK demanding greater space for local difference itself, some of its representatives still harbour a desire for the ECtHR to change the attitudes of other governments so as to align with a certain set of European values.

Furthermore, even after events like the 2012 Brighton Declaration and the 2012–13 conflict between Russia and the CoE over LGBTI rights, proponents of European consensus have continued to rely on the supposed homogeneity

[208] *For Women Scotland Ltd v The Scottish Ministers* [2025] UKSC 16 (16 April 2025).
[209] Athena Stavrou, 'Trans Women to Be Banned from Single-Sex Spaces under New EHRC Guidance' *The Independent* (8 August 2025) <https://www.independent.co.uk/news/uk/home-news/trans-women-ehrc-guidance-banned-single-sex-spaces-b2804202.html>.
[210] See, eg, Moira Dustin, Nuno Ferreira, and Susan Millns (eds), *Gender and Queer Perspectives on Brexit* (Palgrave Macmillan 2019).
[211] See Section 4.4.1 in Chapter 4 of this book.
[212] Mouffe (n 71) 82.
[213] Theresa May quoted in Asthana and Mason (n 137) [emphasis added].

of European states as justification for the ECtHR's use of its comparative interpretive method.[214] Writing in 2015, for example, Dzehtsiarou cited the fact that the CoE Member States 'are much more homogeneous in terms of human rights protection than States worldwide'[215] as a reason why the ECtHR should continue to base its decisions on a European consensus. This demonstrates that while many now appear to be resisting the visions of sameness and agreement that the ECtHR's claims of consensus helped to project onto Europe, sometimes in a violent and hateful register, those visions have not yet completely fallen away either.

6.4 Conclusion: Consensus, Crisis, and the Importance of Difference and Dissent

In the two stories of institutional turbulence told above, an overarching theme emerged. When viewed through the lens of consensus, the difficulties facing both the WTO and ECtHR lie not only in an unravelling of the ideas authorized by their respective uses of consensus, but also in the persistence of those same ideas. That is, even as discontent with the effects of the WTO's consensus procedure and the ECtHR's use of European consensus has mounted, the discourses of democracy and homogeneity that were constructed around those uses of consensus have continued to be deployed. And, as a consequence, neither institution appears willing or able to turn in a different direction.

This situation can be explained, in large measure, by the feature that made consensus a powerful technique of authorization in international law in the first place: its ability to gesture towards a profound, yet unfixed, level of agreement. As we have seen, by holding out the promise of a widespread agreement, the idea of consensus has helped to wrap the WTO and ECtHR in discourses of equality, democracy, unity, and sameness. And yet, by not fixing the number of states or people that need to agree affirmatively with a decision for it to qualify as consensus, both institutions have been able to apply the idea of consensus flexibly. This has included an application of the idea of consensus to procedures that have exacerbated underlying power relations and decisions that were met with substantial dissent. Now, it seems, this mismatch of perception and reality has become more acute. Past narratives of international democracy and ideological consensus are no longer ringing true to many, and people are turning to leaders who are prepared to call out the illusory nature of those narratives and put forward a different story. This has presented a challenge to the authority of the WTO and ECtHR and their legal regimes, which has sometimes taken on an explosive, even violent, form—whether it

[214] On this trend, see Theilen (n 146) 134.
[215] Dzehtsiarou (n 107) 129.

be the US' unilateral decision to paralyze the WTO AB or the worsening treatment of queer people in places such as Russia and the UK in an apparent attempt to re-assert a sense of national identity.

At the same time, the imprecision of the idea of consensus has meant that any problems with the procedures or decisions that carry its name can be dismissed as poor or incorrect use of consensus, rather than a problem with the idea of consensus itself. Consider the ECtHR's decision in *Hirst*. There, the fact that the ECtHR found against the UK, despite there being no 'overwhelming consensus'[216] on prisoner voting rights, has been described by some commentators as a 'questionable'[217] application of ECtHR's comparative method. Likewise, some commentators have called the US' use of the WTO's consensus procedure to paralyze the WTO's judicial branch an '*illegal* blocking of AB nominations'.[218] The implication in these statements is that the events that triggered the crises in the two institutions under analysis were 'poor' or 'wrong' uses of a decision-making method oriented towards consensus. This characterization has allowed various actors to hold on to the idea of a 'right' or 'true' way of achieving consensus; to the promise that there might one day be a way to facilitate an agreement amongst the Members of the WTO or the CoE that will be 'broad' or 'general' enough, if only those institutions would keep trying. As a result, the positive aura surrounding the WTO and ECtHR's use of consensus has not disappeared, making it difficult for those institutions to turn away from consensus, especially after years of it being integral to their authority.

Compounding this situation is the fact that, in both the WTO and ECtHR, the notion of consensus has worked to suppress and conceal difference and dissent. It has done so discursively by generating narratives of unity and sameness. It has also done so procedurally by only officially recording a *lack* of formal disagreement, and never disagreement itself (in the case of the WTO's main consensus procedure),[219] or by smoothing a 'trend' into an 'emerging consensus', rather than lingering in the conflicts and contradictions that may underlie that trend (in the case of the ECtHR).[220] Yet, new ideas are frequently born from disagreement and a diversity of opinion. Conflict between a range of perspectives is often what is required to move from one narrative to another or to find creative solutions to complex problems.[221] By downplaying and papering over difference and dissent, the notion of consensus in the WTO and ECtHR has worked to salt the earth of new ideas, so to speak, leaving both institutions with little upon which to draw in order to reinvent

[216] ibid 63.
[217] ibid.
[218] Petersmann (n 6) [emphasis added]. Petersmann argues that the US' blockage of AB appointments was illegal because it was unilaterally undoing an already agreed-upon institutional structure.
[219] See Section 3.3.1 in Chapter 3 of this book.
[220] Theilen (n 146) 439.
[221] On the need for a vibrant 'agonistic' public sphere of contestation, see Mouffe (n 71) 18.

themselves or reimagine the basis of their authority. Consequently, both the WTO and the ECtHR find themselves trapped within past narratives of democracy and sameness, even as those narratives have begun to crumble. As such, despite the idea of consensus helping to prop up the authority of the WTO and ECtHR for many years, it may now be a source of their undoing.

7

Towards an International Law with Space for Difference

7.1 Introduction: Constructing a World of Many Worlds

What, then, could offer an approach to international law that would better accommodate all the diversity and dissent that exists in the world? In this chapter, I draw on queer and jurisdictional thinking to consider what an international law with space for difference might look like. In my view, overcoming some of the issues described in this book is not as simple as abandoning or reducing the use of decision-making methods called 'consensus'—although moving to a voting system, in the case of the World Trade Organization (WTO),[1] or an alternative method of comparative treaty interpretation, in the case of the European Court of Human Rights (ECtHR),[2] could well provide a better record of disagreement, helping to challenge narratives of sameness and opening up new ways of thinking. Rather, I am of the view that moving beyond the issues described in this book involves a shift in imagination in which the goal of the world or a particular region routinely reaching a widespread agreement is decentred in international law. To achieve this shift, the discourses that have formed around the idea of consensus, in which it is held out as a beacon of democracy and a marker of unity, must be dismantled, such that it no longer operates as a powerful (but fragile) technique of authority. In its place, we require an alternative international legal imaginary that not only allows for diversity but enables it to thrive.

It is my hope that this book has so far helped along the task of puncturing the positive aura that has grown up around the idea of consensus in international law by demonstrating how it has worked to shape and reshape the world in ways that

[1] This is a common proposal made by observers of the WTO's decision-making difficulties. See, eg, see Hector Torres, 'A Tariff Crisis Is Exactly the Right Time to Reform the WTO' (*Centre for International Governance Innovation (CIGI) Online*, 11 April 2025) <https://www.cigionline.org/articles/a-tariff-crisis-is-exactly-the-right-time-to-reform-the-wto/>.

[2] Jens Theilen, for example, has persuasively argued that the ECtHR could use comparative legal reasoning in a way 'which distances itself from the closure-oriented notion of European consensus and instead aims to highlight contradictions within and among the legal systems of the States parties', see Jens T Theilen, *European Consensus Between Strategy and Principle: The Uses of Vertically Comparative Legal Reasoning in Regional Human Rights Adjudication* (Nomos 2021) 438. According to Theilen, using comparative legal reasoning to expose differences and inconsistencies in European public culture could help to unsettle dominant social practices, opening up space for more transformative political agendas.

Consensus in International Law. Claerwen O'Hara, Oxford University Press. © Claerwen O'Hara 2026.
DOI: 10.1093/9780198948643.003.0007

often suppress difference and uphold existing power relations. In this chapter, I now wish to begin the second task of sketching an alternative, queerer international legal imaginary with which we could replace it. In pursuit of such an alternative, I have been influenced by the thinking of the Zapatistas, a left-wing insurgent group in Chiapas, Mexico, who I introduced in Chapter 3 and will discuss again in more detail below. In particular, I have been drawn to the Zapatistas' call for 'a world where many worlds fit'—a vision that has been noted for its resonances with queer theory due to its radical embrace of difference.[3] A world of multiple worlds, or what some have called the 'pluriverse', involves 'heterogeneous worldings coming together as a political ecology of practices, negotiating their difficult being together in heterogeneity'.[4] Rather than seeking out sameness and agreement in order to construct a single world, the pluriverse accepts and celebrates the fact that the world is composed of 'many ontologies, many ways of being in the world, many ways of knowing reality'[5]—and many different laws and legal cultures. For Conway and Singh, this acceptance and celebration of difference gives rise to an 'ethos of non-interference coupled with hospitality and co-operation', which may offer a pathway to realizing a more radical vision of international democracy.[6] For these reasons, the pluriverse could provide an alternative horizon towards which we could begin to reach as we turn away from a consensus-oriented vision of international law.

This chapter begins by considering how the idea of a pluriverse could be translated into international law. It argues that a vision of the international as a 'meeting place' represents a jurisdictional form that could enable a world where many worlds can fit. The chapter then illustrates what this meeting place might look like by providing a series of vignettes of predominantly historical examples in which states or groups of people have attempted to construct the international as a place for encounters between different communities and their laws.

7.2 The International as a Meeting Place for a Plurality of Peoples and Their Laws

How could the idea of the pluriverse be translated into international law? Writing about private international law—that is, the domestic laws that apply where a case

[3] Jamie Heckert, 'Intimacy with Strangers/Intimacy with Self: Queer Experiences of Social Research' in Kath Browne and Catherine J Nash (eds), *Queer Methods and Methodologies Intersecting Queer Theories and Social Science Research* (Routledge 2016) 45.

[4] Mario Blaser and Marisol de la Cadena, 'Pluriverse: Proposals for a World of Many Worlds' in Mario Blaser and Marisol de la Cadena (eds), *A World of Many Worlds* (Duke University Press 2018) 4.

[5] Amaya Querejazu, 'Encountering the Pluriverse: Looking for Alternatives in Other Worlds' (2016) 59 Revista Brasileira de Política Internacional 1, 3.

[6] Janet Conway and Jakeet Singh, 'Radical Democracy in Global Perspective: Notes from the Pluriverse' (2011) 32 Third World Quarterly 689, 702. While Conway and Singh see radical democracy as something that should be rooted in the local, they single out the Zapatistas' 'international of hope' as an example of how this democratic vision could be 'place-based, yet transnationalized', ibid.

has connections to more than one jurisdiction—Ralf Michaels argues that a legal pluriverse should not be conceptualized in a way that 'reduces relations between different (legal) worlds to potential enmity'.[7] Rather, a legal pluriverse should be something that 'creates both freedom, individual and collective, and spaces for interaction and intercultural communication'[8] between different communities, 'while keeping the[ir] respective laws (and worldviews) intact'.[9] Although Michaels' aim is to show how private international law already gives rise to a 'world of many worlds', his insights about facilitating interaction and communication, while keeping diverse legal worlds alive, provide guidance for thinking about how the idea of the pluriverse could be mobilized in (public) international law.

In my view, a vision of international law as a 'meeting place' represents a jurisdictional form that could enable such interactions between worlds. The idea of an international 'meeting place' is already an established way of thinking about international law. According to Shaunnagh Dorsett and Shaun McVeigh, 'since the 17th century, jurists have tended to present the international according to two rival accounts': one of cosmopolitanism, which treats the international domain as having an independent existence (and, in stronger accounts, presents international law as a 'general law of the world'); the other of 'meeting place', which sees the international as a site for encounters between different collectivities and their laws.[10]

Dorsett and McVeigh contend that both of these accounts of international law shaped the 'move to institutions'[11] in the twentieth century, with international organizations being conceived at once as entities with a separate legal existence *and* as spaces for diplomatic encounter.[12] However, in my account, as the emphasis on consensus grew in some international organizations, the notion of international law as an independent sphere came to dominate. This is because both the decision-making procedures that carried the name 'consensus' and the discourses that emanated from those procedures worked to blur the individuated voices of the members, so that they seemed to speak as one.[13] The collective entity that emerged, whether it be the 'international community' or 'Europe', in turn began to take on its own, singular[14] identity, concealing alternative ways of doing and being and giving the impression that the law it spoke was now a 'general' law of the world or a

[7] Ralf Michaels, 'Private International Law and the Legal Pluriverse' in Michael S Green, Ralf Michaels, and Roxana Banu (eds), *Philosophical Foundations of Private International Law* (Oxford University Press 2024) 277.

[8] ibid.

[9] ibid.

[10] Shaunnagh Dorsett and Shaun McVeigh, *Jurisdiction* (Routledge-Cavendish 2012) 118.

[11] David Kennedy, 'The Move to Institutions' (1987) 8 Cardozo Law Review 841.

[12] Dorsett and McVeigh (n 10) 120–21.

[13] Kennedy (n 11) 972.

[14] Here, I am following Margaret Davies in using the term 'singular' to mean something associated 'with the philosophical concepts of universality and totality', rather than 'particular', see Margaret Davies, 'The Ethos of Pluralism' (2005) 27 Sydney Law Review 87, 91.

particular region. One way of creating greater space for difference in international law could thus be to resurrect—and then expand upon—the rival imaginary of 'meeting place' that already lies beneath the surface of the current system.

Just how open or expansive the 'meeting place' is imagined to be in this alternative vision of international law varies, depending on the legal tradition. In European international legal thought, which centres on the Westphalian myth of a 'free meeting of sovereign territorial nation states',[15] the conditions of sociality governing the idea of the international meeting place are constrained.[16] This is because, in order to participate in the European international meeting place, a community must outwardly relate through the juridical form of the nation state and therefore accept, from the outset, the application (and primacy) of European international law.[17] But there have been, and continue to be, other ways of imagining the international as a 'meeting place' that are more open to legal plurality and thus the idea of a 'world of multiple worlds'. For example, Shaun McVeigh and Sundhya Pahuja argue that, for Third World leaders in the mid-twentieth century, 'international law was projected as something like a "meeting place", or open space structured by international law, but not necessarily "full" of law, or fully regulated by law'.[18] Prior to decolonization and in the decades following, these leaders neither believed nor behaved 'as though European international law was the only international law . . . Instead, by word and deed, they described a different world: a world made through lawful encounters.'[19]

Jurisdictional thinkers in the present, who pay attention to the variety of practices through which legal authority is exercised,[20] put forward an even broader vision of the international as a site of 'meeting' or 'encounter'. In McVeigh and Pahuja's own account, the international operates as a 'middle ground' between different communities that 'is law-full in that it marks the point of engagement or creation of relations' but 'also lawless in that the coming together does not follow a *pre-given* law'.[21] In this vision of the international, there is not only space for interactions between the laws of states, but also those of Indigenous peoples, transnational communities, and corporations.[22]

[15] Dorsett and McVeigh (n 10) 118. See also Shaun McVeigh and Sundhya Pahuja, 'Rival Jurisdictions: The Promise and Loss of Sovereignty' in Charles Barbour and George Pavlich (eds), *After Sovereignty: On the Question of Political Beginnings* (Routledge-Cavendish 2009) 100.

[16] McVeigh and Pahuja (n 15) 105.

[17] Sundhya Pahuja, 'Laws of Encounter: A Jurisdictional Account of International Law' (2013) 1 London Review of International Law 63, 74–77.

[18] McVeigh and Pahuja (n 15) 104.

[19] Sundhya Pahuja, 'Letters from Bandung: Encounters with Another International Law' in Luis Eslava, Michael Fakhri, and Vasuki Nesiah (eds), *Bandung, Global History, and International Law: Critical Pasts and Pending Futures* (Cambridge University Press 2017) 568.

[20] Pahuja (n 17) 70.

[21] McVeigh and Pahuja (n 15) 98.

[22] Pahuja (n 17) 92.

These more open visions of the international as a 'meeting place' represent a queerer way of thinking about international law than the notion of the international as an independent domain. This is because they understand international law to be both fluid and relational.[23] In them, the 'inter' or 'between' of *inter*-national law never arrives fully formed.[24] Rather, the emphasis on encounter 'marks out . . . a way of "being with others"',[25] which requires a certain attentiveness to their different laws, practices, and ways of being. As Wiradjuri legal scholar Mark McMillan explains, '[i]n order to understand a jurisdictional boundary or meeting point there must be a recognition of the structured existences of the other to observe (and respect) its jurisdiction'.[26] This need to see, recognize, and respect communities and legal systems other than our own is why an expansive idea of the international as a 'meeting place' holds out the possibility of enabling a world with multiple worlds within it.

In my own thinking, the international could act as an open space in which different collectivities, including those which do not outwardly relate through the form of the state, can come together, interact, and collaborate, all the while holding on to much of what makes them socially, politically, and legally different. While it could be loosely structured by some principles or organizational form(s), there would be no expectation of a widespread agreement. Indeed, I envisage ample room for dissent, as well as the possibility of creating multiple and shifting versions of international law, so that different groups of collectivities can respond to issues of an international nature without having to accept a version of international law with which they fundamentally disagree. In practice, this might resemble what some have called a 'messy multilateralism'[27]—a fluid and overlapping patchwork of international legal and governance arrangements that not only allows for multiple domestic worlds (in whatever form the 'domestic' takes), but multiple international worlds too.

7.3 The International as a Meeting Place in Action: Sketches of Alternative Approaches to International Law

In this section, I illustrate what the international as a meeting place for a plurality of worlds might look like by providing a series of vignettes of predominantly historical examples in which states or groups of people have approached the

[23] On the emphasis on fluidity and relationality in queer theory, see Claerwen O'Hara, 'Queering the International Human Rights Framework Pertaining to Sexuality: Toward the Right to Relate' in Paula Gerber (ed), *Worldwide Perspectives on Lesbians, Gays and Bisexuals*, vol 2 (Praeger 2021) 61.

[24] McVeigh and Pahuja (n 15) 98.

[25] ibid.

[26] Mark McMillan, 'Koowarta and the Rival Indigenous International: Our Place as Indigenous Peoples in the International' (2014) 23 Griffith Law Review 110, 118.

[27] See, eg, Martin Daunton, *The Economic Government of the World 1933–2023* (Allen Lane 2023).

international in ways that come close to resembling—or at least show glimmers of—such a meeting place.[28] Most of these vignettes are drawn from international actors or arrangements already touched upon briefly in this book, including the Zapatistas (in Chapter 3), the United Nations Conference on Trade and Development (in Chapter 2), and the International Tribunal on Crimes against Women (in Chapter 4). One is new: the conduct of the Bolivarian Alliance of the Peoples of Our America, or 'ALBA', in existing international organizations and negotiating frameworks, such as the WTO and UN Framework Convention on Climate Change. As can be seen from this selection, some of these examples are focused on 'official' international organizations while others are concerned with the activities of actors outside the dominant system of international law, allowing us to expand our imaginations beyond that system.

Importantly, none of the vignettes provided in this section perfectly encapsulate the idea of the international as a place of encounter for multiple worlds. All are flawed in some way, and some may even be viewed as 'failed' experiments of the past. But as scholars of queer temporality have taught us, there can be value in looking back to 'the tail end of things, willing to be bathed in the fading light of . . . incomplete, partial, or otherwise failed transformations of the social field'.[29] Not only can seeking out 'past futures' help to challenge the sense of inevitability surrounding present arrangements by showing that it could have been otherwise, but they can also provide a springboard from which we can begin reimagining those arrangements.[30] In this second function, the flaws we encounter may provide important lessons from which we can learn as we chart new pathways towards a still unknown future. As Pickering and Keightley observe, there is 'a distinction between the desire to return to an earlier state or idealized past, and the desire not to return but to recognize aspects of the past as the basis for renewal and satisfaction in the future'.[31] Ultimately, this renewal might take a very different form to the sources of inspiration that we locate in the past.[32]

[28] In ending this book with a series of vignettes, I am influenced by the approach taken by Ratna Kapur in the epilogue of her book, in which she tells a series of stories in order to allow us to sense and feel the alternative for which she is advocating, without constraining that alternative by laying it out in singular or concrete terms, see Ratna Kapur, *Gender, Alterity and Human Rights: Freedom in a Fishbowl* (Edward Elgar Publishing 2018) Epilogue. For a more detailed account of how Kapur's work has inspired y own, see Claerwen O'Hara, 'Disordering, pluralising, queering: reflections on Ratna Kapur's contribution to queer engagements with international law' (forthcoming, 2026) London Review of International Law.

[29] Elizabeth Freeman, *Time Binds: Queer Temporalities, Queer Histories* (Duke University Press 2010) xiii. See also Anthony J Langlois, 'Queer Temporalities and Human Rights' in Kathryn McNeilly and Ben Warwick (eds), *The Times and Temporalities of International Human Rights Law* (Hart Publishing 2022).

[30] For works that take this approach, see eg Julia Dehm, 'Righting Inequality: Human Rights Responses to Economic Inequality in the United Nations' (2019) 10 Humanity 443; Claerwen O'Hara, 'In Search of a Queerer Law: Two People's Tribunals in 1976' (2023) 49 Australian Feminist Law Journal 17.

[31] Michael Pickering and Emily Keightley, 'The Modalities of Nostalgia' (2006) 54 Current Sociology 919, 921.

[32] Davina Cooper, 'Prefiguring the State' (2017) 49 Antipode 335, 343.

7.3.1 The Encounters of the Zapatistas

Let me begin with a vignette of the group that has most inspired my thinking in this chapter: the Zapatista Army of National Liberation, often referred to as just the 'Zapatistas'. Formed in the 1980s through a mingling between the Indigenous communities of Chiapas, Mexico and 'a small group of urban intellectuals with a revolutionary vision',[33] the Zapatistas are best known for staging an armed uprising against the Mexican state on 1 January 1994, the day the North American Free Trade Agreement became law. The Zapatistas are a local movement, who have created their own autonomous communities and solidarity economies in Chiapas, based around principles of mutual aid, collective work, and food sovereignty.[34] However, the Zapatistas have also long been oriented towards the international, forging relationships with a transnational network of activists and communities, and framing their concerns about capitalism, imperialism, and undemocracy in global terms—for example, by emphasizing the unaccountability of international organizations like the WTO.[35] It is through their international orientation that the Zapatistas provide a glimpse of what an international 'meeting place' could look like—in their case, one that exists entirely outside of the structure of the international organization.

As noted earlier, the Zapatistas advocate for '*un mundo donde quepan muchos mundos*' or 'a world where many worlds fit'.[36] In their view, there are already 'many worlds that live and fight within the world' and 'any pretence of homogeneity and hegemony threatens the essence of the human being: freedom'.[37] As such, the Zapatistas fight for a 'respect for difference',[38] both within their own communities and internationally. This not only means attempting to interact with 'those who think differently than we do',[39] but also rendering visible and celebrating that diversity at every turn. For the Zapatistas, it also involves opposing systems and values that they see as incompatible with a pluriverse.[40] Originally, this meant that the Zapatistas would only collaborate with those who opposed globalized neoliberalism. This was captured by the phrase 'one no and many yeses' (the 'no'

[33] Thomas Olesen, 'Globalizing the Zapatistas: From Third World Solidarity to Global Solidarity?' (2004) 25 Third World Quarterly 255, 261.

[34] Levi Gahman, 'Building "A World Where Many Worlds Fit": Indigenous Autonomy, Mutual Aid, and an (Anti-Capitalist) Moral Economy of the (Rebel) Peasant' in Jessica Duncan and Megan Bailey (eds), *Sustainable Food Futures: Multidisciplinary Solutions* (Routledge 2017) 103.

[35] Olesen (n 33) 262.

[36] Judith Schacherreiter, 'Un Mundo Donde Quepan Muchos Mundos: A Postcolonial Legal Perspective Inspired by the Zapatistas' (2009) 9 Global Jurist 1.

[37] 'Part One: A DECLARATION . . . FOR LIFE' (*Enlace Zapatista*, 1 January 2021) <https://enlacezapatista.ezln.org.mx/2021/01/01/part-one-a-declaration-for-life/>.

[38] ibid.

[39] EZLN (2000), quoted in Nicole Gulewitsch, 'Ya Basta! A Cry That Echoes Beyond Borders: Zapatismo and International Solidarity Networks in the Zapatista Uprising' (2011) 2 McGill Sociological Review 77, 83.

[40] Olesen (n 33) 262.

being to neoliberalism, the 'yeses' referring to their openness to a multiplicity of alternatives).[41] However, more recently, this has been updated to an opposition to capitalism more generally. For example, the 2021 Declaration for Life describes its network of co-signatories as united by an understanding that a system is responsible for their pains: 'The executioner is an exploitative, patriarchal, pyramidal, racist, thievish and criminal system: capitalism.'[42]

In their international dealings, the Zapatistas have attempted to give effect to the idea of a 'world of multiple worlds' through the notion of an 'encounter'. Since the mid-1990s, the Zapatistas have hosted multiple 'intergalactic' or 'intercontinental' encounters in order to extend their understanding of, and struggle against, forces such as neoliberal capitalism beyond Chiapas and Mexico.[43] The first of these was the 'Intergalactic Encounter against Neoliberalism and for Humanity' (also known as the 'Intercontinental Encounter against Neoliberalism and for Humanity'). Held in 1996 in the mountains and rainforest of the Mexican Southeast, the event was attended by 4,000 activists and members of civil society from 43 states, including some globally prominent figures, such as Danielle Mitterrand, the wife of the former French president.[44] Since then, the Zapatistas have hosted several other encounters within their territory, including the first and second 'Encounters of Zapatista Peoples with the Peoples of the World' in 2007,[45] the 'Encounter of Indigenous Peoples of America' in 2007,[46] the first and second 'International Encounters of Women who Struggle' in 2009 and 2019,[47] and the 'Encounter of the Zapatistas and the ConSciences for Humanity' in 2016.[48] The Zapatistas have also inspired encounters abroad, such as the 'Second Intergalactic Encounter for Humanity and Against Neoliberalism', which was took place in Madrid, Spain in 1997.[49]

[41] Naomi Klein, 'Farewell to the "End of History": Organization and Vision in Anti-Corporate Movements' (2002) 38 Socialist Register 1, 4.

[42] 'Part One: A DECLARATION ... FOR LIFE' (n 37).

[43] Olesen (n 33) 260.

[44] June Nash, *Mayan Visions: The Quest for Autonomy in an Age of Globalization* (Taylor & Francis 2001) 200.

[45] See, eg, 'II Encounter of the Zapatista Peoples with the Peoples of the World' (*Enlace Zapatista*, June 2007) <https://enlacezapatista.ezln.org.mx/2007/07/01/ii-encounter-of-the-zapatista-peoples-with-the-peoples-of-the-world/>.

[46] See, eg, 'Communiqué from the Indigenous Revolutionary Clandestine Committee—General Command of the Zapatista Army for National Liberation. Mexico' (*Enlace Zapatista*, 22 September 2007) <https://enlacezapatista.ezln.org.mx/2007/09/23/communique-from-the-indigenous-revolutionary-clandestine-committee-general-command-of-the-zapatista-army-for-national-liberation-3/>.

[47] See, eg, 'Invitation to the Second International Gathering of Women Who Struggle' (Enlace Zapatista, 21 September 2019) <https://enlacezapatista.ezln.org.mx/2019/09/21/invitation-to-the-second-international-gathering-of-women-who-struggle/>.

[48] 'Progress on the Encounter "The Zapatistas and the ConSciences for Humanity"' (Enlace Zapatista, 19 March 2016) <https://enlacezapatista.ezln.org.mx/2016/03/19/progress-on-the-encounter-the-zapatistas-and-the-consciences-for-humanity/>.

[49] 'Manifesto for the Convocation of the 2nd Intercontinental Gathering: For a World which Contains All Worlds' (Archives of Global Protests, Nadir, 1997) <https://www.nadir.org/nadir/initiativ/medienbus/was_wir_tun_start_eng.html>.

For the Zapatistas, the notion of an 'encounter' captures the looseness of their events. In their invitation to the first 'Intergalactic Encounter against Neoliberalism and for Humanity', for example, the Zapatistas stressed that the event was 'an encounter, not a congress', by which they meant there was no aim of reaching a particular decision or agreement. They simply intended to 'find one another and see what is the result of this encounter'.[50] They also made it clear that they did not require participants to share their worldview: 'This is not an encounter solely for Zapatistas or sympathizers of Zapatismo.'[51] Rather, their aim was to facilitate interaction and communication between *different* communities and perspectives. In some of their other writings, the Zapatistas have captured this vision through the metaphor of a bridge between two lands that are 'different, special, and distant'.[52] In constructing the bridge, those lands cease to be distant, but they need not cease being different and special.[53] A Zapatista encounter thus presents opportunity for metaphorical bridge-building between worlds, creating openings for interconnections between those worlds, without forcing them to become one. In framing many of these events as 'intergalactic' or 'intercontinental', the Zapatistas have also sought to decentre the nation state, creating space for individuals and communities who outwardly relate in other ways—including, in the case of the 'intergalactic' framing, ways not yet known to Earth.[54]

While it may now be cliché for Western scholars to seek out inspiration in the thought and practices of the Zapatistas,[55] they present a particularly interesting example in the context of this book. This is because they predominantly operate through a non-voting method of decision-making known as 'consensus'.[56] However, unlike many international organizations, the Zapatistas have developed ways to ensure that the voices of those who would ordinarily find themselves marginalized or excluded from such methods of decision-making are heard. According to David Graeber, they have gone about this locally by supplementing their communal assemblies with 'women and youth caucuses to counterbalance the traditional dominance of adult males'.[57] One can also observe a similar model

[50] Model A Invitation, in 'Zapatista Army of National Liberation' (Archives of Global Protests, Nadir, May 1996) <https://www.nadir.org/nadir/initiativ/agp/chiapas1996/en/invite.html>.

[51] ibid.

[52] Quoted in Olesen (n 33) 262.

[53] ibid.

[54] Shukaitis argues that, through the intergalactic framing, the Zapatistas maintain 'an open relation to the actually existing other, the other of the future', see Stevphen Shukaitis, 'Space Is the (Non) Place: Martians, Marxists, and the Outer Space of the Radical Imagination' (2009) 57 The Sociological Review 99, 111.

[55] On the romanticization of the Zapatistas by those on the left in the West, see Christine Unrau, 'A World of Many Walks? Zapatista World Ordering between Center and Margins' (2024) 4 Global Studies Quarterly 1.

[56] On the way this process works, see Amory Starr, María Elena Martínez-Torres, and Peter Rosset, 'Participatory Democracy in Action: Practices of the Zapatistas and the Movimento Sem Terra' (2011) 38 Latin American Perspectives 102, 105.

[57] David Graeber, 'There Never Was a West: Or, Democracy Emerges from the Spaces in Between', *Possibilities: Essays on Hierarchy, Rebellion, and Desire* (AK Press 2007) 362.

at work in the Zapatistas' international encounters, where specific encounters for Indigenous people and women have been held in addition to their more general encounters.[58]

The Zapatistas' encounters have also been marked by an emphasis on listening, reflecting their belief that 'what allows us to move forward is the listening to and the observation of the Other'.[59] For example, the Zapatistas often begin their encounters by listening to their guests' stories, sometimes over many hours, before speaking themselves.[60] On occasion, this exercise in storytelling and listening has even been prioritized over any other plans for the encounter. As one participant at the Second International Encounter of Women who Struggle in 2019 recounts:

> [The Zapatistas' listening to their guests' stories] was supposed to be a one day thing, and it just continued and continued and continued to the very end of the Encuentro. There was an agenda and workshops and everything planned throughout the weekend so that we could meet and organize ourselves but they never said okay, that's enough.[61]

In addition, the Zapatistas attempt to ensure a high level of social and economic equality amongst the participants in their decision-making processes. In their own communities, they have gone about this through a variety of measures, from the establishment of communally-run food gardens to ensure that no one goes hungry to the adoption of the Women's Revolutionary Law in 1993, which safeguards gender equality.[62] In their broader engagements, the Zapatistas have also made public expressions of support for marginalized communities, including those who have had 'their humanness reduced for the simple fact of not being in accord with a nonexistent sexual norm'.[63] Further, the Zapatistas have made efforts to 'queer' their language by 'blend[ing] the masculine and feminine spellings of Spanish pronouns... to be inclusive of everyone along differing gender and sexuality continuums'.[64] For instance, the Zapatistas often begin their international communications with

[58] For example, the Encounter of Indigenous Peoples of America in 2007 and the first and second International Encounters of Women who Struggle in 2009 and 2019.

[59] 'Part One: A DECLARATION ... FOR LIFE' (n 37).

[60] Starr, Martínez-Torres and Rosset (n 56) 108.

[61] Julia Thomas, 'Sowing Solidarity: Reflections on Zapatismo from the International Gathering of Women Who Struggle' (*Peoples Dispatch*, 20 June 2020) <https://peoplesdispatch.org/2020/06/20/sowing-solidarity-reflections-on-zapatismo-from-the-international-gathering-of-women-who-struggle/>. On the importance of listening as a feminist praxis, see, eg Dianne Otto, 'Beyond Legal Justice: Some Personal Reflections on People's Tribunals, Listening and Responsibility' (2017) 5 London Review of International Law 225; Gina Heathcote, *Feminist Dialogues on International Law: Successes, Tensions, Futures* (Oxford University Press 2019) Chapter 6.

[62] Gahman (n 34).

[63] 'Zapatistas on Gay Rights: "Let Those Who Persecute Be Ashamed!"' (*Green Left*, 21 July 1999) <https://www.greenleft.org.au/content/zapatistas-gay-rights-let-those-who-persecute-be-ashamed>.

[64] Gahman (n 34) 112.

'compañer@s'[65] ('companions' or 'comrades' in Spanish, with the '@' symbol representing both the masculine 'o' and feminine 'a'), so as to include men, women, and non-binary people. Along with their use of specific caucuses and encounters for marginalized groups and emphasis on listening, practices such as these likely go some way toward mitigating the silencing effect of non-voting methods of decision-making on those who carry less power.

Even more significantly, the Zapatistas resist the homogenizing effects that can flow from claims of consensus by foregrounding the diversity of those participating in any collective decision or statement. This practice can be seen in the 2021 Declaration for Life, which the Zapatistas co-signed with hundreds of individuals, collectives, and organizations from around the world. The Declaration begins with a statement emphasizing all that makes the signatories different to one another:

> During these previous months, we have established contact between us by various means. We are women, lesbians, gays, bisexuals, transgender, transvestites, transsexuals, intersex, queer and more, men, groups, collectives, associations, organizations, social movements, indigenous peoples, neighbourhood associations, communities and a long etcetera that gives us identity.
>
> We are differentiated and separated by lands, skies, mountains, valleys, steppes, jungles, deserts, oceans, lakes, rivers, streams, lagoons, races, cultures, languages, histories, ages, geographies, sexual and non-sexual identities, roots, borders, forms of organization, social classes, purchasing power, social prestige, fame, popularity, followers, likes, coins, educational level, ways of being, tasks, virtues, defects, pros, cons, buts, howevers, rivalries, enmities, conceptions, arguments, counterarguments, debates, disputes, complaints, accusations, contempts, phobias, philias, praises, repudiations, boos, applauses, divinities, demons, dogmas, heresies, likes, dislikes, ways, and a long etcetera that makes us different and, not infrequently, opposites.[66]

The Declaration then goes on to outline the substance of the agreement, which includes, inter alia, a shared conviction that 'the equality of humanity lies in the respect for difference'.[67] The Declaration also makes plans for future meetings to take place across the 'five continents'.[68] The Zapatistas thus demonstrate that it is possible to go about the creation of a pluriverse while maintaining decision-making methods called 'consensus', should that be of interest to a particular group or organization. The key is unsettling the gesture the idea of consensus makes towards visions of sameness by actively foregrounding and celebrating difference.

[65] See, eg, 'Part One: A DECLARATION ... FOR LIFE' (n 37).
[66] ibid.
[67] ibid.
[68] ibid.

The Zapatistas' encounters have also helped to create transnational networks of rebel and activist groups, which have come to exist independently from the Zapatistas themselves. At the end of the First Intergalactic Encounter in 1996, for example, the Zapatistas issued a declaration calling for the establishment of an 'intercontinental network of resistance' for all who wished to continue the conversations and work they had begun at the encounter.[69] The Zapatistas made it clear that, with this proposal, they were not looking to establish a fixed organization. They stressed that the network would neither have 'an organizing structure' nor any 'central command or hierarchies'.[70] Rather, their aim was to create a 'permanent encounter' of sorts, which could exist across multiple places and times at once:

> We propose that the intercontinental encounter for humanity and against neoliberalism continue on every continent, in every country, in each rural area and city, in each house, school or workplace where human beings live who want a better world.[71]

The Zapatistas' proposal would eventually lead to the creation of the People's Global Action (PGA) in 1998—a decentralized 'worldwide coordination network' of grassroots campaigns and social movements.[72] The PGA came to include a great variety of groups and communities from around the world, including anarchist groups and trade unions in Europe, radical associations of farmers and fisherfolk in India and Indonesia, and the Brazilian Landless Workers' Movement.[73] It also played an important role in the coordination of global protest and direct action initiatives in the late 1990s and 2000s, including the 'Battle of Seattle' against the WTO in 1999.[74] As such, in addition to offering an international 'meeting place' themselves, the Zapatistas' encounters have provided a platform for the creation of new international networks and arrangements amongst willing participants.

There are some shortcomings to the Zapatistas' international practices and engagements. Due to geographical distance and lack of access to resources, people from Asia and Africa have been underrepresented in the encounters and networks created or inspired by the Zapatistas.[75] Linguistic constraints and difficulties accessing online communication tools have also meant that dialogues between

[69] 'Closing Words of the EZLN at the Intercontinental Encounter* 2nd Declaration of La Realidad' (1996) <https://library.uniteddiversity.coop/More_Books_and_Reports/Zapatista_2nd_Declaration_LaRealidad.pdf>.
[70] ibid.
[71] ibid.
[72] 'What is Peoples' Global Action?' (*Archives of Global Protests, Nadir*) <https://www.nadir.org/nadir/initiativ/agp/en/pgainfos/about.html>.
[73] David Graeber, 'The New Anarchists' [2002] New Left Review 4–5.
[74] ibid 4.
[75] Olesen (n 33) 264.

the Zapatistas and solidarity groups around the world have tended to take place through the Zapatistas' educated leadership, rather than everyday members of their autonomous communities.[76] The prominence of 'Subcomandante Insurgente Marcos', an urban intellectual who coordinated the 1994 uprising and became the face of the Zapatistas in their early years, has, at times, seemed inconsistent with the group's anti-hierarchical and pluralistic approach.[77] Further, the fact that the Zapatistas' international activities have mainly taken place in the register of co-ordinating rebellion, rather than establishing a different way of approaching international law, makes it harder to present them as direct alternatives to the practices of the WTO and ECtHR than is the case for some of the other vignettes I offer in this section.

Nevertheless, the Zapatistas still provide a model of internationalism from which it is possible to draw when considering the multiple ways in which international law could be imagined as a 'meeting place'. From their counterbalancing of dominant voices and emphasis on listening to their commitment to diversity and rejection of organizational structures in favour of fluid encounters, the Zapatistas have developed a range of practices and ideas that enable bridge-building between worlds, without requiring those worlds to blend.

7.3.2 UNCTAD: A Meeting Place for the Cold War's Different 'Worlds'

I will now turn to a very different example of an international meeting place, but one that may be more familiar to international lawyers: the United Nations Conference on Trade and Development (UNCTAD) in its early years. As may be recalled from Chapter 2, UNCTAD was created in the mid-1960s by states in the global South, with the backing of the Socialist Bloc, due to a common perception that the General Agreement on Tariffs and Trade (GATT) system favoured Western interests.[78] UNCTAD began as a one-off conference in 1964 but subsequently became a permanent organ of the UN. In Chapter 2, I focused on how states in the South used this body to advocate for a more egalitarian international economic order. I also explored how it became one of the sites through which the global North launched its consensus-based counter-offensive. However, before UNCTAD itself became subsumed by a logic of consensus, it also acted as a place of encounter for the Cold War's different 'worlds'. In this sub-section, I provide

[76] ibid.

[77] Red Marriott, 'A Critique of the Zapatista "Other Campaign"—Grupo Socialista Libertario' (*Libcom*, 25 March 2008) <https://libcom.org/library/a-critique-zapatista-other-campaign-grupo-socialista-libertario>. On the way Subcomandante Marcos has been used to make the movement more intelligible to non-Indigenous audiences, see also Adrienne Russell, 'Myth and the Zapatista Movement: Exploring a Network Identity' (2005) 7 New Media & Society 559.

[78] John Toye, *UNCTAD at 50: A Short History* (United Nations 2014) 7.

a vignette of how UNCTAD performed the role of an international economic meeting place, albeit not always so successfully.

Unlike the GATT, which had a 'restricted composition'[79] in the first few decades of its existence due to its exclusion of many socialist states,[80] UNCTAD was established within the 'universal' UN system. For representatives of states in the South, such as Chilean President Salvador Allende, this enabled UNCTAD to operate as an 'assembly of the world community of nations',[81] in contrast to the GATT, which was 'at odds with the concept of universal participation' and 'essentially concerned with the interests of the powerful countries'.[82] Of course, the UN's membership, and thus that of UNCTAD, was (and continues to be) limited insofar as it is only open to states. In his speech at UNCTAD III in 1972, Allende seemed to recognize this limitation, lamenting that '[u]nfortunately, not yet quite all'[83] could join UNCTAD due to ongoing struggles for decolonization. Nevertheless, the fact that UNCTAD was established as a forum for discussing international economic matters between states with very different economic models during the Cold War was significant, as it enabled it to operate as a site of encounter at a time of great geopolitical hostility.

Indeed, the first UNCTAD in 1964 was attended by figures as diverse as Edward Heath, the United Kingdom's Conservative trade minister, who would later go on to become Prime Minister, and Ernesto 'Che' Guevara, a prominent member of Cuba's revolutionary regime.[84] For many attendees, this coming together signalled the possibility of a new era of peaceful coexistence. In his speech at the first UNCTAD, for example, Che Guevara acknowledged the Cold War context in which they were meeting, stating, '[w]e live in a world that is deeply and antagonistically divided into groupings of nations very dissimilar in economic, social, and political outlook'.[85] In this regard, he noted not only the divisions between the socialist and capitalist worlds, but also those between the 'developed' and

[79] This is how GATT Executive Secretary Wyndham White described the institution in 1957, see Letter from White to Wormser, quoted in Francine McKenzie, 'GATT and the Cold War: Accession Debates, Institutional Development, and the Western Alliance, 1947–1959' (2008) 10 Journal of Cold War Studies 78, 100.

[80] While Czechoslovakia and Cuba were always part of the GATT, having become Contracting Parties before their respective revolutions, the GATT was reluctant to admit other socialist states until the 1960s and, even then, it was not until the 1990s that a state such as Bulgaria was permitted to join. See the chapter '"An Arrow in the Western World's Quiver": The Cold War Challenge to GATT' in Francine McKenzie, *GATT and Global Order in the Postwar Era* (Cambridge University Press 2020).

[81] Address delivered by Mr Salvador Allende Gossens, President of Chile at the Inaugural Ceremony of 13 April 1972, in 'Proceedings of the United Nations Conference on Trade and Development: Third Session: Santiago de Chile, 13 April to 21 May 1972' (1973) Volume I: Report and Annexes 348 [8].

[82] ibid 354 [73].

[83] ibid 348 [8].

[84] Ann J Zammit, 'UNCTAD III: End of an Illusion' (1973) 5 Institute of Development Studies Bulletin 3, 3.

[85] Che Guevara, '"On Development", Speech Delivered March 25, 1964 at the Plenary Session of the United Nations Conference on Trade and Development (UNCTAD)' (*Che Guevara Internet Archive*) <https://www.marxists.org/archive/guevara/1964/03/25.htm>.

'underdeveloped' worlds.[86] However, Guevara stressed that states must be able 'to adopt the form of political and economic organization that suits them best, and to choose their own lines of development and specialization in economic activity, without incurring reprisals of any kind'[87]—including the 'measures aimed at paralyzing the Cuban economy' being perpetuated by the US as he spoke.[88] As such, Cuba had come to the Conference 'ready to join in constructive debate in a setting of peaceful coexistence between countries with different political, economic, and social systems'.[89]

The international body that emerged from this first 'encounter'[90] went about creating a space for interaction between the Cold War's different worlds in at least four ways. First, it sought to accommodate the diversity of political, economic, and social systems of which Guevara spoke. When UNCTAD was made a permanent organ of the UN, for example, its founding resolution listed formulating 'principles and policies on international trade and related problems of economic development' and making 'proposals for putting said principles and policies into effect', '*having regard to differences in economic systems and stages of development*',[91] as some of UNCTAD's principal functions. In this way, an attentiveness to economic difference was baked into the organization's decision-making.

A number of initiatives to come out of UNCTAD in its early years were also directed at accommodating pluralism at both the domestic and international levels. For example, the Charter of Economic Rights and Duties of States, which was first proposed by Mexico at UNCTAD III in 1972 and then drafted by an UNCTAD Working Group, before being adopted by the UN General Assembly (UNGA) in 1974,[92] contains in its first Article the right for each state to choose its own economic model:

> Every State has the sovereign and inalienable right to choose its economic system as well as its political, social and cultural systems in accordance with the will of its people, without outside interference, coercion or threat in any form whatsoever.[93]

[86] ibid.
[87] ibid.
[88] ibid.
[89] ibid.
[90] For the framing of UNCTAD as a site of 'encounter', see Branislav Gosovic, 'UNCTAD: North-South Encounter' (1968) 568 *International Conciliation 1*.
[91] United Nations General Assembly, 'Establishment of the United Nations Conference on Trade and Development as an Organ of the General Assembly, Resolution 1995 (XIX)' (30 December 1964) [3](a) [emphasis added] ('Establishment of UNCTAD Resolution').
[92] For this procedural history, see United Nations, 'Charter of Economic Rights and Duties of States General Assembly Resolution 3281 (XXIX) New York, 12 December 1974' (*Audiovisual Library of International Law*, 2023) <https://legal.un.org/avl/ha/cerds/cerds.html>.
[93] United Nations General Assembly, 'Charter of Economic Rights and Duties of States General Assembly, Resolution 3281 (XXIX)' (12 December 1974) ('CERDS'), Article 1.

Article 4 of the Charter also provides that 'every state has the right to engage in international trade and other forms of economic co-operation irrespective of any differences in political, economic and social systems' and 'is free to choose the forms of organization of its foreign economic relations',[94] embracing a pluralized vision of the international economic order, in which there could be multiple international legal and institutional arrangements.

Second, UNCTAD attempted to construct a more egalitarian international economic system. UNCTAD went about this task in a number of ways, from its Secretariat providing support to states in the global South in trade and development negotiations in recognition of their comparative lack of resources[95] to facilitating the establishment of the Generalized System of Preferences (GSP), under which the wealthy states agreed to provide tariff reductions to the poorer states on a non-reciprocal basis.[96] The South's struggle for greater inter-state equality in UNCTAD and other fora as part of the 'New International Economic Order' (NIEO) was outlined in detail in Chapter 2 and will not be rehashed in this section. But it is worth mentioning here because, in the view of many states in the global South, the push for greater economic equality was also intertwined with the goal of constructing a setting of peaceful coexistence for the Cold War's different worlds. As Che Guevara put it in a speech to the UNGA a few months after the first UNCTAD in 1964: 'peaceful coexistence among nations does not encompass coexistence between the exploiters and the exploited, between the oppressors and the oppressed.'[97] In other words, for Guevara, a baseline of social and material equality was necessary for different worlds to be able to exist side by side and this could only be achieved through a restructuring of the global economy.

Third, UNCTAD sought to facilitate economic relationships between the Cold War's different worlds. This was significant because, during the early Cold War period, there had been a splitting of the international economy along capitalist and socialist lines.[98] This bifurcation of the international economy was accompanied by the establishment of rival trade organizations on each side. On the Western side, there was the Organization for European Economic Co-operation, which later became the Organization for Economic Co-operation and Development (OECD), and the European Economic Community (EEC) in Western Europe. There was also the GATT, which was established before the economic Cold War had begun in earnest but was subsequently transformed into an informal 'western forum and

[94] ibid, Article 4.

[95] On the UNCTAD Secretariat's support for states in the global South, see Toye (n 78) 21–22.

[96] ibid 41.

[97] Che Guevara, '"At the United Nations", Speech Delivered on 11 December 1964, 19th General Assembly of the United Nations in New York' (*Che Guevara Internet Archive*) <https://www.marxists.org/archive/guevara/1964/12/11.htm>.

[98] James K Libbey, 'CoCom, Comecon, and the Economic Cold War' (2010) 37 Russian History 133.

an economic instrument of the capitalist democracies'.[99] On the Eastern side, there was the Council for Mutual Economic Assistance (CMEA), which sought to facilitate economic specialization and trade relations amongst the centrally planned economies of Eastern Europe, and later Mongolia, Cuba, and Vietnam as well.[100] Following the wave of decolonization that took place in the post-war period, a third, non-aligned bloc also emerged in the form of the global South or 'Third World', which was dissatisfied by the trade arrangements on offer from both the East and West.

These different political and economic groupings came to be represented at UNCTAD through the establishment of a 'group system'.[101] For the purpose of elections to the Trade and Development Board, UNCTAD's membership was divided into four groups: A, B, C, and D. Group A was made up of African and Asian states, as well as Yugoslavia; Group B consisted of European, North American, and other Western states; Group C was composed of Latin American and Caribbean states; and Group D comprised the Eastern European states. However, at the first UNCTAD in 1964, Groups A and C decided to operate together via the formation of the Group of 77 (G77). This meant that there were now effectively three groups, which corresponded to what had become the tripartite structure of the Cold War: Group B representing the capitalist West; Group D representing the socialist East; and Groups A and C together representing the global South. Before long, all UNCTAD deliberations were refracted through this group system. States in each group first negotiated a common platform, often externally through their own conferences and organizations, before taking their position to the other groups.[102] As described in Chapter 2, decision-making would then take place through majority voting, with the option of conciliation beforehand—although UNCTAD's conciliation procedure was not actually used in practice.[103]

There were drawbacks to UNCTAD's group system. Most notably, it often worked to obscure the diversity that existed within each Cold War bloc, whether it be the great variety of political orientations and economic positions that existed within the G77,[104] or the situation of a state such as Australia, which, despite being politically aligned with the states in Group B, shared economic similarities with those in the G77 due to its reliance on primary exports.[105] As a result, the

[99] McKenzie (n 80) 65.

[100] Libbey (n 98) 135.

[101] UNCTAD Secretariat, 'UNCTAD: A Brief Historical Overview' (2006) UNCTAD/GDS/2006/1 9–10 <https://digitallibrary.un.org/record/576638?ln=en&v=pdf>.

[102] Toye (n 78) 20–1.

[103] R Krishnamurti, 'UNCTAD as a Negotiating Institution' (1981) 15 Journal of World Trade Law 3,.26.

[104] Giuliano Garavini, *After Empires: European Integration, Decolonization, and the Challenge from the Global South, 1957–1986* (Oxford University Press 2012) 134.

[105] Nicholas Ferns, 'The Middle Zone: The 1964 UN Conference on Trade and Development and the Australian Response' (2021) 32 Journal of World History 465.

group system often helped to reinforce the narrow identities of 'West', 'East', and 'South',[106] preventing new linkages from emerging.[107] In this way, it does not represent the best way of constructing a 'meeting place' for an expansive pluriverse. Nevertheless, within the geopolitical context in which it came about, the group system seemed to enable encounters between the Cold War's worlds by allowing otherwise separate organizations like the OECD and the CMEA to be 'incarnated',[108] and thus interact, within UNCTAD.

In addition to bringing these different groupings into the room, UNCTAD attempted to facilitate trade between them, without requiring them to give up their economic differences. In the resolution establishing UNCTAD as a permanent body, for example, the promotion of 'international trade . . . particularly between countries at different stages of development, between developing countries and between countries with different systems of economic and social organization'[109] was listed as one of the organization's principal functions. Following a report from the Fourth Committee which declared that 'differences of social and economic system need not constitute an obstacle to trade',[110] a resolution encouraging both East–West trade and East–South trade was passed at UNCTAD II in 1968.[111] At UNCTAD III in 1972, the 'Committee on Trade Relations among Countries having Different Economic and Social Systems' was then established, with the aim of enabling greater trade between the different Cold War blocs.[112] However, UNCTAD's work in this area ultimately stagnated. While UNCTAD did end up facilitating East–South trade by providing opportunities for bilateral and multilateral consultations, its work on East–West trade was effectively blocked by the Western states, who made it clear that they did not consider UNCTAD the proper forum for such issues.[113]

[106] On the role of UNCTAD in forging a 'Western' identity, see, eg, Patricia Hongler, 'The Construction of a Western Voice: OECD and the First UNCTAD of 1964' in Matthieu Leimgruber and Matthias Schmelzer (eds), *The OECD and the International Political Economy Since 1948* (Springer 2017).

[107] Toye (n 78) 21.

[108] On the idea of these organizations being 'incarnated' at UNCTAD, see Robert M Cutler, 'East-South Relations at UNCTAD: Global Political Economy and the CMEA' (1983) 37 International Organization 121, 144, observing that the CMEA was 'incarnated at UNCTAD as an autonomous collective entity, "Group D"'. On way the group system was probably unavoidable in that geopolitical context, see Toye (n 78) 21.

[109] Establishment of UNCTAD Resolution (n 91), Article 1.

[110] Report of the Fourth Committee in 'Proceedings of the United Nations Conference on Trade and Development: Second Session: New Delhi, 1 February–29 March 1968' (1968) Volume I: Report and Annexes 451.

[111] Resolution 15(II) on 'Trade relations among countries having different economic and social systems including problems of East-West trade, paying attention particularly to the trade interests of developing countries and taking into account the work in this field of other United Nations organs, including the regional economic commissions' in ibid 32–4.

[112] Vanya Walker-Leigh, 'Was UNCTAD III A Failure?' (1972) 28 The World Today 411, 416.

[113] Krishnamurti (n 103) 13.

Finally, UNCTAD provided a space for encounters between different conceptions of international law. Pahuja and Saunders, for example, have described in detail how UNCTAD III allowed for 'a meeting of, and struggle between'[114] alternative visions of the place of the multinational corporation in international law. In this case, the conflict centred on whether the regulation of multinational corporations belonged in the domestic or international law 'basket'.[115] Whereas the Western capitalist states were of the view that it was states' responsibility to enact domestic legislation to regulate the conduct of multinational corporations, the G77, backed by the Socialist Bloc, saw the regulation of corporate conduct as something that should belong to the international sphere due to 'the essential rootlessness of the multinational corporation'.[116]

UNCTAD's use of majority voting played a role in enabling such encounters between different legal visions. According to Krishnamurti, in UNCTAD's first few decades, voting was commonly used by the G77 as a way to initiate new areas of work and discussion in situations where the Western states were resisting such a move due to a 'desire to restrain UNCTAD's influence and to have the subject either not taken up at all or dealt with in other agencies in which they [had] a much stronger voice'.[117] Moreover, the use of voting in such contexts often yielded constructive results, at least in terms of allowing new and sometimes difficult international conversations to take place. As Krishnamurti explains: 'Despite their initial and sometimes continuing opposition B Group countries [were often] willing to participate in the working groups and other negotiating procedures which emanated from the initial decisions [taken by a vote]'.[118]

However, UNCTAD never flourished as a lawmaking institution. While UNCTAD did facilitate some international agreements on commodities in its early years, these were concluded in specially convened negotiating conferences that took place outside of UNCTAD.[119] In the 1970s, states in the South sought to expand UNCTAD's lawmaking function, with the aim of transforming it into a forum for the negotiation and adoption of trade treaties.[120] However, the Western states pushed back against these efforts, making it clear that they saw UNCTAD as merely a 'consultative organ of the General Assembly' and 'did not consider it constructive to seek to change UNCTAD into an organization dealing with binding

[114] Sundhya Pahuja and Anna Saunders, 'Rival Worlds and the Place of the Corporation in International Law' in Jochen von Bernstorff and Philipp Dann (eds), *The Battle for International Law: South-North Perspectives on the Decolonization Era* (Oxford University Press 2019) 171.
[115] ibid 174.
[116] ibid.
[117] Krishnamurti (n 103) 15.
[118] ibid.
[119] ibid 7. An example is the International Cocoa Agreement (21 October 1972, entered into force provisionally on 30 June 1973 but expired on 30 September 1976) 882 UNTS 67.
[120] Pahuja and Saunders (n 114) 162.

legal instruments',[121] given the GATT's existing competency in the area. This hampered UNCTAD's ability to produce legal agreements, including on a plurilateral basis (i.e. amongst a subset of UNCTAD's membership), preventing the organization from realizing its full potential as an international 'meeting place' in which different organized communities could come together and form their own international legal arrangements.

For a time, the ability to vote on resolutions offered some groups of states a way around this limitation by enabling them to articulate and record different visions of international law, while also giving other states the option to register their dissent against those visions. For example, many of the decisions relating to the Charter of Economic Rights and Duties of States, from the decision to begin drafting it at UNCTAD III to its final adoption in the UNGA, were taken by a vote, with states in the global North either abstaining or voting against.[122] While the legal status of the Charter resolution itself was contested, with states in the South arguing that it represented instant custom or at least 'transitional international law' and states in the North arguing that resolutions have no binding force,[123] it was clear to many that it contained within it a 'vision of international economic law'.[124] Yet, as time went on, voting became less frequent in UNCTAD. Like many other international organizations, UNCTAD eventually came to operate informally through a non-voting method of decision-making known as 'consensus'. From UNCTAD IV in 1987 onwards, it became common practice to end the Conference with one consolidated text adopted by consensus, rather than with a series of resolutions, some of which were adopted by a vote.[125] This move to consensus resulted in a 'drastic dilution of the proposals of the developing countries',[126] as well as a murkier account of the different positions involved.

Eventually, as the twentieth century drew to a close, UNCTAD ceased to play the role of international economic meeting place. Increasing opposition to UNCTAD from states in the global North, combined with a weakening of the G77 over the course of the 1980s, saw UNCTAD transform from a forum for international debate on matters relating to trade and development into a body that provided policy research and technical assistance.[127] As part of this change, UNCTAD began to

[121] Spokesman for Group B countries, Report of Working Group I, in 'Proceedings of the United Nations Conference on Trade and Development: Third Session: Santiago de Chile, 13 April to 21 May 1972' (n 81) 299 [8].

[122] Krishnamurti (n 103) 17. The procedural history is available at United Nations (n 92).

[123] Mohammed Bedjaoui, *Towards a New International Economic Order* (Holmes & Meier 1979) 178–79, 191–92.

[124] On the way the NIEO constituted a 'vision of international economic law', see Antony Anghie, 'Legal Aspects of the New International Economic Order' (2015) 6 Humanity 145, 147. For an example of the view that while the CERDS was 'not a legal instrument', it nevertheless made 'an important contribution to international economic law', see Krishnamurti (n 103) 7.

[125] Toye (n 78) 80–81.

[126] Krishnamurti (n 103) 15.

[127] Massoud Karshenas, 'Power, Ideology and Global Development: On the Origins, Evolution and Achievements of UNCTAD' (2016) 47 Development and Change 664, 679.

resemble a supporting institution to the GATT, which itself came to be viewed as *the* international trade organization.[128] This trajectory has turned UNCTAD into somewhat of a 'cautionary tale'. For example, Rolland and Trubek note that some may fear that, if the WTO were to move in a more pluralist and egalitarian direction, it could 'lose influence, becoming just another relatively powerless version of UNCTAD'.[129] But, in my view, the fact that UNCTAD came close to resembling an international 'meeting place', even if only temporarily, is a source of inspiration. Looking back at how UNCTAD functioned in its early years, from its openness to 'countries having different economic and social systems' to its members' ability to use voting to initiate new areas of discussion and record different visions of international law, helps us to imagine how an international organization—not too dissimilar from the ones we know today—could function as a 'meeting place' for multiple worlds.

7.3.3 ALBA: A Bridge Between Alternative International Laws

My next example of an international 'meeting place' combines aspects of the fluid, non-state-based approach of the Zapatistas' encounters and the institutional approach of UNCTAD. In this subsection, I provide a vignette of how a coalition of Latin American states known as the Bolivarian Alliance of the Peoples of Our America, or 'ALBA' (its acronym in Spanish), approached international law in the late 2000s and 2010s.[130] More specifically, I describe how ALBA used existing international organizations and negotiating frameworks to stage an encounter between the dominant conception of international law and an alternative vision of international law, drawn from ALBA's engagements with everyday people, including climate activists, peasant groups, and Indigenous peoples. In its efforts to bring about this encounter, ALBA did not seek to reform the international organizations or frameworks in which it was operating. The coalition simply acted 'as if' they already functioned as 'meeting places' for a plurality of peoples and their laws. In this way, ALBA demonstrates that the task of (re)imagining the international as a 'meeting place' does not necessarily require a radical overhaul of the current international legal system. It may simply be possible to go about this transformation

[128] Michael Strange, 'Discursivity of Global Governance: Vestiges of "'Democracy'" in the World Trade Organization' (2011) 36 Alternatives: Global, Local, Political 240, 250.

[129] Sonia E Rolland and David M Trubek, 'A Development-Driven Post WTO World' in Meredith Kolsky Lewis and others (eds), *A Post-WTO International Legal Order: Utopian, Dystopian and Other Scenarios* (Springer 2020) 257.

[130] Much of the thinking and research in this subsection on ALBA was developed in collaboration with Valeria Vázquez Guevara, see Claerwen O'Hara and Valeria Vázquez Guevara, '"We, the Peoples of the Earth": ALBA, Populism and the Making of an Alternative International Law' [2025] London Review of International Law 23.

through prefigurative action, whereby actors perform in the present the world they wish to create.[131]

ALBA, which means 'dawn' in Spanish, was created by Cuban President Fidel Castro and Venezuelan President Hugo Chávez, in 2004.[132] Over its lifetime, ALBA has had twelve members. In addition to Cuba and Venezuela, Antigua and Barbuda, Bolivia, Dominica, Ecuador, Grenada, Honduras, Nicaragua, Saint Kitts and Nevis, Saint Lucia, and Saint Vincent and the Grenadines have been part of ALBA at various points in time. ALBA was originally created to counter US influence in the region and offer an alternative to neoliberal economics.[133] To achieve these aims, ALBA undertook a range of regional initiatives in its early years aimed at promoting self-determination, integration, and poverty alleviation, including establishing a regional bank and creating an electronic currency.[134] In the late 2000s, ALBA also began to extend its sights beyond Latin America by operating as a coalition within existing multilateral bodies. ALBA's first appearance as a coalition within a multilateral body was at the UN climate conference in Copenhagen in 2009 (COP15).[135] Over the following decade, ALBA would continue to operate as a coalition in the UN Framework Convention on Climate Change (UNFCCC) negotiations.[136] During this period, it also came to act collectively in other international bodies, including the WTO[137] and UN Human Rights Council.[138] However, it should be noted that ALBA's membership as an international coalition has been more fluid than that of other regional organizations operating within international bodies, with different members of the regional organization signing on to different collective statements made in the name of 'ALBA'.[139]

As an international coalition, ALBA regularly sought to give a voice to those marginalized by the international legal order.[140] At COP15, for example, one of the

[131] On prefigurative politics and the way it can be used by/inside existing institutions, see Davina Cooper, 'Towards an Adventurous Institutional Politics: The Prefigurative "As If" and the Reposing of What's Real' (2020) 68 The Sociological Review 893.

[132] O'Hara and Vázquez Guevara (n 130) 2.

[133] ibid.

[134] Moshen Al Attar and Rosalie Miller, 'Towards an Emancipatory International Law: The Bolivarian Reconstruction' (2010) 31 Third World Quarterly 347, 356.

[135] Joshua Watts and Joanna Depledge, 'Latin America in the Climate Change Negotiations: Exploring the AILAC and ALBA Coalitions' (2018) 9 WIREs Climate Change 1, 6.

[136] See 'Party Groupings', *United Nations Climate Change* <https://unfccc.int/process-and-meetings/parties-non-party-stakeholders/parties/party-groupings>.

[137] See, for example, Rorden Wilkinson, Erin Hannah, and James Scott, 'The WTO in Bali: What MC9 Means for The Doha Development Agenda and Why It Matters' (2014) 35 Third World Quarterly 1032, 1037.

[138] See, for example, Office of the United Nations High Commissioner for Human Rights (OHCHR), 'Intervención de la Alianza Bolivariana para los Pueblos de Nuestra América, Grupo de Trabajo Intergubernamental de Composición Abierta sobre Los Derechos de los Campesinos y Otras Personas Que Trabajan en las Zonas Rurales', Primer período de sesiones (17 July 2013) <https://www.ohchr.org/sites/default/files/Documents/HRBodies/HRCouncil/WGPleasants/ALBA-TCP.pdf>.

[139] O'Hara and Vázquez Guevara (n 130) 7–8.

[140] See generally ibid.

ALBA leaders, Venezuelan President Hugo Chávez, drew attention to the protests of around 100,000 people in the streets of Copenhagen, stating '[t]here are many people outside, you know? Of course, they do not fit in this room, they are too many people.'[141] Chávez claimed that the reason people had come from all over the world to protest the UNFCCC negotiations was because they recognized that global capitalism was driving the climate crisis: 'It's capitalism, the people roar out there. Hear them.'[142] To make this point, Chávez repeated two of the protesters' slogans. One was, 'Don't change the climate, change the system'.[143] The other was, 'If the climate were a bank it would have been saved already'.[144] By repeating these slogans, Chávez helped to bring the voices of the people in the streets into the official UN Conference. A similar approach was taken up by ALBA in its collective Declaration on the Copenhagen Climate Summit. This Declaration was issued at the end of the Conference, after ALBA had helped to block the final Copenhagen Accord on account of it having been drafted without its consultation.[145] ALBA's Declaration provides: 'We recall that while the conference failed in an irreversible way, the voices of the youth who know that the future is theirs grows stronger . . . We join with them and their protests, and we salute and support them.'[146] It also ends by repeating the protesters' slogan, 'Don't change the climate, change the system!'[147]

After COP15, ALBA went even further in its attempts to uplift the voices of those on the outside of formal international institutions. Another of the ALBA leaders, Bolivian President Evo Morales, followed up the coalition's claim that it 'joined with' the people by organizing an alternative international environmental conference, the 'World People's Conference on Climate Change and the Rights of Mother Earth', in which not only governments but also everyday people could participate. An open call was put out for 'peoples of the world, social movements and Mother Earth's defenders, scientists, academics, lawyers and governments that want to work with their citizens'[148] to come to Bolivia and discuss alternative ways of addressing the climate crisis. From the outset, it was made clear that

[141] Hugo Chávez Frías, 'Speech to Copenhagen' (Kiraz Janicke tr) in Socialist Voice, *If the Climate Were a Bank, It Would Have Already Been Saved: Latin America vs Imperialism at the Copenhagen Climate Summit* (Socialist Alliance Australia, 2010) 18.
[142] ibid.
[143] ibid 23.
[144] ibid 18.
[145] 'ALBA Declaration on Copenhagen Climate Summit: Issued by the Bolivarian Alliance for the Peoples of Our America (ALBA) on December 18, 2009, In Response to the Copenhagen Climate Summit (Translated by Tamara Pearson)', in Socialist Voice, *If the Climate Were a Bank, It Would Have Already Been Saved: Latin America vs Imperialism at the Copenhagen Climate Summit* (Socialist Alliance Australia, 2010).
[146] ibid 16.
[147] ibid.
[148] World People's Conference on Climate Change and the Rights of Mother Earth: Building the People's World Movement for Mother Earth, 'Call' (15 January 2010) <https://pwccc.wordpress.com/2010/01/15/call/>.

the conference aimed to articulate a very different international legal vision to that prevailing in the UNFCCC. For example, the references to 'Mother Earth' in both the conference name and its call for attendees displayed a desire to move away from the anthropocentric thinking of the dominant international environmental law framework towards something more closely aligned with Andean Indigenous legal thinking, which centres around respect for '*Pachamama*' ('Mother Earth' in the Aymara and Quechua languages).[149]

The World People's Conference on Climate Change and the Rights of Mother Earth took place in Cochabamba, Bolivia in April 2010. It was attended by around 35,000 people from more than 140 states,[150] including climate activists, peasant alliances, and Indigenous groups, as well as ALBA leaders, such as Chávez and Morales. Through a combination of consensus decision-making and majority voting,[151] the Conference produced a number of collective documents, including a People's Agreement on Climate Change and the Rights of Mother Earth and a Universal Declaration of the Rights of Mother Earth (UDRME). The People's Agreement emphasizes the connection between capitalism and climate change, stating, '[t]he corporations and governments of the so-called "developed" countries, in complicity with a segment of the scientific community, have led us to discuss climate change as a problem limited to the rise in temperature without questioning the cause, which is the capitalist system'.[152] It goes on to explain that, in the view of the Conference participants, '[t]he capitalist system has imposed on us a logic of competition, progress and limitless growth', under which 'Mother Earth is converted into a source of raw materials, and human beings into consumers and a means of production'.[153]

To counter these effects, the People's Agreement states that 'we must recognize Mother Earth as the source of life and forge a new system based on the principles of harmony and balance among all and with all things'.[154] The UDRME then

[149] President Morales, himself an Aymara man, had already undertaken domestic law reform in Bolivia by this point aimed at protecting 'Mother Earth' and giving effect to the communitarian Andean model of 'living well'. Though far from perfect, Kapoor argues that in its refusal of both the neoliberal and state capitalist models, along with its attempts to 'put the country's subalterns first (indigenous groups and the socioeconomically most poor and marginalized)', Bolivia's Morales regime can be seen as 'one of the queerest globally', Ilan Kapoor, 'The Queer Third World' 36(9) (2015) Third World Quarterly 1611, 1622.

[150] 'Statement by the Plurinational State of Bolivia on the Cochabamba Conference' in World Trade Organization Committee on Trade and Environment, Report of the Meeting Held on 9 November 2010, WTO Doc WT/CTE/M/51 (31 May 2011) [56].

[151] Kevin Koenig, 'Cochabamba Chronicles: The World People's Conference on Climate Change and the Rights of Mother Earth' (*Amazon Watch*, 22 April 2010) <https://amazonwatch.org/news/2010/0422-cochabamba-chronicles-the-world-peoples-conference-on-climate-change-and-the-rights-of-mother-earth>.

[152] People's Agreement on Climate Change and the Rights of Mother Earth (22 April 2010), available at <https://daily.jstor.org/cochabamba-peoples-agreement-annotated/>.

[153] ibid.

[154] ibid.

fleshes out this vision by proclaiming a list of rights for Mother Earth.[155] These include 'the right to live and exist'[156] and the right for Mother Earth 'to maintain its identity and integrity as a distinct, self-regulating and interrelated being',[157] as well as more specific rights, such as 'the right not to have its genetic structure modified or disrupted in a manner that threatens its integrity or vital and healthy functioning'.[158]

However, what is particularly significant from the perspective of this chapter is that ALBA did not only help to bring about the articulation of this alternative vision of international law. As with the voices of the Copenhagen protesters, the coalition also made active efforts to ensure that vision would be registered within 'official' international institutions. Following the People's Conference, for example, ALBA made a submission to the UNFCCC, informing its members of the outcome of the Conference and endorsing the People's Agreement and UDRME, stating, '[w]e, the Governments of ALBA . . . make these voices our own'.[159] In addition, Bolivia shared the documents with the UNGA[160] and the WTO.[161] In the WTO, the representative for Bolivia, Angélica Cecilia Navarro Llanos, explained how the vision of international law contained within them differed from the WTO's own rules relating to intellectual property and agriculture. For example, she outlined how the People's Agreement 'rejected any form of enforcing IPRs [intellectual property rights] over life'[162] and endorsed a concept of 'food sovereignty', according to which countries had a right to 'control their own seeds, water, lands, and technology for the production of food products in harmony with Mother Earth'.[163]

In this example, we see ALBA and its members using existing international institutions to facilitate an encounter between the dominant conception of international law and a popular, Earth-centred vision of international law, drawn from its engagements with people on the outside. In doing so, the coalition helped to transform those institutions—even if only fleetingly—into meeting places, in

[155] Universal Declaration for the Rights of Mother Earth (22 April 2010), available at https://www.garn.org/wp-content/uploads/2024/02/ENG-Universal-Declaration-of-the-Rights-of-Mother-Earth.pdf.

[156] ibid Article 2(1)(a).

[157] ibid Article 2(1)(d).

[158] ibid Article 2(1)(i).

[159] Official Submission of the Bolivarian Republic of Venezuela on Behalf of Cuba, Bolivia, Ecuador and Nicaragua; ALBA-PTT Member States, to the UNFCCC Ad-Hoc Working Group on Long-Term Cooperative Action, 26 April 2010, in 'Additional views on which the Chair may draw in preparing text to facilitate negotiations among Parties', Ad Hoc Working Group on Long-Term Cooperative Action under the Convention, United Nations Framework Convention on Climate Change (30 April 2010), 86 <https://unfccc.int/resource/docs/2010/awglca10/eng/misc02.pdf>.

[160] Letter dated 7 May 2010 from the Permanent Representative of the Plurinational State of Bolivia to the United Nations addressed to the Secretary-General, UN Doc. A/64/777 (7 May 2010).

[161] 'Statement by the Plurinational State of Bolivia' (n 150).

[162] ibid [60].

[163] ibid [59].

which different accounts of international law could come together and interact. What is more, this legal encounter has left its mark on the work of some of these institutions. While the legal discourse of 'Mother Earth' did not gain traction within the WTO, it did have some influence within the UNFCCC. For example, the preamble to the 2015 Paris Agreement refers to 'the importance of ensuring the integrity of all ecosystems, including oceans, and the protection of biodiversity, *recognized by some cultures as Mother Earth* . . . .'[164] The Paris Agreement also opened for signature on 22 April 2016[165]—a day that the UNGA had earlier proclaimed the 'International Day of Mother Earth' on the initiative of Bolivia.[166] Further, ALBA was successful in preventing a reference to 'market mechanisms' from being included in the Paris Agreement,[167] thereby avoiding one of the strongest attempts to entrench a capitalist logic into the international climate regime.

References to 'Mother Earth' can now also be found in other international instruments. For example, the preamble to the UNGA's Declaration on the Rights of Peasants and Other People Working in Rural Areas (UNDROP),[168] which was adopted by majority vote in 2018[169] and which ALBA was also instrumental in creating,[170] provides that 'peasants and other people working in rural areas should be supported in their efforts to promote and undertake sustainable practices of agricultural production that support and are in harmony with nature, *also referred to as Mother Earth in a number of countries and regions* . . . .'[171] While these preambular references to Mother Earth may not constitute a particularly strong intervention into the dominant system of international law, the avoidance of universalizing language within them, whereby 'Mother Earth' is described as something recognized by 'some cultures' or 'in a number of countries and regions', at least captures the meeting of different laws and legal traditions that took place. It also demonstrates the possibility of a pluralist approach to international law, in which multiple legal frameworks can exist at once.

As with all of my examples, ALBA's approach to international law has been flawed. For example, scholars have observed that the coalition's embrace of the

[164] Paris Agreement to the United Nations Framework Convention on Climate Change, opened for signature 22 April 2016, [2016] ATS 24 (entered into force 4 November 2016), Preamble [emphasis added].

[165] European Union External Action, 'Mother Earth Day sees signing of Paris Agreement for a more secure and stable world' (22 April 2016) <https://www.eeas.europa.eu/node/3507_en>.

[166] International Mother Earth Day, UN Doc GA Res 63/278 (22 April 2009).

[167] Watts and Depledge (n 135) 6.

[168] United Nations Declaration on the Rights of Peasants and Other People Working in Rural Areas (UNDROP), UN Doc A/RES/73/165 (17 December 2018).

[169] 121 states out of a total of 193 voted in favour of the UNDROP, see the Summary Record of the 53rd Meeting, UN Doc A/C.3/73/SR.53 (31 January 2019) 5. According to Gradoni and Pasquet, this made it the 'most controversial UN-sponsored human rights instrument' see Lorenzo Gradoni and Luca Pasquet, 'Voice under Domination: Notes on the Making and Significance of the United Nations Declaration on the Rights of Peasants' (2022) 33 European Journal of International Law 39, 41, 63.

[170] O'Hara and Vázquez Guevara (n 130) 9–10.

[171] UNDROP (n 168), Preamble [emphasis added].

rights of Mother Earth has sat uneasily with the historically important role of Venezuelan oil wealth in the creation and maintenance of ALBA.[172] There are also reports of activists having been denounced by the group as 'right-wing' when they have criticized the ALBA members' own domestic environmental policies,[173] suggesting that the coalition's willingness to collaborate with social movements has sometimes been more about political expediency than a desire to uplift marginalized voices.[174] Further, since the late 2010s, there has been a notable decline in ALBA's activities as an international coalition. While ALBA still exists as a regional organization, the last official communication from the group to an international organization was to the UN in 2019.[175] ALBA's waning influence as an international force has taken place alongside the descent of some of its members into social and economic crisis. Most notably, since Hugo Chávez's death, Venezuela has experienced hyperinflation, starvation, and disease, as well as an increase in political repression.[176] According to Nolte, these issues have caused ALBA to lose 'most of its attractiveness'[177] for states and groups once within its orbit—a sentiment that has likely only been heightened by the abduction and removal of Venezuelan President Nicolás Maduro by the US in January 2026.[178]

Yet, the tragedy of this narrative arc does should not erase ALBA's demonstration that it may be possible to create a 'meeting place' within the existing institutional structure of international law if actors simply begin treating it as such. The key is prioritizing the recognition of different international legal visions and traditions in international organizations over achieving a widespread agreement. Further, while ALBA's model of internationalism is still limited insofar as it is heavily reliant on states to act as a 'bridge' between formal international institutions and those on the outside, its members' efforts to include the voices of everyday people may make it easier for non-state actors—and thus a wider range of worlds—to be heard in these fora without the medium of the state in the future.

[172] Watts and Depledge (n 135) 9–10.

[173] Alice Cutler and Yasmine Brien, 'Global Struggles for Climate Justice and the ALBA-TCP Council of Social Movements: An Activist Perspective', *Counter-Globalization and Socialism in the 21st Century: The Bolivarian Alliance for the Peoples of Our America* (Routledge 2013) 227.

[174] O'Hara and Vázquez Guevara (n 130) 17.

[175] Letter dated 15 November 2019 from the Permanent Representative of the Bolivarian Republic of Venezuela to the United Nations addressed to the Secretary-General, UN Doc. A/74/556 (19 November 2019).

[176] Steve Ellner, 'Explanations for the Current Crisis in Venezuela: A Clash of Paradigms and Narratives' (2019) 10 Global Labour Journal 159.

[177] Detlef Nolte, 'From the Summits to the Plains: The Crisis of Latin American Regionalism' (2021) 12 LAP: Latin American Policy 181, 183.

[178] For an overview of these events, see Diana Kearne, 'The Abduction of a President: Shock, Illegality, and the Implications for Human Rights Law' (*Opinio Juris*, 2 February 2026) <https://opiniojuris.org/2026/02/02/the-abduction-of-a-president-shock-illegality-and-the-implications-for-human-rights-law/>.

7.3.4 The International Tribunal on Crimes against Women: A Site for Storytelling Across Worlds

My final vignette is focused on the International Tribunal on Crimes against Women. I discussed this people's tribunal briefly in Chapter 4, when reflecting on how social movements in Europe had begun to create their own international bodies in the 1970s to deal with issues of importance to them. In raising it again here, I aim to show how an international court or court-like body focused on social justice matters could also function as a meeting place for a plurality of worlds by creating a space for interaction between different people and their conceptions and experiences of law.[179]

The International Tribunal on Crimes against Women took place in Brussels in 1976. Conceived at an international feminist camp in Denmark in 1974, the Tribunal was presented as a feminist response to international institutions' treatment of the issue of gender equality to date, which many saw as seeking to give 'women equality with men in the system as it exists',[180] rather than reimagining the system itself. The Tribunal took place over five days and was attended by more than 2,000 women from 40 countries.[181] Although most attendees were from the global North, people from Egypt, Guinea, India, Iran, Mexico, Mozambique, the Philippines, Syria, Vietnam, and Yemen also participated.[182] In addition, there was a small group of immigrant and 'Third World' women living in Europe and settler colonies who testified, including a Vietnamese woman living in France, an Indian woman living in Britain, an Aboriginal woman from Australia, a Black South African woman, and a Native American woman.[183] The organizers made active efforts to include the voices of marginalized people. For example, the US committee borrowed funds to pay for the travel of Black and Indigenous attendees.[184] This

[179] In considering how a court could offer a meeting place, I have been influenced by Mark McMillan's account of how the Australian High Court case of *Koowarta v Bjelke-Petersen* (1982) created a 'meeting point' between multiple jurisdictions: international law and domestic law, state and federal law, the Anglo-Australian legal order and Indigenous peoples and their laws, as well as the Indigenous international. In paying attention to how the International Tribunal on Crimes Against Women created opportunities for storytelling, I have also been influenced by McMillan's account of how the possibilities opened up by the jurisdictional encounter in *Koowarta* were not fully realized in that case because the Court 'did not provide an opportunity for Mr Koowarta to actually tell his story, nor the enormity of the harm inflicted on him and the Wik peoples over the denial of access (and ownership) of his/their lands', see McMillan (n 26) 119.

[180] Diana Russell and Nicole Van de Ven, *Crimes against Women: Proceedings of the International Tribunal* (Les Femmes 1976) 151. In particular, it took aim at the UN Conference for International Women's Year in Mexico City in 1975. See, for example, Simone de Beauvoir's opening address, delivered by letter because she was unable to attend in person: 'In contrast to Mexico where women, directed by their political parties, by their nations, were only I seeking to integrate Woman into a male society, you are gathered here to denounce the oppression to which women are subjected in this society', quoted in ibid 5.

[181] ibid 5.

[182] ibid 6.

[183] ibid 67, 76.

[184] ibid 161.

meant that while the Tribunal was still dominated by white, middle-class perspectives from Western Europe and North America, a range of different voices were also able to enter the proceedings.

The main emphasis of the Tribunal was on personal testimony.[185] Each day, different women spoke about their views and experiences in relation to several 'gendered crimes'. For those who wished to participate but could not travel to the Tribunal, letters were read out on their behalf. This emphasis on testimony created opportunities for a meeting of different worlds as women from around the globe shared stories emanating from a range of social, political, and legal contexts. In discussing reproductive justice, for example, an Irish witness explained how the dominance of the Catholic Church in Ireland had produced a different legal landscape to that prevailing in most of Europe at the time:

> While Europe is looking for the legalization of abortion, we in Ireland, as always behind the times, are looking for the legalization of contraception. Irish women are denied this right. It is known in Ireland as 'artificial family planning.' It is a criminal offense to sell contraceptives, to advertise them, or to sell literature on or even related to them. The only methods of family planning legally permissible are those advocated by the Catholic Church: abstention and the rhythm method.[186]

An Aboriginal woman from Australia described the devastating impact of settler colonialism and Western patriarchy on her community. She told the Tribunal that, through 'colonialism, racism and sexism, Aboriginal women's status ha[d] been reduced to the lowest level in the hierarchy of Australian society, and her traditional status in Aboriginal society ha[d] been destroyed'.[187] The participant explained how, under the laws and customs of many Aboriginal communities, 'women were the basic producers of food. Women were economically independent. A woman's daily activities were not under the control of her father or husband but were collectively organized with other women.'[188] However, '[l]ack of understanding and attitudes of superiority and ethnocentricity [had] led to the imposition of the white western model of male/female relations'[189] onto Aboriginal societies, with destructive consequences for their life-worlds.

A lesbian woman from Mozambique reflected on how, under the new Marxist revolutionary regime in her country, 'lesbianism [was] considered a leftover from colonialism and decadent Western civilization'.[190] As a result, '[l]esbians [were] sent to rehabilitation camps to learn through selfcriticism the correct line about

185 ibid 7.
186 Quoted in ibid 13.
187 Quoted in ibid 67.
188 ibid.
189 ibid.
190 Quoted in ibid 46.

themselves'.[191] This perspective contrasted with the accounts of participants from Western Europe and North America, many of whom attributed the persecution of lesbians to the capitalist system.[192] The witness from Mozambique cautioned such participants against uncritically supporting revolutionary alternatives, noting that she was now personally hesitant to offer blanket support to 'struggles for liberation' when they could 'deny my right to existence and reject my collaboration once they gain power'.[193]

Moreover, unlike the ECtHR, the Tribunal did not seek to smooth over this meeting of different legal positions and experiences through any notion of 'consensus'. In fact, as discussed in Chapter 4, the Tribunal opted not to have a central decision-maker in the form of a jury or panel of judges, deciding instead that the participants could all be their 'own judges'.[194] Nor was there any single judgment or list of recommendations handed down. The organizers simply translated and compiled the participants' testimony, as well as the various 'solutions, resolutions, [and] proposals for change' put forward, into a book on the Tribunal proceedings, allowing their voices to stand on their own.[195]

Even the way the Tribunal structured its legal framework provided ample room for difference. As noted above, the Tribunal was organized around several 'gendered crimes'—although it should be noted that its use of the term 'crime' seemed to denote a social or structural wrong, rather than an offence with individual 'victims' and 'perpetrators'. The Tribunal's list of crimes included, inter alia, 'forced motherhood', 'compulsory non-motherhood', 'compulsory heterosexuality', 'economic crimes', 'dual oppression by family and economy', and 'the double oppression of Third World women'. As can be seen from this list, many of the Tribunal's crimes were expressed in such open terms that they allowed the participants themselves to fill them with meaning. Participants at the Tribunal thus took up the opportunity to articulate their own, feminist visions of international law. In the session on the 'dual oppression by family and economy', for example, a group from Canada designated unpaid care work as one of the gravest international crimes against women:

> In our view the crime against us internationally, from which all the other crimes against us flow, is our life centered around servicing men, children, and other women in order to produce and reproduce the working class. For this work, we are never paid a wage. The crime of work and wagelessness brands us for life as the weaker sex and delivers us powerless to employers, government, planners, and legislators, doctors, and the police, prisons and mental institutions, as well as individual men, for a lifetime of servitude and imprisonment.[196]

[191] ibid.
[192] For an overview, see O'Hara (n 30) 24.
[193] Quoted in Russell and Van de Ven (n 180) 46.
[194] ibid 7.
[195] See generally Russell and Van de Ven (n 180).
[196] Quoted in ibid 66.

In filling these crimes with meaning, there was also space for a divergence in views amongst the participants. On the issue of unpaid care work, for example, the Tribunal organizers record that while some participants believed that women should be paid for domestic labour, others were of the view that the role of 'housekeeper' needed to be abolished altogether.[197]

Where the Tribunal's crimes were more specific, they often designated the imposition of a social or legal consensus on women as the *problem*. That is, rather than being underpinned by any claim of regional or international consensus, crimes such as 'compulsory non-motherhood' and 'compulsory heterosexuality' centred on the way in which social and legal expectations about who can be a parent or what kinds of sexual relations are permissible served to harm people and curtail diversity. This practice of designating the norm as the problem led participants to offer an array of narratives about what gender and sexuality meant for them without feeling the need to conform to any pre-given legal narrative. In the session on the crime of 'compulsory heterosexuality', for example, some participants deployed an essentialist construction of sexuality. A witness from Norway told the Tribunal that she 'started to feel attracted to women at the age of 3'[198] and defined a 'lesbian' as 'a women who feels attracted to other women . . . whether we act on it or not'.[199] Others, however, conceived of queerness in more relational or cultural terms. A witness from France stated, 'lesbianism means for me feminine polarity: cultural, psychic, emotional, sexual and creative polarity'.[200] For other participants, it constituted a form of rebellion against the patriarchy. For example, a witness from England stated: 'So we are attacked not as passive victims, but because we ourselves are making an attack—we are refusing to be a service station for men . . . We lesbians have paid a heavy price for our rebellion.'[201]

These diverse accounts of sexuality stand in contrast to the ECtHR's case law, which, through claims of social, legal, and expert consensus, has lent weight to a single, essentialist ontology, which presents a 'sexual orientation' toward a given gender as an immutable characteristic that becomes fixed at a certain age. As discussed in Chapter 5, this has had a performative effect on applicants before the Court, who, in order to make their claims intelligible within that particular discursive landscape, have taken up an essentialist narrative themselves. The result has been an erasure of alternative experiences of sexuality, from those who experience sexuality as something fluid or non-binary to those who experience it as something cultural or political.

The Tribunal proceedings also offered opportunities for outright conflict and disagreement, although many of these were unplanned.[202] By the end of the first

[197] For a summary of this disagreement, see ibid 62.
[198] Quoted in ibid 35.
[199] ibid.
[200] Quoted in ibid 44.
[201] Quoted in ibid 37.
[202] O'Hara (n 30) 31–32.

day, some participants had grown frustrated with the coordinating committee remaining on the platform, the lack of theoretical analysis, and oral testimony being hurried along, and openly denounced these aspects of the Tribunal as authoritarian, hierarchical, and inflexible.[203] By the second day, there were disagreements over issues such as whether to permit male journalists at the Tribunal,[204] and different groups began proposing alternative programmes.[205] On the third day, there was an unscheduled 'lesbian demonstration', in which around '150 women with signs pinned on their backs and fronts announcing "I am a Lesbian," "J'aime les Femmes," "Ich bin Lesbisch," swarmed onto the stage',[206] sang a song, and offered impromptu testimony, including one in the form of a poem.[207] From that point onwards, the coordinating committee relinquished control over the event, permitting 'a basically anarchistic situation to prevail'.[208]

The structurelessness and conflict of the Tribunal attracted disapproval in the press. The UK-based *Guardian* newspaper ran an article on the Tribunal lamenting, 'now, it seems . . . that any international meeting of women is more likely to produce division than cohesion'.[209] Yet, as a group of Australian women participating in the Tribunal stressed, '[t]here are differences among women despite our common oppression and it is constructive and essential to discuss these in order to understand each other'.[210] Indeed, it seems that, for many, the conflicts and debates were what gave the Tribunal its energy. As one of the organizers, Diana Russell, reflected: 'the passive audience of the first day changed into active, involved participants. The Tribunal had come alive.'[211] Moreover, the chaos did not cause the Tribunal to fall apart. Most of the women who had come to testify were still able to do so[212] and although the disorder of the event caused upset amongst some, many others described it 'as one of the most fantastic and meaningful experiences of their lives'.[213] Perhaps owing to this positive experience, the organizers decided to carefully record all the disagreements and protests in their book on the Tribunal proceedings, making them accessible for all.

Another striking feature of the Tribunal was that it balanced the participants' 'stories of oppression, maltreatment, and misery',[214] as well as the disagreements

203 Russell and Van de Ven (n 180) 169.
204 ibid 164–68.
205 ibid 171–72.
206 ibid 11.
207 ibid 44.
208 ibid 172.
209 Quoted in ibid 182.
210 Quoted in ibid 171. This insight resonates with Jodi Dean's concept of 'reflective solidarity'—a feminist approach to solidarity based on an 'openness to difference which lets our disagreements provide the basis for connection', see Jodi Dean, *Solidarity of Strangers: Feminism after Identity Politics* (University of California Press 1996) 17.
211 Russell and Van de Ven (n 180) 178.
212 ibid 173.
213 ibid 190.
214 Marianne Oktober, quoted in ibid 181.

that ensued, with moments of fun. On the Saturday and Sunday nights, parties were held at the Maison des Femmes—a women's centre in Brussels. At these events, '[h]undreds of women, gay and straight, danced exuberantly' to the music of the Flying Lesbians—a feminist rock band from West Germany.[215] According to the organizers, the singing and dancing at these events helped to improve feelings of solidarity and communication between participants, particularly amongst those from different cultural and linguistic backgrounds.[216] As such, in addition to facilitating an encounter between multiple laws and legal experiences, the Tribunal created a space in which different groups and individuals could come together, interact, and build ongoing connections.

As in all of my vignettes, there are criticisms that can be made of the Tribunal. As noted above, there were far fewer participants from the global South and Socialist Bloc than there were from the West, limiting the extent to which it could provide a point of meeting for a plurality of worlds.[217] The Tribunal's exclusive focus on 'women' also worked to paper over the ways in which men, transgender, and non-binary people suffer under the patriarchy. However, these flaws do not take away from the rich repository of legal frames and procedures that the Tribunal offers when seeking to imagine how an international court or tribunal could function as a place of encounter for multiple worlds, from the Tribunal's adoption of a legal framework that designated the imposition of social norms as the problem to its emphasis on personal testimony and embrace of disagreement and dissent.

7.4 Conclusion

The future of international law is uncertain. As I write this concluding chapter, international law already looks very different to when I first began this project in 2018. The post-Cold War neoliberal order, 'marked by ever deepening globalization of commercial relationships, facilitated by the World Trade Organization (WTO) and other post-war international institutions',[218] seems to be collapsing. And yet, the international order that is forming in its ashes appears to be even uglier and full of 'monsters'.[219] Russia's full-scale invasion of Ukraine, which began in 2022, rages on, in defiance of international law's prohibition on the use of force.[220]

215 ibid 12.

216 ibid.

217 On the lack of participants from the Socialist Bloc, see Chiara Bonfiglioli, 'The First UN World Conference on Women (1975) as a Cold War Encounter: Recovering Anti-Imperialist, Non-Aligned and Socialist Genealogies' (2016) 27 Philosophy and Society 521, 528.

218 Eric Hontz, 'The End of the Washington Consensus Interbellum' (2024) 39 Maryland Journal of International Law 8, 8.

219 Eric Loefflad, 'International Law for a Time of Monsters: "White Genocide", The Limits of Liberal Legalism, and the Reclamation of Utopia' (2022) 35 Law and Critique 191; Anne Peters, 'International Law and Its Scholarship in the Time of Monsters' (2025) 2025–05 Max Planck Institute for Comparative Public Law & International Law (MPIL) Research Paper 1.

220 Peters (n 219) 1.

The US, under a second Trump Administration, is withdrawing from multiple international treaties and organizations,[221] applying tariffs to 'virtually all places on earth',[222] engaging in mass deportations,[223] abducting sitting heads of state,[224] and threatening to take over territories such as Greenland.[225] Anti-queer policies and discourses are on the rise.[226] And, in the eyes of many around the world, 'the largely unopposed live-streaming of genocidal violence in Gaza' for two years represented 'a moment of rupture both for international law and for global politics as any hegemonic pretence of universalism and equality is openly abandoned'.[227] What is more, all of this is taking place against a backdrop of a heating planet.

The ugliness of our present moment may create a sense of nostalgia for the discourses of international and regional consensus that once dominated bodies like the WTO and ECtHR. Yet, as I have sought to demonstrate in this book, the consensus order of international law's recent past came with its own set of problems. Not only was it not necessarily a time of widespread agreement, but it also worked to lock in unequal power relations and suppress difference and dissent in ways that have contributed to the aggression, hate, and turn away from international law that we are now witnessing. But we do not face a binary choice between an international order dominated by the idea of consensus and one marked by hostility, aggression and isolation. As I showed in this chapter, there are alternative international legal imaginaries that can facilitate collaboration and solidarity between different peoples, while also allowing space for diversity. One option is conceiving of the international as a 'meeting place' for multiple worlds, built upon an ethos that combines hospitality and cooperation with non-interference. Through a series of vignettes, I sketched out some of the different forms this 'meeting place' could take. While all of the examples I provided are flawed in some way, it is my hope that together, in their multiplicity, they might provide a basis for reimagining international law in more open, plural, and queer directions into the future.

[221] Kalyani Yeola, 'The U.S. Withdrawal from International Organizations: What It Means for Global Order?' *Modern Diplomacy* (10 February 2025) <https://moderndiplomacy.eu/2025/02/10/the-u-s-withdrawal-from-international-organizations-what-it-means-for-global-order/>.

[222] Nicholas Lamp, 'What President Trump's "Reciprocal" Tariffs Mean for International (Trade) Law' (*EJIL: Talk!*, 30 April 2025) <https://www.ejiltalk.org/what-president-trumps-reciprocal-tariffs-mean-for-international-trade-law/>.

[223] On the possible implications of this under international law, see William Worster, 'Trump's Deportations as an Emerging Crime Against Humanity' (*Opinio Juris*, 23 May 2025) <https://opiniojuris.org/2025/05/23/trumps-deportations-as-an-emerging-crime-against-humanity/>.

[224] In February 2026, the US abducted Venezuelan President Nicolás Maduro, see Diana Kearne (n 178).

[225] Ekaterina Antsygina, 'The Legal Debate Surrounding Greenland and Denmark: Unpacking Donald Trump's Statements' (*EJIL: Talk!*, 24 January 2025) <https://www.ejiltalk.org/the-legal-debate-surrounding-greenland-and-denmark-unpacking-donald-trumps-statements/>.

[226] See, eg, Craig McLean, 'The Growth of the Anti-Transgender Movement in the United Kingdom. The Silent Radicalization of the British Electorate' (2021) 51 International Journal of Sociology 473; Paula Gerber, 'One Step Forward, 10 Steps Back: The Rise of Anti-LGBTQ+ Laws in the United States' (*Australian Institute of International Affairs*, 3 May 2022) <https://www.internationalaffairs.org.au/australianoutlook/one-step-forward-10-steps-back-the-rize-of-anti-lgbtq-laws-in-the-united-states/>.

[227] Ntina Tzouvala, 'International Law as a Discipline in Crisis' (2025) 79 Australian Journal of International Affairs 71, 73.

References

A. Bibliography

1. Books and Journal Articles

Ahmed S, *Queer Phenomenology: Orientations, Objects, Others* (Duke University Press 2006)

Aksenova M, 'Quantum Leaps of International Law' in Barrie Sander and Jason Rundall (eds), *Symposium: COVID-19 and International Law* (Opinio Juris 2020) 142.

Al Attar M and Miller R, 'Towards an Emancipatory International Law: The Bolivarian Reconstruction' (2010) 31 Third World Quarterly 347

Alessandrini D, *Developing Countries and the Multilateral Trade Regime: The Failure and Promise of the WTO's Development Mission* (Hart Publishing 2010)

Alves JAL, 'The Declaration of Human Rights in Postmodernity' (2000) 22 Human Rights Quarterly 478

Ammaturo FR, 'The Right to a Privilege? Homonormativity and the Recognition of Same-Sex Couples in Europe' (2014) 23 Social & Legal Studies 175

Ammaturo FR, *European Sexual Citizenship: Human Rights, Bodies and Identities* (Palgrave Macmillan 2017)

Amos M, 'Can European Consensus Encourage Acceptance of the European Convention on Human Rights in the United Kingdom?' in Panos Kapotas and Vassilis P Tzevelekos (eds), *Building Consensus on European Consensus Judicial Interpretation of Human Rights in Europe and Beyond* (Cambridge University Press 2019) 258.

Anghie A, 'Legal Aspects of the New International Economic Order' (2015) 6 Humanity 145

Ansong A, 'Democracy in the World Trade Organization: Are Some Members More Equal Than Others?' (2017) 14 International Organizations Law Review 154

Antsygina E, 'The Legal Debate Surrounding Greenland and Denmark: Unpacking Donald Trump's Statements' (*EJIL: Talk!*, 24 January 2025) <https://www.ejiltalk.org/the-legal-debate-surrounding-greenland-and-denmark-unpacking-donald-trumps-statements/>

Arendt H, *Between Past and Future* (Penguin Books 1997)

Azmeh S, 'Developing Countries and Joint Statement Initiatives at the WTO: Damned If You Join, Damned If You Don't?' (2024) 55 Development and Change 349

Babu R, 'Decision Making in the WTO: From Negotiated Law-Making to Judicial Law- Making' in Julien Chaisse and Tsai-Yu Lin (eds), *International Economic Law and Governance* (Oxford University Press 2016) 487

Bachand R, 'What's Behind the WTO Crisis? A Marxist Analysis' (2020) 31 European Journal of International Law 857

Barfield CE, 'Free Trade, Sovereignty, Democracy: The Future of the World Trade Organization' (2001) 2 Chicago Journal of International Law 403

Bartenev D, 'LGBT Rights in Russia and European Human Rights Standards' in Lauri Mälksoo and Wolfgang Benedek (eds), *Russia and the European Court of Human Rights: The Strasbourg Effect* (Cambridge University Press 2017) 326

Bassok O, 'The European Consensus Doctrine and the ECtHR Quest for Public Confidence' in Panos Kapotas and Vassilis P Tzevelekos (eds), *Building Consensus on European Consensus: Judicial Interpretation of Human Rights in Europe and Beyond* (Cambridge University Press 2019) 236

Bateman BW, 'There Are Many Alternatives: Margaret Thatcher in the History of Economic Thought' (2002) 24 Journal of the History of Economic Thought 307

Bates E, *The Evolution of the European Convention on Human Rights: From Its Inception to the Creation of a Permanent Court of Human Rights* (Oxford University Press 2010)
Bates E, 'The UK and Strasbourg: A Strained Relationship—The Long View' in Katja S Ziegler, Elizabeth Wicks, and Loveday Hodson (eds), *The UK and European Human Rights: A Strained Relationship?* (Hart Publishing 2015) 39
Bates E, 'Consensus in the Legitimacy-Building Era of the European Court of Human Rights' in Panos Kapotas and Vassilis P Tzevelekos (eds), *Building Consensus on European Consensus: Judicial Interpretation of Human Rights in Europe and Beyond* (Cambridge University Press 2019) 42
Beddard R, *Human Rights and Europe: A Study of the Machinery of Human Rights Protection of the Council of Europe* (Sweet & Maxwell 1973)
Bedford K, *Developing Partnerships: Gender, Sexuality, and the Reformed World Bank* (University of Minnesota Press 2009)
Bedjaoui M, *Towards a New International Economic Order* (Holmes & Meier 1979)
Bengtson S, Gonzalez-Salzberg DA, and Johnson P, 'Christine Goodwin v the United Kingdom' in Loveday Hodson and Troy Lavers (eds), *Feminist Judgments in International Law* (Hart Publishing 2019) 175
Benvenisti E, 'Margin of Appreciation, Consensus, and Universal Standards' (1999) 31 New York University Journal of International Law and Politics 843
Bernstorff J von and Dann P (eds), *The Battle for International Law: South–North Perspectives on the Decolonization Era* (Oxford University Press 2019)
Bhala R, 'Chaos: Recent Developments in International Trade Law at the Multilateral, Regional, and U.S. Levels' [2018] Recent Developments in the Law: University of Kansas School of Law
Biddolph C, 'Queering Temporalities of International Criminal Justice: Srebrenica Remembrance and the International Criminal Tribunal for the Former Yugoslavia (ICTY)' (2020) 29 Griffith Law Review 401
Bjorge E, *The Evolutionary Interpretation of Treaties* (Oxford University Press 2014)
Black C, McVeigh S, and Johnstone R, 'Of the South' (2007) 16 Griffith Law Review 299
Blaser AW, 'How to Advance Human Rights Without Really Trying: An Analysis of Nongovernmental Tribunal' (1992) 14 Human Rights Quarterly 339
Blaser M and de la Cadena M, 'Pluriverse: Proposals for a World of Many Worlds' in Mario Blaser and Marisol de la Cadena (eds), *A World of Many Worlds* (Duke University Press 2018) 1
Bockman J, 'Socialist Globalization against Capitalist Neocolonialism: The Economic Ideas behind the New International Economic Order' (2015) 6 Humanity 109
Boer LJM, '"The greater part of jurisconsults": On Consensus Claims and Their Footnotes in Legal Scholarship' (2016) 29 Leiden Journal of International Law 1021
Bogdandy A von and Venzke I, 'In Whose Name? An Investigation of International Courts' Public Authority and Its Democratic Justification' (2012) 23 The European Journal of International Law 7
Bonfiglioli C, 'The First UN World Conference on Women (1975) as a Cold War Encounter: Recovering Anti-Imperialist, Non-Aligned and Socialist Genealogies' (2016) 27 Philosophy and Society 521
Bönnemann M and Bredler EM, '"Wavering Between Hope and Despair": Reflections from within German International Law Scholarship' (*Verfassungsblog*, 20 June 2025) <https://verfassungsblog.de/between-hope-and-despair/>
Bonner D, 'The Beginning of the End for Corporal Punishment?' (1979) 42 Modern Law Review 580
Borowiak C, 'The World Tribunal on Iraq: Citizens' Tribunals and the Struggle for Accountability' (2008) 30 New Political Science 161
Boyle A and Chinkin C, *The Making of International Law* (Oxford University Press 2007)
Brauch JA, 'The Margin of Appreciation and the Jurisprudence of the European Court of Human Rights: Threat to the Rule of Law' (2005) 11 Columbia Journal of European Law 113
Brauch JA, 'The Dangerous Search for an Elusive Consensus: What the Supreme Court Should Learn from the European Court of Human Rights' (2009) 52 Howard Law Journal 277

Bredeson K, 'L'Entrée Libre à L'Ex-Théâtre de France: The Occupation of the Odéon and the Revolutionary Culture of the French Stage' in Julian Jackson, Anna-Louise Milne, and James S Williams (eds), *May 68: Rethinking France's Last Revolution* (Palgrave Macmillan 2011) 299

Brems E, 'The Margin of Appreciation Doctrine of the European Court of Human Rights: Accommodating Diversity within Europe' in David P Forsythe and Patrice C McMahon (eds), *Human Rights and Diversity: Area Studies Revisited* (University of Nebraska Press 2003) 81

Brewster R, 'The Trump Administration and the Future of the WTO' (2018) 44 The Yale Journal of International Law Online 6

Brower CN and Tepe JB, 'The Charter of Economic Rights and Duties of States: A Reflection or Rejection of International Law?' (1976) 9 International Lawyer 295

Browne K and Nash CJ, 'Queer Methods and Methodologies: An Introduction' in Kath Browne and Catherine J Nash (eds), *Queer Methods and Methodologies: Intersecting Queer Theories and Social Science Research* (Routledge 2016) 1

Buergenthal T, 'International Law and the Holocaust' in Michael J Bazyler and Roger P Alford (eds), *Holocaust Restitution: Perspectives on the Litigation and Its Legacy* (New York University Press 2006) 17

Burgess J and Pearlstein S, 'Protests Delay WTO Opening: Seattle Police Use Tear Gas; Mayor Declares a Curfew' *The Washington Post* (1 December 1999) <https://www.washingtonpost.com/wp-srv/WPcap/1999-12/01/089r-120199-idx.html>

Bürli N, 'Amicus Curiae as a Means to Reinforce the Legitimacy of the European Court of Human Rights' in Spyridon Flogaitis, Tom Zwart, and Julie Fraser (eds), *The European Court of Human Rights and its Discontents: Turning Criticism into Strength* (Edward Elgar Publishing 2013) 135

Buss DE, 'Queering International Legal Authority' (2007) 101 Proceedings of the Annual American Society of International Law Meeting 122

Butler J, *Gender Trouble: Feminism and the Subversion of Identity* (Routledge 1990)

Butler J, *Excitable Speech: A Politics of the Performative* (Routledge 1997)

Butler J, *Undoing Gender* (Routledge 2004)

Butler J, *Notes Toward a Performative Theory of Assembly* (Harvard University Press 2015)

Buzan B, 'Negotiating by Consensus: Developments in Technique at the United Nations Conference on the Law of the Sea' (1981) 75 The American Journal of International Law 324

Byrnes A and Simm G, 'International Peoples' Tribunals: Their Nature, Practice and Significance' in Andrew Byrnes and Gabrielle Simm (eds), *Peoples' Tribunals and International Law* (Cambridge University Press 2018) 11

Carozza PG, 'Uses and Misuses of Comparative Law in International Human Rights: Some Reflections on the Jurisprudence of the European Court of Human Rights' (1998) 73 Notre Dame Law Review 1217

Chambers SA, 'A Queer Politics of the Democratic Miscount' (2009) 8(2) Borderlands 1

Charlesworth H, 'International Legal Encounters with Democracy' (2017) 8 Global Policy 34

Charlesworth H, 'The Travels of Human Rights: The UNESCO Human Rights Exhibition 1950–1953' in Sundhya Pahuja and Shane Chalmers (eds), *Routledge Handbook of International Law and the Humanities* (Routledge 2021) 173

Charlesworth H and Chinkin C, *The Boundaries of International Law: A Feminist Analysis* (Manchester University Press 2016)

Charlesworth H and Larking E (eds), *Human Rights and the Universal Periodic Review: Rituals and Ritualism* (Cambridge University Press 2015)

Charney J, 'United States Interests in a Convention on the Law of the Sea: The Case for Continued Efforts' (1978) 11 Vanderbilt University Journal of Transnational Law 39

Chimni BS, 'Political Economy of the Uruguay Round of Negotiations: A Perspective' (1992) 29 International Studies 135

Chimni BS, 'International Institutions Today: An Imperial Global State in the Making' (2004) 15 European Journal of International Law 1

Chimni BS, 'World Trade Organization, Democracy and Development: A View from the South' (2006) 40 Journal of World Trade 5

Cho S, 'The Demise of Development in the Doha Round Negotiations' (2010) 45 Texas International Law Journal 573
Chomsky N, *Occupy* (Penguin 2012)
Chorev N, 'The Institutional Project of Neo-Liberal Globalism: The Case of the WTO' (2005) 34 Theory and Society 317
Chowdhury N, 'The Quest for Universal Human Rights: A Brief Comparative Study of Universal Declarations of Human Rights by the UN and the Islamic Council of Europe' (2008) 12 International Journal of Human Rights 347
Cichowski RA, 'Civil Society and the European Court of Human Rights' in Jonas Christoffersen and Mikael Rask Madsen (eds), *The European Court of Human Rights between Law and Politics* (Oxford University Press 2011) 77
Clifford R, Gildea R, and Mark J, 'Awakenings' in Robert Gildea, James Mark, and Anette Warring (eds), *Europe's 1968: Voices of Revolt* (Oxford University Press 2013) 21
Cohn T, *Governing Global Trade: International Institutions in Conflict and Convergence* (Routledge 2002)
Conway J and Singh J, 'Radical Democracy in Global Perspective: Notes from the Pluriverse' (2011) 32 Third World Quarterly 689
Cooper D, 'Prefiguring the State' (2017) 49 Antipode 335
Cooper D, 'Towards an Adventurous Institutional Politics: The Prefigurative "as If" and the Reposing of What's Real' (2020) 68 The Sociological Review 893
Council of Europe, *The Conscience of Europe: 50 Years of the European Court of Human Rights* (Third Millennium Publishing Limited 2010)
Craven M, Pahuja S, and Simpson G, 'Reading and Unreading a Historiography of Hiatus' in Matthew Craven, Sundhya Pahuja, and Gerry Simpson (eds), *International Law and the Cold War* (Cambridge University Press 2019) 1
Cronin B, *Purging the Odious Scourge of Atrocities: The Limits of Consent in International Law* (Oxford University Press 2023)
Croome J, *Reshaping the World Trading System: A History of the Uruguay Round* (World Trade Organization 1995)
Cutler A and Brien Y, 'Global Struggles for Climate Justice and the ALBA-TCP Council of Social Movements: An Activist Perspective', *Counter-Globalization and Socialism in the 21st Century: The Bolivarian Alliance for the Peoples of Our America* (Routledge 2013)
Cutler RM, 'East–South Relations at UNCTAD: Global Political Economy and the CMEA' (1983) 37 International Organization 121
Daunton M, *The Economic Government of the World 1933–2023* (Allen Lane 2023)
Davies M, 'The Ethos of Pluralism' (2005) 27 Sydney Law Review 87
Dean J, *Solidarity of Strangers: Feminism after Identity Politics* (University of California Press 1996)
Dehm J, 'Righting Inequality: Human Rights Responses to Economic Inequality in the United Nations' (2019) 10 Humanity 443
Dembour M-B, 'What Are Human Rights? Four Schools of Thought' (2010) 32 Human Rights Quarterly 1
Derrida J, *Specters of Marx: The State of the Debt, the Work of Mourning and the New International* (Peggy Kamuf tr, Routledge 1994)
Dillon K, 'Divorce and Remarriage as Human Rights: The Irish Constitution and the European Convention on Human Rights at Odds in Johnston v Ireland' (1989) 22 Cornell International Law Journal 63
Dingwerth K, 'Democracy' in Klaus Dingwerth and Clara Weinhardt (eds), *The Language of World Trade Politics: Unpacking the Terms of Trade* (1st edn, Routledge 2018) 80
Donnelly J, *Universal Human Rights in Theory and Practice* (3rd edn, Cornell University Press 2013)
Dorsett S and McVeigh S, *Jurisdiction* (Routledge-Cavendish 2012)
Doty KA, 'From Fretté to E.B: The European Court of Human Rights on Gay and Lesbian Adoption' (2009) 18 Law & Sexuality 121

Dowrick FE, 'Juristic Activity in the Council of Europe—25th Year' (1974) 23 International and Comparative Law Quarterly 610

Drahos P, 'Weaving Webs of Influence: The United States, Free Trade Agreements and Dispute Resolution' (2007) 41 Journal of World Trade 191

Drahos P and Braithwaite J, *Information Feudalism: Who Owns the Knowledge Economy?* (Earthscan 2002)

Drzemczewski A, 'The Sui Generis Nature of the European Convention on Human Rights' (1980) 29 International and Comparative Law Quarterly 54

Duffy S, 'Moral Panics and Legal Projects: Echoes of Section 28 in United Kingdom Transgender Discourse and Law Reform' (2025) 1 Gender and Justice 78

Duggan L, *The Twilight of Equality? Neoliberalism, Cultural Politics, and the Attack on Democracy* (Beacon Press 2003)

Dunkley G, *The Free Trade Adventure: The WTO, the Uruguay Round, and Globalism—A Critique* (Zed Books 2000)

Dunoff JL and Pollack M, 'The Judicial Trilemma' (2017) 111 American Journal of International Law 225

Duranti M, '"A Blessed Act of Oblivion": Human Rights, European Unity and Postwar Reconciliation' in Birgit Schwelling (ed), *Reconciliation, Civil Society, and the Politics of Memory: Transnational Initiatives in the 20th and 21st Century* (Transcript 2012) 115

Duranti M, *The Conservative Human Rights Revolution: European Identity, Transnational Politics, and the Origins of the European Convention* (Oxford University Press 2017)

Dyer KJ, 'The Need to Re-Evaluate Incest in the Age of Assisted Reproductive Techniques: Stübing v Germany' (2012) 42 Family Law 1144

Dustin M, Ferreira N, and Millns S (eds), *Gender and Queer Perspectives on Brexit* (Palgrave Macmillan 2019)

Dzehtsiarou K, 'European Consensus and the Evolutive Interpretation of the European Convention on Human Rights' (2011) 12 German Law Journal 1730

Dzehtsiarou K, *European Consensus and the Legitimacy of the European Court of Human Rights* (Cambridge University Press 2015)

Ehlermann C-D and Ehring L, 'Are WTO Decision-Making Procedures Adequate for Making, Revising, and Implementing Worldwide and "Plurilateral" Rules?' in Ernst-Ulrich Petersmann and James Harrison (eds), *Reforming the World Trading System: Legitimacy, Efficiency, and Democratic Governance* (Oxford University Press 2005) 497

Ellner S, 'Explanations for the Current Crisis in Venezuela: A Clash of Paradigms and Narratives' (2019) 10 Global Labour Journal 159

Elsig M and Pollack M, 'Agents, Trustees, and International Courts: The Politics of Judicial Appointment at the World Trade Organization' (2014) 20 European Journal of International Relations 391

Eslava L, 'The Developmental State: Independence, Dependency, and the History of the South' in Jochen von Bernstorff and Philipp Dann (eds), *The Battle for International Law: South–North Perspectives on the Decolonization Era* (Oxford University Press 2019) 71

Fabri HR, 'The WTO Appellate Body or Judicial Power Unleashed: Sketches from the Procedural Side of the Story' (2017) 27 European Journal of International Law 1075

Falk RA, *Status of Law in International Society* (Princeton University Press 1970)

Feichtner I, 'The Waiver Power of the WTO: Opening the WTO for Political Debate on the Reconciliation of Competing Interests' (2009) 20 European Journal of International Law 615

Feichtner I, *The Law and Politics of WTO Waivers: Stability and Flexibility in Public International Law* (Cambridge University Press 2011)

Ferns N, 'The Middle Zone: The 1964 UN Conference on Trade and Development and the Australian Response' (2021) 32 Journal of World History 465

Fitzpatrick P, *The Mythology of Modern Law* (Routledge 1992)

Flett J, 'From the Green Room to the Court Room (And Back): Judicial Clarification of Ambiguity in WTO Law and the Effects on Subsequent Negotiations' (2011) 1 Oñati Socio-Legal Series 1

Footer ME, 'The Role of Consensus in GATT/WTO Decision-Making' (1997) 17 Northwestern Journal of International Law & Business 653
Ford J, *A Social Theory of the WTO: Trading Cultures* (Palgrave Macmillan 2003)
Foucault M, *The History of Sexuality Vol 1: An Introduction* (Robert Hurley tr, Pantheon 1980)
Foucault M, *Discipline and Punish: The Birth of the Prison* (Alan Sheridan tr, Penguin 1991)
Fraser N, *The Old Is Dying and the New Cannot Be Born: From Progressive Neoliberalism to Trump and Beyond* (Verso 2019)
Freeman E, *Time Binds: Queer Temporalities, Queer Histories* (Duke University Press 2010)
Fukuyama F, 'The End of History?' (1989) 16 The National Interest 3
Gahman L, 'Building "A World Where Many Worlds Fit": Indigenous Autonomy, Mutual Aid, and an (Anti-Capitalist) Moral Economy of the (Rebel) Peasant' in Jessica Duncan and Megan Bailey (eds), *Sustainable Food Futures: Multidisciplinary Solutions* (Routledge 2017) 103
Galindo GRB and Yip C, 'Customary International Law and the Third World: Do Not Step on the Grass' (2017) 16 Chinese Journal of International Law 251
Garavini G, *After Empires: European Integration, Decolonization, and the Challenge from the Global South, 1957–1986* (Oxford University Press 2012)
Getachew A, *Worldmaking after Empire: The Rise and Fall of Self-Determination* (Princeton University Press 2019)
Gibson-Graham JK, 'Queer(y)Ing Capitalism in and out of the Classroom' (1999) 23 Journal of Geography in Higher Education 80
Gibson-Graham JK, *A Postcapitalist Politics* (University of Minnesota Press 2006)
Gibson-Graham JK, *The End of Capitalism (As We Knew It): A Feminist Critique of Political Economy* (2nd edn, University of Minnesota Press 2006)
Gildea R and Mark J, 'Introduction' in Robert Gildea, James Mark, and Anette Warring (eds), *Europe's 1968: Voices of Revolt* (Oxford University Press 2013) 1
Gildea R, Mark J, and Warring A (eds), *Europe's 1968: Voices of Revolt* (Oxford University Press 2013)
Gilleri G, *Sex, Gender and International Human Rights Law: Contesting Binaries* (Routledge 2023)
Gilman N, 'The New International Economic Order: A Reintroduction' (2015) 6 Humanity 1
Golder B and Fitzpatrick P, *Foucault's Law* (Routledge-Cavendish 2009)
Goldhaber MD, *A People's History of the European Court of Human Rights* (Rutgers University Press 2007)
Golsong HI, 'The European Commission of Human Rights' (1987) 2 Connecticut Journal of International Law 285
Gonzalez-Salzberg DA, *Sexuality and Transsexuality under the European Convention on Human Rights: A Queer Reading of Human Rights Law* (Hart Publishing 2019)
Goodman N, *Ways of Worldmaking* (Hackett Publishing 1978)
Gradoni L and Pasquet L, 'Voice under Domination: Notes on the Making and Significance of the United Nations Declaration on the Rights of Peasants' (2022) 33 European Journal of International Law 39
Graeber D, 'The New Anarchists' [2002] New Left Review
Graeber D, 'There Never Was a West: Or, Democracy Emerges from the Spaces in Between', *Possibilities: Essays on Hierarchy, Rebellion, and Desire* (AK Press 2007)
Gramsci A, *Selections from the Prison Notebooks* (Quentin Hoare and Geoffrey Nowell Smith eds, 2014 edn, International Publishers 1971)
Griffiths C, 'Gay Activism in Modell Deutschland' (2015) 22 European Review of History 60
Grigolo M, 'Sexualities and the ECHR: Introducing the Universal Sexual Legal Subject' (2003) 14 European Journal of International Law 1023
Grigorescu A, *Democratic Intergovernmental Organizations: Normative Pressures and Decision-Making Rules* (Cambridge University Press 2015)
Grimmett JJ, *WTO Dispute Settlement: Status of U.S. Compliance in Pending Cases* (US Congressional Research Service 2011)
Grolimund AC, 'Sadomasochism at the European Court of Human Rights: Rights to Sex and Drawing the Line between Privacy and Public Interest' in Tamsin Phillipa Paige and Claerwen

O'Hara (eds), *Queer Encounters with International Law: Lives, Communities, Subjectivities* (Routledge 2024) 127
Gruszczynski L and Lawrence J, 'Trump, International Trade and Populism', *Netherlands Yearbook of International Law 2018* (TMC Asser Press 2019)
Gulewitsch N, 'Ya Basta! A Cry That Echoes Beyond Borders: Zapatismo and International Solidarity Networks in the Zapatista Uprising' (2011) 2 McGill Sociological Review 77
Gunewardene RM, 'GATT and the Developing World: Is a New Principle of Trade Liberalization Needed?' (1991) 15 Maryland Journal of International Law 45
Halperin DM, *Saint Foucault: Towards a Gay Hagiography* (Oxford University Press 1995)
Hamzić V, 'International Law, Coloniality, and the Temporal Otherwise' in Claerwen O'Hara and Tamsin Phillipa Paige (eds), *Queer Engagements with International Law: Times, Spaces and Imaginings* (Routledge 2024) 85
Haritaworn J, 'Wounded Subjects: Sexual Exceptionalism and the Moral Panic on "Migrant Homophobia" in Germany' in Encarnacion Gutierrez Rodriguez and Manuela Boatcă Costa Sérgio (eds), *Decolonizing European Sociology: Transdisciplinary Approaches* (Routledge 2010) 135
Harzl B, 'Nativist Ideological Responses to European/Liberal Human Rights Discourses in Contemporary Russia' in Lauri Mälksoo and Wolfgang Benedek (eds), *Russia and the European Court of Human Rights: The Strasbourg Effect* (Cambridge University Press 2017) 355
Healey D, *Russian Homophobia from Stalin to Sochi* (Bloomsbury Academic 2018)
Heathcote G, *Feminist Dialogues on International Law: Successes, Tensions, Futures* (Oxford University Press 2019)
Heathcote G, 'Oceans versus Ghost Fleets' in Claerwen O'Hara and Tamsin Phillipa Paige (eds), *Queer Engagements with International Law: Times, Spaces and Imaginings* (Routledge 2024) 39
Heckert J, 'Intimacy with Strangers/Intimacy with Self: Queer Experiences of Social Research' in Kath Browne and Catherine J Nash (eds), *Queer Methods and Methodologies: Intersecting Queer Theories and Social Science Research* (Routledge 2016) 41
Heinze E, 'Sexual Orientation and International Law: A Study in the Manufacture of Cross-Cultural Sensitivity' (2001) 22 Michigan Journal of International Law 283
Hekma G and Giami A, *Sexual Revolutions* (Palgrave Macmillan 2014)
Helfer LR, 'Finding a Consensus on Equality: The Homosexual Age of Consent and the European Convention on Human Rights' (1990) 65 New York University Law Review 1044
Helfer LR, 'Lesbian and Gay Rights as Human Rights: Strategies for a United Europe' (1991) 32 Virginia Journal of International Law 157
Helfer LR, 'Consensus, Coherence and the European Convention on Human Rights' (1993) 26 Cornell International Law Journal 133
Helfer LR, 'The Burdens and Benefits of Brighton' (*European Society for International Law (ESIL) Reflections*, 8 June 2012) <https://scholarship.law.duke.edu/cgi/viewcontent.cgi?article=5348&context=faculty_scholarship>
Herzog D, *Sexuality in Europe: A Twentieth-Century History* (Cambridge University Press 2012)
Hillman J, 'Three Approaches to Fixing the World Trade Organization's Appellate Body: The Good, the Bad and the Ugly?' [2018] Institute of International Economic Law Issue Brief 1
Hines S, 'Hands towards the Right: UK Gender-Critical Feminism and Right-Wing Coalitions' (2025) 34 Journal of Gender Studies 699
Hodson L, 'The European Court of Human Rights and Same-Sex Marriage: Incompatible Bedfellows?' (2025) 47 Journal of Social Welfare and Family Law 69
Hongler P, 'The Construction of a Western Voice: OECD and the First UNCTAD of 1964' in Matthieu Leimgruber and Matthias Schmelzer (eds), *The OECD and the International Political Economy Since 1948* (Springer 2017) 137
Hontz E, 'The End of the Washington Consensus Interbellum' (2024) 39 Maryland Journal of International Law 8
Hoover J, 'Rereading the Universal Declaration of Human Rights: Plurality and Contestation, Not Consensus' (2013) 12 Journal of Human Rights 217

Hopewell K, *Breaking the WTO: How Emerging Powers Disrupted the Neoliberal Project* (Stanford University Press 2016)
Howse R, 'How to Begin to Think About the "Democratic Deficit" at the WTO' in Stefan Griller (ed), *International Economic Governance and Non-Economic Concerns: New Challenges for the International Legal Order* (Springer 2003) 79
Howse R, 'The World Trade Organization 20 Years On: Global Governance by Judiciary' (2016) 27 European Journal of International Law 9
Howse R and Langille J, 'Continuity and Change in the World Trade Organization: Pluralism Past, Present, and Future' (2023) 117 American Journal of International Law 1
Hudes KA, 'Towards a New International Economic Order' (1975) 2 Yale Journal of International Law 88
Hunt A and Wickham G, *Foucault and Law: Towards a Sociology of Law as Governance* (Pluto Press 1994)
Irwin DA, Mavroidis PC, and Sykes AO, *The Genesis of the GATT* (Cambridge University Press 2011)
Jackson J, *World Trade and the Law of GATT: A Legal Analysis of the General Agreement on Tariffs and Trade* (Bobbs-Merrill 1969)
Jackson J, 'Review: Oliver Long, Law and Its Limitations in the GATT Multilateral Trade System' (1988) 82 American Journal of International Law 653
Jackson J, 'Designing and Implementing Effective Dispute Settlement Procedures: WTO Dispute Settlement, Appraisal and Prospects' in Anne O Krueger (ed), *The WTO as an International Organization* (University of Chicago Press 1998) 161
Jackson J, *Sovereignty, the WTO and Changing Fundamentals of International Law* (Cambridge University Press 2006)
Jenks WC, 'Unanimity, the Veto, Weighted Voting, Special and Simple Majorities and Consensus as Modes of Decision in International Organisations', *Cambridge Essays in International Law—Essays in Honour of Lord McNair* (Cambridge University Press 1965)
Jones E, 'Challenging International Environmental Law's Heteronormativity and Anthropocentrism: Towards Queer Kinship' in Claerwen O'Hara and Tamsin Phillipa Paige (eds), *Queer Engagements with International Law: Times, Spaces and Imaginings* (Routledge 2024) 17
Johnson P, *Homosexuality and the European Court of Human Rights* (Routledge 2013)
Johnson P, 'Sociology and the European Court of Human Rights' (2014) 62 The Sociological Review 547
Johnson P, '"Homosexual Propaganda" Laws in the Russian Federation: Are They in Violation of the European Convention on Human Rights?' (2015) 3 Russian Law Journal 37
Johnson P, *Going to Strasbourg: An Oral History of Sexual Orientation Discrimination and the European Convention on Human Rights* (Oxford University Press 2016)
Kapoor I, 'The Queer Third World' (2015) 36 Third World Quarterly 1611
Kapotas P and Tzevelekos VP, 'How (Difficult Is It) to Build Consensus on (European) Consensus?' in Panos Kapotas and Vassilis P Tzevelekos (eds), *Building Consensus on European Consensus: Judicial Interpretation of Human Rights in Europe and Beyond* (Cambridge University Press 2019) 1
Kapur R, 'Post-Colonial Economies of Desire: Legal Representations of the Sexual Subaltern' (2001) 78 Denver University Law Review 855
Kapur R, *Gender, Alterity and Human Rights: Freedom in a Fishbowl* (Edward Elgar Publishing 2018)
Karshenas M, 'Power, Ideology and Global Development: On the Origins, Evolution and Achievements of UNCTAD' (2016) 47 Development and Change 664
Kastner P and Trudel ER, 'Unsettling International Law and Peace-Making: An Encounter with Queer Theory' (2020) 33 Leiden Journal of International Law 911
Kauffman LA, 'A Short History of Radical Renewal' in Benjamin Shephard and Ronald Hayduk (eds), *From ACT UP to the WTO: Urban Protest and Community Building in the Era of Globalization* (Verso 2002) 35

Kaya A, 'Designing the Multilateral Trading System: Voting Equality at the International Trade Organization' (2016) 15 World Trade Review 25

Keil R, 'From Los Angeles to Seattle: World City Protests and the New Global Resistance' in Benjamin Shephard and Ronald Hayduk (eds), *From ACT UP to the WTO: Urban Protest and Community Building in the Era of Globalization* (Verso 2002) 326

Kelly JP, 'The Twilight of Customary International Law' (2000) 40 Virginia Journal of International Law 449

Kelsey J, *Serving Whose Interests? The Political Economy of Trade in Services Agreements* (Routledge-Cavendish 2008)

Kelsey J, 'The Illegitimacy of Joint Statement Initiatives and Their Systemic Implications for the WTO' (2022) 55 Journal of International Economic Law 2

Kennedy D, 'The Move to Institutions' in Jan Klabbers (ed), *International Organizations* (2nd edn, Routledge 2016) 3

Khasnabish A, *Zapatistas: Rebellion from the Grassroots to the Global* (Zed Books 2010)

Klein N, 'Farewell to the "End of History": Organisation and Vision in Anti-Corporate Movements' (2002) 38 Socialist Register 1

Klein N, *The Shock Doctrine: The Rise of Disaster Capitalism* (Penguin Press 2008)

Kleinlein T, 'Consensus and Contestability: The ECtHR and the Combined Potential of European Consensus and Procedural Rationality Control' (2017) 29 European Journal of International Law 871

Knox R and Kotiaho P, 'Beyond Competing Liberalisms: The World Trade Organization as Class Project' (2014) 23 Social & Legal Studies 426

Koch IE and Vedsted-Hansen J, 'International Human Rights and National Legislatures—Conflict or Balance?' (2006) 75 Nordic Journal of International Law 3

Kotz DM, 'Russia's Financial Crisis: The Failure of Neoliberalism?' *Z Magazine* (January 1999) 28 <http://people.umass.edu/dmkotz/R_Fin_Crisis_99.pdf>

Kock K, *International Trade Policy and the Gatt 1947–1967* (Almqvist & Wiksell 1969)

Krever T, 'Remembering the Russell Tribunal' (2017) 5 London Review of International Law 483

Krishnamurti R, 'UNCTAD as a Negotiating Institution' (1981) 15 Journal of World Trade Law 3

Kuijper PJ, 'From the Board: The US Attack on the WTO Appellate Body' (2018) 45 Legal Issues of Economic Integration 1

Lamp N, 'What President Trump's "Reciprocal" Tariffs Mean for International (Trade) Law' (*EJIL: Talk!*, 30 April 2025) <https://www.ejiltalk.org/what-president-trumps-reciprocal-tariffs-mean-for-international-trade-law/>

Lamy P, *The Geneva Consensus: Making Trade Work for All* (Cambridge University Press 2013)

Lang A, *World Trade Law After Neoliberalism: Re-Imagining the Global Economic Order* (Oxford University Press 2011)

Lang A, 'Protectionism's Many Faces' (2018) 44 The Yale Journal of International Law Online 54

Lang A, 'Heterodox Market Orders in the Global Trade System' in Alvaro Santos, Chantal Thomas and David Trubek (eds), *World Trade and Investment Law Reimagined: A Progressive Agenda For An Inclusive Globalization* (Anthem Press 2019) 73

Lang A and Scott J, 'The Hidden World of WTO Governance' (2009) 20 The European Journal of International Law 575

Langlois AJ, 'Queer Temporalities and Human Rights' in Kathryn McNeilly and Ben Warwick (eds), *The Times and Temporalities of International Human Rights Law* (Hart Publishing 2022) 159

Laruelle M, *In the Name of the Nation: Nationalism and Politics in Contemporary Russia* (Palgrave Macmillan 2009)

Libbey JK, 'CoCom, Comecon, and the Economic Cold War' (2010) 37 Russian History 133

Letsas G, 'The Truth in Autonomous Concepts: How to Interpret the ECHR' (2000) 15 European Journal of International Law 279

Lewis MK, 'The Lack of Dissent in WTO Dispute Settlement' (2006) 9 Journal of International Economic Law 895

Lindgren T, 'An International Law of Peoples: The International Rights of Nature Tribunal and International Law' (University of Melbourne 2024)
Lixinski L, 'The Consensus Method of Interpretation by the Inter-American Court of Human Rights' (2017) 3 Canadian Journal of Comparative & Contemporary Law 65
Loefflad E, 'International Law for a Time of Monsters: "White Genocide", The Limits of Liberal Legalism, and the Reclamation of Utopia' (2022) 35 Law and Critique 191
Long O, *Law and Its Limitations in the GATT Multilateral Trade System* (Kluwer Academic Publishers 1987)
Lucas I, *OutRage! An Oral History* (Cassell 1998)
MacMillan E, 'Explaining Rising Regionalism and Failing Multilateralism: Consensus Decision-Making and Expanding WTO Membership' (2014) 11 International Economics and Economic Policy 599
Madsen MR, 'From Cold War Instrument to Supreme European Court: The European Court of Human Rights at the Crossroads of International and National Law and Politics' (2007) 32 Law and Social Inquiry 137
Madsen MR, 'The European Court of Human Rights: From the Cold War to the Brighton Declaration and Backlash' in Karen J Alter and Laurence R Helfer (eds), *International Court Authority* (Oxford University Press 2018) 243
Madsen MR, 'Rebalancing European Human Rights: Has the Brighton Declaration Engendered a New Deal on Human Rights in Europe?' (2018) 9 Journal of International Dispute Settlement 199
Madsen MR, 'Two-Level Politics and the Backlash against International Courts: Evidence from the Politicisation of the European Court of Human Rights' (2020) 22 The British Journal of Politics and International Relations 728
Maeckelbergh M, 'The Road to Democracy: The Political Legacy of "1968"' (2011) 56 International Review of Social History 301
Mälksoo L, 'The Human Rights Concept of the Russian Orthodox Church and Its Patriarch Kirill I: A Critical Appraisal' in Benedek Wolfgang and others (eds), *European Yearbook on Human Rights* (Neuer Wissenschaftlicher Verlag 2013) 403
Mälksoo L, 'Russia's Constitutional Court Defies the European Court of Human Rights: Constitutional Court of the Russian Federation Judgment of 14 July 2015, No 21-П/2015' (2016) 12 European Constitutional Law Review 377
Mälksoo L, 'Introduction: Russia, Strasbourg and The Paradox of a Human Rights Backlash' in Benedikt Harzl, Lauri Mälksoo, and Wolfgang Benedek (eds), *Russia and the European Court of Human Rights: The Strasbourg Effect* (Cambridge University Press 2017) 3
Marceau G, 'Never Waste a Good Crisis: The End of the WTO Dream, or the Beginning of Something Greater?' (2020) 17 International Organizations Law Review 345
Matsushita M, 'Reflections on the Functioning of the Appellate Body', *A History of Law and Lawyers in the GATT/WTO: The Development of the Rule of Law in the Multilateral Trading System* (Cambridge University Press 2015)
Matsushita M, *The World Trade Organization: Law, Practice, and Policy* (3rd edn, Oxford University Press 2015)
McKenzie F, 'GATT and the Cold War: Accession Debates, Institutional Development, and the Western Alliance, 1947–1959' (2008) 10 Journal of Cold War Studies 78
McKenzie F, *GATT and Global Order in the Postwar Era* (Cambridge University Press 2020)
McLean C, 'The Growth of the Anti-Transgender Movement in the United Kingdom: The Silent Radicalization of the British Electorate' (2021) 51 International Journal of Sociology 473
McMillan M, 'Koowarta and the Rival Indigenous International: Our Place as Indigenous Peoples in the International' (2014) 23 Griffith Law Review 110
McNeilly K, *Human Rights and Radical Social Transformation: Futurity, Alterity, Power* (Routledge 2018)
McVeigh S, 'Critical Approaches to Jurisdiction and International Law' in Stephen Allen and others (eds), *The Oxford Handbook of Jurisdiction in International Law* (Oxford University Press 2019) 183

McVeigh S and Pahuja S, 'Rival Jurisdictions: The Promise and Loss of Sovereignty' in Charles Barbour and George Pavlich (eds), *After Sovereignty: On the Question of Political Beginnings* (Routledge-Cavendish 2009) 100

McVeigh S and Pahuja Sundhya, 'Thinking with Jurisdiction: Shaun McVeigh and Sundhya Pahuja in Conversation' (2022) 82 Zeitschrift für ausländisches öffentliches Recht und Völkerrecht/Heidelberg Journal of International Law 299

Mercer B, *Student Revolt in 1968: France, Italy and West Germany* (Cambridge University Press 2020)

Michaels R, 'Private International Law and the Legal Pluriverse' in Michael S Green, Ralf Michaels, and Roxana Banu (eds), *Philosophical Foundations of Private International Law* (Oxford University Press 2024) 277

Moore M, 'Global Health Policy' (2000) 356 The Lancet 680

Moore M, 'The Democratic Roots of the World Trade Organization' in Patrick FJ Macrory, Arthur E Appleton, and Michael G Plummer (eds), *The World Trade Organization: Legal, Economic and Political Analysis*, vol 1 (Springer 2005)

Moores C, *Civil Liberties and Human Rights in Twentieth-Century Britain* (Cambridge University Press 2017)

Morgan W, 'Queering International Human Rights Law' in Carl Stychin and Didi Herman (eds), *Law and Sexuality* (University of Minnesota Press 2000) 208

Mosley H, 'Third International Russell Tribunal on Civil Liberties in West Germany' (1978) 14 New German Critique 178

Mouffe C, *The Democratic Paradox* (Verso 2000)

Mouffe C, *On the Political* (Routledge 2005)

Mouffe C, *For a Left Populism* (Verso 2018)

Moynihan D, 'The United States in Opposition' (1975) 59 Commentary

Moyn S, *The Last Utopia: Human Rights in History* (Harvard University Press 2010)

Moyn S, *Christian Human Rights* (University of Pennsylvania Press 2015)

Narlikar A, 'WTO Decision-Making and Developing Countries' (2001) 11 South Centre Working Paper

Narlikar A, 'The Politics of Participation: Decision-Making Processes and Developing Countries in the World Trade Organisation' (2002) 91 The Round Table 171

Narlikar A, *International Trade and Developing Countries: Bargaining Coalitions in the GATT & WTO* (Taylor & Francis 2005)

Nash J, *Mayan Visions: The Quest for Autonomy in an Age of Globalization* (Taylor & Francis 2001)

Nolte D, 'From the Summits to the Plains: The Crisis of Latin American Regionalism' (2021) 12 LAP: Latin American Policy 181

Nozawa J, 'Drawing the Line: Same-Sex Adoption and the Jurisprudence of the ECtHR on the Application of the European Consensus Standard under Article 14' (2013) 29 Merkourios Utrecht Journal of International and European Law 66

Ó Laoghaire T, 'Making Offers They Can't Refuse: Consensus and Domination in the WTO' (2018) 5 Moral Philosophy and Politics 227

Odell JS, 'Breaking Deadlocks in International Institutional Negotiations: The WTO, Seattle, and Doha' (2009) 53 International Studies Quarterly 273

O'Donnell TA, 'The Margin of Appreciation Doctrine: Standards in the Jurisprudence of the European Court of Human Rights' (1982) 4 Human Rights Quarterly 474

O'Hara C, 'Queering the International Human Rights Framework Pertaining to Sexuality: Toward the Right to Relate' in Paula Gerber (ed), *Worldwide Perspectives on Lesbians, Gays and Bisexuals*, vol 2 (Praeger 2021)

O'Hara C, 'In Search of a Queerer Law: Two People's Tribunals in 1976' (2023) 49 Australian Feminist Law Journal 17

O'Hara C, 'Queer Approaches to International Economic Law', *Elgar Encyclopedia of International Economic Law: Expanded Edition* (Edward Elgar 2024)

O'Hara C, 'Queer Legal Theory' in Harry Hobbs and Jeremy Patrick (eds), *Beyond Doctrine: Alternative and Critical Approaches to Law* (Federation Press 2025) 221

O'Hara C, 'Disordering, pluralising, queering: reflections on Ratna Kapur's contribution to queer engagements with international law' (forthcoming, 2026) London Review of International Law.

O'Hara C and Paige TP, 'Reaching Out Towards the Horizon: Queer Engagements with International Law Beyond Queer Theory's Site of Origin', *Queer Engagements with International Law: Times, Spaces, Imaginings* (Routledge 2024)

O'Hara C and Vázquez Guevara V, '"We, the Peoples of the Earth": ALBA, Populism and the Making of an Alternative International Law' (2025) 13(2) London Review of International Law 201

Olesen T, 'Globalising the Zapatistas: From Third World Solidarity to Global Solidarity?' (2004) 25 Third World Quarterly 255

Oomen BM, 'A Serious Case of Strasbourg-Bashing? An Evaluation of the Debates on the Legitimacy of the European Court of Human Rights in the Netherlands' (2016) 20 International Journal of Human Rights 407

Orford A, *International Authority and the Responsibility to Protect* (Cambridge University Press 2011)

Orford A, 'Broken Bargains' (*London Review of Books Blog*, 5 May 2021) <https://www.lrb.co.uk/blog/2021/may/broken-bargains>

Osterweil M, 'Place-Based Globalists: Rethinking the Global in the Alternative Globalization Movement' [2004] Unpublished paper, Department of Anthropology, University of North Carolina, Chapel Hill

Ostry S, 'The Uruguay Round North-South Grand Bargain: Implications for Future Negotiations', *The Political Economy of International Trade Law: Essays in Honor of Robert E. Hudec* (Cambridge University Press 2002)

Oswald RF, Blume LB, and Marks SR, 'Decentering Heteronormativity: A Proposal for Family Studies' in Vern L Bengtson and others (eds), *Sourcebook of Family Theories and Methods: An Interactive Approach* (Thousand Oaks 2005) 143

Otto D, 'Subalternity and International Law: The Problems of Global Community and the Incommensurability of Difference' (1996) 5 Social & Legal Studies 337

Otto D, 'Queering Gender [Identity] in International Law' (2015) 33 Nordic Journal of International Law 299

Otto D, 'Impunity in a Different Register: People's Tribunals and Questions of Judgment, Law, and Responsibility' in Karen Engle, Zinaida Miller, and DM Davis (eds), *Anti-Impunity and the Human Rights Agenda* (Cambridge University Press 2016) 316

Otto D, 'Beyond Legal Justice: Some Personal Reflections on People's Tribunals, Listening and Responsibility' (2017) 5 London Review of International Law 225

Otto D, 'Introduction: Embracing Queer Curiosity' in Dianne Otto (ed), *Queering International Law: Possibilities, Alliances, Complicities, Risks* (Routledge 2018)

Otto D, 'Resisting the Heteronormative Imaginary of the Nation-State: Rethinking Kinship and Border Protection' in Dianne Otto (ed), *Queering International Law: Possibilities, Alliances, Complicities, Risks* (Routledge 2018) 236

Otto D, 'Rethinking "Peace" in International Law and Politics From a Queer Feminist Perspective' (2020) 126 Feminist Review 19

Otto D, 'Queerly Troubling International Law's Vision of "Peace"' (2022) 116 AJIL Unbound 22

Otto D, 'Fearless Speech: A Portrait of UN Typist Shirley Hazzard', *Portraits of Women in International Law* (Oxford University Press 2023)

Pahuja S, 'Laws of Encounter: A Jurisdictional Account of International Law' (2013) 1 London Review of International Law 63

Pahuja S, 'Letters from Bandung: Encounters with Another International Law' in Luis Eslava, Michael Fakhri, and Vasuki Nesiah (eds), *Bandung, Global History, and International Law: Critical Pasts and Pending Futures* (Cambridge University Press 2017) 568

Pahuja S and Saunders A, 'Rival Worlds and the Place of the Corporation in International Law' in Jochen von Bernstorff and Philipp Dann (eds), *The Battle for International Law: South–North Perspectives on the Decolonization Era* (Oxford University Press 2019) 141

Paige TP, *Petulant and Contrary: Approaches by the Permanent Five Members of the UN Security Council to the Concept of 'Threat to the Peace' Under Article 39 of the UN Charter* (Brill Nijhoff 2019)
Paige TP and O'Hara C (eds), *Queer Encounters with International Law: Lives, Communities, Subjectivities* (Routledge 2024)
Pal M, *Jurisdictional Accumulation: An Early Modern History of Law, Empires, and Capital* (Cambridge University Press 2020)
Papadogiannis N and Gehrig S, '"The Personal Is Political": Sexuality, Gender and the Left in Europe During the 1970s' (2015) 22 European Review of History 1
Parmentier S and Malfliet K (eds), *Russia and the Council of Europe: 10 Years After* (Palgrave Macmillan 2010)
Pascual-Vives F, *Consensus-Based Interpretation of Regional Human Rights Treaties* (Brill 2019)
Paternotte D, 'Pedophilia, Homosexuality and Gay and Lesbian Activism' in G Hekma and A Giami (eds), *Sexual Revolutions* (Palgrave Macmillan 2014)
Patterson G, 'The GATT and Negotiating International Trade Rules' in Alan K Henrikson (ed), *Negotiating World Order: The Artisanship and Architecture of Global Diplomacy* (Scholarly Resources 1986) 181
Pauwelyn J, 'The Sutherland Report: A Missed Opportunity for Genuine Debate on Trade, Globalization and Reforming the WTO' (2005) 8 Journal of International Economic Law 329
Payosova T, Hufbauer GC, and Schott Jeffrey J, 'The Dispute Settlement Crisis in the World Trade Organization: Causes and Cures' (2018) 18-5 Policy Brief: Peterson Institute for International Economics 1
Peat D, 'The Tyranny of Choice and the Interpretation of Standards: Why the ECtHR Uses Consensus' (2021) 53 New York University Journal of International Law and Politics 381
Peters A, 'International Law and Its Scholarship in the Time of Monsters' (2025) Max Planck Institute for Comparative Public Law & International Law (MPIL) Research Paper 2025–26, 1
Petersmann E-U, 'Human Rights and International Economic Law in the 21st Century: The Need to Clarify Their Interrelationships' (2001) 4 Journal of International Economic Law 3
Petersmann E-U, 'How Should WTO Members React to Their WTO Crises?' [2019] World Trade Review 1
Petkova B, 'The Notion of Consensus as a Route to Democratic Adjudication?' (2012) 14 Cambridge Yearbook of European Legal Studies 663
Pickering M and Keightley E, 'The Modalities of Nostalgia' (2006) 54 Current Sociology 919
Pleyers G, *Alter-Globalization: Becoming Actors in the Global Age* (Polity Press 2010)
Polgari E, 'European Consensus: A Conservative and a Dynamic Force in European Human Rights Jurisprudence' (2018) 12 Vienna Journal on International Constitutional Law 59
Popelier P, Lambrecht S, and Lemmens K (eds), *Criticism of the European Court of Human Rights: Shifting the Convention System: Counter-Dynamics at the National and EU Level* (Intersentia 2016)
Prearo M, 'The 1970s Moment in Sexual Politics' in Julian Jackson, Anna-Louise Milne, and James S Williams (eds), *May 68: Rethinking France's Last Revolution* (Palgrave Macmillan 2011) 137
Prince S, *Northern Ireland's '68: Civil Rights, Global Revolt and the Origins of the Troubles* (Irish Academic Press 2007)
Puar JK, 'Rethinking Homonationalism' (2013) 45 International Journal of Middle East Studies 336
Puar JK, *Terrorist Assemblages: Homonationalism in Queer Times* (2nd edn, Duke University Press 2017)
Puckett AL and William L Reynolds, 'Rules, Sanctions and Enforcement under Section 301: At Odds with the WTO?' (1996) 90 American Journal of International Law 675
Querejazu A, 'Encountering the Pluriverse: Looking for Alternatives in Other Worlds' (2016) 59 Revista Brasileira de Política Internacional 1
Qureshi AH, *The World Trade Organization: Implementing International Trade Norms* (Manchester University Press 1996)

Raghavan C, *Recolonization: GATT, the Uruguay Round & the Third World* (Zed Books 1990)
Ramírez C, 'Ethos and Critical Discourse Analysis: From Power to Solidarity' (2013) 13 Contextes 1
Rancière J, *Disagreement: Politics and Philosophy* (Julie Rose tr, University of Minnesota Press 1999)
Rancière J, *Chronicles of Consensual Times* (Steven Corcoran tr, Continuum International Publishing Group 2010)
Rancière J, *Dissensus: On Politics and Aesthetics* (Steven Concoran tr, Continuum International Publishing Group 2010)
Rao R, *Third World Protest: Between Home and the World* (Oxford University Press 2010)
Rao R, 'Global Homocapitalism' (2015) 194 Radical Philosophy 38
Rao R, *Out of Time: The Queer Politics of Postcoloniality* (Oxford University Press 2020)
Renkin HZ and Trofimov V, 'The Global Dialectics of Homonationalism and Homophobia' (2023) 27 Sexuality & Culture 1987
Riabov O and Riabova T, 'The Remasculinization of Russia? Gender, Nationalism, and the Legitimation of Power Under Vladimir Putin' (2014) 61 Problems of Post-Communism 23
Rodríguez Mendoza M and Wilke M, 'Revisiting the Single Undertaking: Towards a More Balanced Approach to WTO Negotiations' in Carolyn Deere Birkbeck (ed), *Making Global Trade Governance Work for Development: Perspectives and Priorities from Developing Countries* (Cambridge University Press 2011) 490
Rodrik D, *The Globalization Paradox: Democracy and the Future of the World Economy* (WW Norton 2011)
Roffee JA, 'No Consensus on Incest? Criminalisation and Compatibility with the European Convention on Human Rights' (2014) 14 Human Rights Law Review 541
Rolland SE and Trubek DM, 'A Development-Driven Post WTO World' in Meredith Kolsky Lewis and others (eds), *A Post-WTO International Legal Order: Utopian, Dystopian and Other Scenarios* (Springer 2020) 241
Ross K, *May '68 and Its Afterlives* (The University of Chicago Press 2002)
Rozakis C, 'Foreword' in Panos Kapotas and Vassilis P Tzevelekos (eds), *Building Consensus on European Consensus: Judicial Interpretation of Human Rights in Europe and Beyond* (Cambridge University Press 2019) x
Rubin G, 'Thinking Sex: Notes for a Radical Theory of the Politics of Sexuality' in Guy Parker and Peter Aggleton (eds), *Culture, Society and Sexuality: A Reader* (University College London Press 1999) 143
Rush P, 'An Altered Jurisdiction: Corporeal Traces of Law' (1997) 6 Griffith Law Review 144
Russell A, 'Myth and the Zapatista Movement: Exploring a Network Identity' (2005) 7 New Media & Society 559
Ryssdal R, 'The Coming of Age of the ECHR' (1996) 1 European Human Rights Law Review 18
Sargent DJ, 'North/South: The United States Responds to the New International Economic Order' (2015) 6 Humanity 201
Saunders I, 'Populism, Backlash and the Ongoing Use of the World Trade Organization Dispute Settlement System: State Responses to the Appellate Body Crisis' (2021) 35 Maryland Journal of International Law 172
Schacherreiter J, 'Un Mundo Donde Quepan Muchos Mundos: A Postcolonial Legal Perspective Inspired by the Zapatistas' (2009) 9 Global Jurist 1
Schermers HG and Blokker NM, *International Institutional Law* (5th edn, Martinus Nijhoff 2011)
Scherpe JM, 'Same-Sex Couples Have Family Life' (2010) 69 Cambridge Law Journal 463
Schulz-Forberg H, 'Claiming Democracy: The Paris 1968 May Revolts in the Mass Media and Their European Dimensions' (2009) 31 Cuadernos de Historia Contemporánea 27
Sedgwick EK, *Tendencies* (Duke University Press 1993)
Sedgwick EK, *Epistemology of the Closet* (1st edn, University of California Press 2008)
Shaffer G, Elsig M, and Puig S, 'The Extensive (but Fragile) Authority of the WTO Appellate Body' (2016) 79 Law and Contemporary Problems 237

Shahid M, 'The Right to Same-Sex Marriage: Assessing the European Court of Human Rights' Consensus-Based Analysis in Recent Judgments Concerning Equal Marriage Rights' (2017) 10 Erasmus Law Review 184
Shephard B and Hayduk R (eds), *From ACT UP to the WTO: Urban Protest and Community Building in the Era of Globalization* (Verso 2002)
Shukaitis S, 'Space Is the (Non)Place: Martians, Marxists, and the Outer Space of the Radical Imagination' (2009) 57 The Sociological Review 99
Sibalis M, '"And What Then about 'Our' Problem?"—Gay Liberation in the Occupied Sorbonne in May 1968' in Julian Jackson, Anna-Louise Milne, and James S Williams (eds), *May 68: Rethinking France's Last Revolution* (Palgrave Macmillan 2011) 122
Sibalis M, 'The Gay Liberation Movement in France' in Gert Hekma and Alain Giami (eds), *Sexual Revolutions* (Palgrave Macmillan 2014) 188
Simm G, 'Peoples' Tribunals, Women's Courts and International Crimes of Sexual Violence' in Andrew Byrnes and Gabrielle Simm (eds), *Peoples' Tribunals and International Law* (Cambridge University Press 2018) 61
Simpson AWB, *Human Rights and the End of Empire: Britain and the Genesis of the European Convention* (Oxford University Press 2001)
Sinclair GF, *To Reform the World: International Organizations and the Making of Modern States* (Oxford University Press 2017)
Singh KM, *World Trade Organization and the Third World* (Mittal Publications 2005)
Slaughter J, 'Hijacking Human Rights: Neoliberalism, the New Historiography, and the End of the Third World' (2018) 40 Human Rights Quarterly 735
Sleptcov N, 'Political Homophobia as a State Strategy in Russia' (2018) 12 Journal of Global Initiatives: Policy, Pedagogy, Perspective 140
Slobodian Q, *Globalists: The End of Empire and the Birth of Neoliberalism* (Harvard University Press 2018)
Sohn LB, 'Voting Procedures in United Nations Conferences for the Codification of International Law' (1975) 69 The American Journal of International Law 310
Spano R, 'Universality or Diversity of Human Rights? Strasbourg in the Age of Subsidiarity' (2014) 14 Human Rights Law Review 487
Spano R, 'The Future of the European Court of Human Rights—Subsidiarity, Process-Based Review and the Rule of Law' (2018) 18 Human Rights Law Review 473
Spencer JR, 'Incest and Article 8 of the European Convention on Human Rights' (2013) 72 Cambridge Law Journal 5
Spijkerboer T, 'Gender, Sexuality, Asylum and European Human Rights' (2018) 29 Law and Critique 221
Starr A, Martínez-Torres ME, and Rosset P, 'Participatory Democracy in Action: Practices of the Zapatistas and the Movimento Sem Terra' (2011) 38 Latin American Perspectives 102
Steger D, 'The Future of the WTO: The Case for Institutional Reform' (2009) 12 Journal of International Economic Law 803
Steinberg RH, 'In the Shadow of Law or Power? Consensus-Based Bargaining and Outcomes in the GATT/WTO' (2002) 56 International Organization 339
Steinberg RH, 'The Impending Dejudicialization of the WTO Dispute Settlement System?' (2018) 112 American Society for International Law Proceedings 316
Stern B, 'Custom at the Heart of International Law' (2001) 11 Duke Journal of Comparative and International Law 89
Stiansen Ø and Voeten E, 'Backlash and Judicial Restraint: Evidence from the European Court of Human Rights' (2020) 64 International Studies Quarterly 770
Stone TW, 'Margin of Appreciation Gone Awry: The European Court of Human Rights' Implicit Use of the Precautionary Principle in Frette v France to Backtrack on Protection from Discrimination on the Basis of Sexual Orientation' (2003) 3 Connecticut Public Interest Law Journal 271
Storr C, *International Status in the Shadow of Empire: Nauru and the Histories of International Law* (Cambridge University Press 2020)

Strange M, 'Discursivity of Global Governance: Vestiges of "'Democracy'" in the World Trade Organization' (2011) 36 Alternatives: Global, Local, Political 240
Strange M, *Writing Global Trade Governance: Discourse and the WTO* (Routledge 2014)
Sullivan N, *A Critical Introduction to Queer Theory* (New York University Press 2003)
Suri J, *Power and Protest: Global Revolution and the Rise of Detente* (Harvard University Press 2003)
Sutherland P and others, *The Future of the WTO: Addressing Institutional Challenges in the New Millennium* (World Trade Organization 2005)
Suy E, 'The Meaning of Consensus in Multilateral Diplomacy' in Robert J Akkerman, Peter J Krieken and Charles O Pannenbourg (eds), *Declarations on Principles: A Quest for Universal Peace* (A W Sijthoff 1977) 259
Theilen JT, *European Consensus Between Strategy and Principle: The Uses of Vertically Comparative Legal Reasoning in Regional Human Rights Adjudication* (Nomos 2021)
Theilen JT, 'Civilizational Hierarchies and the Notion of "Europe" in the European Convention on Human Rights' (2025) 36 European Journal of International Law 113
Thomas C, 'The Death of Doha? Forensics of Democratic Governance, Distributive Justice, and Development in the WTO' in Chi Carmody, Frank J Garcia, and John Linarelli (eds), *Global Justice and International Economic Law: Opportunities and Prospects* (Cambridge University Press 2012) 185
Torres H, 'A Tariff Crisis Is Exactly the Right Time to Reform the WTO' (*Centre for International Governance Innovation (CIGI) Online*, 11 April 2025) <https://www.cigionline.org/articles/a-tariff-crisis-is-exactly-the-right-time-to-reform-the-wto/>
Toye J, 'Assessing the G77: 50 Years After UNCTAD and 40 Years After the NIEO' (2014) 35 Third World Quarterly 1759
Toye J, *UNCTAD at 50: A Short History* (United Nations 2014)
Tzevelekos VP and Dzehtsiarou K, 'International Custom Making and the ECtHR's European Consensus Method of Interpretation' (2016) 16 European Yearbook of Human Rights 313
Tzouvala N, 'Neoliberalism as Legalism: International Economic Law and the Rise of the Judiciary' in Ben Golder and Daniel McLoughlin (eds), *The Politics of Legality in a Neoliberal Age* (Routledge 2017) 116
Tzouvala N, 'Book Review: World Trade and Investment Law Reimagined: A Progressive Agenda for an Inclusive Globalization' (2020) 31 European Journal of International Law 1166
Tzouvala N, *Capitalism As Civilisation: A History of International Law* (Cambridge University Press 2020)
Tzouvala N, 'International Law as a Discipline in Crisis' (2025) 79 Australian Journal of International Affairs 71
Unrau C, 'A World of Many Walks? Zapatista World Ordering between Center and Margins' (2024) 4 Global Studies Quarterly 1
Van Damme I, 'Treaty Interpretation by the WTO Appellate Body' (2010) 21 European Journal of International Law 605
VanGrasstek C, *The History and Future of the World Trade Organization* (World Trade Organization 2013)
Větrovský J, 'Determining the Content of the European Consensus Concept: The Hidden Role of Language' in Panos Kapotas and Vassilis P Tzevelekos (eds), *Building Consensus on European Consensus: Judicial Interpretation of Human Rights in Europe and Beyond* (Cambridge University Press 2019) 120
Villani U, 'Conciliation and Consensus in UNCTAD' (1976) 2 Italian Yearbook of International Law 61
Vinen R, *The Long '68: Radical Protest and Its Enemies* (Allen Lane 2018)
Vleuten A van der, 'Transnational LGBTI Activism and the European Courts: Constructing the Idea of Europe' in Philip M Ayoub and David Paternotte (eds), *LGBT Activism and the Making of Europe: A Rainbow Europe?* (Palgrave Macmillan 2014) 119
Waites M, *The Age of Consent: Young People, Sexuality and Citizenship* (Palgrave Macmillan 2005)
Waites M, 'Critique of "Sexual Orientation" and "Gender Identity" in Human Rights Discourse: Global Queer Politics Beyond the Yogyakarta Principles' (2009) 51 Contemporary Politics 137

Walker-Leigh V, 'Was UNCTAD III A Failure?' (1972) 28 The World Today 411
Warner M, *Publics and Counterpublics* (Zone Books 2005)
Watts J and Depledge J, 'Latin America in the Climate Change Negotiations: Exploring the AILAC and ALBA Coalitions' (2018) 9 WIREs Climate Change 1
Weintraub S, 'North–South Dialogue at the United Nations: How the UN Votes on Economic Issues' (1977) 53 International Affairs 188
Werner WG, 'Regulating Speed: Social Acceleration, and International Law' in Moshe Hirsch and Andrew Lang (eds), *Research Handbook on the Sociology of International Law* (Edward Elgar Publishing 2018) 86
Wildhaber L, Hjartarson A, and Donnelly S, 'No Consensus on Consensus? The Practice of the European Court of Human Rights' (2013) 33 Human Rights Law Journal 248
Whyte J, *The Morals of the Market: Human Rights and the Rise of Neoliberalism* (Verso 2019)
Wildhaber L, Hjartarson A, and Donnelly S, 'No Consensus on Consensus? The Practice of the European Court of Human Rights' (2013) 33 Human Rights Law Journal 248
Wilkinson R, Hannah E, and Scott J, 'The WTO in Bali: What MC9 Means for the Doha Development Agenda and Why It Matters' (2014) 35 Third World Quarterly 1032
Williamson J, 'From Reform Agenda to Damaged Brand Name: A Short History of the Washington Consensus and Suggestions for What to Do Next' (2003) 40 Finance and Development 10
Williamson J, 'A Short History of the Washington Consensus' (2009) 15 Law and Business Review of the Americas 7
Wilson J and Swyngedouw E, 'Seeds of Dystopia: Post-Politics and the Return of the Political' in Japhy Wilson and Erik Swyngedouw (eds), *The Post-Political and Its Discontents: Spaces of Depoliticization, Spectres of Radical Politics* (Edinburgh Scholarship 2014) 1
Wintemute R, *Sexual Orientation and Human Rights: The United States Constitution, the European Convention, and the Canadian Charter* (Clarendon Press 1995)
Wolfrum R and Pichon J, 'Consensus', *Max Planck Encyclopaedia of Public International Law* (Oxford University Press 2010)
Wu M, 'The "China, Inc." Challenge to Global Trade Governance' (2016) 57 Harvard International Law Journal 261
Yildiz E, 'Enduring Practices in Changing Circumstances: A Comparison of the European Court of Human Rights and the Inter-American Court of Human Rights' (2020) 34 Temple International and Comparative Law Journal 309
Yourow HC, 'Margin of Appreciation Doctrine in the Dynamics of European Human Rights Jurisprudence' (1987) 3 Connecticut Journal of International Law 111
Yourow HC, *Margin of Appreciation Doctrine in the Dynamics of European Human Rights* (Brill 1996)
Zamora S, 'Voting in International Economic Organizations' (1980) 74 American Journal of International Law 566
Zammit AJ, 'UNCTAD III: End of an Illusion' (1973) 5 Institute of Development Studies Bulletin 3
Zellick G, 'Corporal Punishment in the Isle of Man' (1978) 27 International and Comparative Law Quarterly 665
Zieck M, 'The European Refugee Crisis from a Vantage Point of View' (2016) 45 Netherlands Journal of Legal Philosophy 3
Ziemele I, 'European Consensus and International Law', *The European Convention on Human Rights and General International Law* (Oxford University Press 2018)

2. Speeches

Address by Mr Donald Trump, President of the United States of America, UN GAOR, 72nd sess, 3rd plen mtg, Agenda Item 110, UN Doc A/72/PV.3 (19 September 2017)
Address by Mr Donald Trump, President of the United States of America, UN GAOR, 74th sess, 3rd plen mtg, Agenda Item 8, UN Doc A/74/PV.3 (24 September 2019)
Albuquerque PP de, 'Is the ECHR Facing an Existential Crisis?' (Speech delivered at the Mansfield College, Oxford, 28 April 2017) <https://www.law.ox.ac.uk/sites/files/oxlaw/pinto_opening_presentation_2017.pdf>

Beatrix, Queen of the Netherlands, 'Speech to the Parliamentary Assembly' (25 June 2002) <http://assembly.coe.int/nw/xml/Speeches/Speech-XML2HTML-EN.asp?SpeechID=135>

Bildt C, Prime Minister of Sweden, 'Speech Made to the Parliamentary Assembly of the Council of Europe' (1 October 1992) <http://www.assembly.coe.int/nw/xml/Speeches/Speech-XML2HTML-EN.asp?SpeechID=22>

Cameron D, 'Speech Made by the Prime Minister of the United Kingdom to the Parliamentary Assembly of the Council of Europe' (25 January 2012) <http://www.assembly.coe.int/nw/xml/Speeches/Speech-XML2HTML-EN.asp?SpeechID=31&a1=0&p2=0&lang=EN>

Castro F, 'Cuba Statement, Geneva Ministerial' (1998) <https://www.wto.org/english/thewto_e/minist_e/min98_e/anniv_e/castro_e.htm>

Chávez Frías, H, 'Speech to Copenhagen' (Kiraz Janicke tr) in Socialist Voice, *If the Climate Were a Bank, It Would Have Already Been Saved: Latin America vs Imperialism at the Copenhagen Climate Summit* (Socialist Alliance Australia, 2010).

Churchill W, 'A Four Year Plan for England' (*Broadcast from London over the BBC*, 21 March 1943) <http://www.ibiblio.org/pha/policy/1943/1943-03-21a.html>

Clinton B, 'Statement, Geneva Ministerial' (*Geneva Ministerial*, 18 May 1998) <https://www.wto.org/english/thewto_e/minist_e/min98_e/anniv_e/clinton_e.htm>

Clinton B, 'Speech on China Trade Bill' (*Johns Hopkins University*, 9 March 2000) <https://www.iatp.org/sites/default/files/Full_Text_of_Clintons_Speech_on_China_Trade_Bi.htm>

'Donald Trump's Speech on Trade' *Time* (28 June 2016) <https://time.com/4386335/donald-trump-trade-speech-transcript/>

Guevara C, '"At the United Nations", Speech Delivered on 11 December 1964, 19th General Assembly of the United Nations in New York' (*Che Guevara Internet Archive*) <https://www.marxists.org/archive/guevara/1964/12/11.htm>

Guevara C, '"On Development", Speech Delivered March 25, 1964 at the Plenary Session of the United Nations Conference on Trade and Development (UNCTAD)' (*Che Guevara Internet Archive*) <https://www.marxists.org/archive/guevara/1964/03/25.htm>

Hoffman LL, 'The Universality of Human Rights' (Judicial Studies Board Annual Lecture, 19 March 2009) <https://www.judiciary.uk/announcements/speech-by-lord-hoffmann-the-universality-of-human-rights/>

Lamy P, 'Statement, WTO Director-General Selection Process' (26 January 2005) <https://www.wto.org/english/thewto_e/dg_e/stat_lamy_e.htm>

Lamy P, 'It's Time for a New "Geneva Consensus" on Making Trade Work for Development' (*New York*, 30 October 2006) <https://www.wto.org/english/news_e/sppl_e/sppl45_e.htm>

Lamy P, 'Speech to the European Parliament Committee on International Trade' (29 May 2008) <https://www.wto.org/english/news_e/sppl_e/sppl90_e.htm>

Lamy P, 'Negotiations Can Find Compromise on the Safeguards Issue' (13 December 2008) <https://www.wto.org/english/news_e/sppl_e/sppl98_e.htm>

Lamy P, 'Trade and Human Rights Go Hand in Hand' (26 September 2010) <https://www.wto.org/english/news_e/sppl_e/sppl172_e.htm>

Lamy P, 'Crisis Is Opportunity to Restore Coherence in Global Economic Governance' (8 December 2010) <https://www.wto.org/english/news_e/sppl_e/sppl181_e.htm>

Lamy P, 'L'Organisation Mondiale Du Commerce et Le Droit' (18 January 2016) <https://academiesciencesmoralesetpolitiques.fr/2016/01/18/lorganisation-mondiale-du-commerce-et-le-droit/>

Mandela N, 'Statement, Geneva Ministerial' (19 May 1998) <https://www.wto.org/english/thewto_e/minist_e/min98_e/anniv_e/mandela_e.htm>

Moore M, 'The WTO: The Challenge Ahead' (1 July 1999) <https://www.wto.org/english/news_e/spmm_e/spmm01_e.htm>

Moore M, 'Trade for Development–The Way Ahead' (14 September 1999) <https://www.wto.org/english/news_e/spmm_e/spmm04_e.htm>

Moore M, 'Challenges for the Global Trading System in the New Millennium' (28 September 1999) <https://www.wto.org/englIsh/news_e/spmm_e/spmm08_e.htm>

Moore M, 'Executive Session of the Senate Finance Committee' (28 September 1999) <https://www.wto.org/english/news_e/spmm_e/spmm09_e.htm>

Moore M, 'The WTO Is Back On Track for Trade and Development' (16 February 2000) <https://www.wto.org/english/news_e/spmm_e/spmm24_e.htm>

Moore M, 'Moore Urges Trade Package for Poorest Countries' (13 April 2000) <https://www.wto.org/english/news_e/spmm_e/spmm27_e.htm>

Moore M, 'The Backlash against Globalization?' (*Ottawa*, 26 October 2000) <https://www.wto.org/english/news_e/spmm_e/spmm39_e.htm>

Moore M, 'Trade, Development and Democracy: The Need for Reform of the WTO' (10 April 2001) <https://www.wto.org/english/news_e/spmm_e/spmm57_e.htm>

Moore M, 'The WTO and LDCs: Delivering a Better Future Through Trade' (17 May 2001) <https://www.wto.org/english/news_e/spmm_e/spmm63_e.htm>

Moore M, 'Promoting Openness, Fairness and Predictability in International Trade for The Benefit of Humanity' (8 June 2001) <https://www.wto.org/english/news_e/spmm_e/spmm64_e.htm>

Moore M, 'Globalisation: The Impact of the Doha Development Agenda on the Free Market Process' (*Florida*, 2002) <https://www.wto.org/english/news_e/spmm_e/spmm77_e.htm>

Moore M, 'Democracy, Development and the WTO' (26 March 2002) <https://www.wto.org/english/news_e/spmm_e/spmm82_e.htm>

Oshima S, 'Farewell Speech' (13 June 2012) <https://www.wto.org/english/news_e/news12_e/speech_shotaro_e.doc>

Panitchpakdi S, 'The WTO after 10 Years: The Lessons Learned and the Challenges Ahead' (11 March 2005) <https://www.wto.org/english/news_e/spsp_e/spsp35_e.htm>

Ruggiero R, 'The Road Ahead: International Trade Policy in the Era of the WTO' (28 May 1996) <https://www.wto.org/english/news_e/pres96_e/pr049_e.htm>

Ruggiero R, 'Trading towards Peace' (12 November 1996) <https://www.wto.org/english/news_e/pres96_e/pr058_e.htm>

Ruggiero R, 'An Enabling Environment for Development: The Contribution of the Multilateral Trading System: Address to ECOSOC' (2 July 1997) <https://www.wto.org/english/news_e/sprr_e/ecosoc_e.htm>

Ruggiero R, 'Opening Statement, Geneva Ministerial' (1998) <https://www.wto.org/english/thewto_e/minist_e/min98_e/anniv_e/dg_e.htm>

Ruggiero R, 'The Multilateral Trading System at Fifty' (16 January 1998) <https://www.wto.org/english/news_e/sprr_e/london_e.htm>

Ruggiero R, 'From Vision To Reality: The Multilateral Trading System At Fifty' (26 February 1998) <https://www.wto.org/english/news_e/sprr_e/sanjos_e.htm>

Ruggiero R, 'The Future of the World Trading System' (15 April 1998) <https://www.wto.org/english/news_e/sprr_e/bergen_e.htm>

Ruggiero R, 'Address to the Second Summit of the Americas' (18 April 1998) <https://www.wto.org/english/news_e/sprr_e/santia_e.htm>

Ruggiero R, 'The Next 50 Years: Challenges and Opportunities For the Multilateral Trading System' (11 June 1998) <https://www.wto.org/english/news_e/sprr_e/hambur_e.htm>

Ruggiero R, 'Address to the University of Trieste MIB—School of Management' (22 September 1998) <https://www.wto.org/english/news_e/sprr_e/triest_e.htm>

Shea D, 'Statement by Deputy U.S. Trade Representative and U.S. Permanent Representative to the WTO, WTO General Council' (8 May 2018) <https://geneva.usmission.gov/2018/05/08/ambassador-dennis-sheas-statement-at-the-wto-general-council/>

Sørensen M, 'Do the Rights Set Forth in the European Convention on Human Rights In 1950 Have the Same Significance in 1975?' *Proceedings of the Fourth Annual International Colloquy about the European Convention on Human Rights* (Ministry of Foreign Affairs of Italy and the Secretariat General of the Council of Europe 1975)

Statement by President Macri, Buenos Aires Ministerial, WT/MIN(17)/75, 10 December 2017.

Statement by the Plurinational State of Bolivia on the Cochabamba Conference in World Trade Organization Committee on Trade and Environment, Report of the Meeting Held on 9 November 2010, WTO Doc WT/CTE/M/51 (31 May 2011)

Statement by the Representative of Egypt, GATT Doc CG.IS/W/6 (24 February 1976)

Statement of the Representative of India, GATT Doc CG.18/WA (25 November 1975)

Stiglitz JE, 'Keynote Address: More Instruments and Broader Goals: Moving Toward the Post-Washington Consensus' [1998] Villa Borsig Workshop Series

Sumption, Lord, 'The Limits of Law' (27th Sultan Azlan Shah Lecture, Kuala Lumpur, 20 November 2013) <https://www.supremecourt.uk/docs/speech-131120.pdf>

Sutherland P, 'Global Trade—The Next Challenge: Address to the World Economic Forum' (GATT Press Release, 28 January 1994)

Thatcher M, 'Speech to Conservative Women's Conference' (21 May 1980) <https://www.margaretthatcher.org/document/104368>

Unterhalter D, 'Farewell Speech' (22 January 2014) <https://www.wto.org/english/tratop_e/dispu_e/unterhalterspeech_e.htm>

Wolfensohn J, 'Opening Remarks at the Shanghai Conference on Scaling Up Poverty Reduction (26 May 2004)' in Andrew Kircher (ed), *Voice for the World's Poor: Selected Speeches and Writings of World Bank President James D. Wolfensohn, 1995–2005* (The World Bank 2005) 473

Wolff A, 'International Cooperation Must Balance Freedom of Action and Respect for Others' (13 September 2019) <https://www.wto.org/english/news_e/news19_e/ddgaw_13sep19_e.htm>

Yeo GY-B, 'Singapore Statement, Seattle Ministerial' (30 November 1999). WTO Doc. WT/MIN(99)/ST/1

3. Newspaper articles

Asthana A and Mason R, 'UK Must Leave European Convention on Human Rights, Says Theresa May' *The Guardian* (26 April 2016) <https://www.theguardian.com/politics/2016/apr/25/uk-must-leave-european-convention-on-human-rights-theresa-may-eu-referendum>

Bowcott O, 'Council of Europe Accepts UK Compromise on Prisoner Voting Rights' *Guardian* (8 December 2017) <https://www.theguardian.com/politics/2017/dec/07/council-of-europe-accepts-uk-compromise-on-prisoner-voting-rights>

'China Becomes World's No 1 Exporter, Passing Germany' *New York Times* (10 January 2010) <https://www.nytimes.com/2010/01/11/business/global/11chinatrade.html>

Diekmann K, 'Hungary's Prime Minister Says Accepting Syrian Refugees "Also Means Importing Terrorism, Criminalism Anti-Semitism and Homophobia"' *Business Insider* (Online, 25 February 2016) <https://www.businessinsider.com.au/viktor-orban-interview-refugee-migrant-hungary-2016-2?r=US&IR=T>.

'Donald Trump Extends China's 145pc Tariff Deadline for Another 90 Days' *ABC News* (12 August 2025) <https://www.abc.net.au/news/2025-08-12/donald-trump-extends-tariff-truce-with-china/105640320>

'ECHR under Pressure on Swiss Anniversary' *Swiss Info* (27 November 2014) <https://www.swissinfo.ch/eng/politics/40-years_echr-under-pressure-on-swiss-anniversary/41132266>

'Former WTO Head Michael Moore Talks About Who Benefits From Trade Reforms' *Radio Free Europe/ Radio Liberty* (11 October 2005) <https://www.rferl.org/a/1062035.html>

'Gay Parades Banned in Moscow for 100 Years' *BBC News* (17 August 2012) <https://www.bbc.com/news/world-europe-19293465>

Inside US Trade, 'For Appellate Body Candidates, USTR Prioritized Willingness To Dissent' *World Trade Online* (7 September 2011) <https://insidetrade.com/daily-news/appellate-body-candidates-ustr-prioritized-willingness-dissent>

Kinstler L, 'Are We Witnessing the Death of International Law?' *The Guardian* (London, 26 June 2025) <https://www.theguardian.com/law/2025/jun/26/are-we-witnessing-the-death-of-international-law>

Lane P, 'Time for Another Round' *The Economist* (3 October 1998) <https://www.economist.com/special-report/1998/10/01/time-for-another-round>

McHardy A, 'Ban on Homosexual Acts Denies Rights' *The Guardian* (23 October 1981)

'Russia Bans Popular LGBT Website for "Propaganda of Nontraditional Sexual Relations"' *The Moscow Times* (30 March 2018) <https://themoscowtimes.com/news/russia-bans-popular-lgbt-website-propaganda-nontraditional-sexual-relations-61007

Rodrik D, 'The WTO Has Become Dysfunctional' *Financial Times* (5 August 2018) <https://www.ft.com/content/c2beedfe-964d-11e8-95f8-8640db9060a7>

Rubin AJ, 'May 1968: A Month of Revolution Pushed France Into the Modern World' *New York Times* (5 May 2018) <https://www.nytimes.com/2018/05/05/world/europe/france-may-1968-revolution.html>

Seo B, 'WTO Urges Australia to Look Beyond Regional Trade' *Australian Financial Review* (23 September 2019) <https://www.afr.com/politics/federal/wto-urges-australia-to-look-beyond-regional-trade-20190919-p52sy2>

Slobodian Q, 'Trump, Populists and the Rise of Right-Wing Globalization' *New York Times* (22 October 2018) <https://www.nytimes.com/2018/10/22/opinion/trump-far-right-populists-globalization.html>

Slobodian Q, '20 Years After Seattle, the Clash of Globalizations Rages On' *The Nation* (29 November 2019) <https://www.thenation.com/article/activism/seattle-trade-globalization/>

Stavrou A, 'Trans Women to Be Banned from Single-Sex Spaces under New EHRC Guidance' *The Independent* (8 August 2025) <https://www.independent.co.uk/news/uk/home-news/trans-women-ehrc-guidance-banned-single-sex-spaces-b2804202.html>

Swanson A, 'Trump's Trade War With China Is Officially Underway' *New York Times* (5 July 2018) <https://www.nytimes.com/2018/07/05/business/china-us-trade-war-trump-tariffs.html>

Tatchell P, 'A Gayer Place than You Think: If Homosexuals Were Afforded Equal Rights, Bisexuality Would Be the Norm in Britain, Argues Peter Tatchell' *Independent* (24 January 1994) <https://www.independent.co.uk/voices/a-gayer-place-than-you-think-if-homosexuals-were-afforded-equal-rights-bisexuality-would-be-the-norm-in-britain-argues-peter-tatchell-1402224.html?r=67833>

'The Doha Round Finally Dies a Merciful Death' *Financial Times* (21 December 2015) <https://www.ft.com/content/9cb1ab9e-a7e2-11e5-955c-1e1d6de94879>

'Thousands Attend Geneva Anti-Globalisation Protest' *Institute for Agriculture and Trade Policy News* (25 June 2000) <https://www.iatp.org/news/thousands-attend-geneva-anti-globalisation-protest>

Watt N and Mason R, 'Cameron "Committed to Breaking Link with European Court of Human Rights"' *Guardian* (1 June 2015) <https://www.theguardian.com/law/2015/jun/01/david-cameron-european-court-of-human-rights>

'Who Elected the WTO?' *The Economist* (29 September 2001) <https://www.economist.com/special-report/2001/09/29/who-elected-the-wto>

4. Other

'ALBA Declaration on Copenhagen Climate Summit: Issued by the Bolivarian Alliance for the Peoples of Our America (ALBA) on December 18, 2009, In Response to the Copenhagen Climate Summit (Translated by Tamara Pearson)', *If the Climate Were a Bank, It Would Have Already Been Saved: Latin America vs Imperialism at the Copenhagen Climate Summit* (Socialist Alliance Australia, 2010)

Antonis Paschalides & Co LLC, '"New Families"? The Case of Schalk and Kopf v Austria on Same-Sex Unions and the Current Legal Situation of Cyprus' (30 January 2013) <https://www.paschalides.com/articles/family-law/124-new-families-the-case-of-schalk-and-kopf-v-austria-on-same-sex-unions-and-the-current-legal-situation-of-cyprus>

Bacchus J, 'The Future of the WTO: Multilateral or Plurilateral?' (*CATO Institute*, 25 May 2023) <https://www.cato.org/policy-analysis/future-wto>

'Closing Words of the EZLN at the Intercontinental Encounter* 2nd Declaration of La Realidad' (1996) <https://library.uniteddiversity.coop/More_Books_and_Reports/Zapatista_2nd_Declaration_LaRealidad.pdf>

'Communiqué from the Indigenous Revolutionary Clandestine Committee—General Command of the Zapatista Army for National Liberation. Mexico' (*Enlace Zapatista*, 22 September 2007) <https://enlacezapatista.ezln.org.mx/2007/09/23/communique-from-the-indigenous-revolutionary-clandestine-committee-general-command-of-the-zapatista-army-for-national-liberation-3/>

Duranti M, 'The Strasbourg Court Is Anti-Democratic, Just as Its Founders Intended' (*OpenDemocracy*, 13 July 2013) <https://www.opendemocracy.net/en/opendemocracyuk/strasbourg-court-is-anti-democratic-just-as-its-founders-intended/>

Gerber P, 'One Step Forward, 10 Steps Back: The Rise of Anti-LGBTQ+ Laws in the United States' (*Australian Institute of International Affairs*, 3 May 2022) <https://www.internationalaffairs.org.au/australianoutlook/one-step-forward-10-steps-back-the-rise-of-anti-lgbtq-laws-in-the-united-states/>

Hartmann J, 'A Danish Crusade for the Reform of the European Court of Human Rights' (*EJIL: Talk!*, 14 November 2017) <https://www.ejiltalk.org/a-danish-crusade-for-the-reform-of-the-european-court-of-human-rights/>

Hosking M, 'Enforcing the Right to Vote: UK Government Given Deadline to Reinstate Prisoners' Right to Vote' (*Human Rights Law Centre*, 23 November 2010) <https://www.hrlc.org.au/human-rights-case-summaries/greens-and-mt-v-united-kingdom-2010-echr-1826-23-november-2010>

'Invitation to the Second International Gathering of Women Who Struggle' (*Enlace Zapatista*, 21 September 2019) <https://enlacezapatista.ezln.org.mx/2019/09/21/invitation-to-the-second-international-gathering-of-women-who-struggle/>

Kearne D, 'The Abduction of a President: Shock, Illegality, and the Implications for Human Rights Law' (*Opinio Juris*, 2 February 2026) <https://opiniojuris.org/2026/02/02/the-abduction-of-a-president-shock-illegality-and-the-implications-for-human-rights-law/>

Koenig K, 'Cochabamba Chronicles: The World People's Conference on Climate Change and the Rights of Mother Earth' (*Amazon Watch*, 22 April 2010) <https://amazonwatch.org/news/2010/0422-cochabamba-chronicles-the-world-peoples-conference-on-climate-change-and-the-rights-of-mother-earth>

'Manifesto for the Convocation of the 2nd Intercontinental Gathering: For a World which Contains All Worlds' (*Archives of Global Protests, Nadir*, 1997) <https://www.nadir.org/nadir/initiativ/medienbus/was_wir_tun_start_eng.html>

Marriott R, 'A Critique of the Zapatista "Other Campaign" - Grupo Socialista Libertario' (*Libcom*, 25 March 2008) <https://libcom.org/library/a-critique-zapatista-other-campaign-grupo-socialista-libertario>

Milanovic M, 'Incest in the European Court' (*EJIL: Talk!*, 15 April 2012) <https://www.ejiltalk.org/incest-in-the-european-court/>

Modifying Reciprocal Tariff Rates to Reflect Trading Partner Retaliation and Alignment, Executive Order, White House (9 April 2025), available at: <https://www.whitehouse.gov/presidential-actions/2025/04/modifying-reciprocal-tariff-rates-to-reflect-trading-partner-retaliation-and-alignment/>.

'Part One: A DECLARATION . . . FOR LIFE' (*Enlace Zapatista*, 1 January 2021) <https://enlacezapatista.ezln.org.mx/2021/01/01/part-one-a-declaration-for-life/>

'Progress on the Encounter "The Zapatistas and the ConSciences for Humanity"' (*Enlace Zapatista*, 19 March 2016) <https://enlacezapatista.ezln.org.mx/2016/03/19/progress-on-the-encounter-the-zapatistas-and-the-consciences-for-humanity/>

Reyes-Torres AA, 'Oliari v Italy: The First Step to Equal Marriage in Europe?' (*Jurist*, 17 August 2015) <https://www.jurist.org/commentary/2015/08/Amaury-Reyes-Torres-Equal-Marriage/>

Russell D and Van de Ven N, *Crimes against Women: Proceedings of the International Tribunal* (Les Femmes 1976)

Sokol D, 'What's So Wrong with Incest? The Case of Stübing v Germany' (*UK Human Rights Blog*, 15 April 2012) <https://ukhumanrightsblog.com/2012/04/15/whats-so-wrong-with-incest-the-case-of-stubing-v-germany/>

'Statement from Ambassador Katherine Tai on the Covid-19 Trips Waiver' (*Office of the United States Trade Representative*, 5 May 2021) <https://ustr.gov/about-us/policy-offices/press-office/press-releases/2021/may/statement-ambassador-katherine-tai-covid-19-trips-waiver>

Thomas J, 'Sowing Solidarity: Reflections on Zapatismo from the International Gathering of Women Who Struggle' (*Peoples Dispatch*, 20 June 2020) <https://peoplesdispatch.org/2020/06/20/sowing-solidarity-reflections-on-zapatismo-from-the-international-gathering-of-women-who-struggle/>

Tzouvala N, 'On Tariffs and the Ends of International Economic Law' (*LPE Project*, 29 April 2025) <https://lpeproject.org/blog/on-tariffs-and-the-ends-of-international-economic-law/>

United States Trade Representative, Report on the Appellate Body of the World Trade Organization (February 2020) 9, available at: <https://ustr.gov/sites/default/files/Report_on_the_Appellate_Body_of_the_World_Trade_Organization>

United States Trade Representative, Trade Policy Agenda of the President of the United States (2018)

United States Trade Representative, Trade Policy Agenda of the President of the United States (2019)

Universal Declaration of the Rights of Mother Earth (22 April 2010), available at https://www.garn.org/wp-content/uploads/2024/02/ENG-Universal-Declaration-of-the-Rights-of-Mother-Earth.pdf.

'What is Peoples' Global Action?' (*Archives of Global Protests, Nadir*) <https://www.nadir.org/nadir/initiativ/agp/en/pgainfos/about.html>

Worster W, 'Trump's Deportations as an Emerging Crime Against Humanity' (*Opinio Juris*, 23 May 2025) <https://opiniojuris.org/2025/05/23/trumps-deportations-as-an-emerging-crime-against-humanity/>

Yeola K, 'The U.S. Withdrawal from International Organisations: What It Means for Global Order?' *Modern Diplomacy* (10 February 2025) <https://moderndiplomacy.eu/2025/02/10/the-u-s-withdrawal-from-international-organisations-what-it-means-for-global-order/>

Zago G, 'Oliari and Others v Italy: A Stepping Stone Towards Full Legal Recognition of Same-Sex Relationships in Europe' (*Strasbourg Observers*, 16 September 2015) <https://strasbourgobservers.com/2015/09/16/oliari-and-others-v-italy-a-stepping-stone-towards-full-legal-recognition-of-same-sex-relationships-in-europe/>

'Zapatista Army of National Liberation' (*Archives of Global Protests, Nadir*, May 1996) <https://www.nadir.org/nadir/initiativ/agp/chiapas1996/en/invite.html>

'Zapatistas on Gay Rights: "Let Those Who Persecute Be Ashamed!"' (*Green Left*, 21 July 1999) <https://www.greenleft.org.au/content/zapatistas-gay-rights-let-those-who-persecute-be-ashamed>

'II Encounter of the Zapatista Peoples with the Peoples of the World' (*Enlace Zapatista*, June 2007) <https://enlacezapatista.ezln.org.mx/2007/07/01/ii-encounter-of-the-zapatista-peoples-with-the-peoples-of-the-world/>

B. Cases

1. European Court of Human Rights

Alekseyev v Russia, App Nos 4916/07, 25924/08, and 14599/09, Eur Ct HR (21 October 2010)

B v France, App No 13343/87, Eur Ct HR (25 March 1992)

Bayev and Others v Russia, App nos. 67667/09, 44092/12 and 56717/12, Eur Ct HR (13 November 2017)

Bruggemann and Scheuten v Federal Republic of Germany, App No 6959/75, Eur Ct HR (12 July 1977)

Chapin and Charpentier v France, App No 40183/07, Eur Ct HR (9 June 2016)

Christine Goodwin v United Kingdom, App No 28957/95, Eur Ct HR (11 July 2002)

Cossey v United Kingdom, App No 10843/84, Eur Ct HR (27 September 1990)

Dudgeon v United Kingdom, App No 7525/76, 25 Eur Ct HR (22 October 1981)

Engel and Others v Netherlands, App Nos 5100/71; 5101/71; 5102/71; 5354/72; 5370/72, Eur Ct HR (8 June 1976)

Fretté v France, App No 36515/97, Eur Ct HR (26 February 2002)

Greens and MT v United Kingdom, App Nos 60041/08 and 60054/08, Eur Ct HR (23 November 2010)

Handyside v United Kingdom, App No 5493/72 Eur Ct HR (7 December 1976)

Hirst v United Kingdom, App No 74025/01, Eur Ct HR (6 October 2005)

Johnston and Others v Ireland, App No 9697/82, Eur Ct HR (18 December 1986).

Laskey, Jaggard and Brown v United Kingdom, App Nos 21627/93, 21628/93, and 21974/93, Eur Ct HR (19 February 1997)
Marckx v Belgium, App No 6833/74, Eur Ct HR (13 June 1979)
Marlow v United Kingdom, App No 42015/98, Eur Ct HR (5 December 2000)
Mata Estevez v Spain, App No 56501/00, Eur Ct HR (10 May 2001)
Norris v Ireland, App No 10581/83, Eur Ct HR (26 October 1988)
Oao Neftyanaya Kompaniya Yukos v Russia, App No 14902/04, Eur Ct HR (31 July 2014)
Oliari and Others v Italy, App Nos. 18766/11 and 36030/11, Eur Ct HR (31 July 2015)
Patrick Stübing, 'Application No 43547/08: Stübing vs Federal Republic of Germany', Submission in Stübing v Germany, 14 January 2011
Pay v United Kingdom, App No 32792/05, Eur Ct HR (16 September 2008)
Rees v United Kingdom, App No 9532/81, Eur Ct HR (17 October 1986)
SL v Austria, App No 45330/99, Eur Ct HR (9 January 2003)
Schalk and Kopf v Austria, App No 30141/04, Eur Ct HR, (24 June 2010)
Sheffield and Horsham v United Kingdom, App Nos 22985/93 and 23390/94, Eur Ct HR (30 July 1998)
Soering v United Kingdom, App No 14038/88, 161 Eur Ct HR (7 July 1989)
Stübing v Germany, App No 43547/08, Eur Ct HR (12 April 2012)
Sutherland v United Kingdom, App No 25186/94, Eur Commn HR (1 July 1997)
Tyrer v United Kingdom, App No 5856/72, 26 Eur Ct HR (25 April 1978)
Valliantos and Others v Greece, App Nos. 29381/09 and 32684/09, Eur Ct HR (7 November 2013)
Wilde, Greenhalgh and Parry v the United Kingdom, App No 22382/93, Eur Commn HR (19 January 1995)
X v Federal Republic of Germany, App No 5935/72, Eur Commn HR (30 September 1975)
X v United Kingdom, App No 7215/75, Eur Commn HR (Report) (12 October 1978)
X, Y and Z v United Kingdom, App No 21830/93, Eur Ct HR (22 April 1997)

2. World Trade Organization

WTO, United States—Definitive Anti-Dumping and Countervailing Duties on Certain Products from China—Report of the Appellate Body, WT/DS379/AB/R (11 March 2011)
WTO, United States—Laws, Regulations and Methodology for Calculating Dumping Margins (Zeroing)—Report of the Appellate Body, WT/DS294/AB/R (18 April 2006)

3. Other

For Women Scotland Ltd v The Scottish Ministers [2025] UKSC 16 (16 April 2025)

C. Treaties, Resolutions, and Other Institutional Documents

1. Council of Europe

European Convention on Human Rights and Fundamental Freedoms, as amended by Protocols Nos 11 and 14, opened for signature 4 November 1950, ETS 5 (entered into force 3 September 1953)
European Court of Human Rights, Annual Report 2001 (Registry of the European Court of Human Rights 2002)
Protocol 11 to the European Convention for the Protection of Human Rights and Fundamental Freedoms, Restructuring the Control Machinery Established Thereby, opened for signature 11 May 1994, ETS 155 (entered into force 1 November 1998)
Protocol No 15 Amending the Convention for the Protection of Human Rights and Fundamental Freedoms, opened for signature 24 June 2013, CETS 213, 2013 (entered into force 1 August 2021)

Statute of the Council of Europe, opened for signature 5 May 1949, 87 UNTS 103; ETS 1 (entered into force 3 August 1949)
The Brighton Declaration (20 April 2012), available at <https://www.echr.coe.int/Documents/2012_Brighton_FinalDeclaration_ENG.pdf>
The Copenhagen Declaration (13 April 2018), available at <https://rm.coe.int/copenhagen-declaration/16807b915c>

2. General Agreement on Tariffs and Trade and World Trade Organization

Agreement on Trade-Related Aspects of Intellectual Property Rights, Marrakesh Agreement Establishing the World Trade Organization, Annex 1C, opened for signature 15 April 1994, 1869 UNTS 299 (entered into force 1 January 1995)
Amendment of the Agreement on Trade-Related Aspects of Intellectual Property Rights, WTO Doc WT/L/641 (6 December 2005) (entered into force 23 January 2017)
Bolivia et al, Strengthening the WTO to Promote Development and Inclusivity, WT/GC/W/778, 11 July 2019
China, Proposal on WTO Reform, WT/GC/W/773, 13 May 2019
Communication from India and South Africa, Waiver from Certain Provisions of the TRIPS Agreement for the Prevention, Containment and Treatment of COVID-19, Council for Trade-Related Aspects of Intellectual Property Rights, WTO Doc. IP/C/W/669 (2 October 2020)
Decision on Differential and More Favourable Treatment, Reciprocity and Fuller Participation of Developing Countries, GATT Doc. L/4903 (28 November 1979)
GATT Analytical Index (World Trade Organization, 6th edn, 1995)
GATT Annual Session Acts on Tokyo Round Results and Sets Future Work Programme, GATT Doc GATT/1253 (30 November 1979)
General Agreement on Tariffs and Trade, opened for signature 30 October 1947, 55 UNTS 194
Generalized System of Trade Preferences, GATT Doc L/3545 (25 June 1971)
India et al, Outcome of the WTO Ministerial Meeting of Developing Countries, WT/L/1062, 27 May 2019
Marrakesh Agreement Establishing the World Trade Organization, opened for signature 15 April 1994, 1867 UNTS 154 (entered into force 1 January 1995)
Nairobi Ministerial Declaration, WTO Doc. WT/MIN(15)/DEC (19 December 2015)
Negotiations on the Dispute Settlement Understanding: Proposal by the LDC Group, WTO Doc TN/DS/W/17 (9 October 2002)
Participation of Switzerland in the Thirteenth Session of the Contracting Parties: Recommendation by the Intersessional Committee, GATT Doc W.13/3 (16 October 1958)
Protocol of Provisional Application to the General Agreement on Tariffs and Trade, 30 October 1947, 55 UNTS 308 (entered into force 1 January 1948)
Summary of the Tenth Meeting, Contracting Parties Fourteenth Session, GATT Doc SR.14/10 (10 June 1959)
Trade Facilitation Agreement, WTO Doc WT/L/931, 2014 (27 November 2014) (entered into force 22 February 2017)
Understanding on Rules and Procedures Governing the Settlement of Disputes, Marrakesh Agreement Establishing the World Trade Organization, Annex 2, opened for signature 15 April 1994, 1869 UNTS 401 (entered into force 1 January 1995)
Working Procedures for Appellate Review, WTO Doc WT/AB/WP/6 (16 August 2010)
World Trade Organization, Annual Report (2001)

3. Other

Additional views on which the Chair may draw in preparing text to facilitate negotiations among Parties, Ad Hoc Working Group on Long-Term Cooperative Action under the Convention, United Nations Framework Convention on Climate Change (30 April 2010)
Charter of Economic Rights and Duties, GA Res 3281(XXIX), UN Doc A/RES/3281(XXIX) (12 December 1974)

Declaration on Permanent Sovereignty Over Natural Resources, GA Res 1803 (XVII), UN Doc. A/RES/1803/(XVII) (14 December 1962)

Declaration on the Establishment of a New International Economic Order, GA Res. 3201 (S-VI), UN Doc A/RES/3201/(S-VI) (1 May 1974)

Drafting Committee of the Preparatory Committee of the United Nations Conference on Trade and Employment, Suggested Amendments to the Draft General Agreement Submitted by the Delegate for the United States and the Draft Declaration Submitted by the Delegate for the United Kingdom, UN Doc E/PC/T/C.6/65 (10 February 1947)

Drafting Committee of the Preparatory Committee of the United Nations Conference on Trade and Employment, First Report of the Administrative Sub-Committee (Report on Executive Board Membership and Voting), UN Doc E/PC/T/C.6/62 (10 February 1947)

European Union, Concept Paper on WTO Modernisation (18 September 2018) <https://trade.ec.europa.eu/doclib/docs/2018/september/tradoc_157331.pdf>

European Union, The New European Consensus on Development—'Our World, Our Dignity, Our Future': Joint Statement by the Council and Representatives of the Governments of the Member States Meeting within the Council, the European Parliament and the European Commission (8 June 2017) <https://ec.europa.eu/europeaid/new-european-consensus-development-our-world-our-dignity-our-future_en>

Final Act and Related Documents, United Nations Conference on Trade and Employment, Havana Cuba, 21 November 1947– 24 March 1948, UN Doc E/CONF.2/78

First Committee, Third United Nations Conference on the Law of the Sea, 1929th Meeting, UN Doc A/C.1/PV.1929 (18 October 1973)

First Committee, Third United Nations Conference on the Law of the Sea, 1932nd Meeting, UN Doc A/C.1/PV.1932 (22 October 1973)

Letter dated 7 May 2010 from the Permanent Representative of the Plurinational State of Bolivia to the United Nations addressed to the Secretary-General, UN Doc A/64/777 (7 May 2010).

Paris Agreement to the United Nations Framework Convention on Climate Change, opened for signature 22 April 2016, [2016] ATS 24 (entered into force 4 November 2016)

Proceedings of the United Nations Conference on Trade and Development: Geneva, 23 March–16 June 1964: Final Act and Report (Vol 2) (1964)

Proceedings of the United Nations Conference on Trade and Development: Second Session: New Delhi, 1 February–29 March 1968 (Vol 1) (1968)

Proceedings of the United Nations Conference on Trade and Development: Third Session: Santiago de Chile, 13 April to 21 May 1972 (Vol 1) (1973)

Programme of Action on the Establishment of a New International Economic Order, GA Res 3202 (S-VI), UN Doc A/RES/3202/(S-VI) (1 May 1974)

Recent Trends in International Trade and Development, UNCTAD Res 91(IV), UN Doc TD/218 (30 May 1976)

Reservations Entered by the United States, German Federal Republic, France, Japan, and the United Kingdom to the Declaration on the Establishment of a New International Economic Order and Programme of Action, 13 ILM 744 (1974)

Resolution on Development and International Economic Co-Operation, GA Res. 3362 (S-VII), UN Doc A/RES/3362/(S-VII) (16 September 1975)

UNCTAD Secretariat, 'UNCTAD: A Brief Historical Overview' (2006) UNCTAD/GDS/2006/1 <https://digitallibrary.un.org/record/576638?ln=en&v=pdf>

United Nations Declaration on the Rights of Peasants and Other People Working in Rural Areas (UNDROP), UN Doc A/RES/73/165 (17 December 2018)

United Nations, 'Charter of Economic Rights and Duties of States General Assembly Resolution 3281 (XXIX) New York, 12 December 1974' (*Audiovisual Library of International Law*, 2023) <https://legal.un.org/avl/ha/cerds/cerds.html>

United Nations, The Monterrey Consensus: Report of the International Conference on Financing for Development, UN Doc A/CONF.198/11 (18–22 March 2002)

Universal Declaration of Human Rights, GA Res A/RES/3/217 A (10 December 1948)

Vienna Declaration and Programme of Action, UN Doc A/CONF.157/23 (12 July 1993)

Index

For the benefit of digital users, indexed terms that span two pages (e.g., 52–53) may, on occasion, appear on only one of those pages.

Introductory Note
As the entire work is about 'consensus', the 'World Trade Organisation' and the 'European Court of Human Rights', the use of these terms, and certain others which occur repeatedly throughout the book, such as 'European consensus', have not been indexed.